Jean Desmet's Dream Factory

The Adventurous Years of Film (1907–1916)

Edited by
Marente Bloemheuvel
Jaap Guldemond
Mark-Paul Meyer

EYE Filmmuseum
nai010 publishers

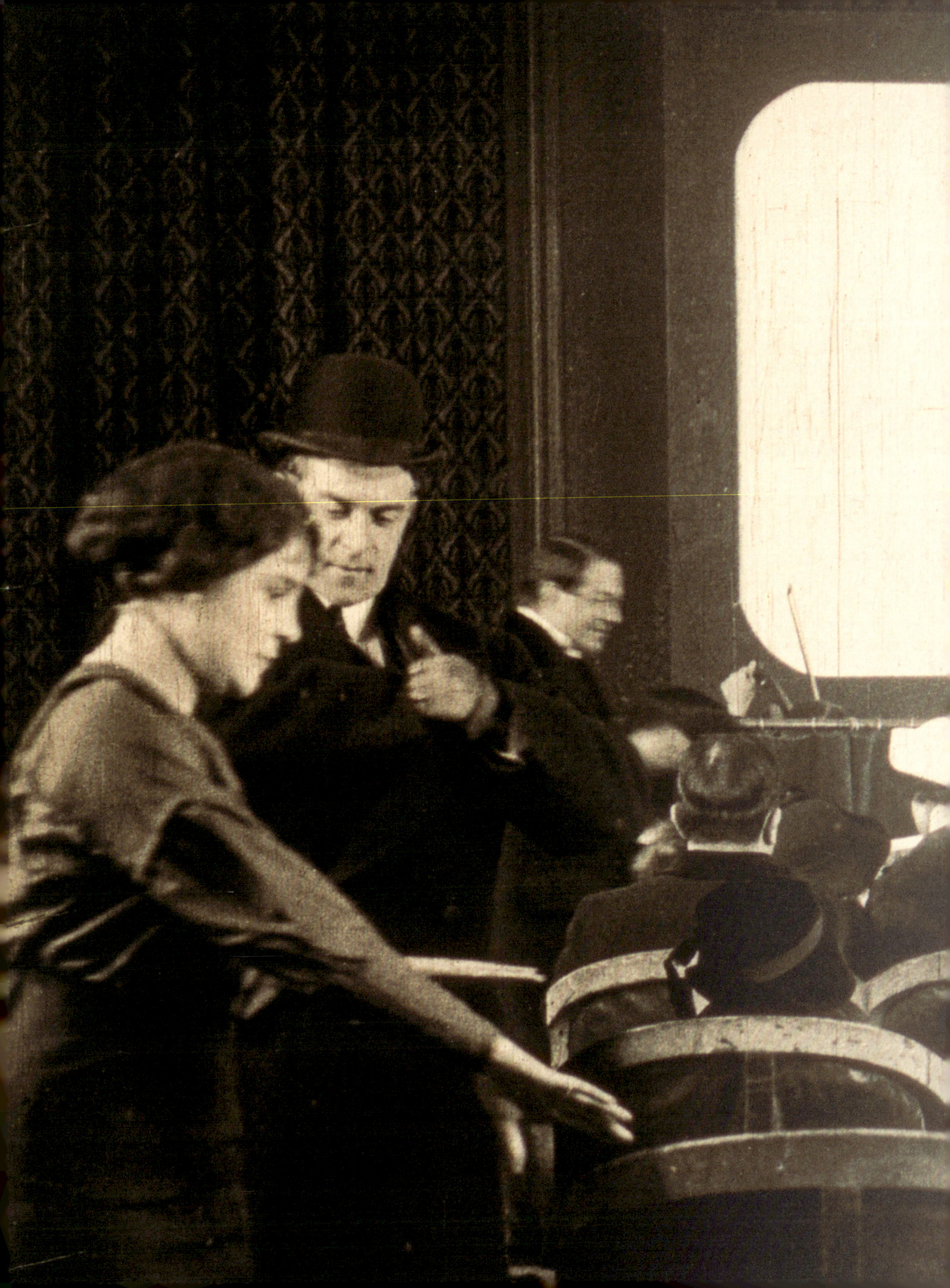

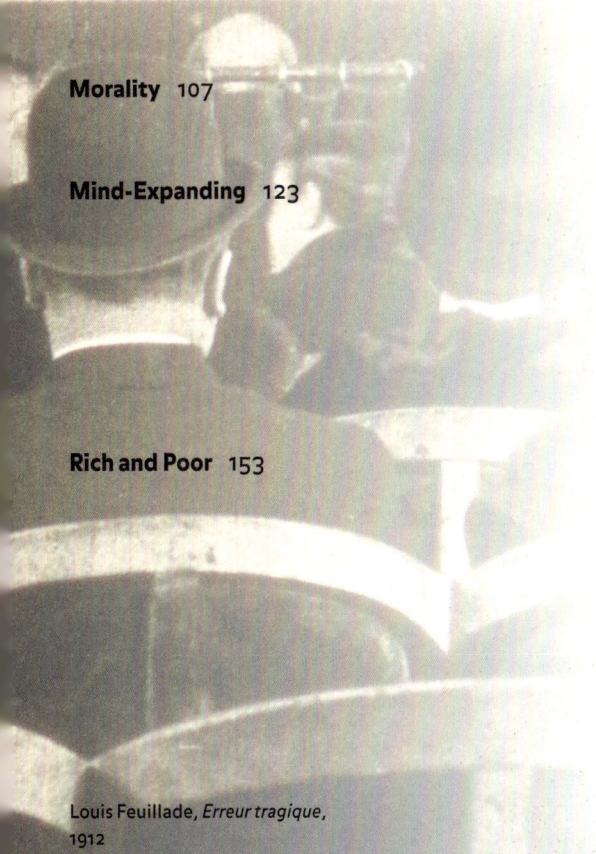

Louis Feuillade, *Erreur tragique*, 1912

Cinema 21

Speed 37

Exoticism 69

Historical Stories 87

Morality 107

Mind-Expanding 123

Rich and Poor 153

Contents

In Our Sight, in Our Mind 4
Sandra den Hamer

Jean Desmet's Dream Factory 8
The Adventurous Years of Film (1907-1916)
Jaap Guldemond

Jean Desmet in His Time 12
Sanne Baar

A Treasure Trove of Adventure and Experimentation 29
Mark-Paul Meyer

The Desmet Collection 47
A Perspective from Abroad
David Robinson

The Wondrous Images of Silent Film 55
Mark-Paul Meyer

'Femmes Fatales' and Film Divas 79
The Decadent Sense of Life
Peter Delpeut

Terrifying, Modern and Artistic 97
The Film Posters in the Desmet Collection
Ivo Blom

The Forgotten Modernism of Vitagraph 115
Peter Delpeut

Jean Desmet and the Transition Years 129
From a Travelling Cinema to a Picture Palace
Rommy Albers and Leanne van Schijndel

Jean Desmet's Time Capsule 139
From Company Archive to Cultural Heritage
Elif Rongen-Kaynakçi and Soeluh van den Berg

Films and Posters in the Desmet Collection in the EYE Filmmuseum 161
Films 163
Posters 176
Cinemas 189

Selected bibliography 190

In Our Sight, in Our Mind

Sandra den Hamer
EYE Director

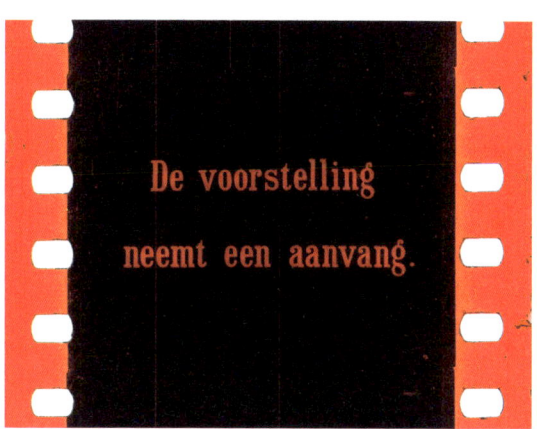

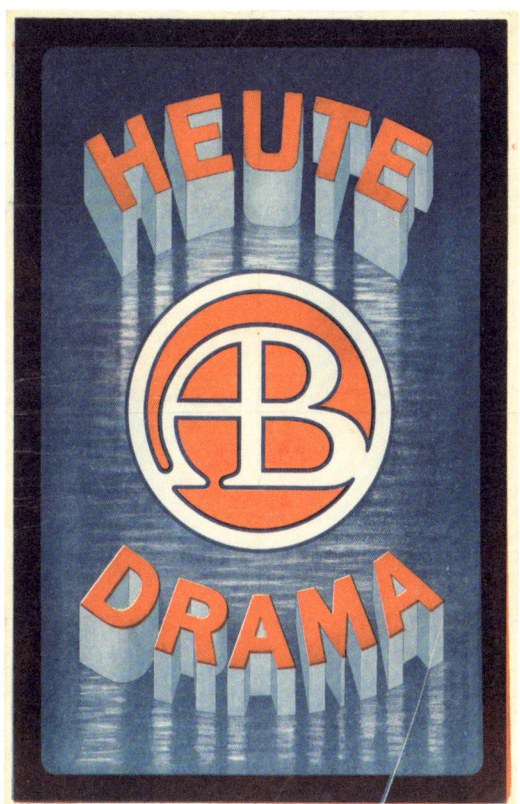

Intertitle from *Al cinematografo guardate – ma non toccate*, 1912

German poster for films by American Biograph
104 x 70 cm

EYE is very proud to present *Jean Desmet's Dream Factory: The Adventurous Years of Film (1907-1916)*, published to accompany a major exhibition of the same name and based on the film collection and company archive of cinema entrepreneur Jean Desmet (1875-1956).

Over the past half century the Desmet Collection has acquired an almost mythical status. Although its name and fame are well established, only a few individuals are aware of exactly what treasures the collection contains. There was of course the wonderful 1990 film *Lyrical Nitrate* by Peter Delpeut, and the important study in 2003 by Ivo Blom entitled *Jean Desmet and the Early Dutch Film Trade*. Many people from Amsterdam also cherish fond memories of the atmospheric Cinema Parisien founded by Jean Desmet, once incorporated into our former home in the Vondelpark pavilion, and now gracing the FilmHallen in Amsterdam West. Worldwide fame came the way of EYE in 2011 when the Desmet Collection was inscibed on UNESCO's Memory of the World Register. But it is only now, at our new home on the north bank of the IJ, and after years of research and restoration work, that the Desmet Collection can be presented to the public in all its glory.

The collection includes hundreds of films, posters and photographs and gives a glance at film culture from 1907 to 1916. This was an exceptionally adventurous period for film pioneers like Desmet, whose eye for both business and art made him a cultural entrepreneur even before the term existed. It was also an adventurous period of experimentation for the art of film itself. The works in the Desmet Collection are an eclectic mixture of styles, genres, colour techniques and narrative strategies. It is therefore not only the historical importance but also the marvellous artistry and cinematography of the films from this era that form the point of departure for both the exhibition and this book.

We could only make an exhibition and a publication such as this because Jean Desmet's family and heirs granted this richness to us, and we are immensely grateful for the trust they have bestowed. Our gratitude goes primarily to Jeanne Hughan-Desmet, Jean Desmet's youngest daughter, who in 1957 ensured that the films were handed over to the then Filmmuseum.

My special thanks also go to the granddaughter of Jean Desmet, Ilse Hughan. Not only because she ensured that the original interior of Cinema Parisien was preserved and donated to EYE. Nor because she, as a former museum employee, played a vital role in setting up the distribution activities at the Filmmuseum and acquiring new classics. Nor even because she, as an internationally active producer of bold filmmakers, makes a genuine contribution to the international film canon presented at EYE. But also because, to this very day, she has always followed and supported our work with tremendous commitment and flamboyant enthusiasm: thank you dear Ilse!

And we would not have been able to make an exhibition like this if my predecessors had not carefully looked after the collection. It is only through their work and dedication that we can do our work today, which is to show you what was collected, restored and conserved during all those years. In this regard I would especially like to thank two of them posthumously. First, Jan de Vaal, who in 1957, when the Filmmuseum operated out of a tiny room at the Stedelijk Museum, immediately recognized the significance of the collection and, despite limited resources, ensured that the films were preserved properly. Moreover, he succeeded in convincing the Desmet family of the importance of keeping the entire collection together, including the publicity material and paper archives. Under the directorship of Hoos Blotkamp, efforts to conserve and provide access to the films gained momentum from 1988 on, and a thorough inventory of the archives was drawn up. Now all of us can reap the benefits of the work of Jan de Vaal and Hoos Blotkamp.

The exhibition 'Jean Desmet's Dream Factory: The Adventurous Years of Film (1907-1916)' is accompanied by a varied and lively programme of film screenings, Cinema Concerts, workshops, lectures and educational activities. So, go forth and enjoy! And there is of course this publication, which can be considered an integral part of the exhibition as well as a lasting continuation of it.

The Desmet Collection is the beating heart of EYE. Numerous colleagues – in fact everybody working at EYE, each in their own way – worked with deep devotion and expertise in recent months and years to ensure the restoration and availability of these works. We turned the vaults inside out, opened the depots and bunkers as wide as possible. We examined the films and viewed them again and again. We cleaned, restored and digitized them. We took the posters out of the protective paper and boxes in which they had been conserved for years. We picked our way through Desmet's company archive, including the receipts and order lists. We spent years studying and researching every item. We consulted countless sources before publishing. We drew up programme proposals and exhibition concepts. We designed publicity campaigns, developed educational projects for our youngest visitors and made digital presentations for those unable to come to the museum. We rolled out the red carpet, and now at last we are ready. More than a century later, Jean Desmet's Dream Factory is about to open.

Honoured guests, ladies and gentlemen, welcome!

Georges Denola, *La Légende des ondines*, 1911

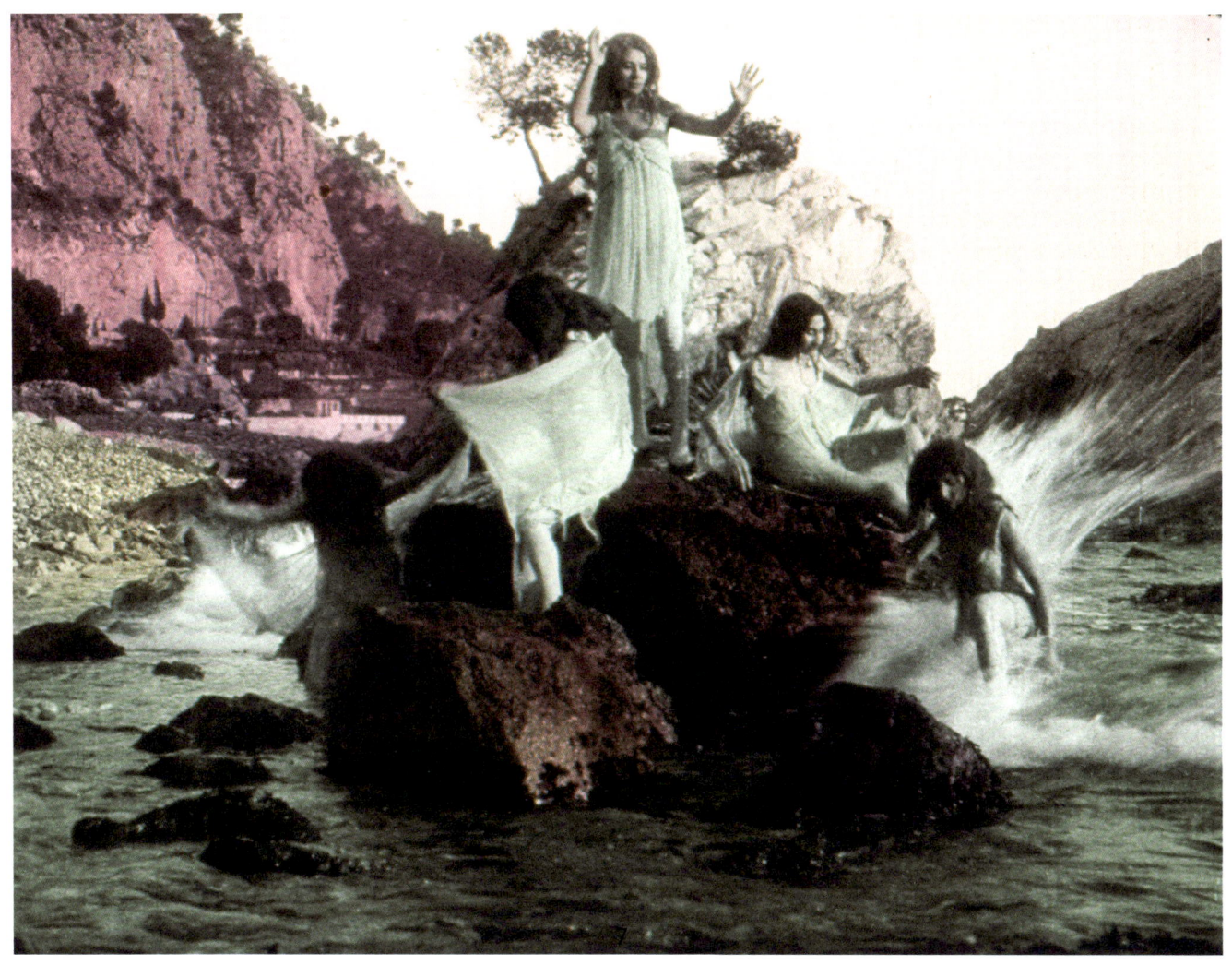

# Jean Desmet's Dream Factory

The Adventurous Years of Film (1907-1916)

Jaap Guldemond

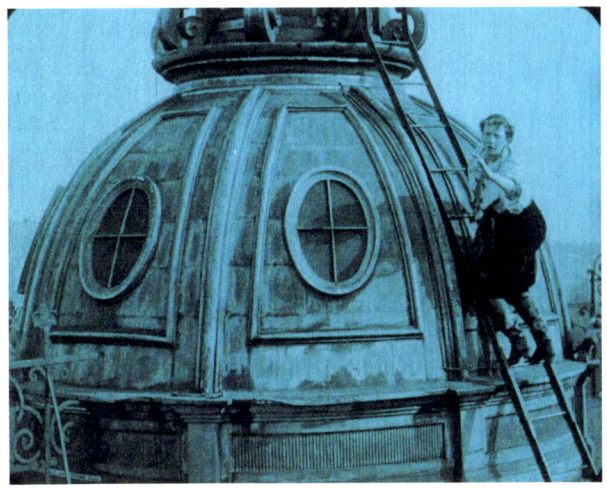

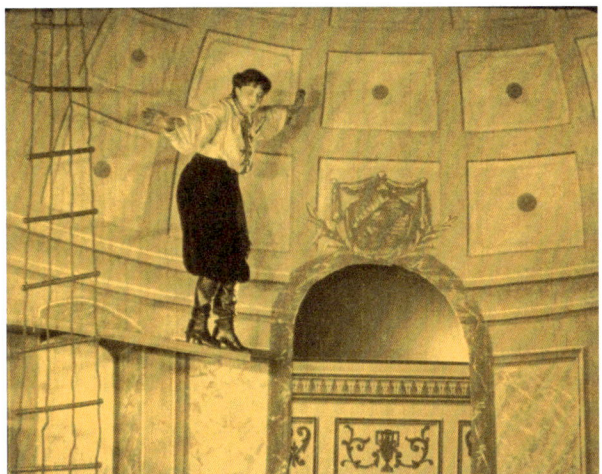

Franz Hofer, *Die Schwarze Natter*, 1913

The exhibition 'Jean Desmet's Dream Factory: The Adventurous Years of Film (1907-1916)' is made up entirely of material from the collection at EYE. The aim of the exhibition policy pursued by EYE is not only to display items from its collection but also to set them in context. In a sense, that is easy in the case of Jean Desmet, precisely because of the completeness of this collection. As far as is known, it is the most exhaustive archive from the early cinema period, containing not only more than 900 films but also more than 1,000 posters, almost 1,500 photographs and tens of thousands of documents that complement and enhance one another. There is no other known collection in the world that presents such an insightful picture of the adventurous early years of film culture in the Netherlands and far beyond. For UNESCO this was one of the main reasons to inscribe the Desmet Collection on the Memory of the World Register. What is remarkable about the collection is that the films come from all over the world. In addition to operating cinemas, Desmet was active internationally as a film distributor. That is why many wonderful early films from Italy and France, not to mention the USA, Denmark, Germany and Britain, ended up in his collection.

The exhibition not only highlights the emergence of cinema and film culture in the Netherlands through the activities of Jean Desmet as a cinema exhibitor and distributor, but also demonstrates the artistic qualities of the films made during that period. More than mere entertainment, these works are mature artistic products whose makers experimented with the possibilities offered by a new medium.

The central proposition of 'Jean Desmet's Dream Factory' is that early cinema – viewed retrospectively – was a nonconformist and a modern cinema. Particularly in Europe, what mattered most was the very art of 'showing' instead of telling a story, which has become the custom since Hollywood started to dominate. Early European cinema was more about showing an event, an 'exotic' land, an unknown city, more about exploring the particular visual and photographic qualities of the new medium, such as the use of double exposure and split screen. According to most historians, this so-called 'cinema of attractions' was already giving way to narrative cinema by 1907. While this is certainly true of films made in the US at the time, it applied much less to films made in Europe, where the 'cinema of attractions' developed into what we today might call a hotbed of forms, styles and new techniques. So this was no 'primitive' cinema that would only reach maturity with the narrative strategies of the United States, where the representation of space and time was dominated by one system. It was, instead, a very different cinema, much closer to the way artists and filmmakers experiment these days, and also much closer to the way millions of mobile telephone users employ film and moving images every day.

In addition to spectacular posters and a selection of documents and publicity material, the exhibition includes a large number of films shown on large screens and grouped according to themes that demonstrate the modern and adventurous nature of early cinema. To this end, the exhibition lets the films themselves speak. And what they speak of is a sense of wonder and pleasure – wonder at the view through the camera, the use of special effects, the ingenious application of colour, the different narrative approaches, the form of representation and staging; and pleasure in filmmaking, in seducing the viewer through the power of imagination.

Presenting these films at EYE as part of an exhibition is a perfect way to underline the current relevance of these early films and to experience them in a totally different way than is possible in a cinema auditorium. The exhibition therefore reflects the exhibition policy that EYE is pursuing: a policy that focuses on the artistic quality of film in all its diversity, and that calls attention not so much to telling a story *about* film but to film *itself*.

On the basis of eight articles, this publication paints a picture of the life and work of Jean Desmet, of the era in which he screened and distributed films, of the historical and international importance of the Desmet Collection, and of the artistic significance of these films. It constitutes both an introduction to early cinema culture in the Netherlands and an invitation to the reader to discover the exceptional qualities of the cinema from the second decade of the last century.

As an international authority on early cinema, David Robinson demonstrates the historical significance of the collection. Peter Delpeut and Mark-Paul Meyer examine the artistic qualities of the films. Ivo Blom, a pre-eminent Desmet authority, spotlights the artistic qualities of the posters. Elif Rongen-Kaynakçi, Soeluh van den Berg, Rommy Albers and Leanne van Schijndel offer an overview of the life and work of Jean Desmet, and his place in and importance to Dutch cinema history. They also describe the history and composition of the collection left behind by Desmet. Sanne Baar uses a historical timeline to show how Desmet's story relates to important world events and developments. The book also contains a comprehensive overview of all films and posters in the Desmet Collection. Finally, seven visual essays represent seven substantive themes embedded in the Desmet Collection. Most of these images are stills from films that Jean Desmet himself once held in his hands.

Mario Roncoroni, *Filibus*, 1915

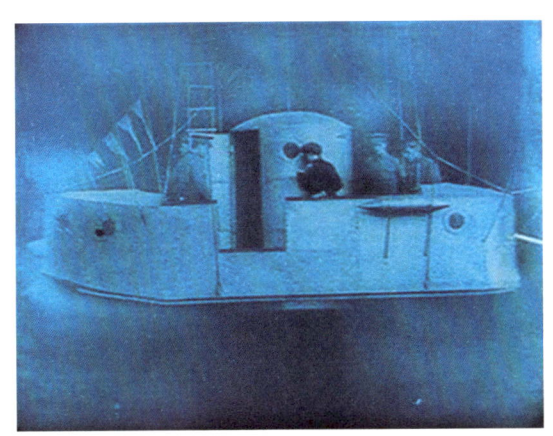

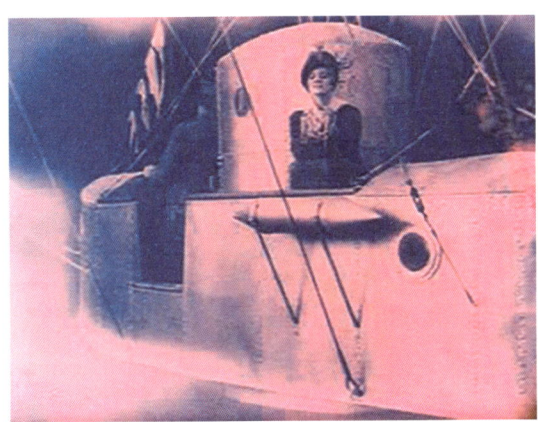

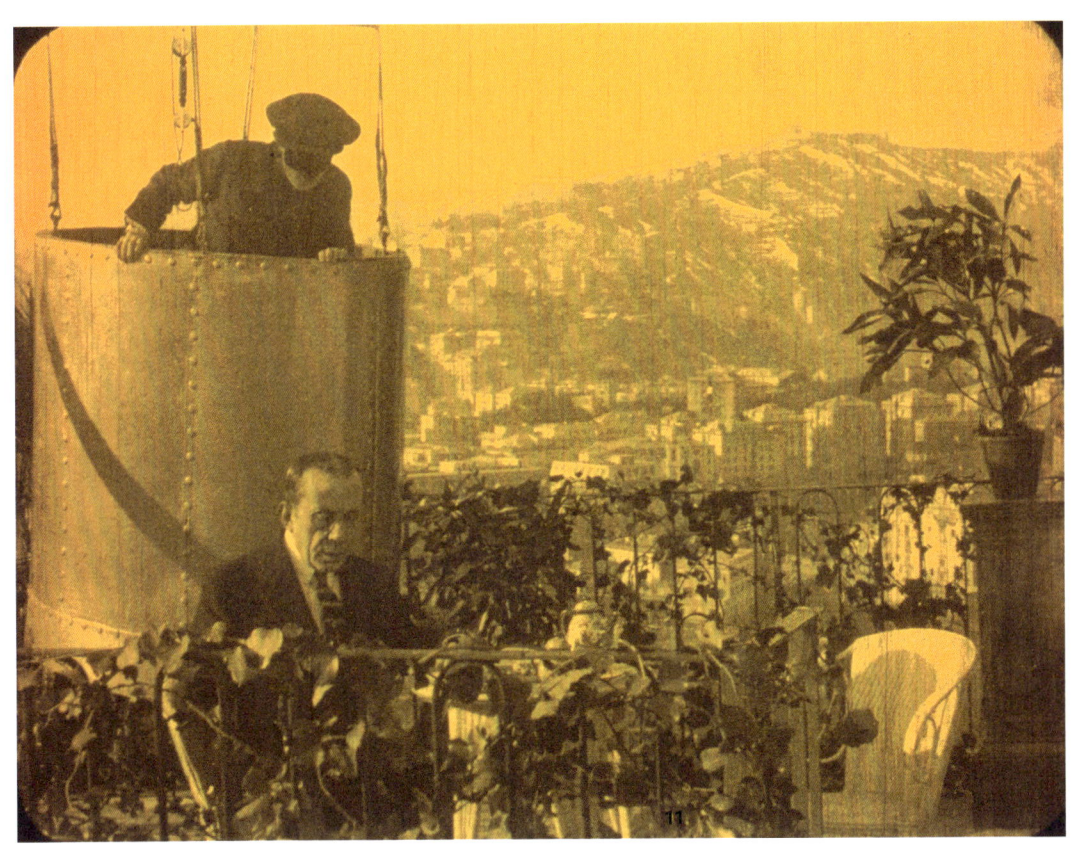

Jean Desmet in His Time

Sanne Baar

History		Jean Desmet	Film History
	1875	**26 August 1875** ▶1 Jean Desmet is born in Ixelles, a suburb of Brussels. He is the eldest in a family of six children. His father Maréchal is a merchant from Renaix (BE). His mother, Petronella, comes from Oss (NL).	
	1877	**1877** The Desmet family moves to Den Bosch (NL).	
1889 ▶2 Exposition Universelle in Paris, construction of the Eiffel Tower.	**1889**		
1890 Rise of Art Nouveau.	**1890**		
1893 The municipality of Rotterdam establishes the first power station in the Netherlands. 1893-1910 ▶3 Edvard Munch produces his series *The Scream*.	**1893**	**1893** Death of Maréchal Desmet. Desmet's mother tries to support her family by selling porcelain and pottery at fairs.	
	1894	**1894** Desmet's mother, too, dies. At the age of 19, Jean Desmet must care for his younger brothers and sisters. They would later hold many positions in his businesses. In the following years, Desmet operates barrel organs at fairs to provide for his family.	
14 September 1895 The Stedelijk Museum opens in Amsterdam.	**1895**		28 December 1895 Film screening by the Lumière brothers, in a salon in Paris. This is regarded as the first public film screening.
	1896	**30 April 1896** Desmet marries Catharina Dahrs, from Germany. They have three children: Jean, Catharina and Maréchal.	12 March 1896 The Belgian Camille Cerf organizes the first film screening in the Netherlands, in a commercial building at Kalverstraat 220 in Amsterdam. 16 July 1896 Christiaan Slieker starts the first travelling cinema in the Netherlands.
	1897	**1897** Desmet now operates a wheel of fortune at fairs.	1896-1897 Founding of Vitagraph (US), Gaumont (FR) and Pathé (FR), three of the earliest film production and distribution companies. An international film industry begins to take shape.

History

6 September 1898
Investiture of Queen Wilhelmina of the Netherlands. A film of the event is shown throughout the country.

1899
Sigmund Freud develops his theory of the unconscious in his book *Die Traumdeutung* (*The Interpretation of Dreams*).

1900
Exposition Universelle in Paris; 1.4 million people visit the Lumière brothers' tent.

2 July 1900 ▶ 6
First zeppelin flight.

1901
Wilhelm Conrad Röntgen receives the first Nobel Prize for chemistry. Röntgen's X-rays soon come into use for entertainment purposes at variety theatres.

1901
Karl Landsteiner describes the different blood types for the first time.

1901
Guglielmo Marconi sends the first transatlantic radio signal.

1903 ▶ 7
Opening of the Beurs van Berlage in Amsterdam.

July 1904
Completion of the Trans-Siberian Railway.

1905
Albert Einstein publishes his theory of relativity: $E=mc^2$.

1898

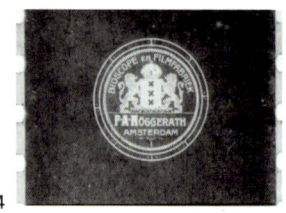

4

1899

5

1900

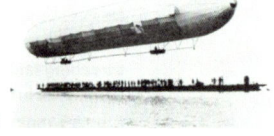

6

1901

7

1903

1904

1905

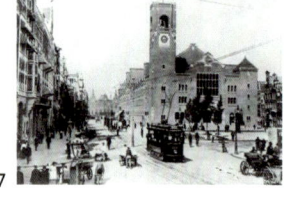

8

Jean Desmet

1905 ▶ 8
When the new Lottery Act prohibits the operation of wheels of fortune, Desmet buys a Canadian Toboggan for the fairgrounds.

Film History

1898 ▶ 4
F.A. Nöggerath establishes FAN Film in Amsterdam and begins to sell films.

1898
The breakthrough year for film in the Netherlands. There are daily screenings in theatres in the major cities. Travelling cinemas rapidly grow in popularity at fairs.

1899 ▶ 5
The Mullens brothers establish their travelling cinema Alberts Frères. They later produce their own films too. In addition to Albert Frères and Slieker's travelling cinema, there are many others.

In 1900, 1904, 1908 and 1911, there are showings of movies with sound (provided by gramophones).

10 October 1903
Opening of the Tivoli Wintertuin in Rotterdam, the first permanent location for film screenings that were not interspersed with variety acts.

c. 1904/1905
Emergence of intertitles and narrators.

1905
Pathé produces c. 240 films.

December 1905
Pathé opens a branch in Amsterdam where film equipment and films are sold.

History

1905 ▶9
In Paris, the Fauves hold their first exhibition. The group's leader is Henri Matisse.

1905
First Russian Revolution; mutiny on the battleship Potemkin on the Black Sea near Odessa.

1906
Formation of the German artists' group Die Brücke. Its members include Erich Schmidt-Rottluff and Ernst Ludwig Kirchner.

20 February 1907
The SS Berlin disaster: the London-Berlin ferry crashes into the breakwater at Hook of Holland; c. 150 people die in the accident. This event in the Netherlands is world news and the images can be seen throughout Europe.

October 1907 ▶11
First Cubist exhibition in Paris. The leading painters in this movement are Pablo Picasso and Georges Braque.

1907
Leo Hendrik Baekeland develops bakelite, the earliest synthetic plastic.

1908
Rotterdam bans funfairs because of the disorder and excesses associated with them. Other cities will follow its example. Amsterdam has had a ban on funfairs since 1876.

1908
Gustav Klimt, *The Kiss*

1908
Henry Ford introduces the Model T.

20 February 1909 ▶12
Filippo Marinetti's *Futurist Manifesto* is published in the French newspaper *Le Figaro*.

6 April 1909
Robert Peary is the first person to reach the North Pole.

1906

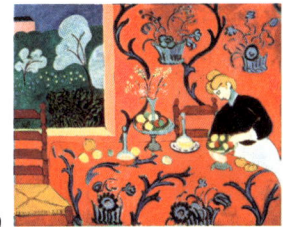
9

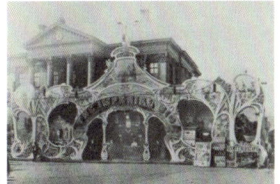
10

1907

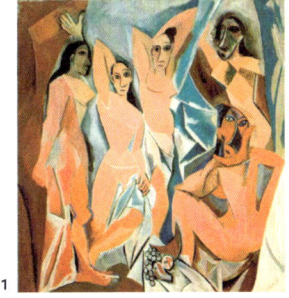
11

1908

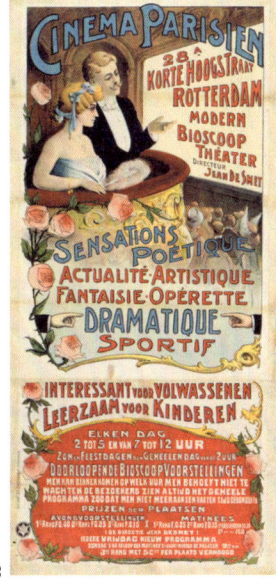
12

1909

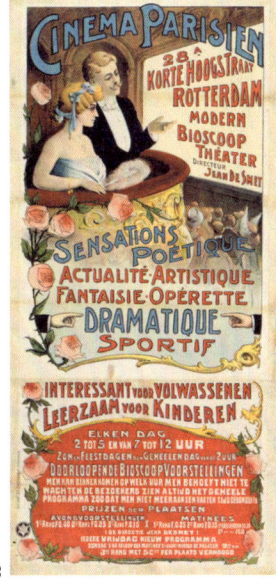

Jean Desmet

1907 ▶10
Desmet buys the travelling cinema Imperial Bio. His first screening takes place at the Leiden fair in the summer. Albert Sonneville designs a 25-m-wide façade decorated with Art Nouveau motifs for the occasion. In the winter months, Desmet presents films in theatres and concert halls throughout the country.

16 September 1907
Death of Desmet's first wife Catherine Dahrs.

13 March 1909 ▶13
Desmet opens his first permanent cinema, in Rotterdam: the Cinema Parisien at Korte Hoogstraat 28.

Film History

1906
The American Andrew Rawson Jennings opens the Nickelodeon Bijou Biograph Theater on Damstraat, Amsterdam. Nickelodeons were small, inexpensive cinemas.

1906/1907
Pathé establishes separate production, distribution and exhibition divisions, setting a new standard for the industry.

7 September 1907
Franz Anton Nöggerath opens his first permanent cinema in Amsterdam: the Bioscope Theater on Reguliersbreestraat.

1909
Invention of the motorized film camera, which replaces hand-cranked cameras.

History

25 July 1909 ▶14
Louis Blériot is the first to fly an aircraft across the English Channel.

September 1910
The Vatican issues an Oath against Modernism and requires all priests to take it before ordination.

1911 ▶15
Formation of the artists' group Der Blaue Reiter, whose members include Paul Klee, Wassily Kandinsky (one of the pioneers of abstract art) and Franz Marc.

1911 ▶17
In Great Britain, the suffragettes fight for equal rights for men and women.

15 April 1912 ▶19
The Titanic crashes into an iceberg and sinks. Approximately 1,500 people die in the shipwreck.

September 1912
The new Poor Act comes into force in the Netherlands. Its objective is to organize poor relief more effectively.

19 September 1912
The Netherlands becomes a party to the Berne Convention on copyright, which recognizes film and photography as art forms.

1910

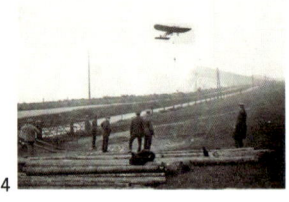
14

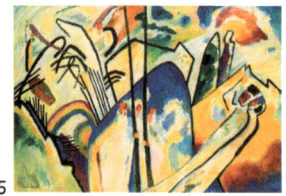
15

1911

16

17

1912

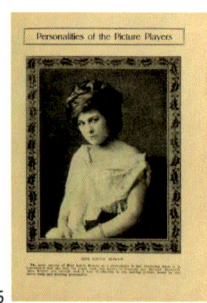
18

19

Jean Desmet

26 March 1910
Desmet opens the Cinema Parisien at Nieuwendijk 69 in Amsterdam. He gradually shifts his focus to permanent cinemas and closes his travelling cinema.

1910
Desmet goes into the film distribution business. At first, he mainly purchases ready-made film programmes already screened in Germany.

Late 1911
Desmet installs an illuminated sign at the Cinema Parisien.

8 March 1912 ▶18
Desmet marries Rika (Hendrika) Klabou, and they have a daughter, Jeanne.

Early 1912
Desmet begins to purchase films directly from distributors and producers in Berlin and Brussels, rather than second-hand.

1912
Desmet starts adding Dutch titles and intertitles to his films.

Film History

1910
Rise of the long fiction film as the main element of film programmes.

1910
Cities such as Berlin, Brussels, Paris and London become centres where films from any country, producer or genre can be obtained.

1911 ▶16
The Motion Picture Story Magazine comes on the market in America. This is the first magazine devoted to stardom and the great film actors and actresses.

1911
Pathé sets up the production company Hollandsche Film and produces 15 short fiction films.

15 July 1911
Opening of the Pathé Theater on Kalverstraat, Amsterdam, where Pathé films premiere before they are screened elsewhere. The well-known Pathé newsreels are also shown here. It becomes the first theatre in the Netherlands without a narrator but with a small orchestra.

August 1911
Opening of the first Dutch film studio by F.A. Nöggerath, Jr.

1912
Dutch local authorities adopt stricter fire safety requirements for cinemas.

1912
The first local motion picture rating systems are established in the Netherlands. Mayors and the police are responsible for the motion picture rating committees.

October 1912
Fritz Burckhardt establishes the Wilhelmina distribution company, which focuses mainly on German and Italian films.

History

29 May 1913
World premiere of Igor Stravinsky's *Le Sacre du Printemps*, performed by Sergei Diaghilev's Ballets Russes in Paris.

1913 ▶ 22
Kazimir Malevich, *Black Square*

1913 ▶ 23
Marcel Duchamp, *Roue de Bicyclette*

28 June 1914 ▶ 26
Archduke Franz Ferdinand and his wife, Duchess Sophie, are shot and killed in Sarajevo. This leads to the outbreak of the First World War in August.

1 August 1914
Mobilization of the Dutch army. The Netherlands will remain neutral throughout the war.

23 November 1914
Establishment of the NOT (Netherlands Overseas Trust), which streamlines Dutch trade with other countries and the colonies.

1913

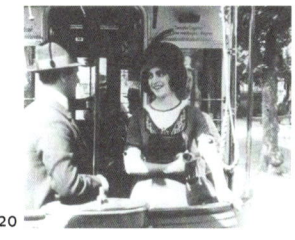
20

21

22

23

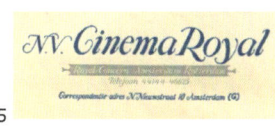
24

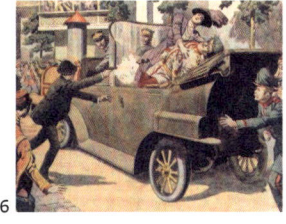
25

26

1914

Jean Desmet

27 December 1912
Opening of Desmet's luxurious Cinema Palace on Kalverstraat, Amsterdam.

1913
Desmet gradually expands as a film exhibitor in Flanders.

1913
Because of the monopoly system and growing competition from other film distributors, some films are unavailable to Desmet. He does not specialize in one genre or country but buys films largely for commercial reasons.

3 May 1913
Desmet opens the Royal Palace on Havenstraat, Bussum (NL). In the years that follow, he opens cinemas across the Netherlands in Vlissingen, Delft, Amersfoort, Eindhoven, Hilversum and Oostzaan.

June 1913 ▶ 24
Desmet's greatest hit this year is *Richard Wagner* (directed by Carl Froelich). He rents the film out to other exhibitors, such as the Mullens brothers.

1 August 1913 ▶ 25
Opening of the Cinéma Royal Elite Bioscope at Coolsingel 17 in Rotterdam.

1913/1914
Desmet sells an increasing number of films in other countries after they have gone out of circulation in the Netherlands. Demand for films is particularly great in the Dutch East Indies, where there are two film releases a week. In the Netherlands, the norm is one release a week.

April 1914
Abraham Tuschinski becomes the manager of the Cinéma Royal Elite Bioscope in Rotterdam. He takes over this cinema in 1916.

Film History

1912 ▶ 20
Johan Gildemeijer founds the Union Filmverhuurkantoor (Film Rental Office). He distributes mainly German films. Gildemeijer acquires the exclusive rights to films starring Asta Nielsen. This can be seen as the start of the film monopoly in the Netherlands; distributors begin to demand exclusive exhibition rights.

1913
In the Netherlands, there is growing interest in German films, especially literary dramas with Albert Bassermann and melodramas starring Asta Nielsen and Henny Porten.

March 1913 ▶ 21
Enrico Guazzoni's *Quo Vadis?*, considered to be the first full-length feature film, appears in cinemas. This film is distributed by Nöggerath.

1913
J. Godefroa establishes the Algemeen Internationaal Filmbureau (World's International Film Office) in Amsterdam, becoming a new competitor to Desmet.

1914–1918 ▶ 27
As a result of the war, fewer foreign films are available and Dutch producers make more films of their own. In the war years, the Hollandia Filmfabriek (Film Factory) in Haarlem alone produces over 20 films.

1914
Eclair and other production and distribution companies open branches in the Dutch East Indies so that the latest films can be shown there. This eats into Desmet's sales.

History		Jean Desmet	Film History
	1915	**1914** The war severely limits the availability of national and international transport, making it increasingly difficult for Desmet to obtain new films.	
22 April 1915 ▶ 28 The Germans are the first to use poison gas, near Gravenstafel, outside the Belgian town of Ypres.		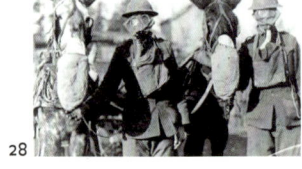 27	October 1915 Germany categorically bans the export of films. In March 1916, Britain bans the export of films without special licences from organizations such as NOT.
	1916	28 **1916** Desmet ends his active film distribution activities to concentrate on the property business. He will will continue to rent films until 1922.	
15 March 1917 During the Russian Revolution, tsar Nicholas II is forced to abdicate.	**1917**		
11 November 1918 ▶ 30 Armistice Day. The First World War officially comes to an end on 28 June 1919, with the signing of the Treaty of Versailles.	**1918**	29 **8 November 1918 ▶ 29** Desmet places an advertisement in the newspapers: 'In view of the sale of the Cinema Palace, Kalverstraat 224, the undersigned has decided to sell his other cinemas as well.' **16 November 1918** Desmet writes to Eclipse, Itala, Vitagraph and Gaumont to request a discount on the films not released in the Netherlands during the war. 30	**1918** During the First World War, the United States grows into a superpower in the film industry. Film production in Europe comes to a virtual halt.
15 March 1919 The Netherlands Overseas Trust removes the restrictions on the import and export of films.	**1919**		
	1920	**1920** In the early 1920s, Desmet still owns three cinemas in the Netherlands: the Cinema Parisien in Amsterdam and two others in Amersfoort and Bussum.	
	1921		21 October 1921 Opening of Theater Tuschinski on Reguliersbreestraat, Amsterdam.
	1923	**April 1923** Desmet writes to a number of film companies in Berlin, Brussels and Paris in the hope of starting up a new business.	

History		Jean Desmet	Film History
	1927	**1927/1930 ▶31** Cloud project: Desmet invests in an invention for projecting advertisements onto clouds. The project falls apart after one of the partners declares bankruptcy.	October 1927 *The Jazz Singer* (directed by Alan Crosland, USA) is one of the first sound films ever released.
	1928 31	**21 December 1928 ▶32** Desmet buys the Flora theatre from Anton Nöggerath. Much of the complex is destroyed in a fire in February 1929. The plan for an entertainment complex with cinemas and a roller-skating rink will never become a reality.	
24 October 1929 ▶33 Black Thursday. Stock exchanges crash and many speculators lose all their savings. This is the start of the economic crisis of the 1930s.	**1929** 32		
	1938 33	**7 August 1938** A fire in the storage area of the Cinema Parisien destroys many posters and part of the company archive. Few films are lost, however. Desmet makes an inventory of his archive afterwards; this is the start of the Desmet Collection.	
1939–1945 Second World War.	**1939**		
	1956 34	**21 November 1956 ▶34** Death of Jean Desmet.	

1957

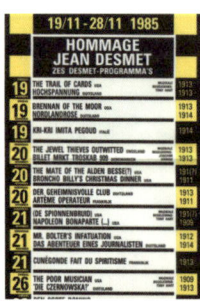

1985

1957
The Desmet Collection comes into the possession of the Nederlands Filmmuseum.

1985 ▶ 35
Exhibition on the Desmet Collection in the Nederlands Filmmuseum. The first steps are taken towards making the company archive accessible and preserving the colours of the films. Frank van der Maden is appointed as the collection curator.

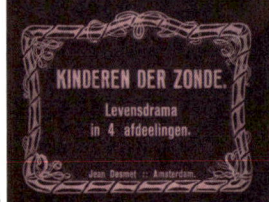

1986

1986 ▶ 36
Fior di male (1915, Carmine Galloneo) is shown at the Pordenone Silent Film Festival in Italy. The collection becomes the focus of growing international attention and interest.

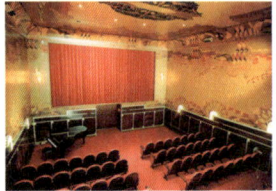

1991

1991 ▶ 37, 38
The interior of the Cinema Parisien (1924) is installed in the Filmmuseum's Vondelpark Pavilion in Nieuwendijk. After the relocation in 2012, EYE builds a modern version of the Parisien interior in its new location. The original Parisien interior is installed in a new location in FilmHallen cinema in Amsterdam in 2014.

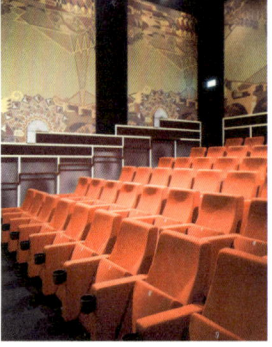

2007

Summer 2007
The film programme 'Jean Desmet's Cinema of Sensation and Sentiment' is presented at the MoMA in New York. In 2011, a second programme follows: 'Cruel and Unusual Comedy from the Desmet Collection of the EYE Institute, Amsterdam'. Every year, many Desmet films are shown at the festivals in the Italian cities Pordenone and Bologna.

2011

May 2011 ▶ 39
The Desmet Collection is inscibed on UNESCO'S Memory of the World Register.

2014

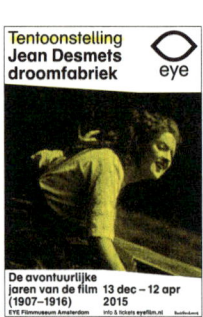

2014–2015 ▶ 40
A major Desmet exhibition is held at the EYE Filmmuseum, with an accompanying programme of films, talks, concerts and this publication.

Cinema

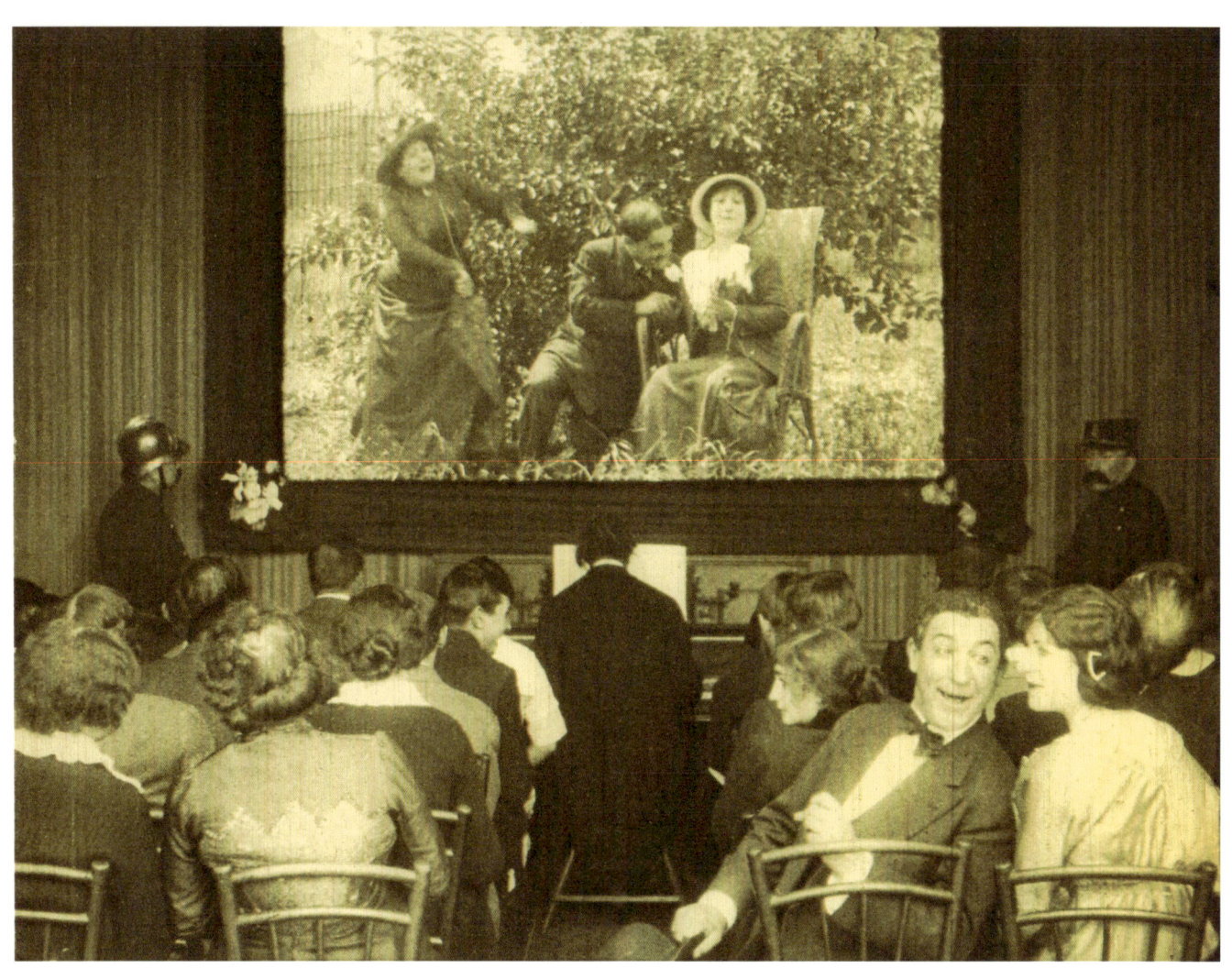

p. 22
Ernest Servaes, *Arthème promène son oncle*, 1913

p. 23
Al cinematografo guardate – ma non toccate, 1912

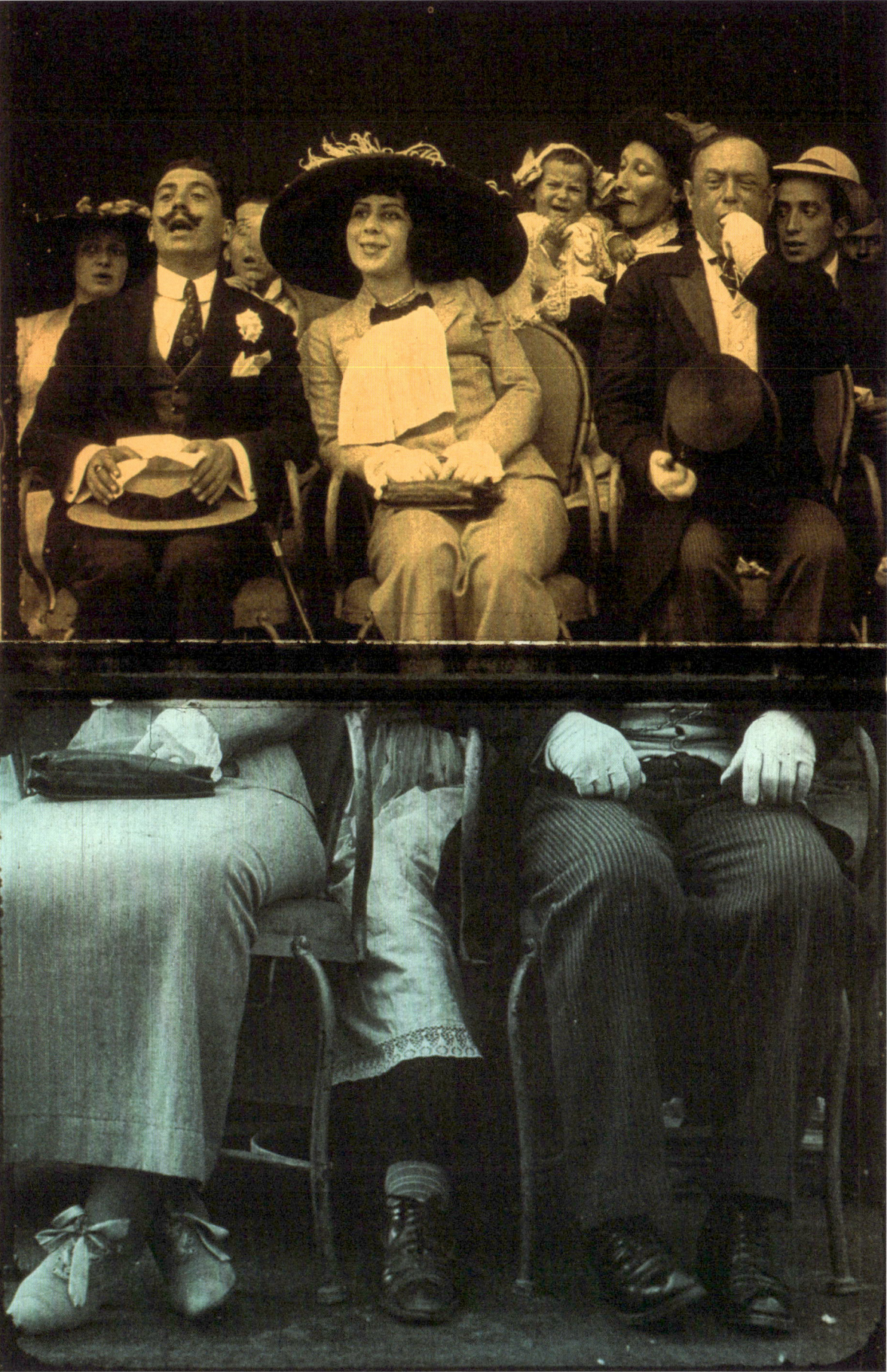

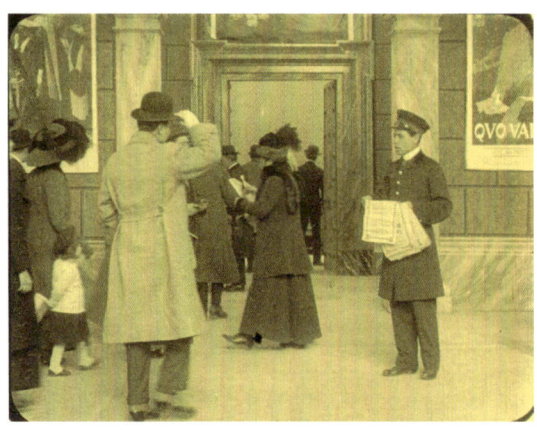
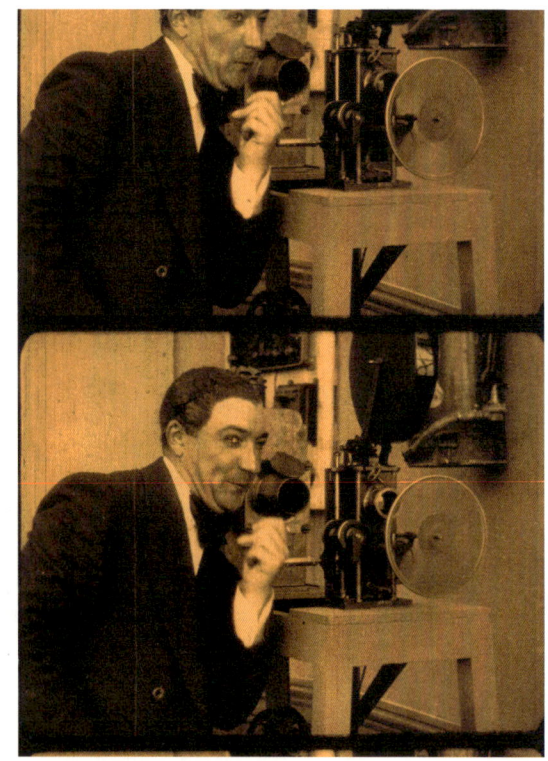
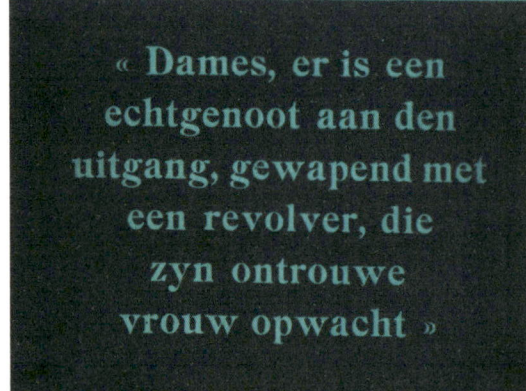
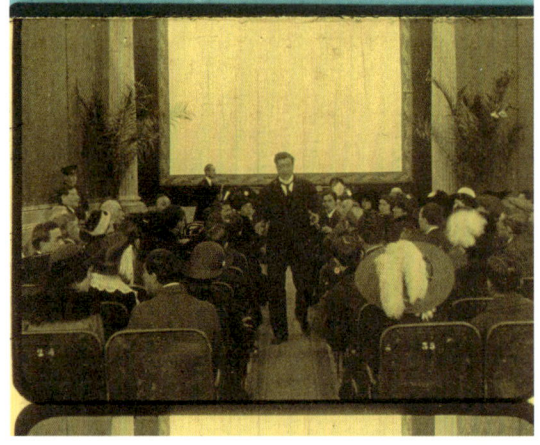
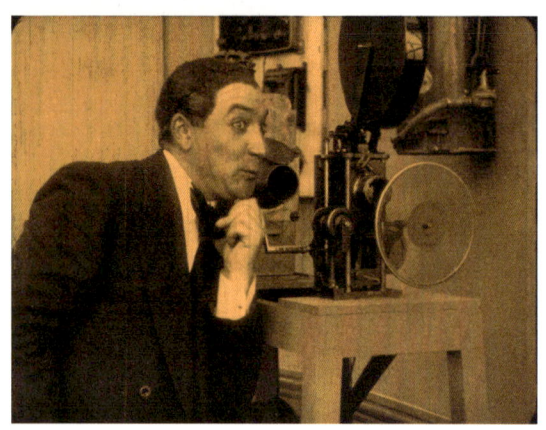
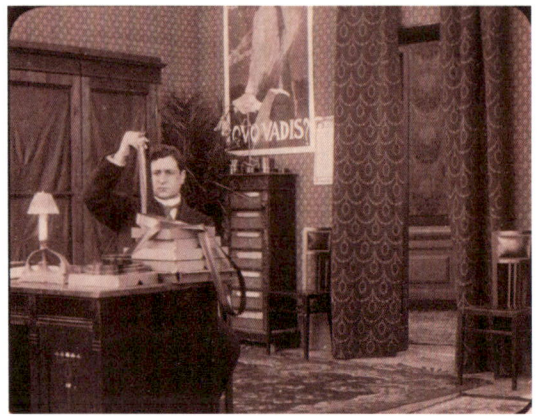

p. 24 l
Filmstrip with intertitle from
Enrico Guazzoni, *Una tragedia al cinematografo*, 1913

pp. 24 r, 25
Ernest Servaes, *Arthème opérateur*, 1913

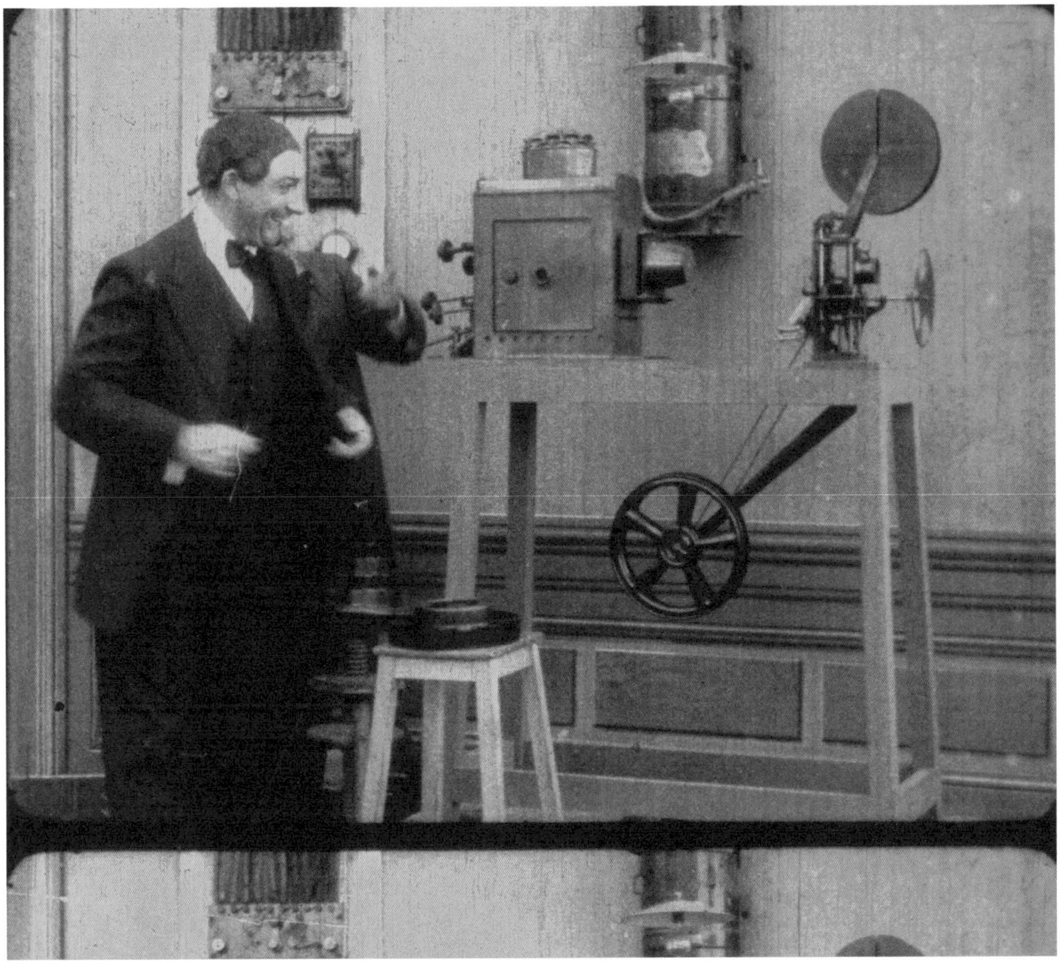

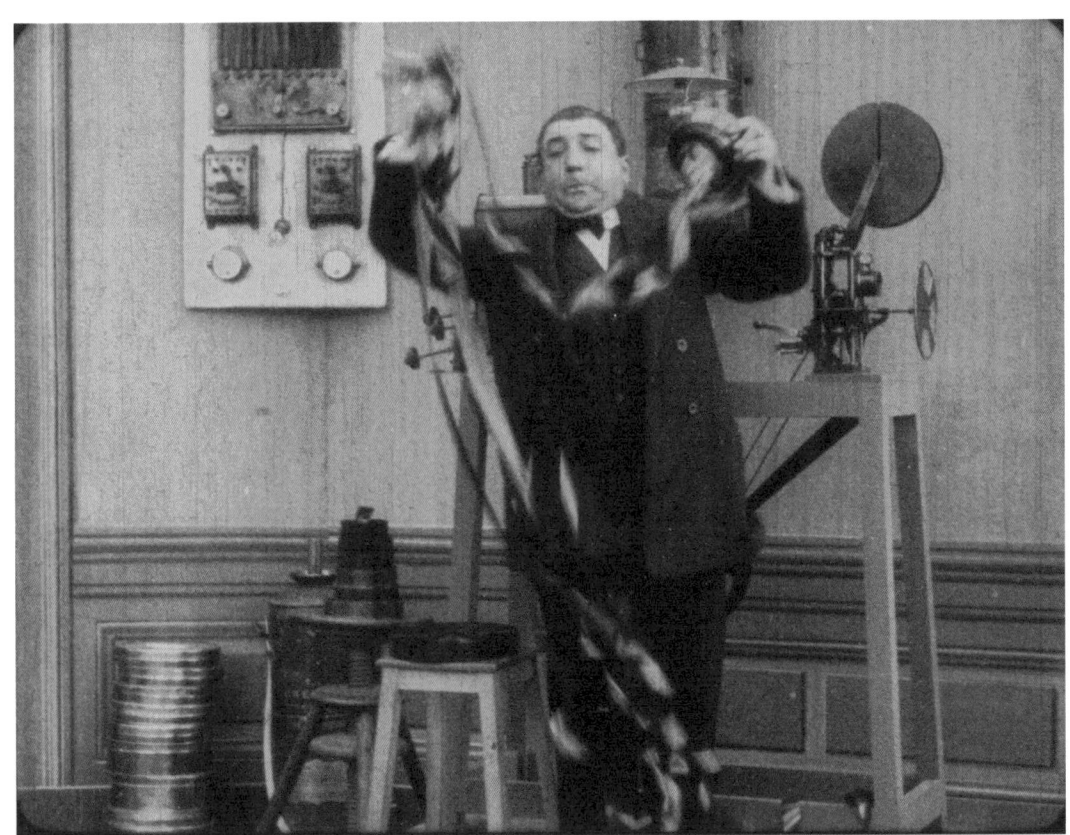

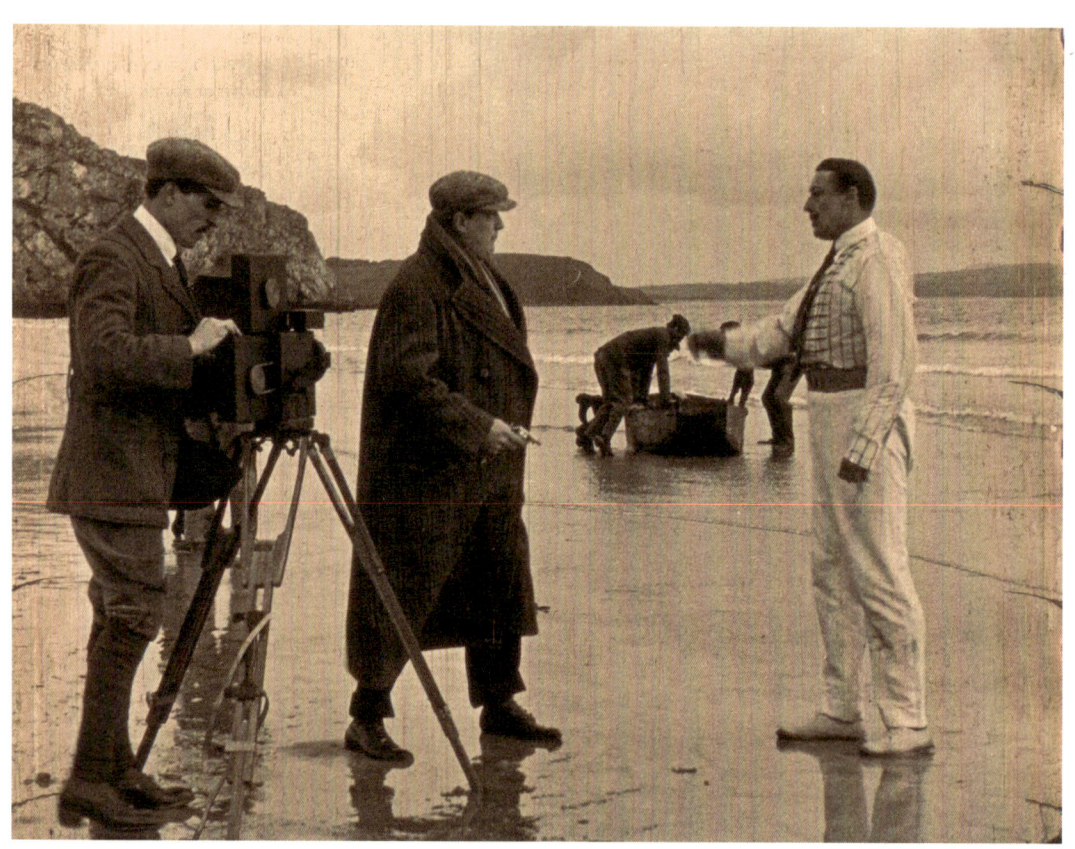

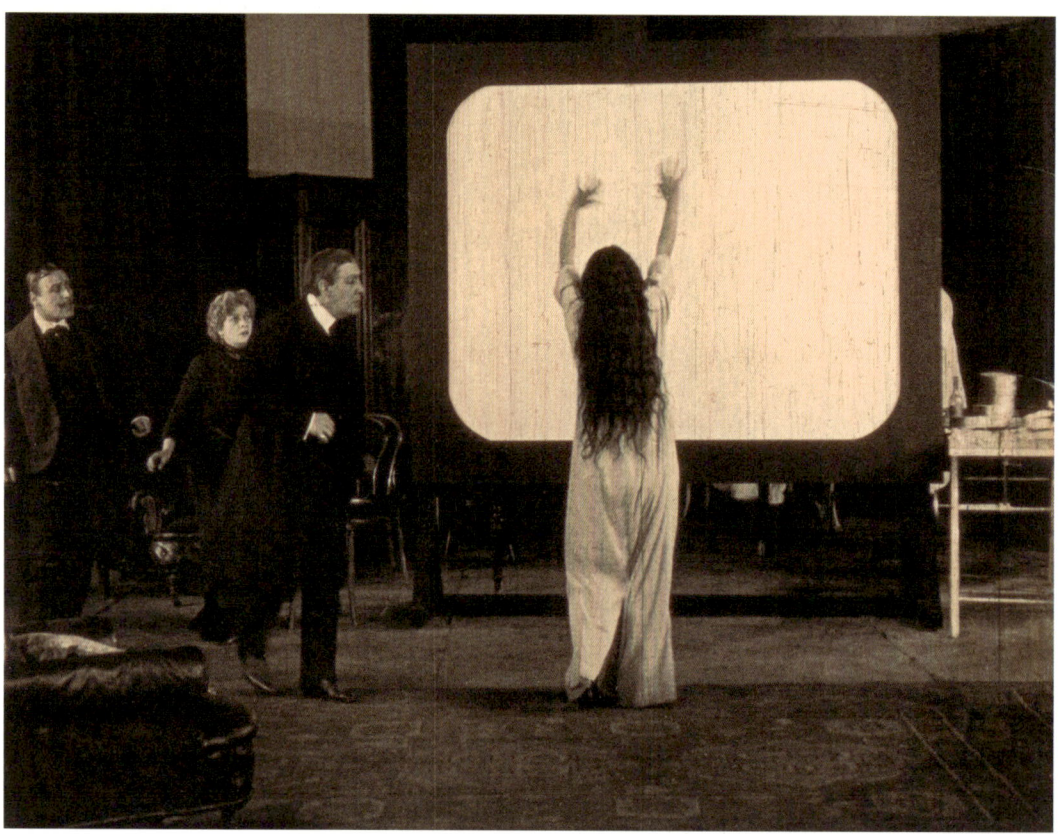

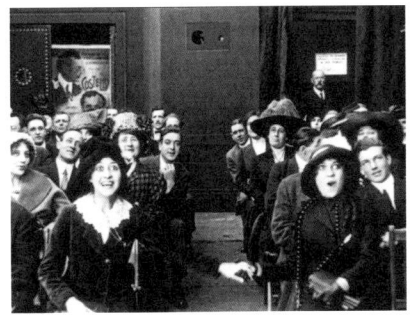
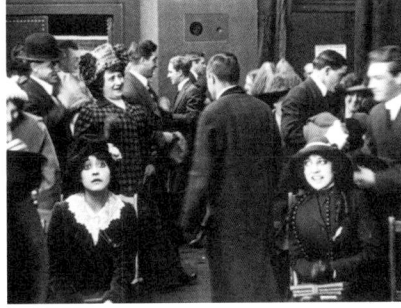
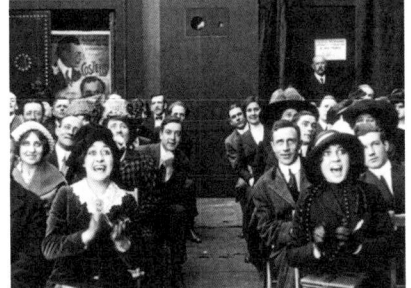
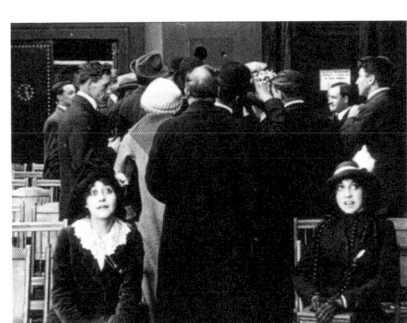

p. 26
Léonce Perret, *Le mystère des Roches de Kador*, 1912

p. 27
James Young, *The Picture Idol*, 1912

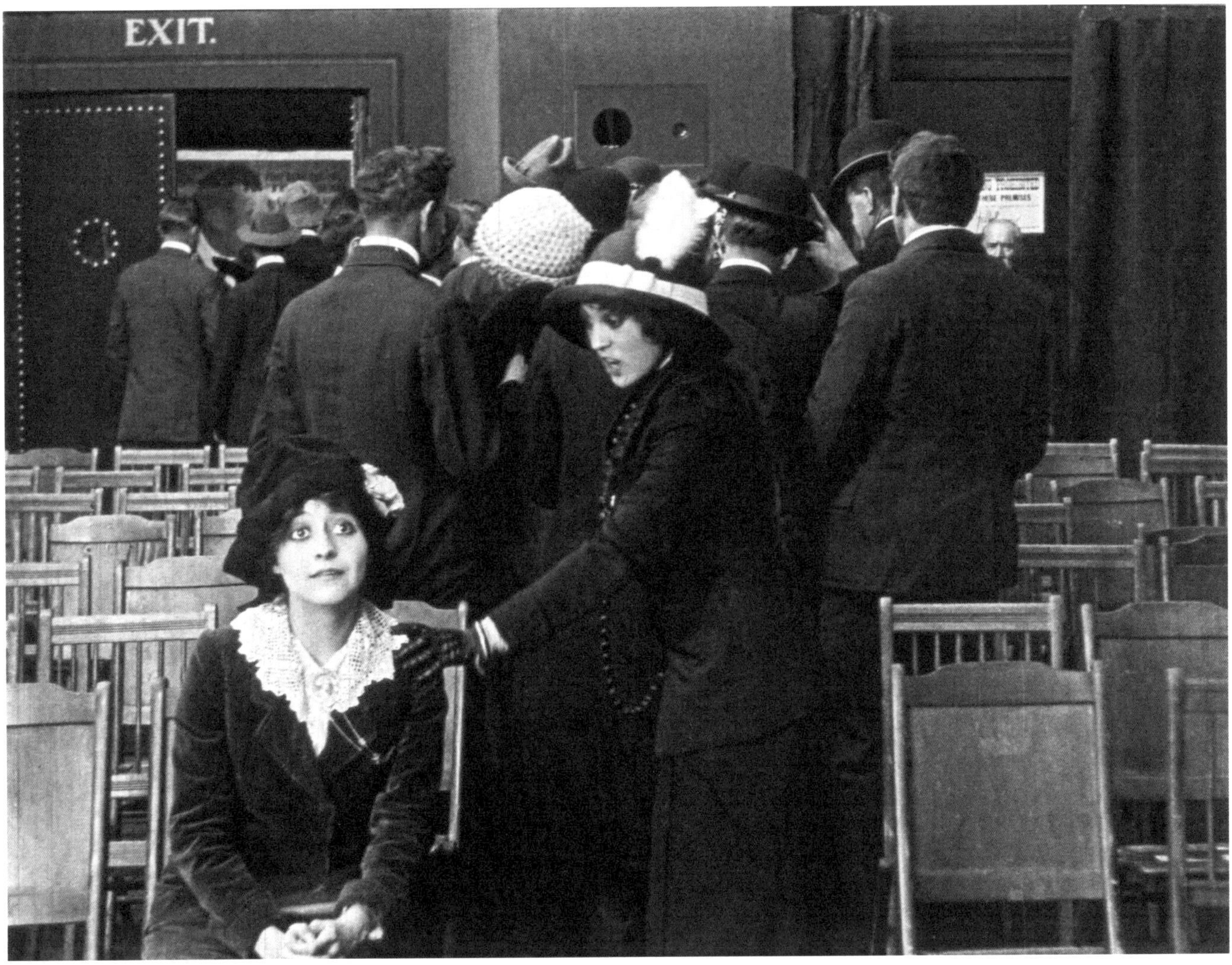

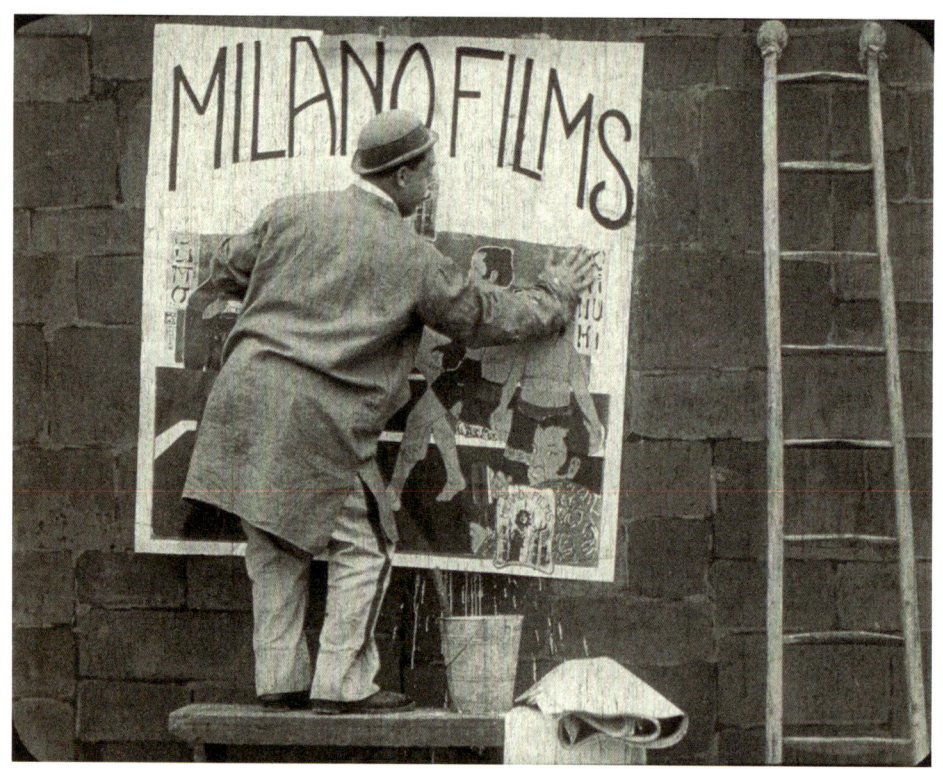

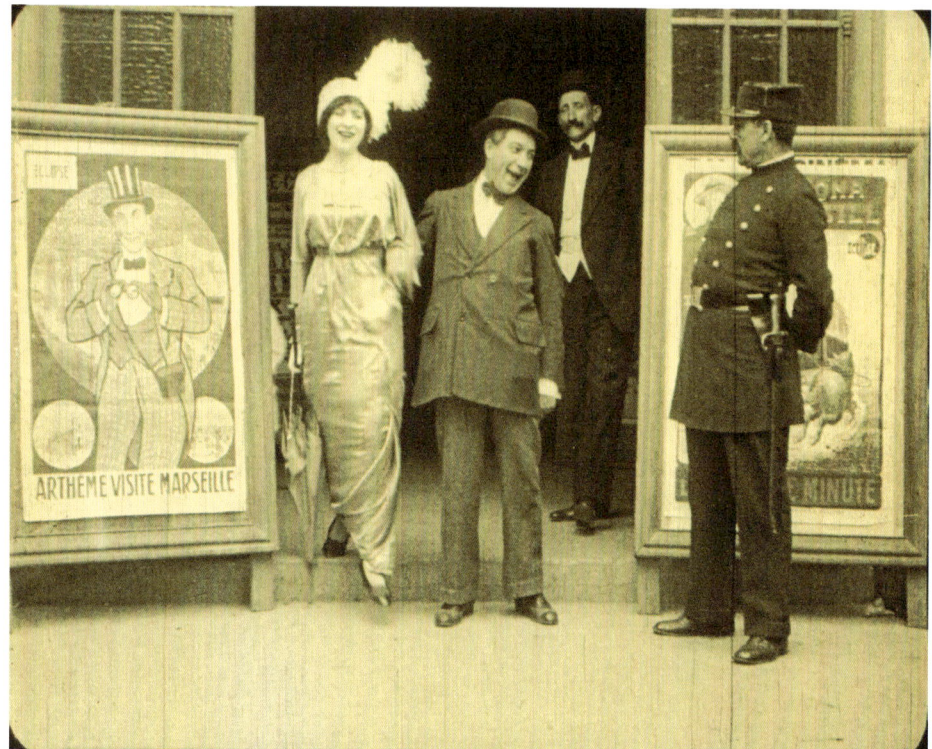

Cocciutelli affissatore, 1911

Ernest Servaes, *Arthème promène son oncle*, 1913

A Treasure Trove of Adventure and Experimentation

Mark-Paul Meyer

Segundo de Chomón, *La maison ensorcelée*, 1907

Between the time of the invention of the basic device (between 1890 and 1895) and the period of the institution (beginning around 1915), kinematography was a wide-open field of experimentation.

André Gaudreault [1]

The rediscovery and reappraisal of early cinema, from the first film screening by the Lumière brothers in 1895 until 1916, when Jean Desmet closed down his film distribution business, has been one of the most important developments in the study of film history over the past 30 years. While we used to believe that early films were clumsy and primitive, this image has changed completely: we now see them as adventurous and experimental. The early decades of film could be compared to the introduction of the Internet in our own day: a medium that had not yet settled into a definite form turns out, in retrospect, to have been a breeding ground of creativity, experimentation and entrepreneurial initiative.

From 1895 to 1916, all sorts of experiments explored the new technology and the possibilities of the medium, in contexts ranging from carnival attractions to high-class theatres. But early filmmakers were also intent on exploring potential modes of filmic representation. How could foreign cultures or everyday reality be depicted on the silver screen? How could the medium be used to narrate a historical drama or fictional love story, or to make tricks and illusions believable to the audience? Because there were not yet any institutionalized strategies for these purposes, we can now admire these films for their surprising and adventurous approaches to cinematic representation.

In the middle of this adventurous period, Jean Desmet decided to begin screening films. After buying a travelling cinema in 1907, he built up an empire of film theatres in just a few years' time. By also distributing his films to other exhibitors, he made it possible for millions of people to see his films and discover the dream factory of the cinema. Many of the films have been preserved, and the film collection and archive managed and made accessible by EYE offer a unique look at developments in this period and are of inestimable value to anyone who wishes to study and enjoy these audacious films.

In the film context, the phrase 'dream factory' typically refers to classic Hollywood cinema, known for transporting audiences into another world, creating an illusion in which they could lose themselves. From the 1920s to the 1960s, the Hollywood mode of representation and narration became the norm that determined how films had to be made. That same 'language of film' still dominates most major productions and is found in related genres such as the television drama. This is the film language that we all effortlessly understand. The classic Hollywood film tends to have a linear narrative – except for flashbacks or flash-forwards – and often involves a conflict that must be resolved, characters who develop in the course of the film and actions motivated by the psychological makeup of the characters. For audiences, such films provide clarity about the unities of place and time. Continuity is crucial and each scene is designed so that every detail plays a role in telling the story. Mise-en-scène, editing, lighting, sound (including music), props and other parameters all serve a narrative purpose.

The cinema of the Jean Desmet period (1907-1916) adhered to few or none of the conventions of classic Hollywood films. That explains why these films from the first two decades of the medium received so little attention for such a long time. For decades, these early films were hardly ever screened and our understanding of this period in film history was based largely on the studies of a small number of renowned film historians, who based their writings mainly on their personal recollections. This resulted in a preponderantly negative image of early film culture as primitive by the later standards of classic cinema. It was not until 1978 that this opinion began to be questioned and gradually reversed.

The immediate source of the renewed interest in early film was a conference in Brighton, England, organized in 1978 by the International Federation of Film Archives (known by its French acronym FIAF). Around 500 fictional films from the period 1900-1906 were shown to a group of internationally renowned film historians and theoreticians. For many of them the experience was a revelation and the years that followed saw a resurgence of research in the area. New generations of film historians and theoreticians have gone on studying early cinema to this day and the project is nowhere near complete. Not only are films still being discovered, but they are also becoming much more easily accessible to many more people, thanks to digitization. Not only films, but also posters, publicity materials and archival documents have been made available for study in digital form. The films and archives in the Desmet Collection are a case in point.

The fact that FIAF organized such a conference was a sign of changes in the world of film archives. The realization had hit home that the old nitrate films were on the verge of disintegration and that urgent action was required to preserve them for future generations. This new perspective on film heritage was underscored in 1980 when UNESCO published its Recommendation for the Safeguarding and Preservation of Moving Images, the product of eight years of work. This document, formally endorsed and accepted by

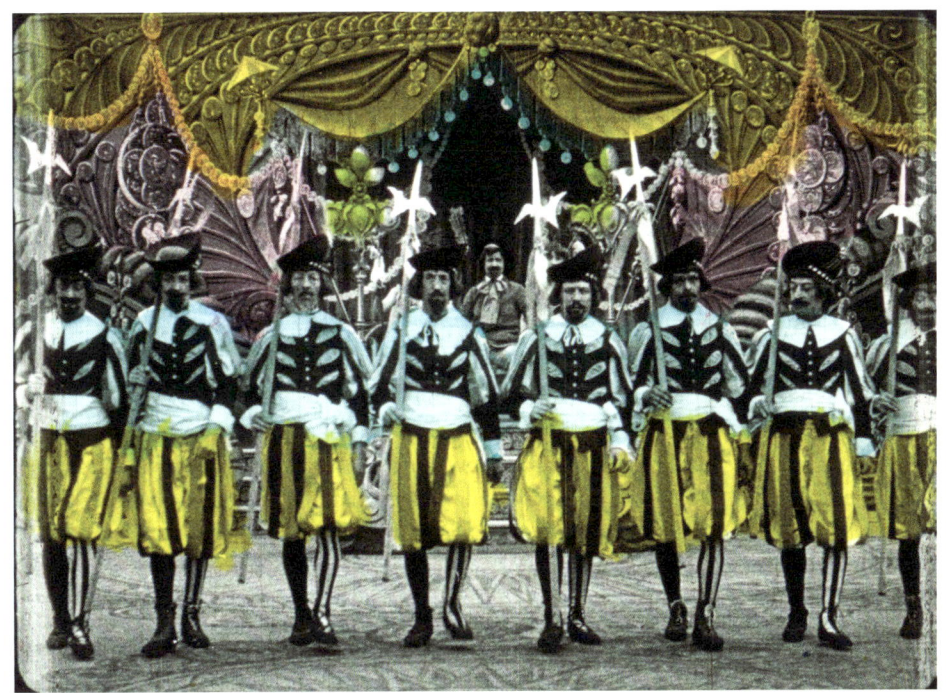

Lucien Nonguet, *L'obsession d'or*, 1906

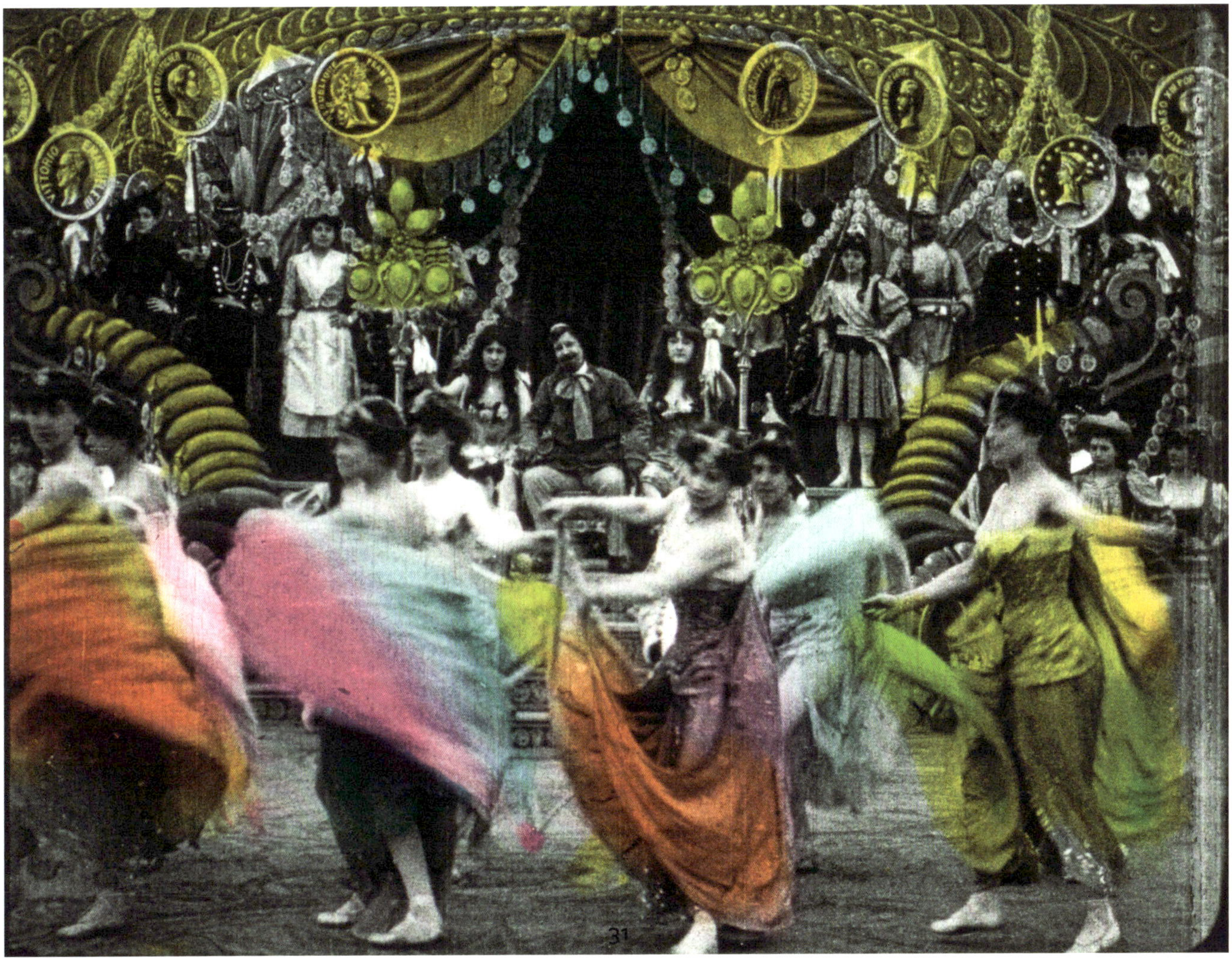

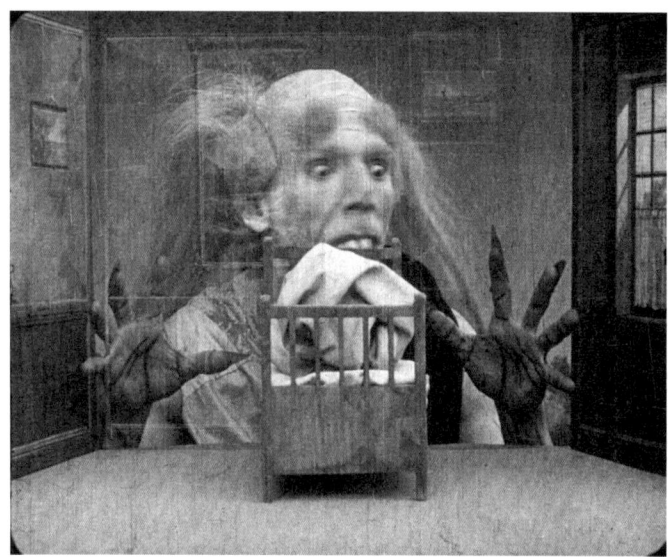

Segundo de Chomón, *La maison ensorcelée*, 1907

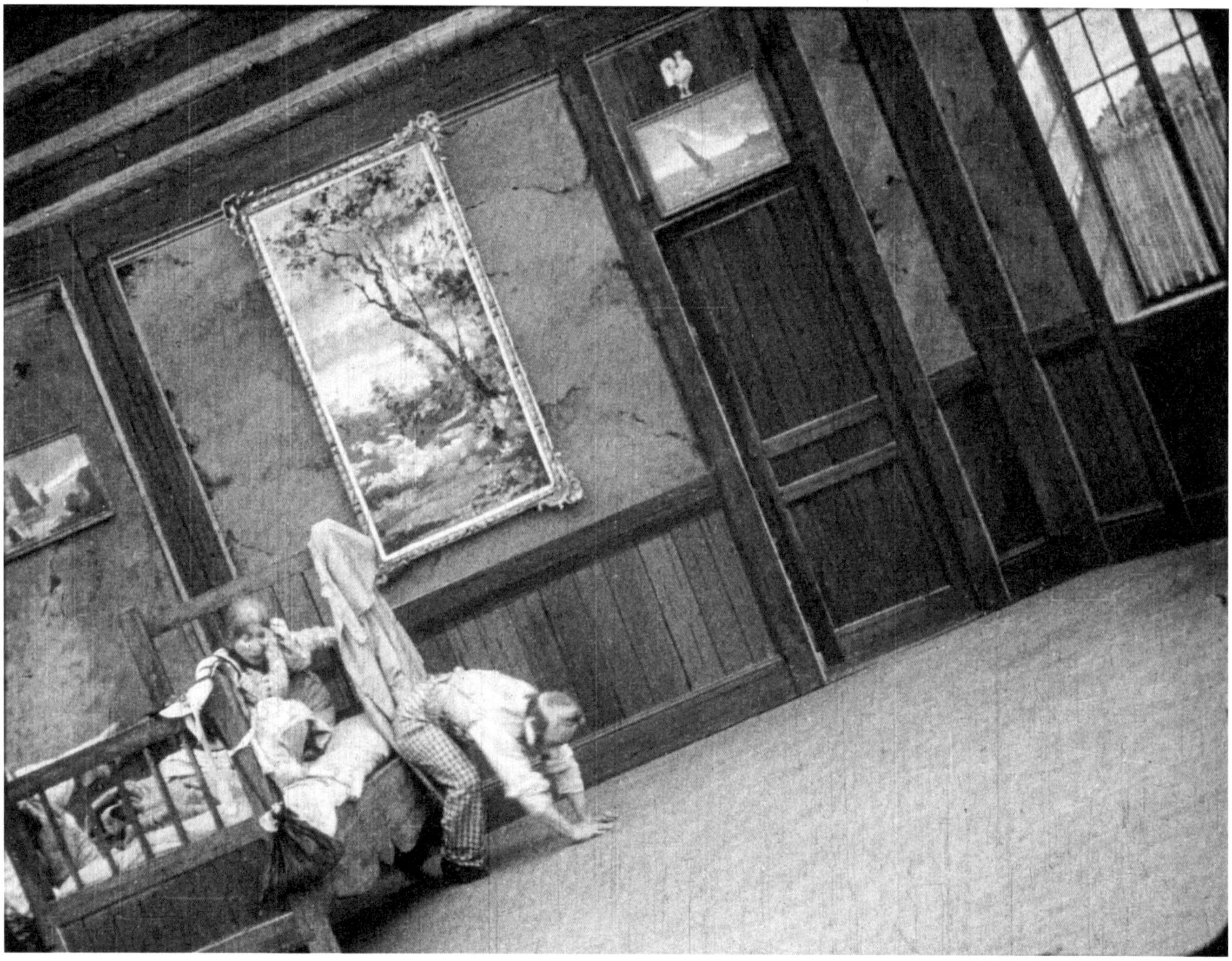

153 UN member states, placed film firmly on the international heritage agenda in the early 1980s.[2]

The conference in Brighton was seen as the start of what has been called 'The New Film History'. One hallmark of this new approach to historical writing was the insight that early cinema differed in essential ways from what followed, and was not simply a more primitive form. Furthermore, scholars paid greater attention to the context of production and presentation, rather than regarding films as autonomous works of art. A primarily art-historical approach made way for a broader cultural-historical approach, in which film was regarded as being embedded in a living culture of theatre, illustration, photography, scholarship and science.

In Brighton, filmmaker and critic Noël Burch gave a talk on the films of Edwin S. Porter (1870-1941), one of the pioneers of American cinema.[3] Burch criticized the linear perspective from which film history was written and the normative implications of that perspective. In other words, he was fed up with film history as the story of the 'first close-up', 'first use of parallel editing', first this, first that. He used Porter's early films, most of which date from around 1903, to illustrate that the development of early film was anything but linear. This set the tone for the up-and-coming generation of film historians and theoreticians. Along with the understanding that early film history could be written and rewritten only by watching and studying early films, there was also an understanding that a linear or teleological approach to film history was simply not justified by the facts.

Two scholars of the new generation who also attended the conference would later become the protagonists of the New Film History: Tom Gunning and André Gaudreault.[4] In the 1980s, they published analyses suggesting that a major shift had occurred around 1907. Before then, films had emphasized showing, displaying, but after 1907, a more narrative form of cinema became dominant. This was the start of a tendency that would later lead to classic Hollywood cinema.

Gunning and Gaudreault dubbed pre-1907 cinema the 'cinema of attractions', meaning cinema that emphasized showing rather than telling, presenting rather than representing.[5] This 'exhibiting' aspect is what makes these films so modern. In many respects, these early films explore the same artistic strategies as present-day art films. They are not films that attempt to transport the viewers to another reality, that present an invisible window on a fictional world; on the contrary, they seem to consistently emphasize the intervening medium. The framing is eccentric, the intertitles halt the forward movement of the action, the colours are unrealistic, many images have no narrative purpose or significance but are there simply to be admired, and occasionally an actor or actress addresses the cinema audience directly. All this would become taboo in classic cinema, but we can appreciate these fascinating examples of adventure and experimentation.

Gunning and Gaudreault have observed that there was a turning point around 1907, when a few films that can be seen as forerunners of classic narrative cinema first came to the screen. Regardless of how much truth there may be in their claim, this was not a root-and-branch shift, not visible in all films produced. Most of the films shown between 1907 and 1916 still had one foot, and usually both, in 'the era of the cinema of attractions'. The film world did not change from one moment to the next. Furthermore, film production was a very complex business at that time, involving many production studios, many nationalities and many practices specific to one country or studio. In other words, the differences between studios were vast, and while film was a highly international industry, developments in different places certainly did not follow the same timeline.

Because the proponents of the New Film History focused specifically on the very earliest period of cinema, the period from 1907 to 1916 has not been studied as exhaustively as the preceding decade. This happens to be the exact period in which Jean Desmet was active. The films in the Jean Desmet Collection illustrate the complexities involved in making any firm generalization about this period, because it was such a confusing, unclear epoch. To be sure, the harbingers of Hollywood cinema were already in evidence, but a very great deal remained as it had been. That is what makes the Desmet Collection so interesting: Desmet bought and distributed films not to illustrate lines of artistic development, but to entertain a wide audience for financial gain. He was first and foremost a businessman, and when he purchased films, the first thing on his mind was profit rather than art. As a result of this pragmatism, his collection offers an admirable cross section of the mainstream cinema of the day.

This period, when many things remained fluid and uncertain, offers present-day viewers a real adventure as well. Styles, genres, forms, techniques and strategies – they are all interwoven. What we find is not a preliminary stage on the way to a fixed system, but an exploration of the possibilities inherent in the film medium and a quest to push the limits as far as possible. Both formally and stylistically, it was a period of tremendous freedom, a time of experimentation on which we can look back in admiration and amazement 100 years later. At this juncture, it is tempting to draw a comparison to the situation in classical music at the dawn of the twentieth century. Classical composition was undergoing revolutionary transformations and in 1907 the composer and musicologist Ferruccio Busoni declared that music had been born free and aspired to regain its freedom.[6] The cinema of the 1910s was free – 'a wide-open field of experimentation' – but the system of classic Hollywood cinema placed it in shackles. Now, 100 years later, we might say that cinema has regained its freedom. The strategies of classic Hollywood film are still on display in our cinemas, but we are also open to other forms of cinematic representation, to Japanese, Russian and African films, to experimental films and art films, to films in art galleries and museum exhibitions – and thus to early cinema as well. To be sure, these 'free-style' films are not always immediately comprehensible, but that is inherent in the fact that their cinematic language is foreign to us.

In 1992, Eric de Kuyper, filmmaker, writer and former deputy director of the Netherlands Filmmuseum, wrote a thought-provoking article about 'the foreign language of the silent film'.[7] He compared the experience of watching a silent film to that of speaking a foreign language. You have to learn the fundamentals and acquire a basic vocabulary before you can communicate. Learning a foreign language requires a modicum of effort, and even with a decent command of the language you often find yourself a little rusty if you haven't spoken it in a while. Early cinema is somewhat comparable: you have to learn to watch it. Over time, you take a growing pleasure in it and it reveals secrets that are not apparent on the surface.

Eric de Kuyper has also provided a noteworthy explanation of the distinction between showing and telling, based on the fact that cinema was embedded in a much broader visual culture and that traditions and cultural expressions do not transform from one thing to another overnight. De Kuyper's point of departure is the difference between dramatic and epic theatre. Dramatic theatre provides the model for the later Hollywood film, which relies heavily on causality and in which the characters set the plot in motion. In contrast, epic theatre consists of tableaux, often with many primary and secondary characters, and is less focused on particular actions and dialogues. De Kuyper also points out that the major events in epic theatre often occur offstage, between the acts, out of sight of the audience.

Many films from the 1910s have this epic quality. This is most obvious in the case of historical drama, with its magnificent, compelling images. Many of the stories were part of the intellectual baggage of the average spectator in those days and it was therefore possible to tell them through minimalistic means. But if you watched these films without intertitles or prior knowledge of the story, you would hardly be able to follow them.

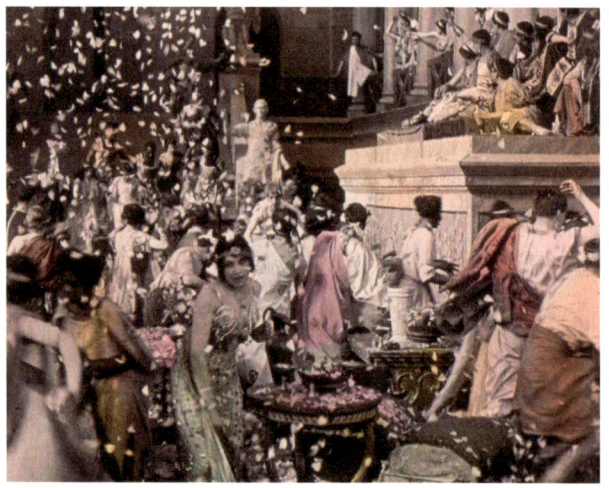

p. 34
Louis Feuillade, *L'orgie romaine*
(*Die Löwen des Tyrannen*), 1911

p. 35
Concorso di bellezza fra bambini a Torino, 1909

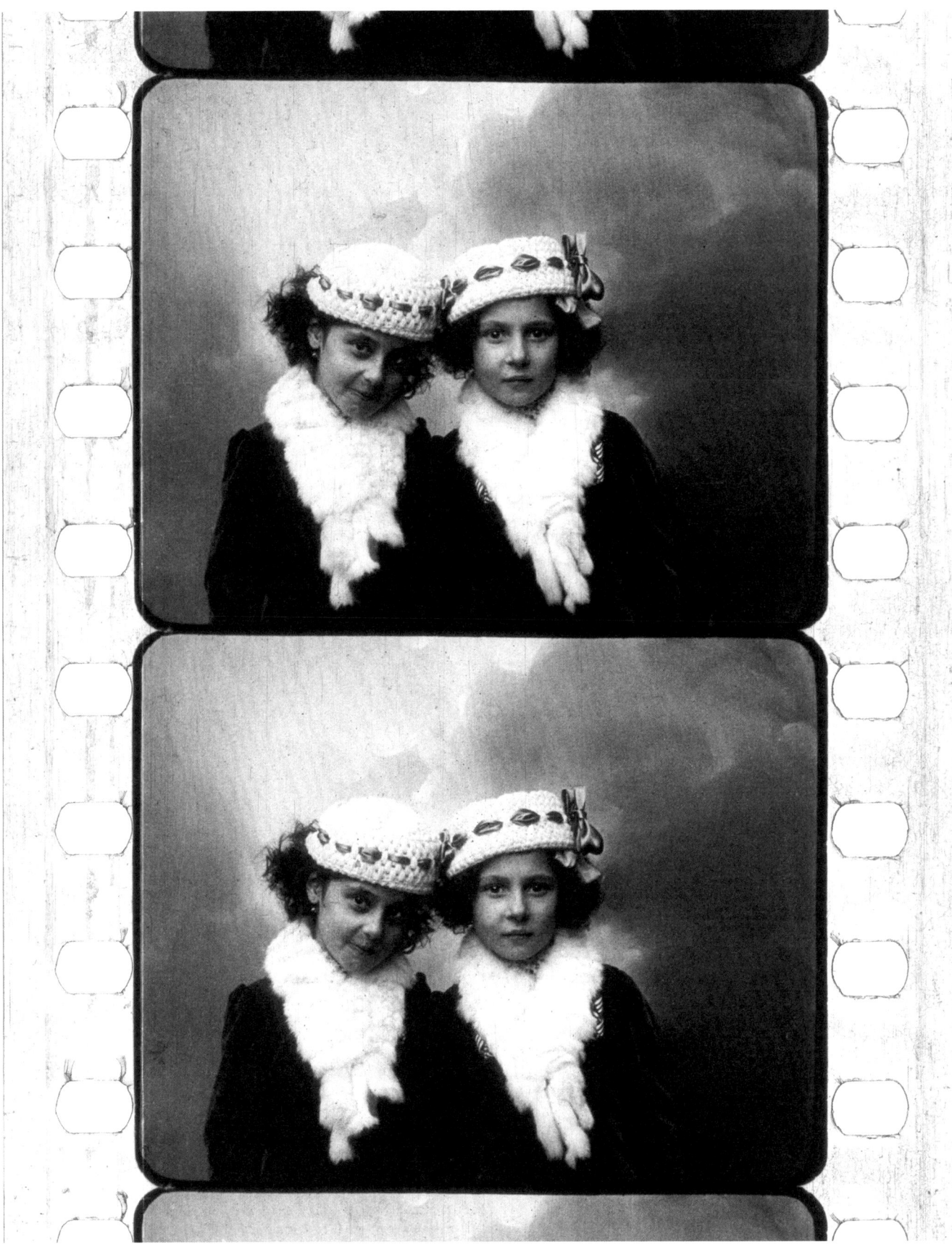

Their power lies not in drawing the viewer into the story or into an illusionistic world, but in visualizing and enacting the key moments in the drama. That explains what today's viewers admire in these films: they are visual galleries of carefully composed moving photography.

What do these observations imply for the rediscovered continent of silent film? Firstly, that we should not see these films as primitive, but judge them on their own merits and recognize that they still speak to us – in particular, their photographic and filmic strategies, which are not dominated by the classic Hollywood system. Tom Gunning called the early cinema a 'Coney Island of the avant-garde'.[8] The image of early cinema as a carnival, a breeding ground for experimentation and innovation, may be more relevant than ever. Now is the time to return to these films for a closer look and to begin our search for the essence of film with the experimentation and freedom of the early cinema. What makes these films so interesting to us today is the fact that, in their own way, they reflect on the specificity of the medium; they express a visual culture that can enrich our own. Seen in this light, early cinema is not a relic from the distant past, but a resource that can easily be put to use in the present. This ease of use is illustrated by found-footage films, in which filmmakers and visual artists reuse old film footage to make new films and generate new meanings, by screenings of silent films with live music by present-day composers and musicians, or by the use of these films by VJs, theatre ensembles and dance troupes. The Desmet Collection is one of the treasure troves of EYE and a superlative source for historical research, but above all it is a collection that can tell us a great deal about the essence of film. Therein lies the relevance of this unique collection today.

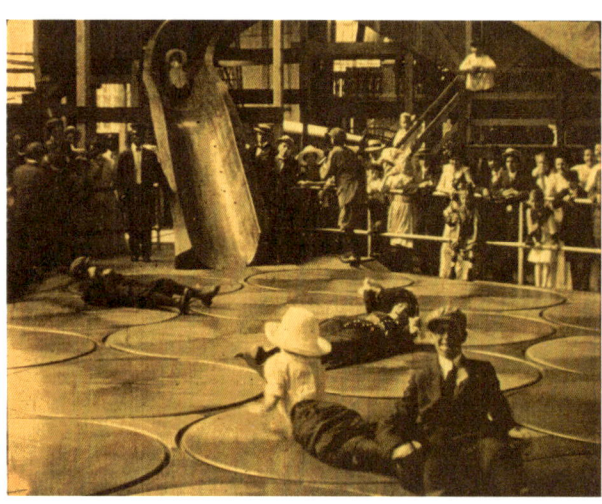

Mack Sennett, *At Coney Island*, 1912

1
A. Gaudreault et al., *Film and Attraction: From Kinematography to Cinema* (Urbana, 2011), 39.

2
C. Frick, *Saving Cinema: The Politics of Preservation* (Oxford, 2011), 111.

3
N. Burch, 'Porter, or Ambivalence', *Screen*, vol. 19 no. 4 (1978), 91-106.

4
The most relevant sources can be found in the collection W. Strauven (ed.), *The Cinema of Attractions Reloaded* (Amsterdam, 2006).

5
'Monstration (showing) is to narration (telling) what presentation is to representation.' Ibid., 15.

6
'Frei ist die Tonkunst geboren und frei zu werden ihre Bestimmung', in: Ferruccio Busoni, *Entwurf einer neuen Ästhetik der Tonkunst* (Leipzig, 1916).

7
E. de Kuyper, *De vreemde taal van de stomme film. Film in de periode 1910-1915* (NFM theme series; 4) (Amsterdam, 1992).

8
T. Gunning, 'The Cinema of Attraction[s]. Early Film, Its Spectator and the Avant-Garde', in: Strauven, *The Cinema of Attractions Reloaded*, op. cit. (note 4), 387.

Speed

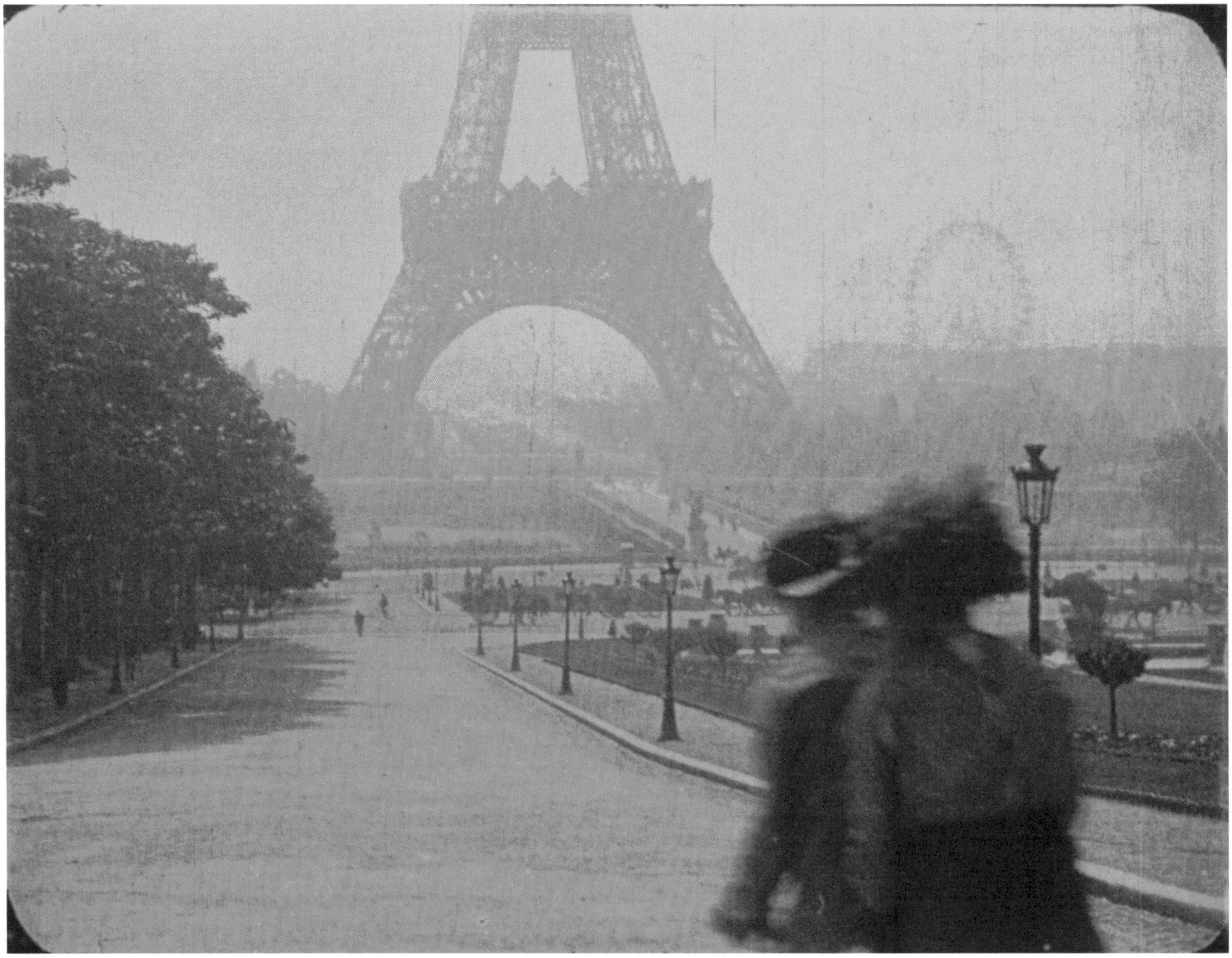

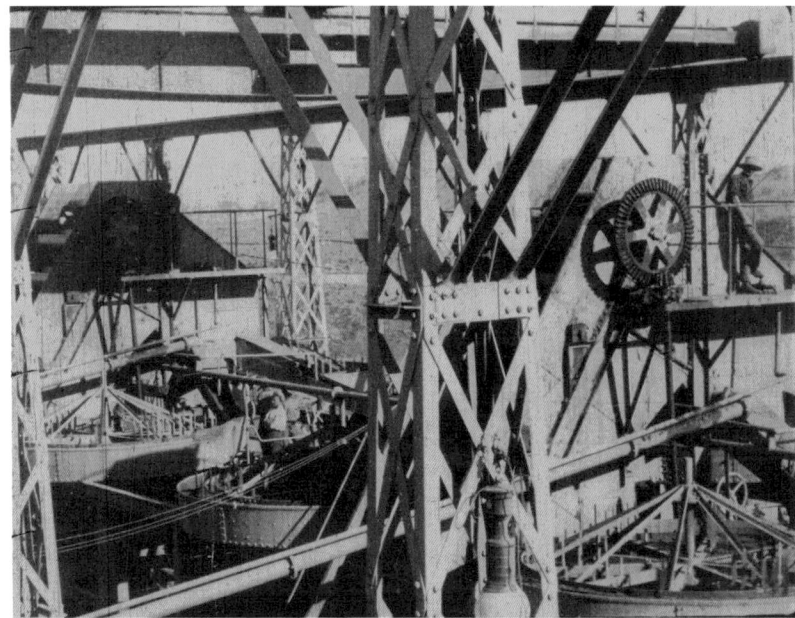

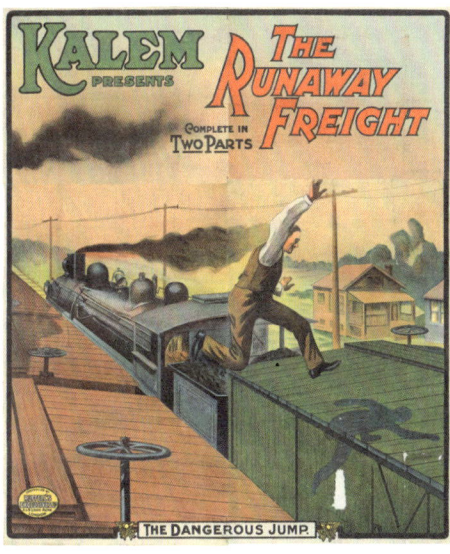

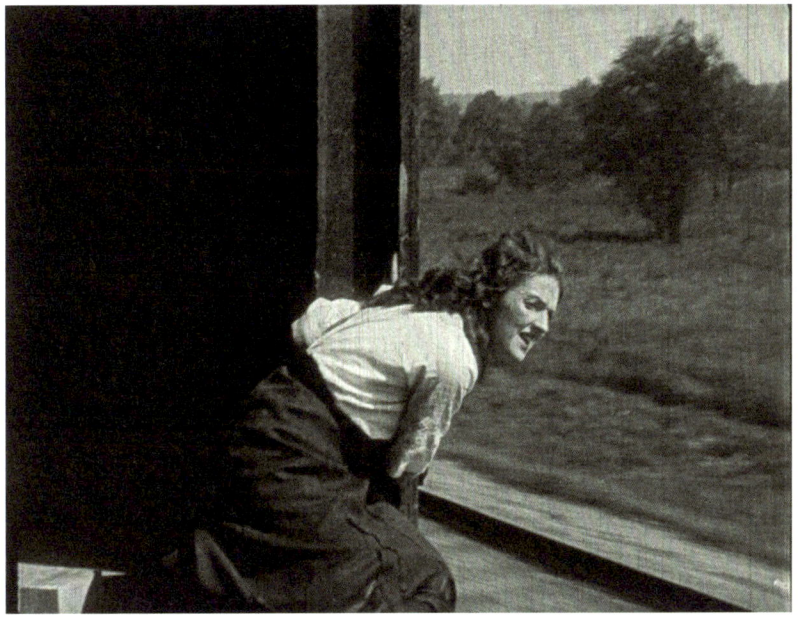

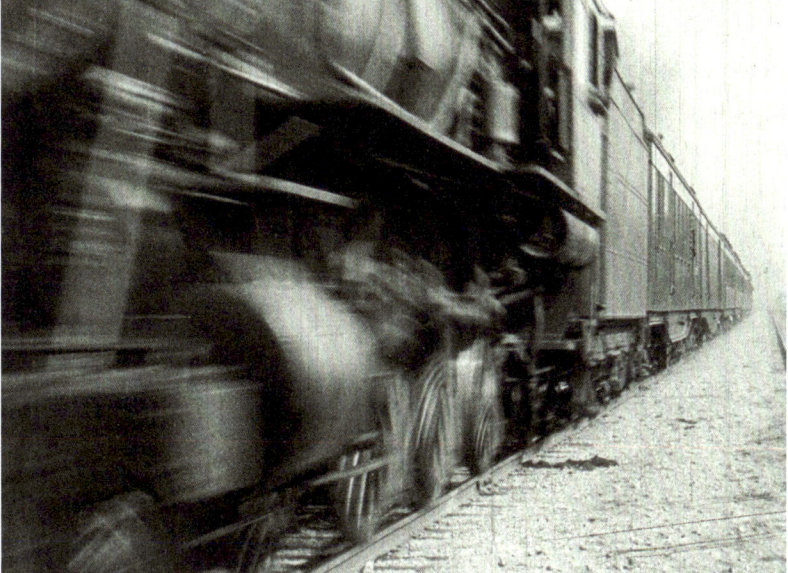

p. 38
Une partie de tandem, 1909

Binnenland van Afrika (The interior of Africa), 1910

p. 39
Poster for *The Runaway Freight*, 1913
222 x 196 cm

A Freight Train Drama, 1912

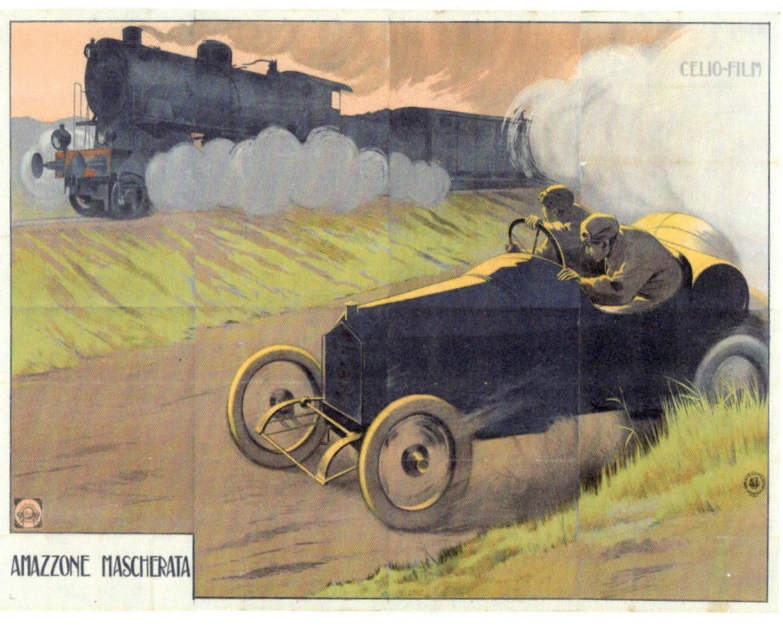

p. 40
Poster for *L'amazzone mascherata*, 1914
277 x 400 cm

Baldassarre Negroni,
L'amazzone mascherata, 1914

p. 41
Poster for *The Streets of New York*, 1913
106 x 71 cm

Poster for *Hochspannung*, 1913
210 x 150 cm

Tefft Johnson, *Love Finds a Way*, 1912

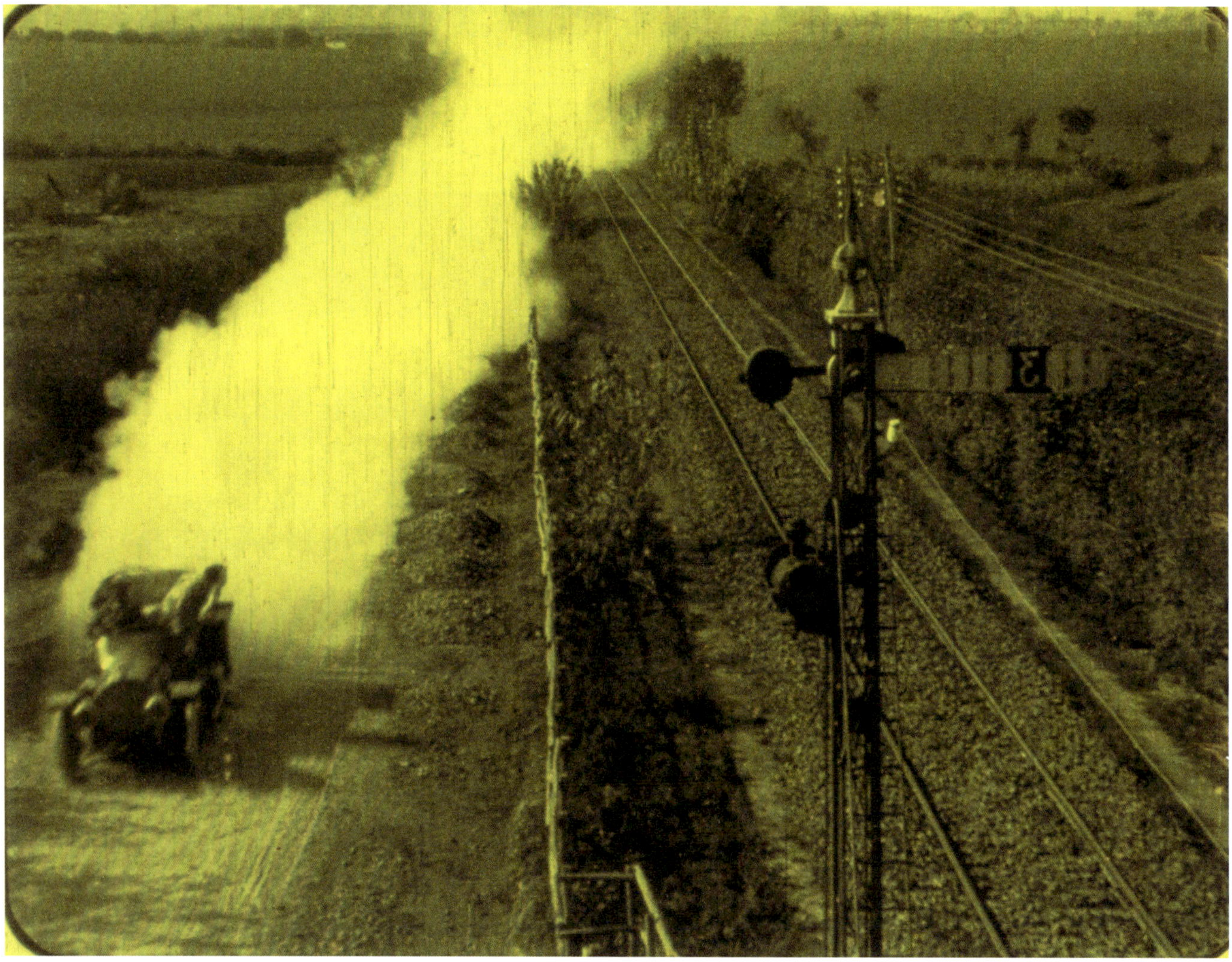

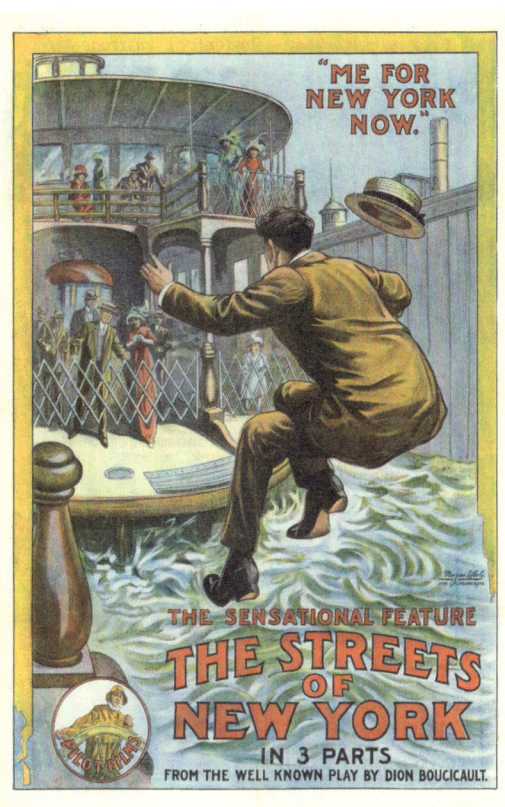
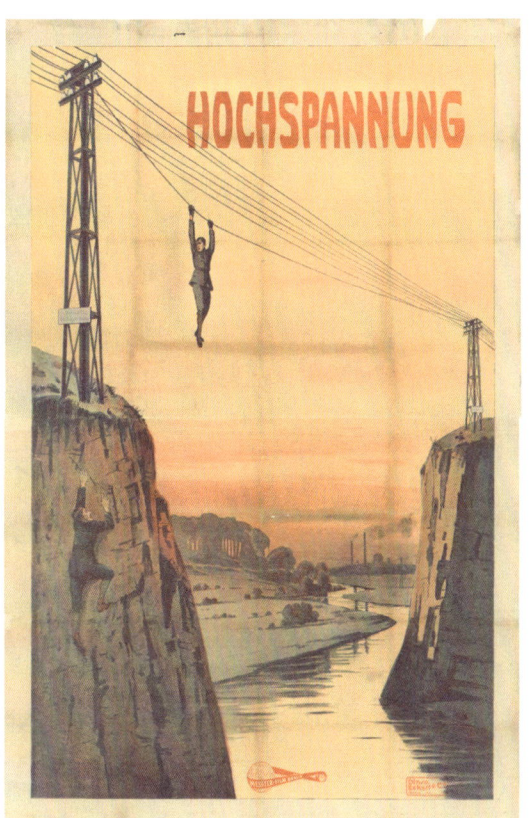
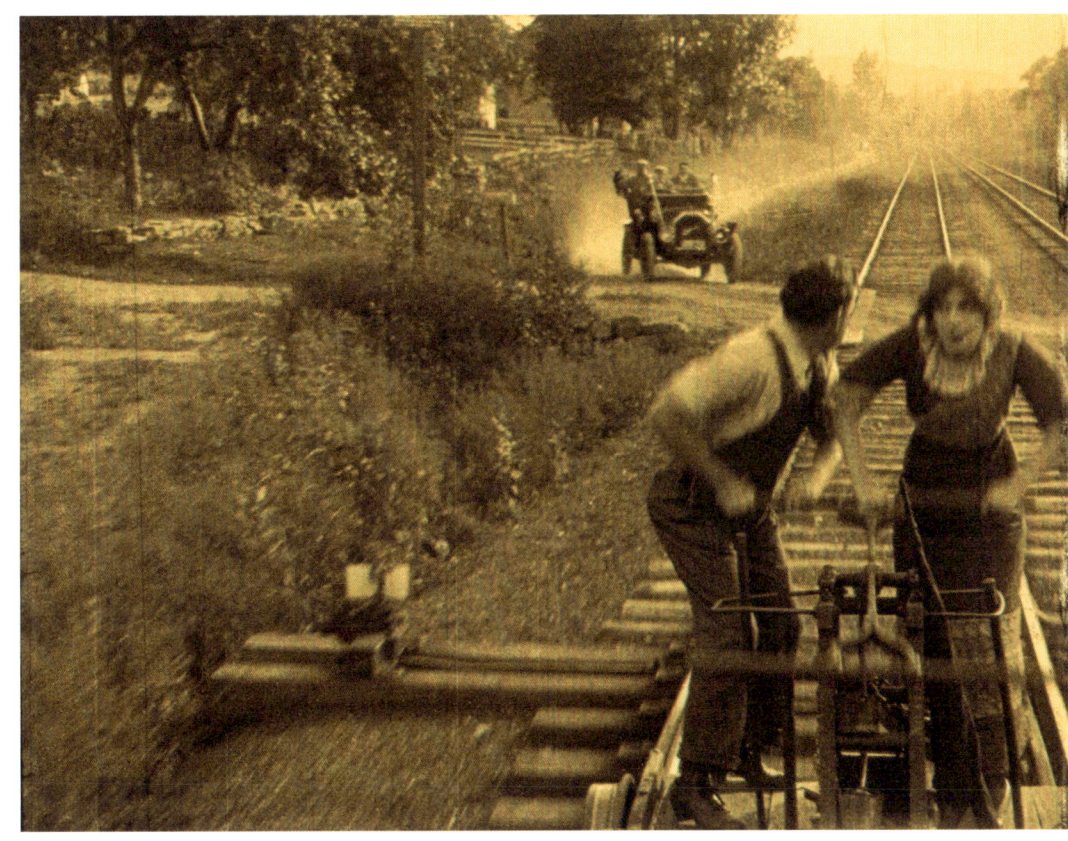

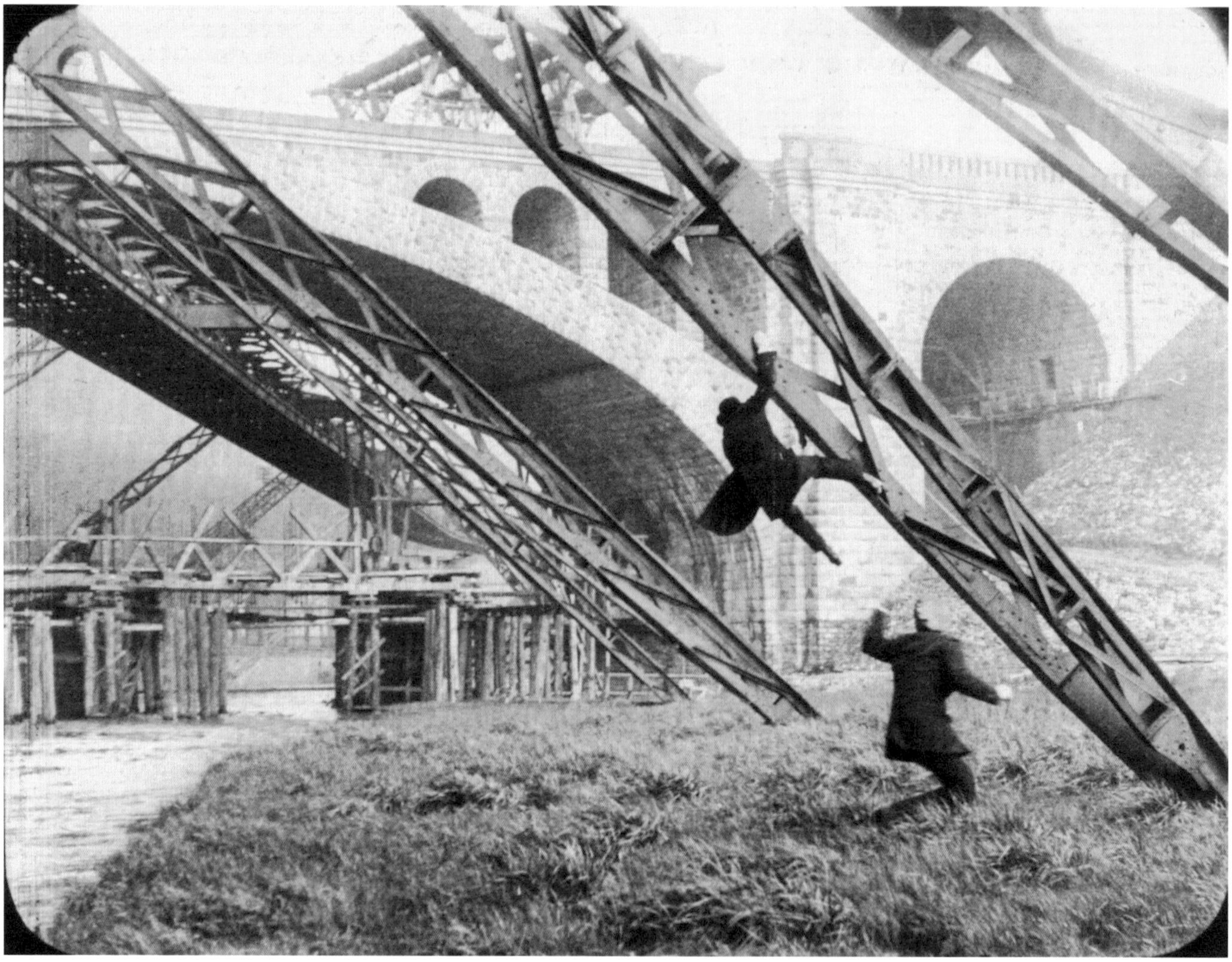

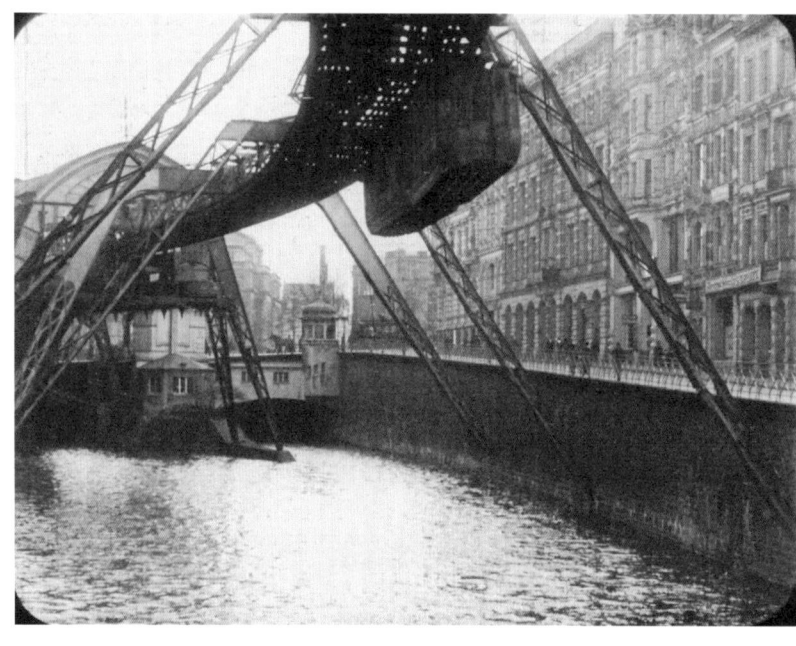

Das Abenteuer eines Journalisten, 1914

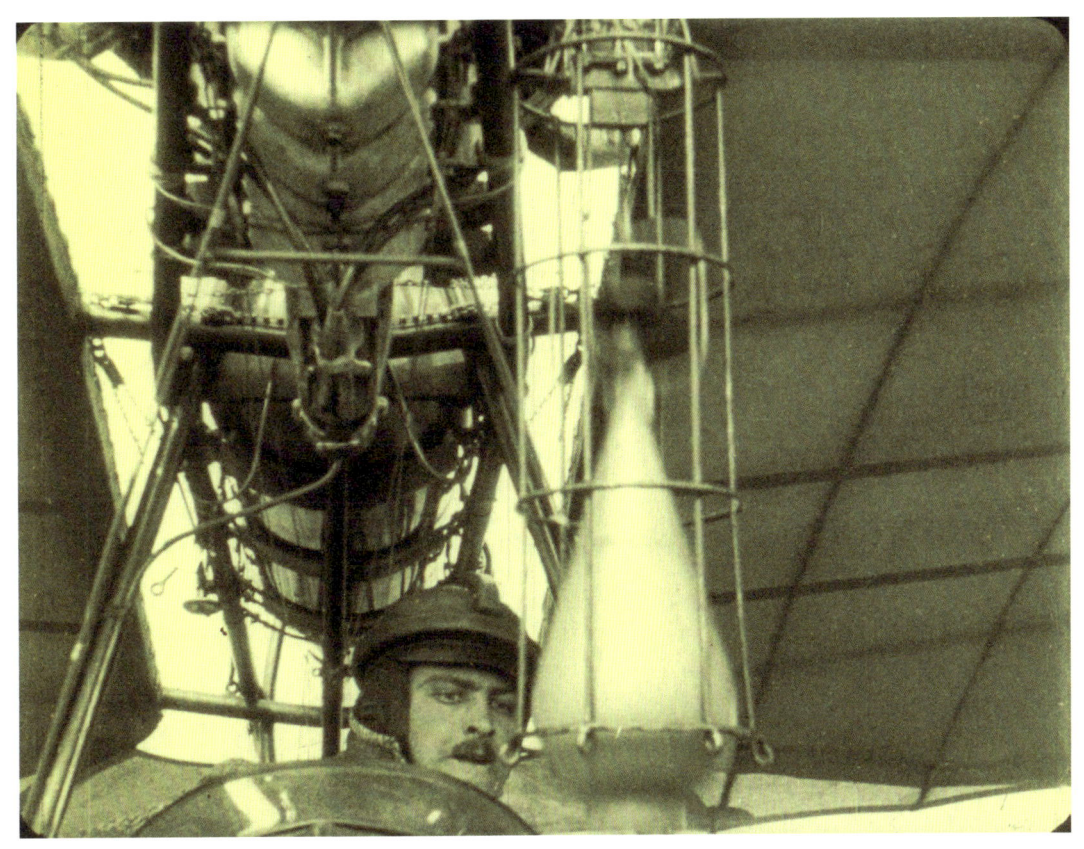
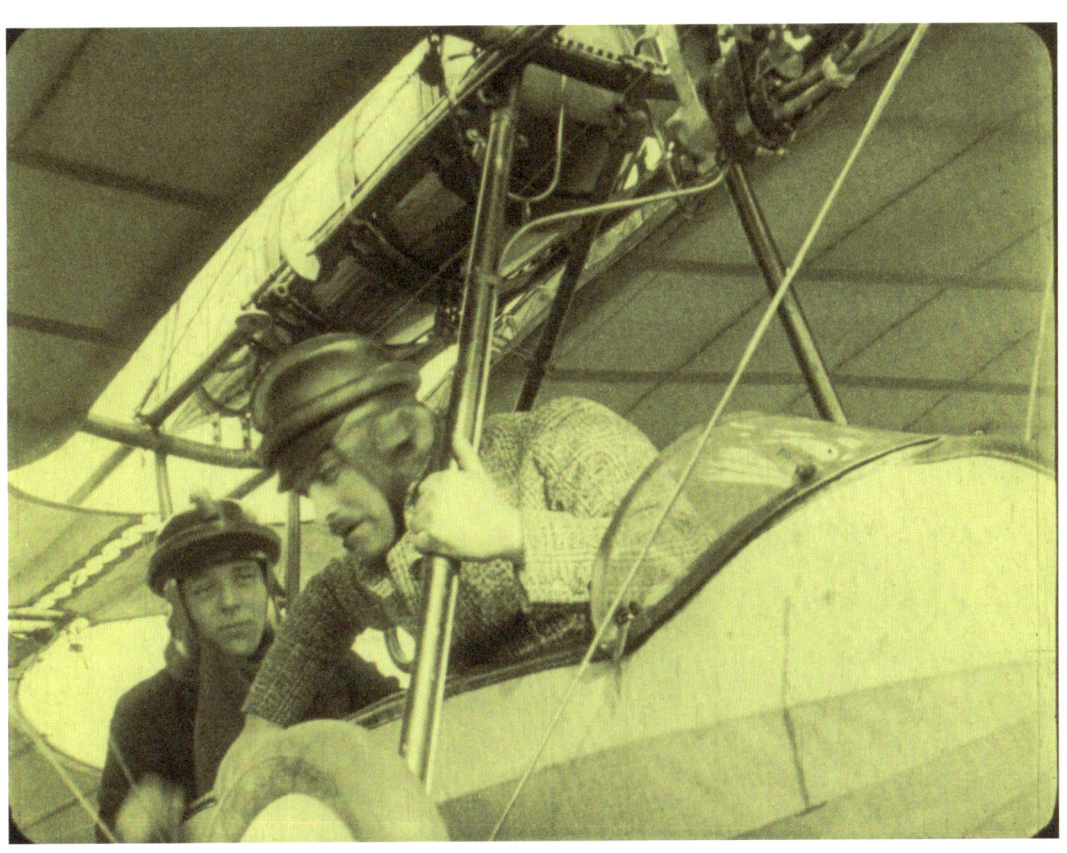

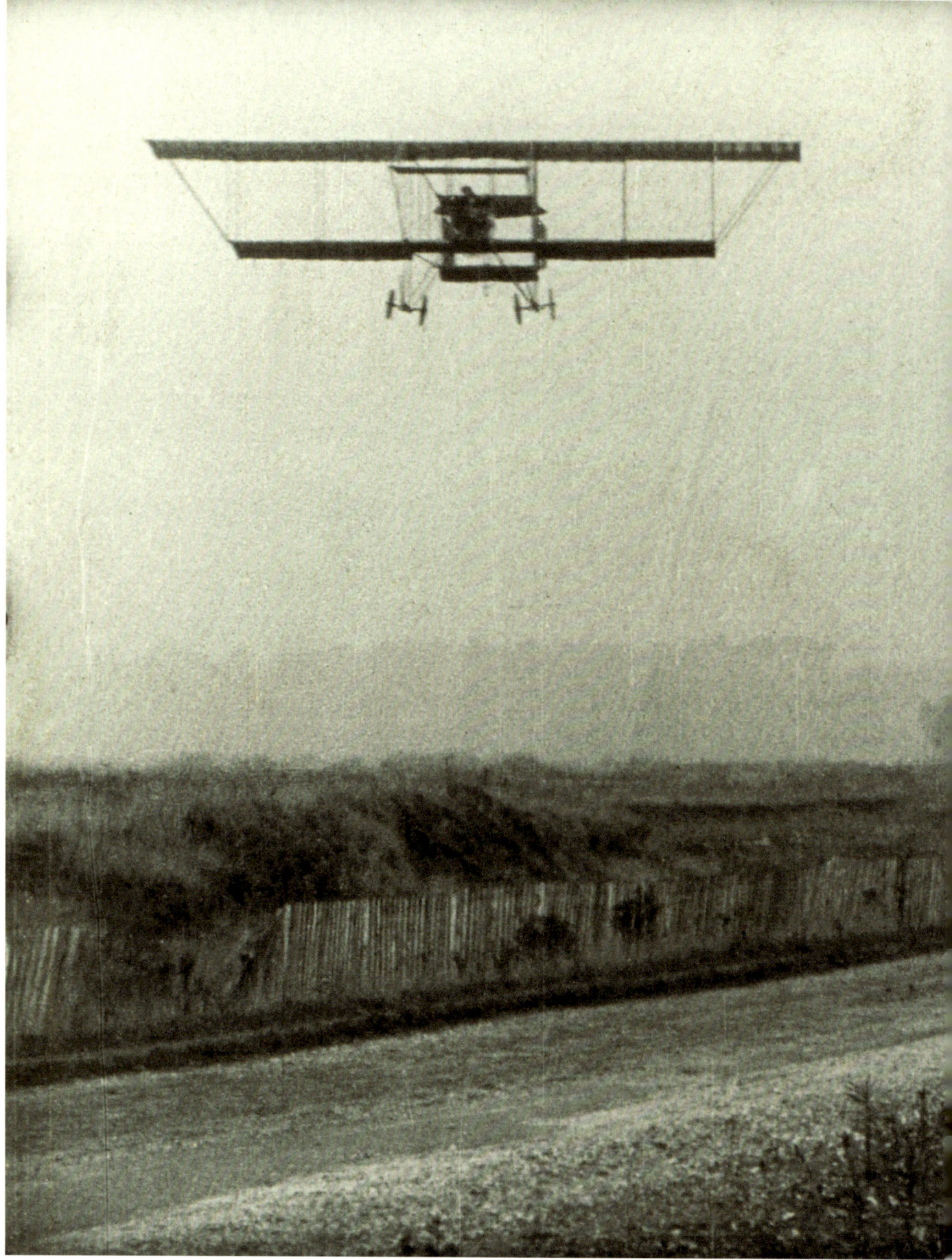

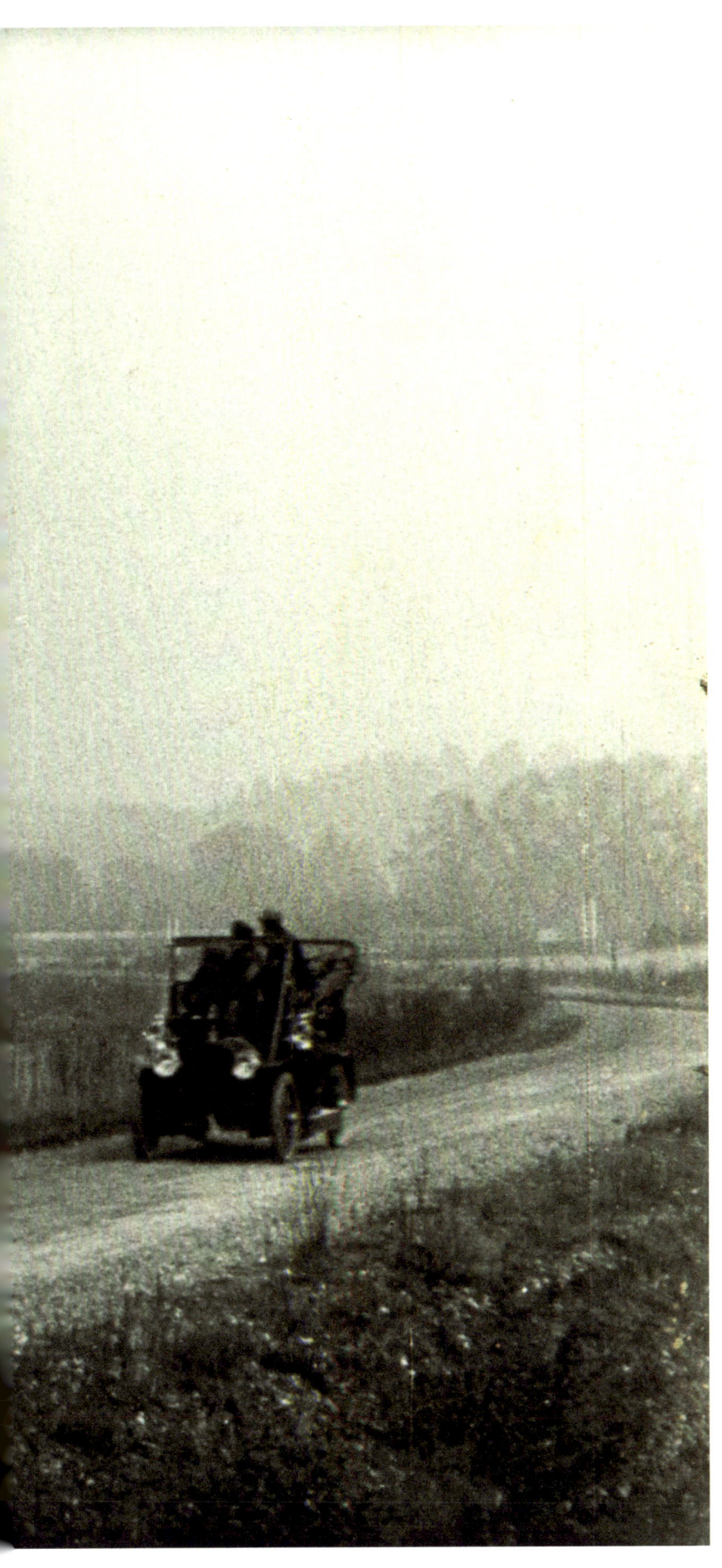

Frank Wilson, *The Jewel Thieves Outwitted*, 1913

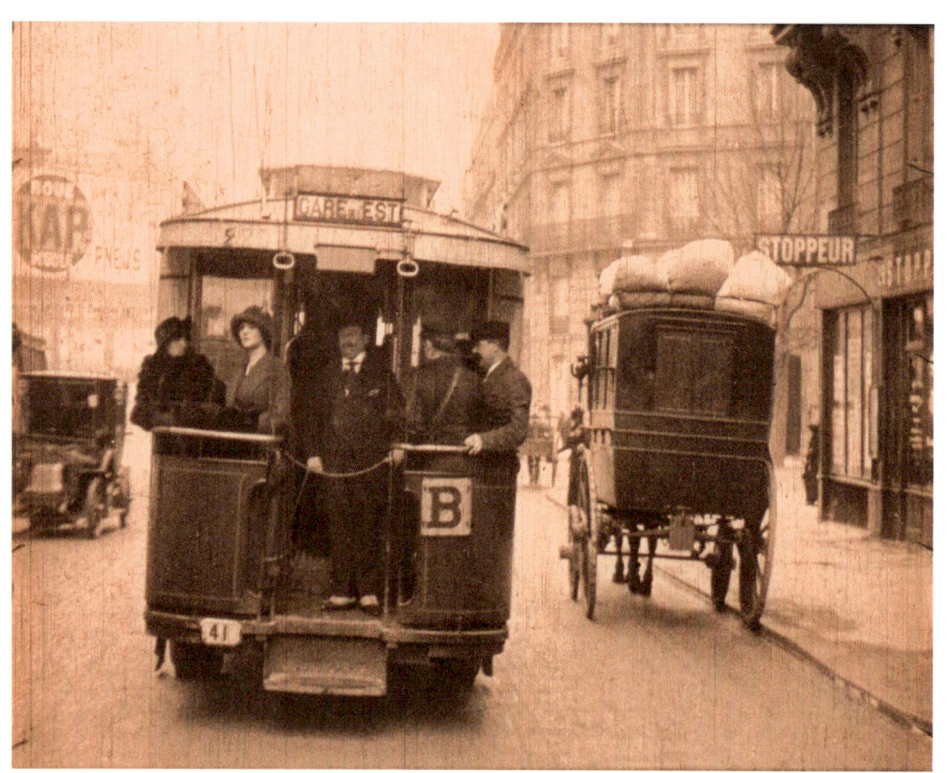

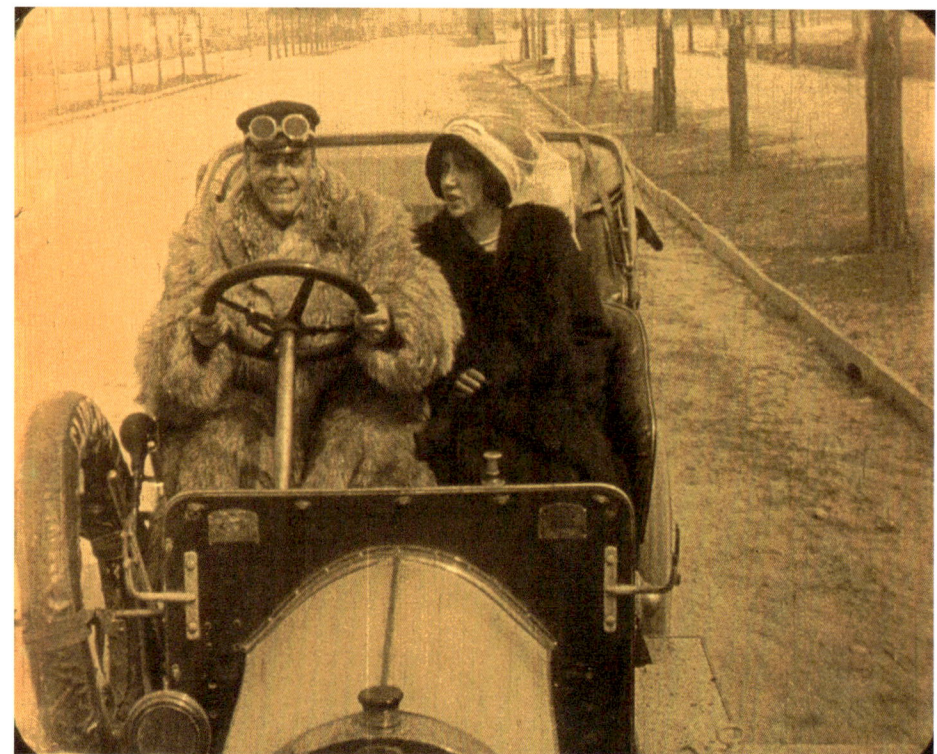

Raoul d'Auchy, *Les demoiselles des PTT*, 1913

L'automobile della morte, 1912

The Desmet Collection

A Perspective from Abroad

David Robinson

Still of *Fior di male*, 1915

My first personal encounter with the Desmet Collection was around 1970, when I was gathering photographs for a history of film posters, which never materialized (posters were not yet in fashion). I was advised that the largest collection of early posters was at the Nederlands Filmmuseum. It was; and to encounter it was staggering. I learned that it was the stock of an early Dutch film distributor called Jean Desmet, and that there were other materials from his collection too, including films – but the thousands of cans had still to be examined, sorted, catalogued and restored. For the moment the posters – a thousand or more of them, many in multiple duplicates – were as much as anyone could cope with. At that time they were principally in the care of the enthusiastic and endearing Nico Diemer, who was to die young. Poster conservation was still a new discipline: at that time London's Victoria and Albert Museum collection (including a rich cache of Lautrecs) looked much like a stack of soiled hotel laundry. But in Amsterdam Diemer and his collaborators were experimenting and innovating, and even published a little booklet on the principles of conservation. They had got it wrong, with a system that involved attaching the posters to cardboard hangers with scotch tape (a sure formula for conservation disaster), but things moved fast: they learned their lessons and have bequeathed a system and a collection that is incomparable in its range, variety, condition – and accessibility. Here in 1970 history was already being written and rewritten thanks to the Desmet bequest. Nowhere before seen together in such quantity, these posters represented all the major film production countries, at the exact moment, the end of the first decade of the century, when the dedicated pictorial film poster was fast discovering and exploiting its arts of seduction.

The rest of the collection – and particularly the films – still remained an intriguing mystery. The secrets were only gradually revealed over the years, as the painstaking and costly process of restoration progressed. The whole Desmet story would only emerge with the publication in 2003 – 46 years after the collection had passed to the Netherlands Filmmuseum (now EYE) – of Ivo Blom's meticulously researched and bewitching book *Jean Desmet and the Early Dutch Film Trade*. With dazzling simplicity, Blom defines the Desmet phenomenon: 'A remarkable combination of business sense, thrift, unsaleable stock, respect and chance secured one of the finest and most varied collections of film in the world for the Netherlands Filmmuseum.'[1]

Could Belgian-born Desmet have anticipated his future place in cultural history (could he indeed have imagined that film itself would have a history) as he set out on his career on the Dutch fairgrounds of the beginning of the

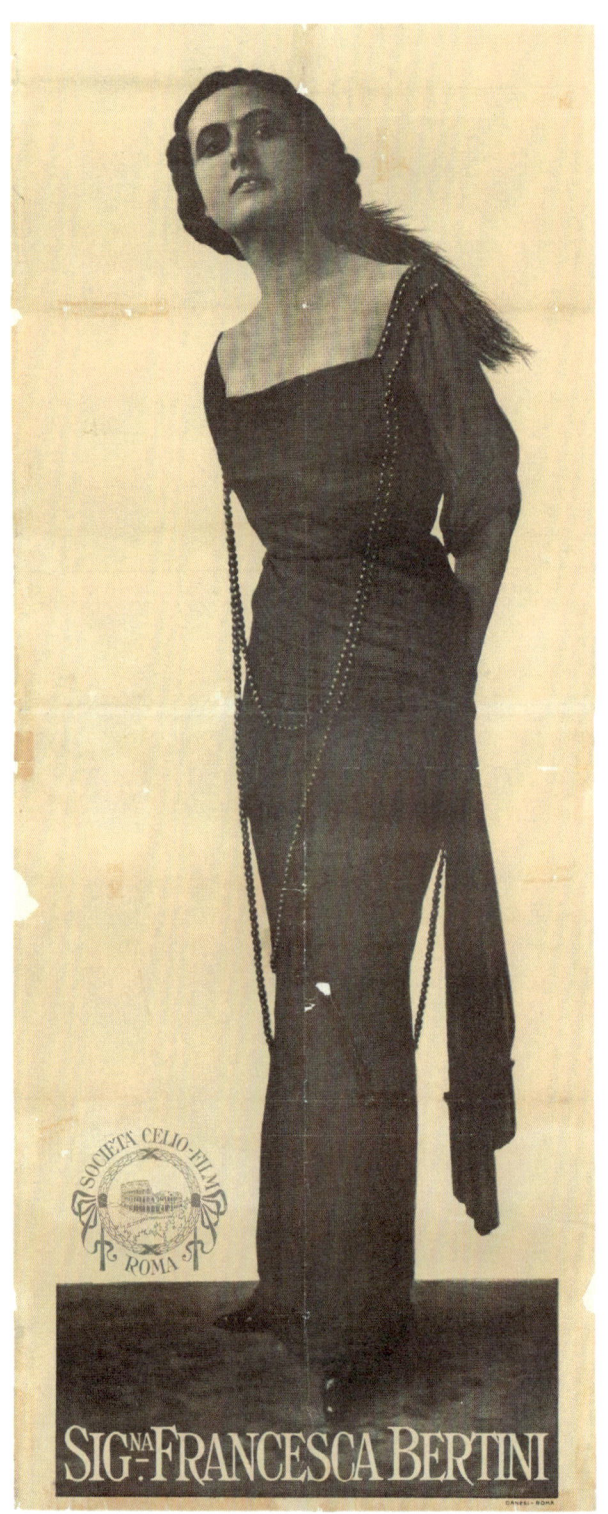

twentieth century; as he supplemented his popular helter-skelter with a tent cinema in 1907; as he gradually moved into the big cities and permanent cinemas; as he extended his exhibition activities to a pioneer distribution business; as in his mid-forties he made the decision largely to give up the cinema business to go on to success in real estate? To elaborate Blom's summation of the metamorphosis of career to collection: Desmet's fairground showman's business sense gave him a nose for the films that would sell, and these were the films that most accurately caught the tastes and desires of the audience of those times. His thrift meant that he seems never to have discarded anything that could possibly retain a future value. His collection was at times eroded by fires and occasional lucky sales – but fortunately there was still the unsaleable stock, which has guaranteed that some 900 films (along with duplicate prints) have come down to us. And Blom's word 'respect' is important. Like most of the best and most successful film magnates down to the present, there is a sure sense that Desmet really cared for his theatres, for his public and for the films he could show them.

The only collection of comparable scale and date is the accumulation of Swiss Jesuit priest Josef Joye, who omnivorously gathered films by the hundred for use in his pioneer audio-visual educational presentations in Basel, which had begun as magic lantern lectures at the end of the nineteenth century. Some 1,200 of Joye's films survive, the majority in the British Film Institute's National Archive. The collection is nearly contemporary with Desmet, with the years 1908-1912 most strongly represented. Although his collection, like Desmet's, vividly demonstrates the multinational character of the cinema of the period, Joye collected, in the phrase of his chronicler Joshua Yumibe, 'like a ragpicker', acquiring, whether by gift or purchase, prints discarded by German and Swiss distributors as no longer showable in terms of condition or topicality. Many of the fiction films acquired in this chancy way must have been quite unsuitable for Joye's 'improving' lectures.

Jean Desmet was certainly no 'ragpicker'. He selected his films personally, with a keen sense of his audience's desires and tastes, and of the way that audience was changing in its social composition. His first audiences on the fairgrounds were more than content with one-reel chase films and scenes of exotic places: his later city audiences encountered the *films d'art* from France and Italy, Italian divas and classical spectacles, and, from Germany, the contrasting appeal of Asta Nielsen and Henny Porten and the massive centenary tribute to Richard Wagner. So Desmet has left not just a history of a brief but dramatically changing era of film history, but a mirror of the society of the time and its relation to the still new entertainment art. The collection belongs to demographic as well as film history.

Amsterdam's dedicated custody and restoration of the collection (with the frequent support of Haghe-

p. 48
Poster for *L'amazzone mascherata*, 1914
175 x 70 cm

p. 49
Poster for *L'amazzone mascherata*, 1914
200 x 280 cm

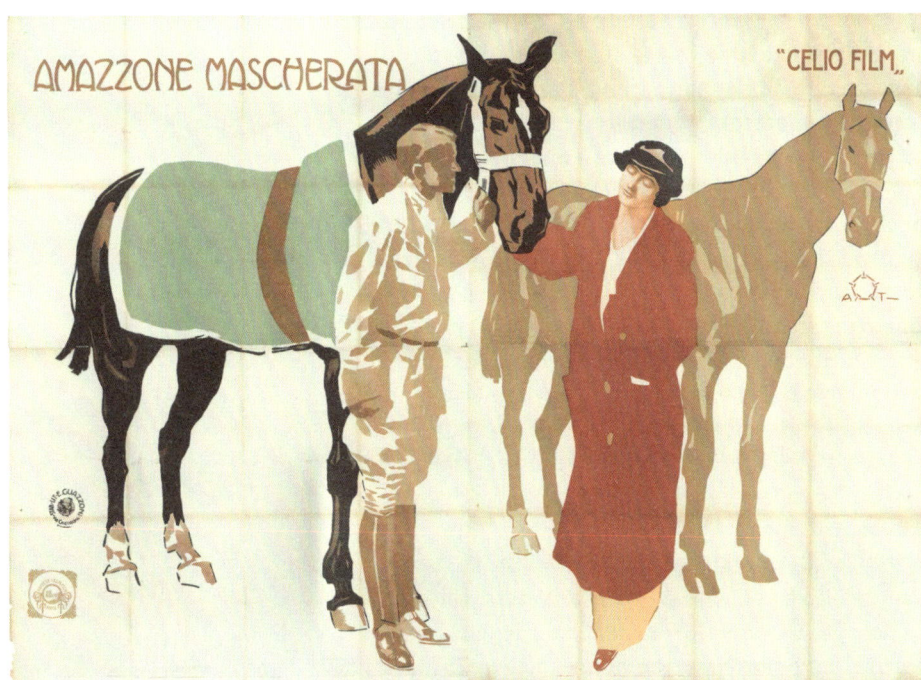

film film laboratory) has helped to revolutionize aspects of film conservation. Today it is hard to believe that for decades the pioneer archivists saw contemporary chemical colouring – tinting, toning and stencil colouring – as a regrettable historical defacement of the pure monochrome nitrate, to be ignored and effaced, as they made their careful black-and-white preservation dupes. Yet in Desmet's day, colour was a significant feature of marketing; and the Amsterdam archive – working with a variety of techniques including that of the coincidentally named Belgian Noël Desmet – has consistently striven to restore the richness of the Desmet Collection's coloured prints. It was an enterprise not immediately welcomed, however. Peter Delpeut recalls, in Blom's book, that at the 1987 Pordenone Festival, out of 300 films screened only ten had colour, and eight of these were new restorations from the Desmet Collection – still stirring the lingering indignation of diehards at this regrettable period 'defacement'.[2] Attitudes have changed since then.

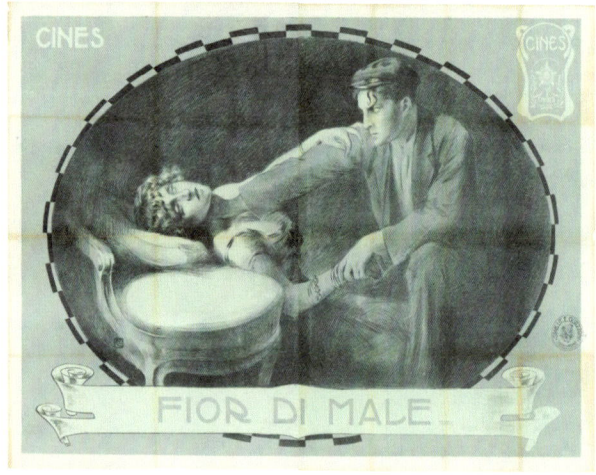

The 1986 Pordenone screening of *Fior di male* (1915) in a way represented the Desmet Collection's prestigious debut on the international festival scene. The Italian divas had enjoyed huge popularity with the early twentieth-century Dutch audience, and Desmet's publicity had pithily and irresistibly styled *Fior di male* (distributed under the title of *Children of Sin*) as the story of 'a deeply fallen and socially elevated woman'. Again its rediscovery was to change received history, which had always celebrated *Cabiria* and Italy's classical spectacles, but generally consigned the *diva* genre to the nostalgists, with their treasured picture postcards of Bertini, Menichelli, Borelli and Jacobini. Carmine Gallone's film *Fior di male*, however, obliged historians to revalue the derided stereotypes of overheated sentiment, melodramatic acting, the larger-than-life star: these elements were there, certainly, but integrated into their own genre – operatic, psychologically expressive and 'sentimental' in the most positive sense. The revaluation of the genre was further emphasized by Peter Delpeut's 1999 film *Diva Dolorosa*, whose appreciation of its visual and poetic potential was inspired by Desmet discoveries. *Fior di male* was also a further revelation of the elusive genius of its writer Nino Oxilia – a war fatality at 28, in 1917, previously remembered as a director only for his collaboration with Mascagni on *Rapsodia satanica* (1917) and his legendary but vanished debut film *Addio giovinezza!* (1913).

The Desmet Collection's second Oxilia feature, *Sangue bleu* (1914), was shown at the 1991 manifestation of Bologna's Cinema Ritrovato. Begun in 1986, this festival has been one of the most dedicated explorers of

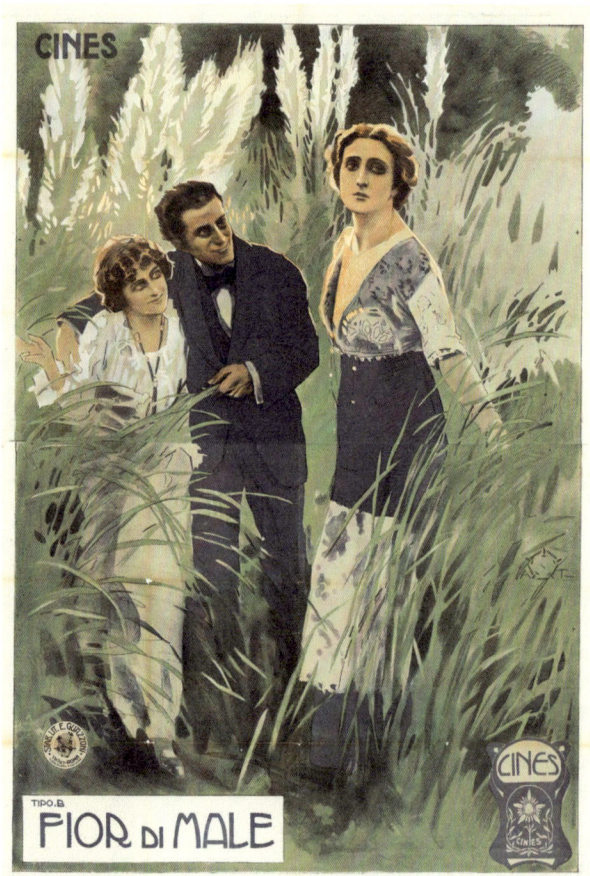

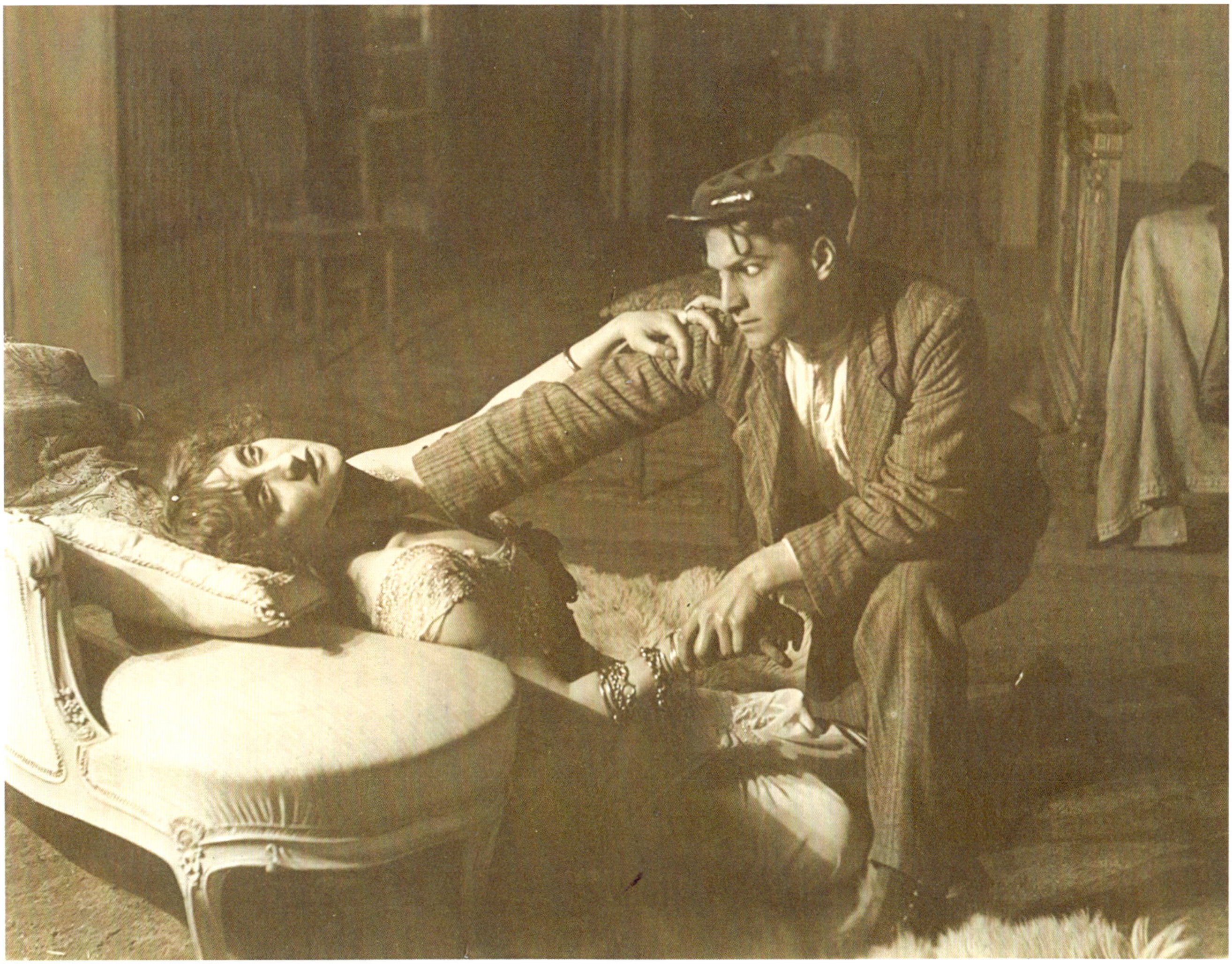

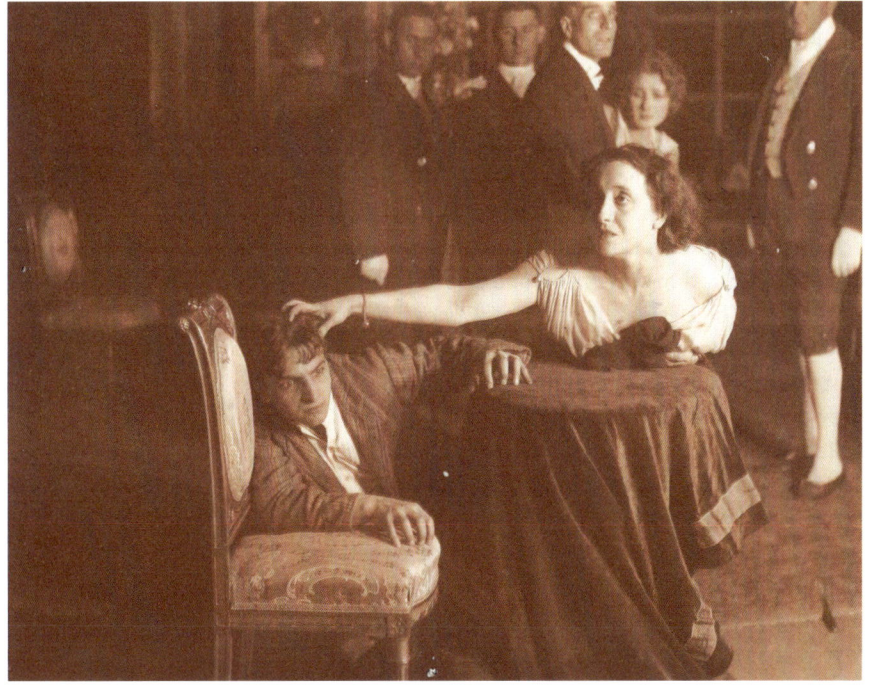

p. 50
Poster for *Fior di male*, 1915
141 x 198 cm

Poster for *Fior di male*, 1915
197 x 140 cm

p. 51
Stills of *Fior di male*, 1915

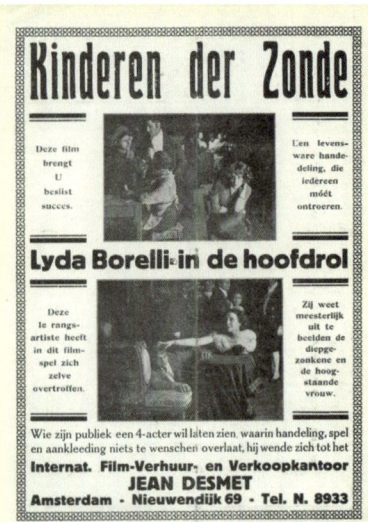

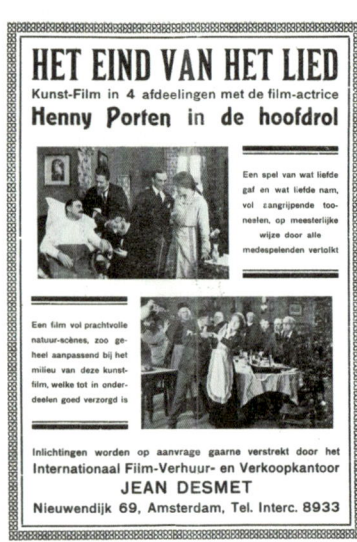

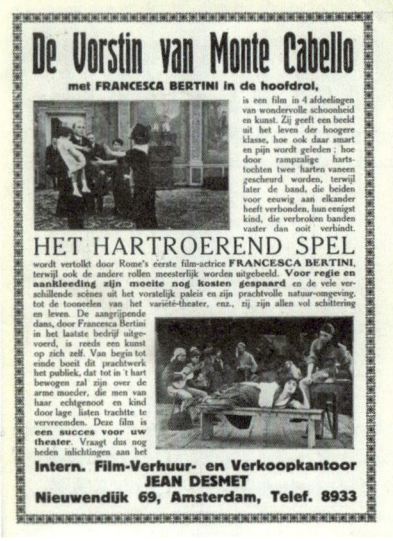

the Desmet Collection. Since 1996, Desmet has been an increasingly vital contributor to Mariann Lewinsky's spectacular annual presentation of films 'Cento anni fà' (A Hundred Years Ago). In the context of this programme *Sangue bleu* was shown again at the 2014 edition of Cinema Ritrovato, and honoured with a DVD release.

Since the revelation of 1986, archival festivals have relied heavily on Amsterdam and Desmet: no retrospective of the cinema's second decade can be complete without its resources. In 1987 Pordenone attempted a complete retrospective of the surviving productions of the Vitagraph Company. The Desmet Collection includes more than 80 Vitagraph films from the years 1907-1914, and though at that moment many of these were not yet restored, the Desmet prints shown included many titles not preserved in the USA, while the coloured prints were again a revelation. In 2002 Pordenone again drew heavily upon the collection for its historic programme of 'Funny Ladies', revealing the delights of long-neglected comediennes of the silent screen. The collection has been the major resource for exploring early-vanished American companies like Selig or Thanhouser.

Since then Pordenone has regularly paid tribute to Desmet. 2011 saw a small but revelatory series of hitherto unknown Italian films of the 1910s; and since that year also Elif Rongen has presented a highly popular series of themed programmes, 'The Desmet Annual'. The series has light-heartedly explored the manner in which the collection reflects the social mores of its era, inevitably commentated by the ironic comedy of the early clowns, to whom this kind of programming gives a new context. The subjects so far have been the early movie-going experience and contemporary views of 'Perils of the Pictures', the oppressive family structures reflected in 'Oh, Mother-in-Law!' and varied misfortunes of 'Suffering Men' of the pre-war world. The 2014 'Annual' was dedicated to the social impact of the motor car in the Desmet era. Yet with all its enthusiasm even Pordenone has explored barely 10 per cent of the collection. The sheer size of it is such that, more than a century after it was formed and six decades since it came into the keeping of the Filmmuseum, the collection is continuously being explored and exploited. Its immediate and passionate curator, Elif Rongen, constantly discovers new marvels, and fights for opportunities to expose them. A few dedicated international programmes have celebrated Desmet. In 2007 the Museum of Modern Art, New York presented the exhibition, 'Jean Desmet's Cinema of Sensation and Sentiment' and in 2011, 'Cruel and Unusual Comedy from the Desmet Collection of the EYE Institute, Amsterdam'.

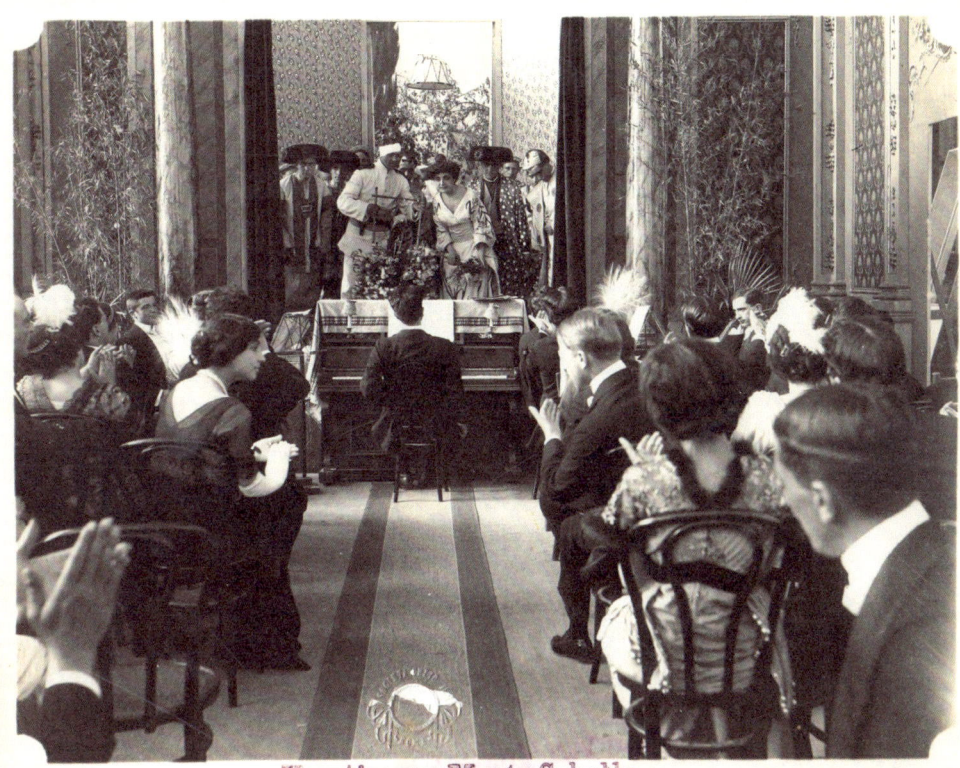

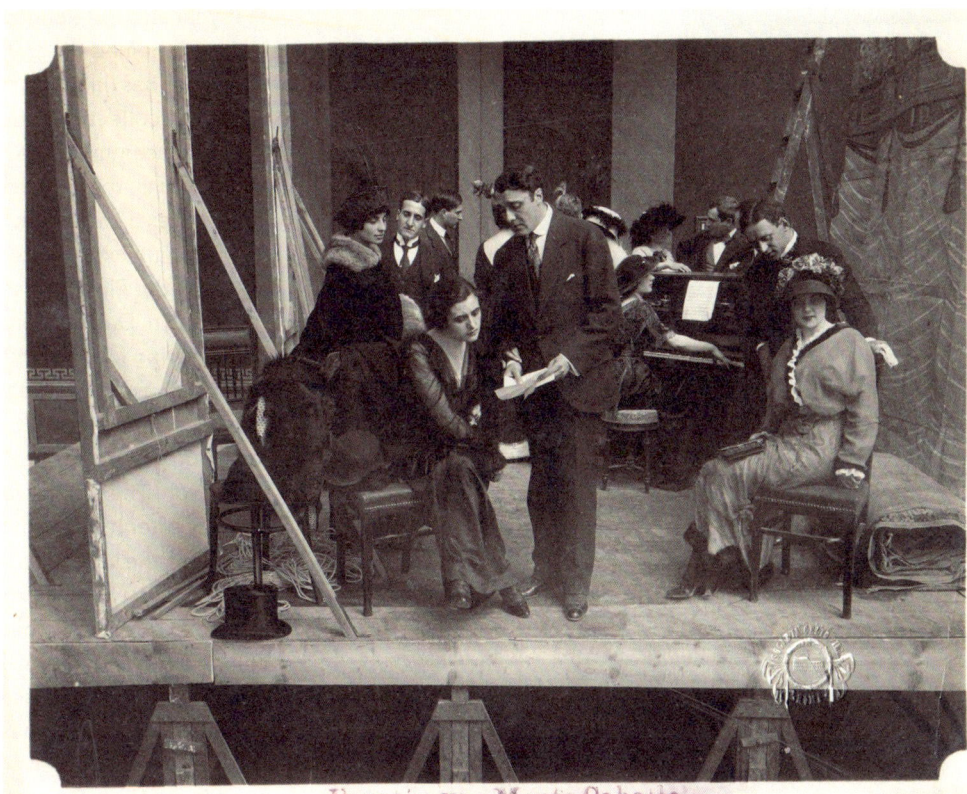

p. 52
Advertisement for *Kinderen der Zonde* (*Fior di male*) in *Bioscoop Courant*, 25 February 1916

Advertisement for *Het eind van het lied* (*Das Ende vom Liede*) in *Bioscoop Courant*, 7 April 1916

Advertisement for *De vorstin van Monte Cabello* (*Sangue bleu*) in *Bioscoop Courant*, 10 December 1915

p. 53
Stills of *Sangue bleu* with imprint of Dutch title 'Vorstin van Monte Cabello', 1914

Stills of *Sangue bleu* with imprint of Dutch title 'Vorstin van Monte Cabello', 1914

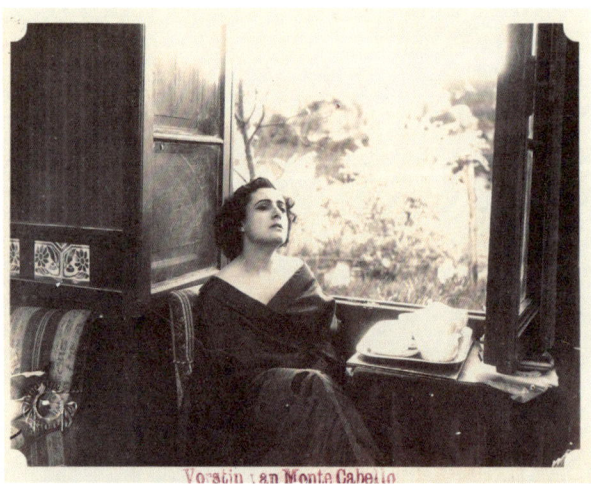

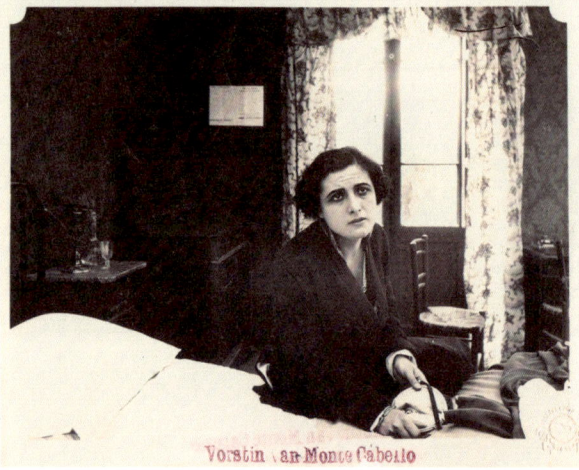

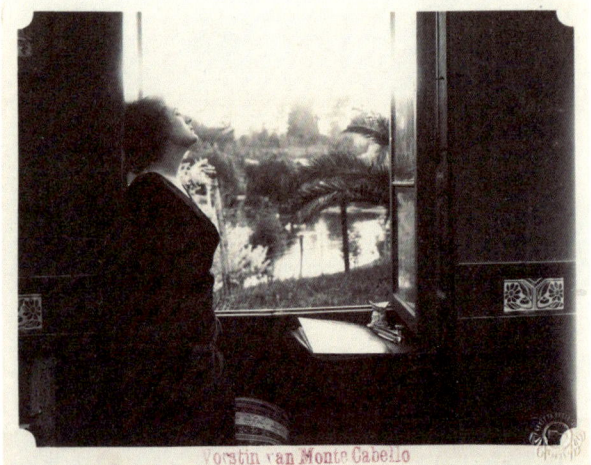

In 2011 UNESCO inscribed the collection on their Memory of the World Register – one of the first film collections to have been so recognized. The words of the UNESCO citation cannot be bettered as an evaluation of the full significance – and future – of the legacy of Jean Desmet:

> The Desmet Collection consists mainly of an exceptional group of films, company documents, posters and film stills from the 1910s. The collection contains a large number of unique film prints including many masterpieces that were formerly presumed lost. It also exceeds the boundaries of film history and has great value for the socio-historical description and appreciation of one of the most important decades in modern history as it reflects cinematographic changes and many stories about the 1910s that still need to be unveiled.[3]

1
I. Blom, *Jean Desmet and the Early Dutch Film Trade* (Amsterdam: Amsterdam University Press, 2003), 335.

2
Ibid., 20.

3
http://www.unesco.org/new/en/communication-and-information/flagship-project-activities/memory-of-the-world/register/full-list-of-registered-heritage/registered-heritage-page-2/desmet-collection/.

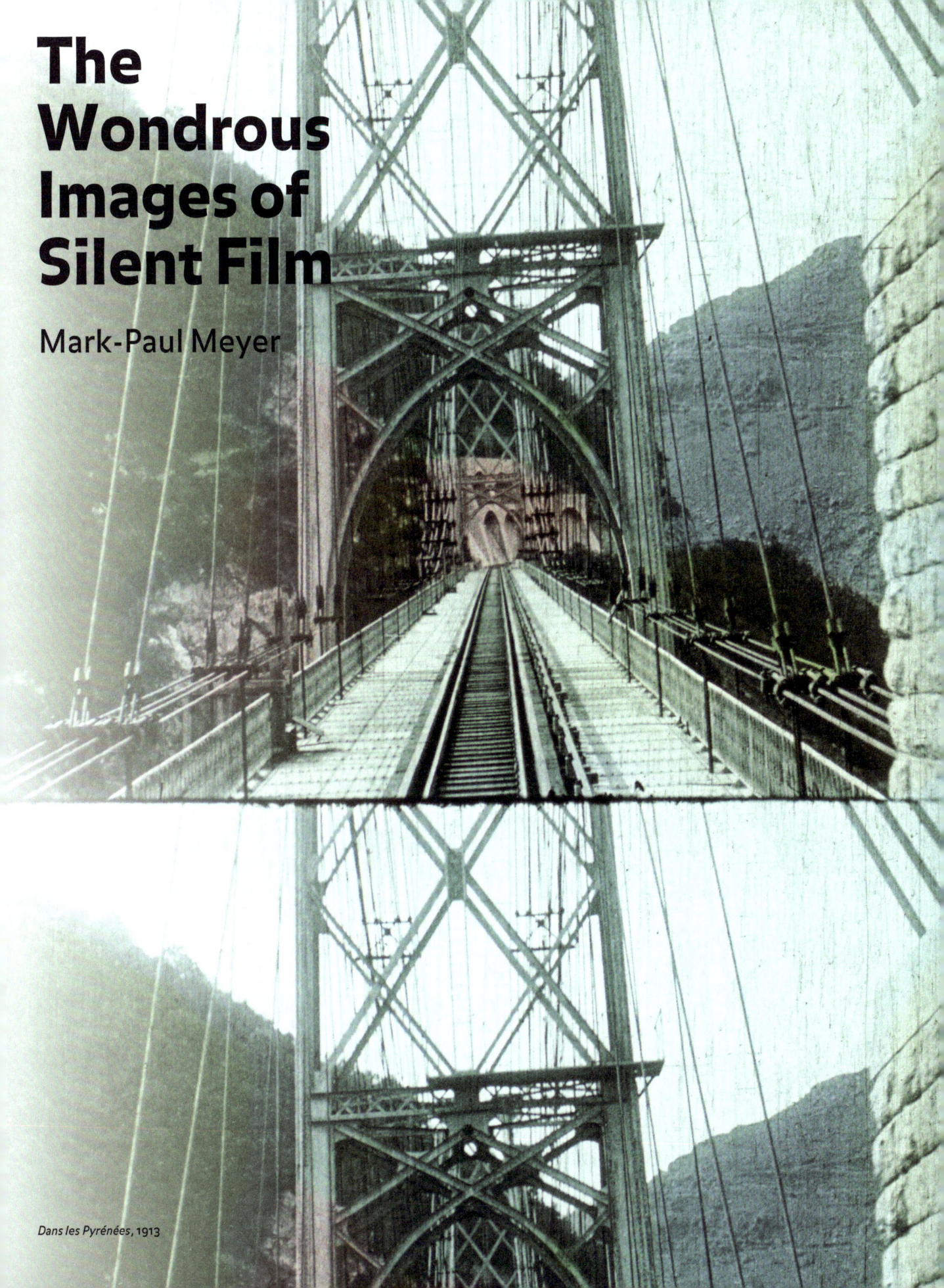

The Wondrous Images of Silent Film

Mark-Paul Meyer

Dans les Pyrénées, 1913

Cinema culture in the period when Jean Desmet worked as a film exhibitor and distributor, from 1907 to 1916, was a fascinating mix of old and new. This was a time of sweeping changes in many areas. The automobile industry, aviation, the electrification of the railway network, radio telegraphy, the vacuum tube – all sorts of new technologies were gradually becoming part of everyday life. It was also a productive period in the arts. In classical music the atonal revolution was in progress, and in the visual arts abstract painting had arrived. The cinema was part of this exhilarating period. Yet although the phenomena of the film camera, the film projector and screenings of 'living photography' belonged to the new age, films from the first two decades of the cinema show the influence of old cultural traditions. Strategies from the theatre, magic lantern shows, illusionist acts and other forms of nineteenth-century entertainment persisted in films. Gradually, however, film wrote a history of its own, with the classic cinema that emerged in the 1920s as one of its dominant forms.

As argued in the article 'A Treasure-Trove of Adventure and Experimentation', it is easy to overlook the bold originality of early cinema when you watch from the perspective of later films. Rather than clumsy or primitive, the use of elements and formal devices alien to the film medium is actually very modern and refreshing. One of Peter Delpeut's contributions to this collection explicitly discusses the modernity of the Vitagraph films. The present article sheds light on several other characteristics of the cinema in Jean Desmet's day, with verbal and pictorial illustrations. It cannot provide anything like a complete survey, partly because some characteristics are difficult to express in a book. The fascination with moving pictures is one such element, hard to capture in a book with only stills. One popular genre in the earliest years of film was the phantom ride. The films in question can be seen as cinematic adaptations of nineteenth-century panoramas: a camera was placed in an automobile, train or boat, and the spectators in the cinema saw a moving landscape passing by them. This minimalistic variety of cinema remained popular in the 1910s (see, for example, the French productions *Le port de Barcelone*, 1913; *Les bords de l'Yerres*, 1912; and *Dans les Pyrénées*, 1913) and has again become a frequently used stylistic technique in art firms in the past 40 years. A case in point is the much-imitated travelling shot in *Der Bräutigam, die Komödiantin und der Zuhälter* (1968), by Jean-Marie Straub and Danièle Huillet, in which images of a Munich shopping street by night, filmed from a moving car, go on for several minutes.

Another aspect of silent film that cannot be expressed on paper is how film screenings sounded. Despite the term 'silent film', the early cinema was

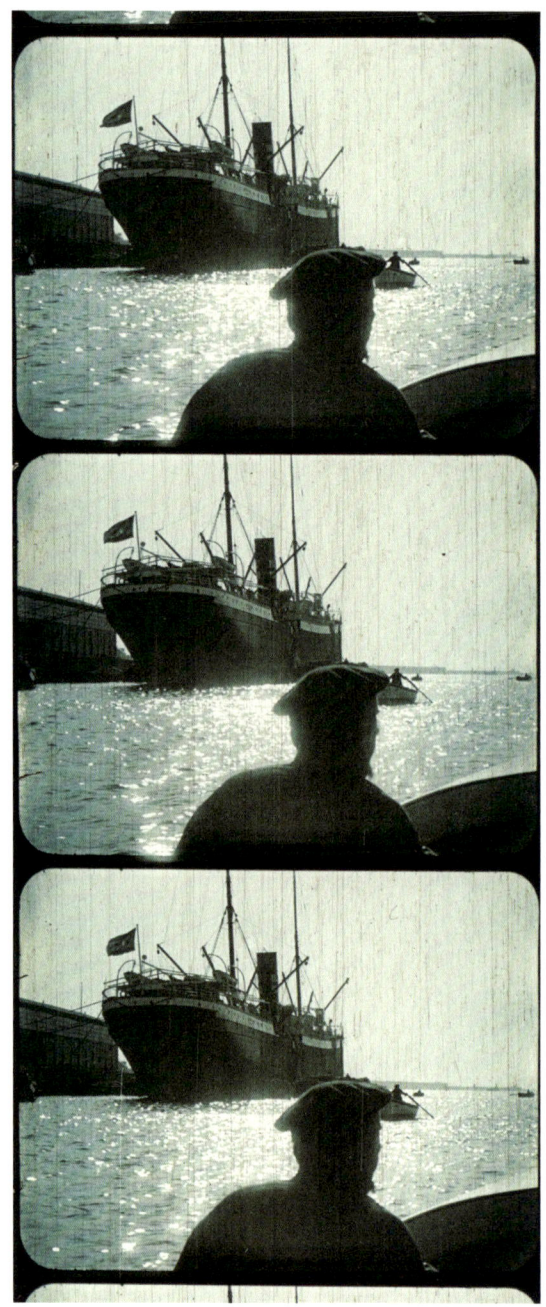

p. 56
Le port de Barcelone, 1913

p. 57
Santa Lucia, 1910

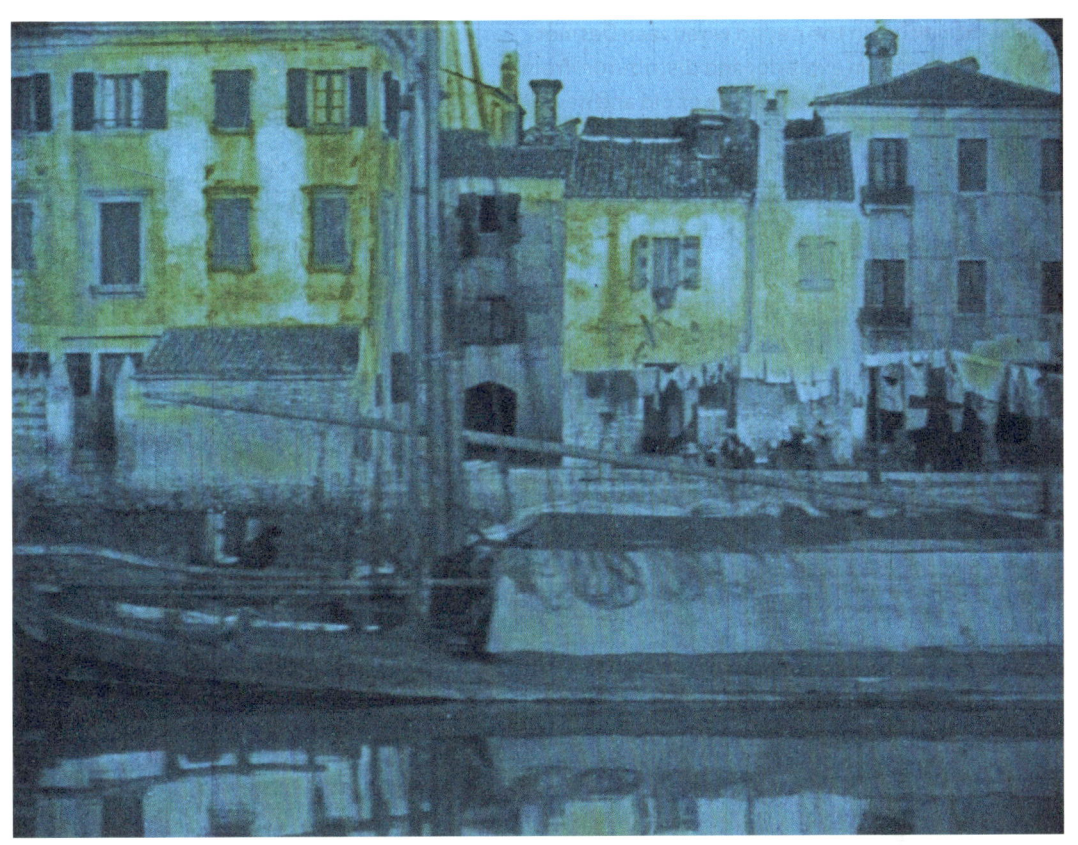

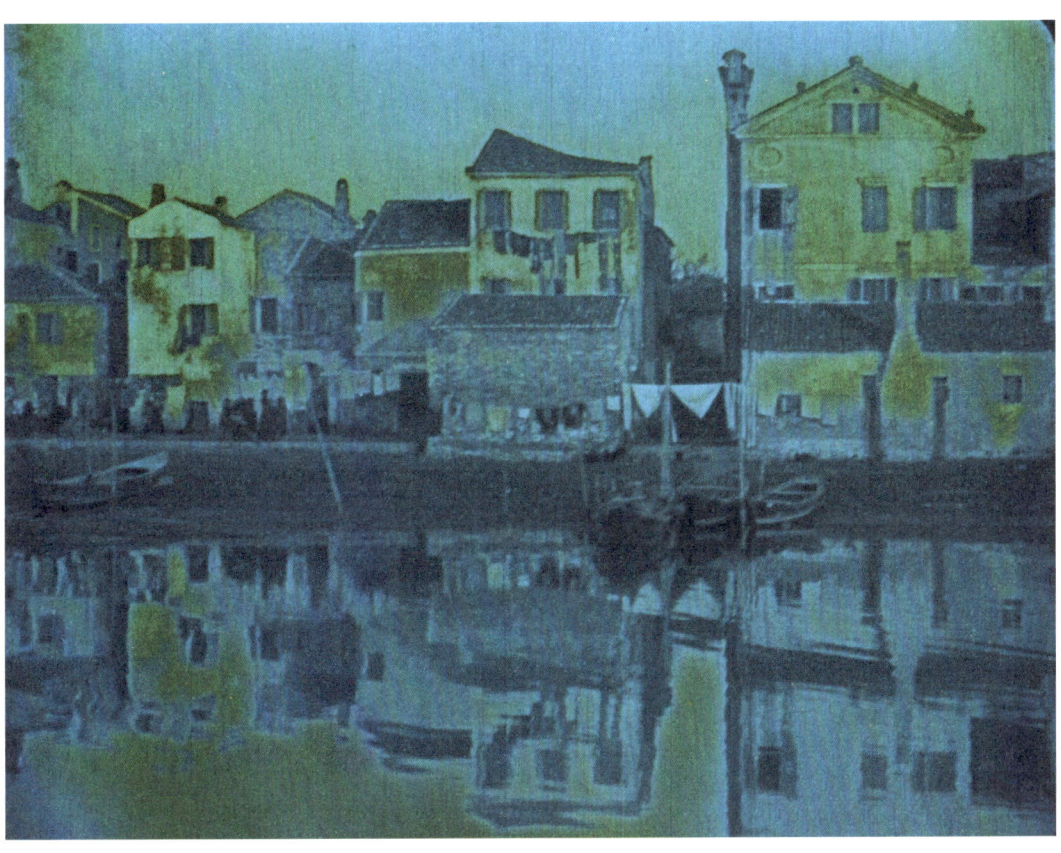

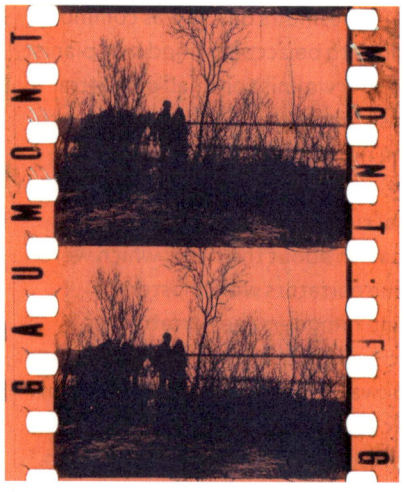
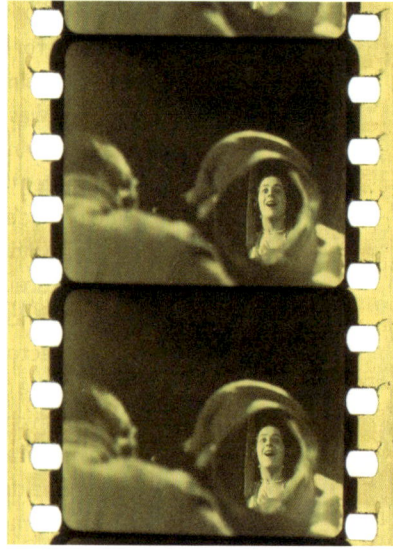
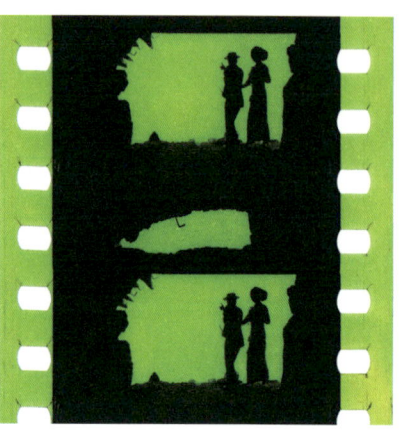

p. 58
Filmstrip with red tinting: *Coeur ardent*, 1912

Filmstrip with pink tinting and blue toning: *Sur la mer Caspienne*, 1912

Filmstrip with green tinting: *Wenn Völker streiten*, 1915

Filmstrip with switch from blue to yellow tinting (character turns on light): *La pipe d'opium*, 1912

Filmstrip with yellow tinting: *Die Schwarze Natter*, 1913

Filmstrip with red tinting: *Die Schwarze Natter*, 1913

Filmstrip with green tinting: *Tra le pinete di Rodi*, 1912

p. 59
Filmstrip with orange and blue toning: *Petites causes, grands effets*, 1912

Filmstrip with blue toning: *Petites causes, grands effets*, 1912

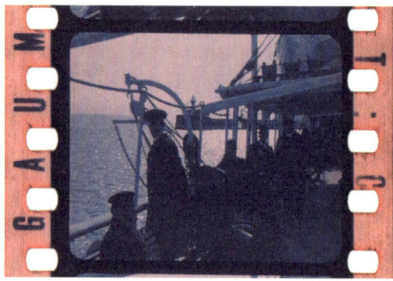
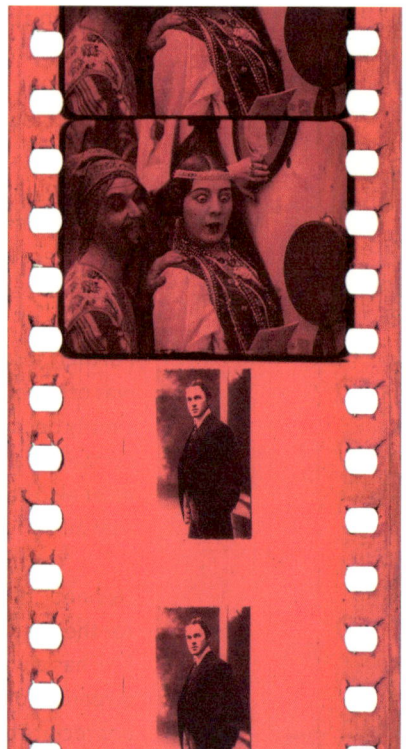
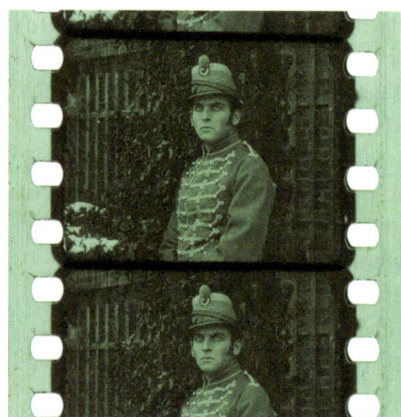
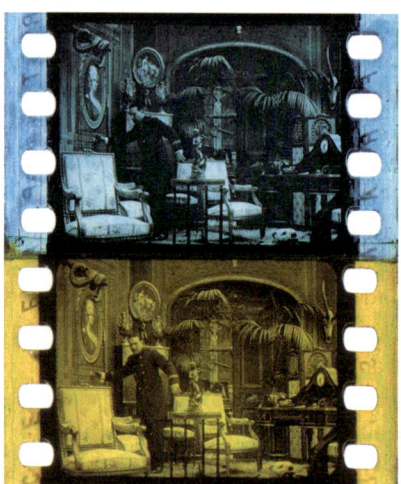

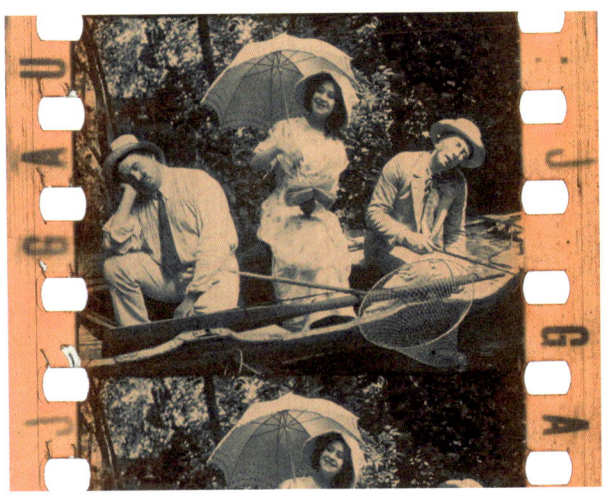

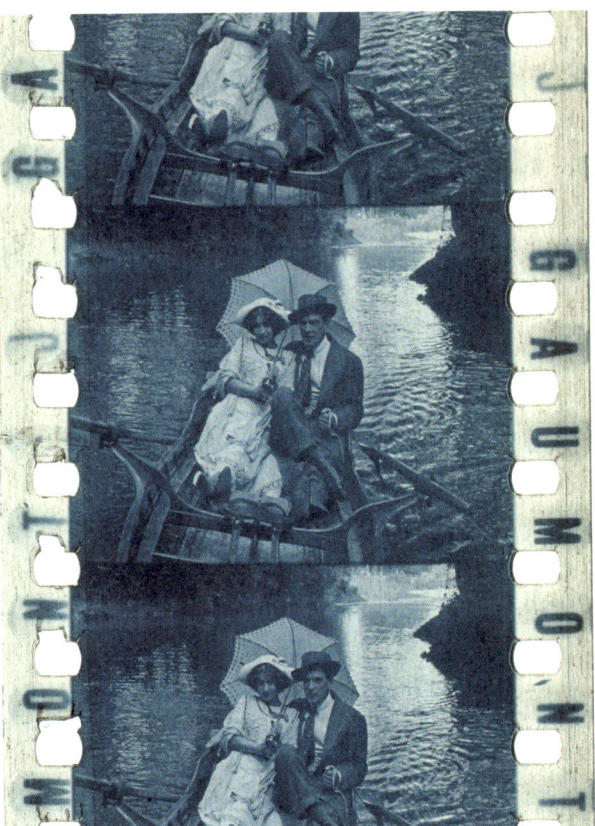

anything but silent. In Desmet's day, it was common practice for screenings to be accompanied by a pianist, and sometimes also by a violinist or small orchestra. Often it was the musician who decided what music to play, drawing on the rich repertoire of popular nineteenth-century favourites. Then there was the narrator, who provided verbal support during screenings and background information about the films, which were mostly foreign. Some narrators were masters of oratory, and for some filmgoers the narrator was a crucial factor in decisions about which cinema to go to. In 1913, the narrator was a generally accepted part of the Dutch cinematic experience; in 1916, *De Kinematograaf* reported that there were 375 of them.[1]

Besides the sound and the 'phantom ride' genre, there are many other distinctive features of films from the period 1907-1916. Several of these formal and stylistic characteristics of early cinema are examined below, in a brief introduction to the astonishing world of silent film.

Colour

One popular misconception about early cinema is that all early films were black and white. That idea arose partly because in the 1960s and 1970s film archives made copies of early films on black-and-white film. For many years, only these black-and-white copies were available. Furthermore, the classic cinema of the 1930s and 1940s was often black and white for aesthetic reasons, or simply because that was less expensive than the colour systems available at the time. Black-and-white television must also have contributed to the widespread belief that all early films were in black and white.

Yet the opposite is true. Almost all films in the Desmet Collection involve some form of colour – and for the past 25 years, their colours have been preserved. EYE has always led the way in the conservation and screening of silent films in colour.[2] The only way to fully appreciate the films in the Desmet Collection is to see them in their original colours.

From the very start, filmmakers strove towards the use of colour, and hand-coloured films were shown frequently in the first ten years of film history. Less labour-intensive techniques quickly followed and soon dominated the market. Two common procedures were tinting and toning. Tinting involved immersing the black-and-white film in a dye bath, giving it a uniform colour. Rather than black and white, the resulting film might be black and red, for example, or black and yellow. Toning meant chemically transforming the black particles of silver in the emulsion into particles of coloured material. Black and white might then become blue and white, for instance. A combination of tinting and toning could achieve spectacular results. Obviously, these were not naturalistic colours, and that certainly contributes – from our perspective – to the artistic quality of the images. There was also a very freewheeling attitude towards conventions. Although in many films, a blue scene is set at dusk, or a red scene heightens the drama of a fire, the use of colour sometimes had no symbolic or associational meaning whatsoever. Its sole purpose was then to make cinematic images even more spectacular.

The 1910s were also a time of intense experimentation with more naturalistic uses of colour. Some of these experiments paved the way for the later colour film. One widespread technique for achieving multiple colours in a single image was known as the stencil process. In fact, this was the semi-automatic successor to hand-coloured film: entire sequences of images could be coloured with the aid of stencils. One stencil might be used to colour the roof of a house red, for example, and another to colour the lawn green. This made it possible to use five or six different colours, and the effect was extraordinarily naturalistic. The French Gaumont and Pathé film studios put this technique to extremely effective use. Among the most refined and breathtaking examples are the historical dramas produced in the Serie d'art Pathé Frères and by the Film d'Arte Italiana, Pathé's Italian subsidiary.

Parallel Editing

One important feature of the cinema as we know it today is parallel editing, or cross-cutting: the technique of rapidly alternating between two scenes, either to draw a parallel between actions or to suggest a connection between events in different places. This editing technique puts the audience in the privileged position of being in two places at once. In the days of silent film, this technique was not in common use. There are early examples of parallel editing, but most films had a linear narrative structure in which entire scenes were placed one after another, without any mixing. That made it difficult to portray events in two or more locations as taking place simultaneously, a problem that sent filmmakers in search of creative and generally visual solutions. The simplest way to show two places at the same time was an old trick from the theatre: making both places visible to the spectators in a single image, with a wall, a curtain, or even a ceiling dividing them. This puts the audience in a more privileged position than the characters, who are privy only to part of the action. The Italian film *Le acque miracolose* (1914) is in a class of its own, showing a cross section of a house as if the viewer were peering into a doll's house.

A still more interesting situation arises when the two places are far apart. The metaphor for connect-

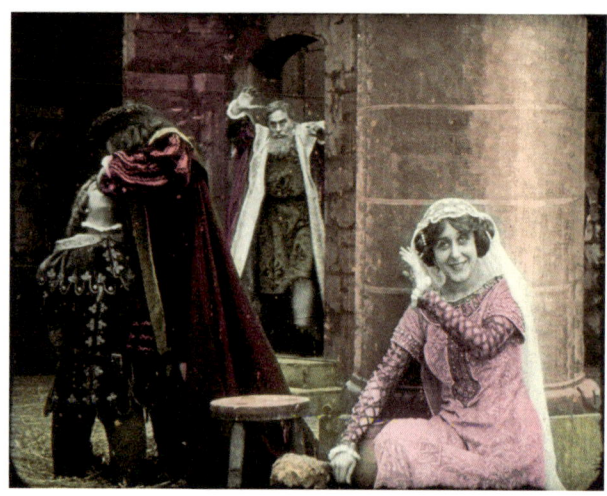

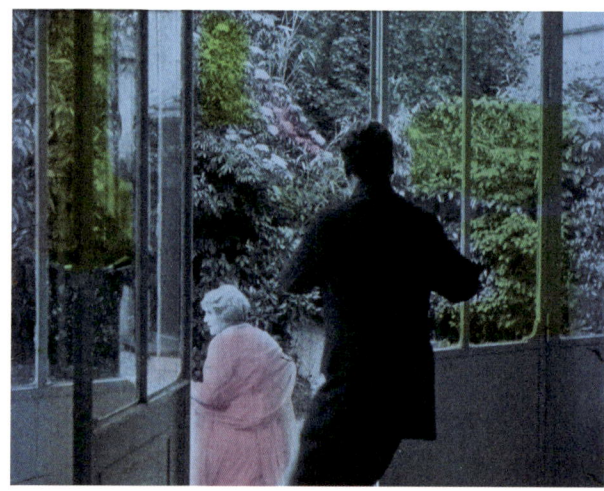

p. 60
Film with stencil colour process: *Amour de page*, 1911

Combination of blue tinting and stencil colour process: *Léonce à la campagne*, 1913

p. 61
Film with stencil colour process: *Une leçon d'amour*, 1912

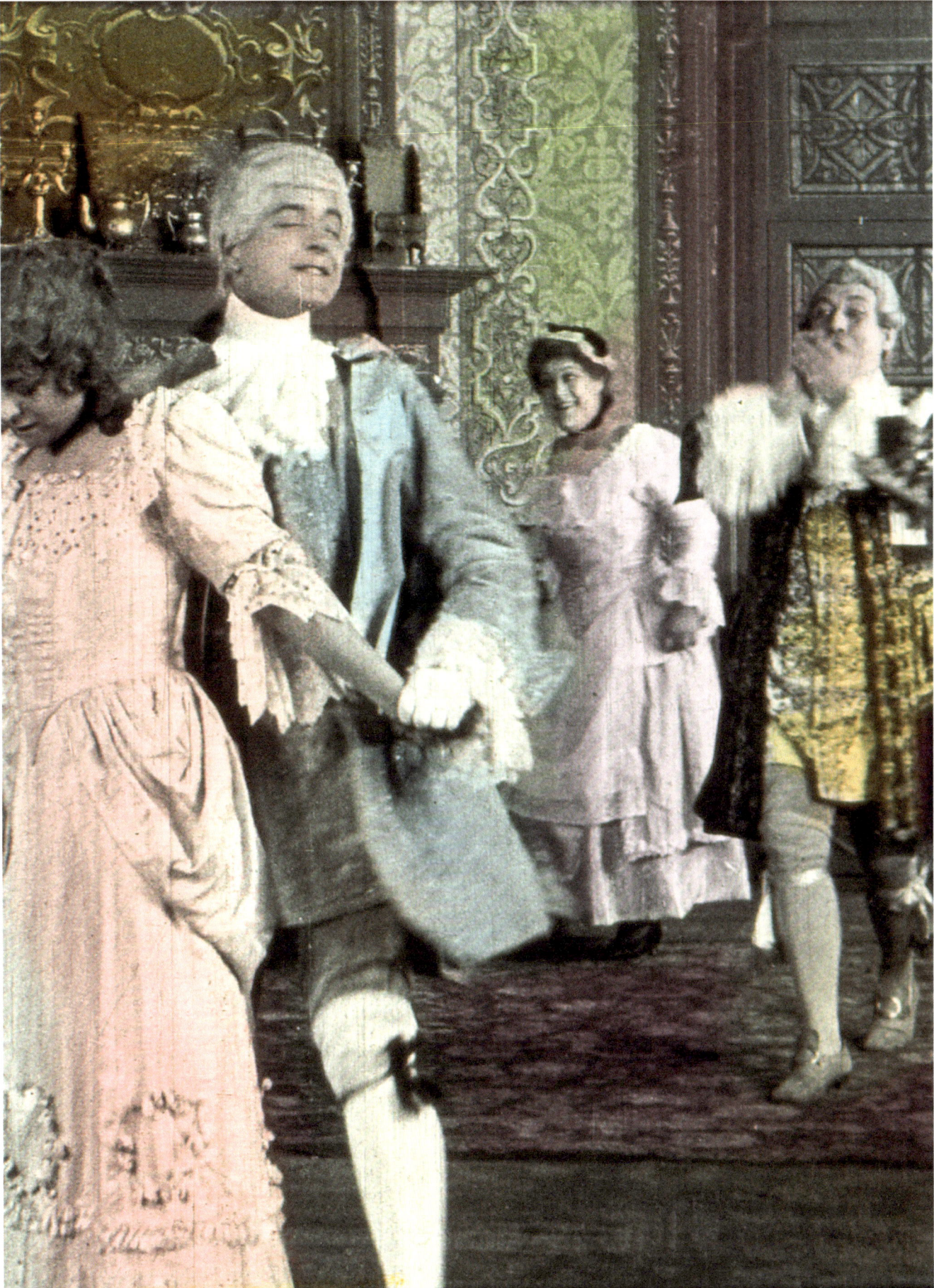

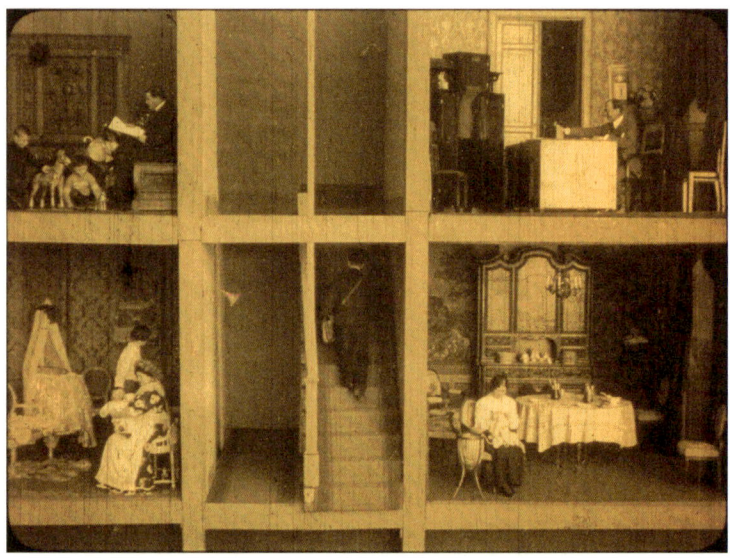

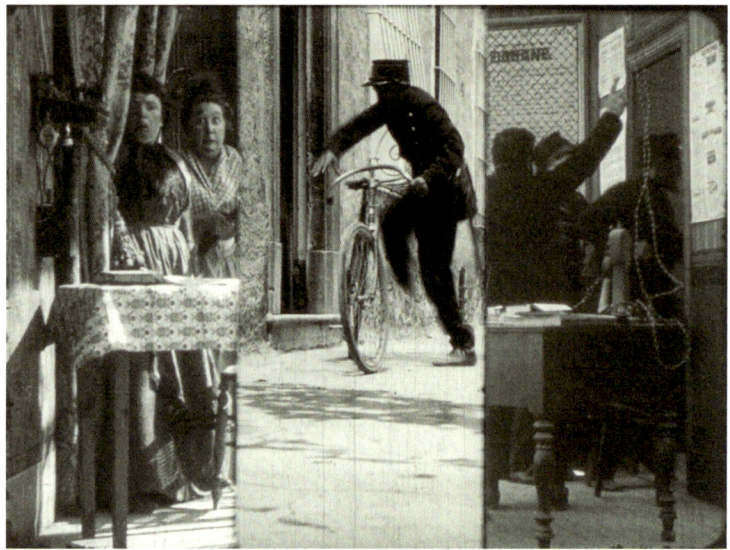

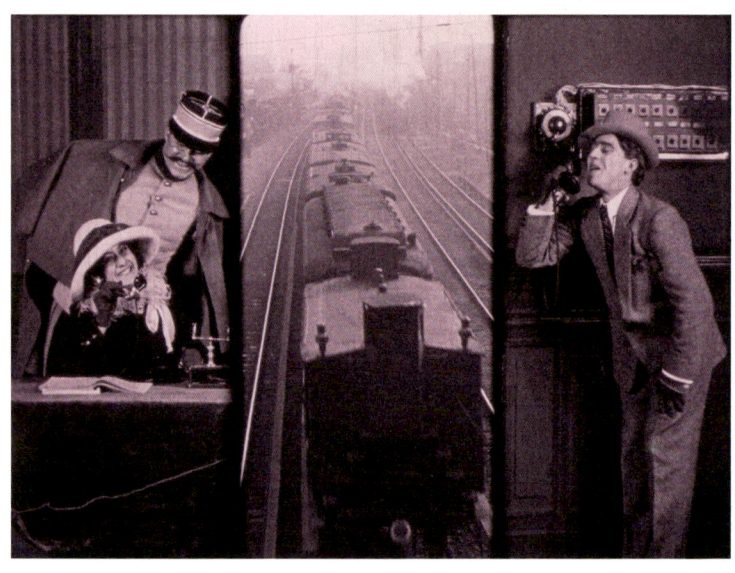

p. 62
Eleuterio Rodolfi, *Le acque miracolose*, 1914

La peur des ombres, 1911

En voyage de noces, 1912

p. 63
Intertitles from various films

ing the two places is often the telephone. This modern communication device was ideally suited to the representation of simultaneous events in two different locations. You see the two parties to the conservation, united photographically in a diptych. Sometimes a triptych is used, and a third image is placed between the two people on the phone: perhaps the telephone line carrying the conversation, or perhaps the image of a city, emphasizing the distance between the two parties. Or it might be a scene or image that reveals something about the relationship between the two characters or the content of their conversation. Triptychs of this kind are sometimes impressive feats of visual ingenuity.

Intertitles

When we speak of film and storytelling, we usually talk about the organization of space and time, about the use of editing, continuity, framing and *mise en scène* to create an illusionistic world that is credible to the viewers. The fascinating thing about silent film is that the written language of the intertitles is an important tool for telling the story.

In the early years of film, intertitles were used sparingly. Often the only title card was at the start of the film, a familiar practice from magic lantern shows. As title cards gradually came into use at other points in the film, the titles were very short at first and limited in function to signalling key moments. They were sometimes the punctuation of the film, so to speak, or else they allowed a leap in time or in the storyline. Some titles summarized the action; when the film leapt from one scene to the next, an intertitle briefly described the action that took place between the two scenes.

By about 1910, the use of title cards with somewhat longer titles had become generally accepted.[3] There was also criticism of such titles, however, because they were thought to disrupt the illusion and pull the spectator out of the story, as it were. Many titles explained or described a situation rather than forming an integrated part of it. For example, dialogue intertitles were not yet embedded in scenes at this stage. Instead, a title card at the start of the scene would give the topic of conversation, and then the scene would be shown, without any precise indication of what words were being uttered. Some intertitles do not even seem to bear any causal relationship to the scene. Such title cards seem to be in an illogical place – much too early on, for example. Some titles are eye-catching because of their odd phrasing or poor spelling. When Dutch intertitles for foreign films were produced in the same country as the film, the resulting misspellings could be fascinating.

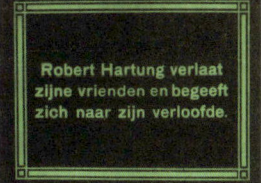
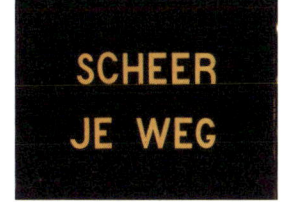
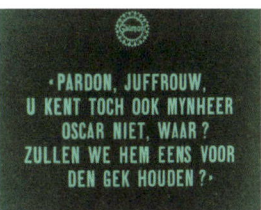
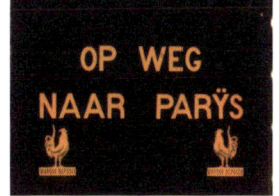
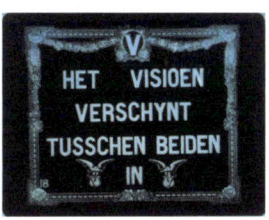
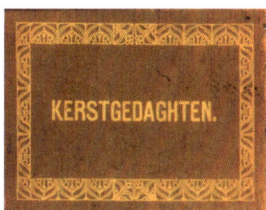
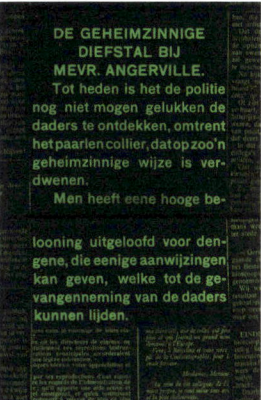

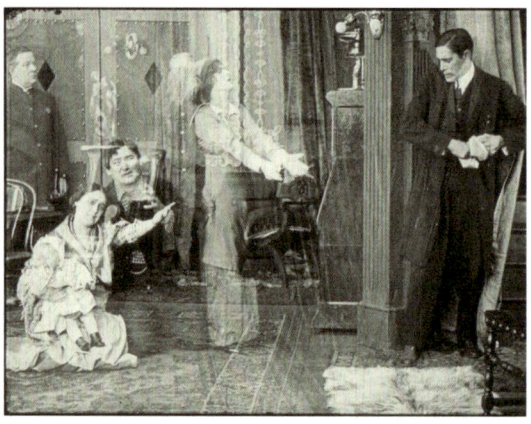

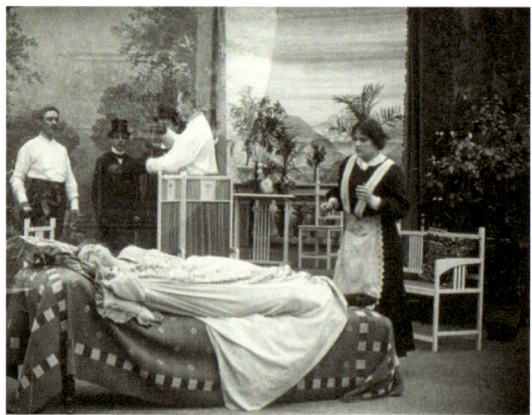

p. 64
Arthur V. Johnson, *The District Attorney's Conscience*, 1913

Eine Herzenseroberung, 1911

Paul Bertho, *Gavroche rêve de grandes chasses*, 1912

p. 65
Poster for *Schatten des Lebens*, 1912
151 x 110 cm

Emile Cohl, *La vengeance des esprits* (*Die Rache der Geister*), 1911

The Red Barrier, 1912

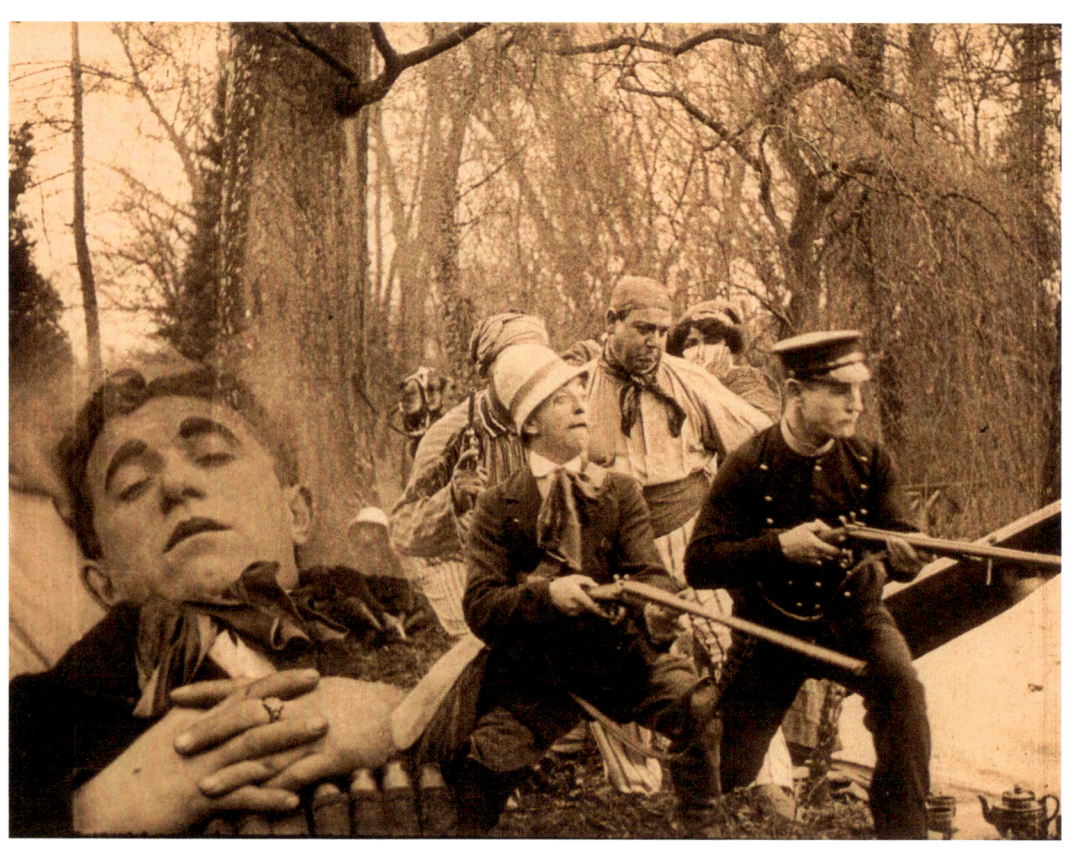

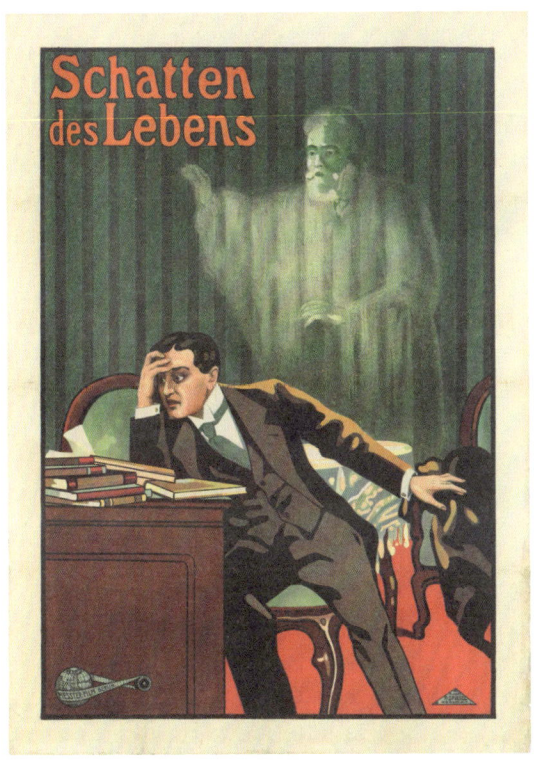

This is exactly what makes these titles seem interesting and modern to us. In relation to the visual style of the cinematic image, the linguistic nature of the titles is sometimes unsettling. It requires a different sort of effort to read a title card than it does to watch moving pictures. Because intertitles interrupt the film, the viewers have to keep shifting their attention back and forth between words and images. That makes it difficult to lose oneself completely in the visual representation of the story. You have to be alert and devote continuous attention to both the titles and the images. Although this was not a deliberate strategy, it resembles an effect that might be pursued by a modern experimental filmmaker.

Spirits, Dreams, Memories and Visions

The late nineteenth century was a time of widespread fascination with making the invisible visible, with phenomena that could not be observed by the naked eye. The discovery of X-rays, for which Wilhelm Röntgen received the first Nobel Prize in 1901, not only had scientific implications, but was also put to use in variety acts.[4] Photography was put to use for capturing invisible phenomena. Photographs were taken through microscope and telescope lenses, and there were

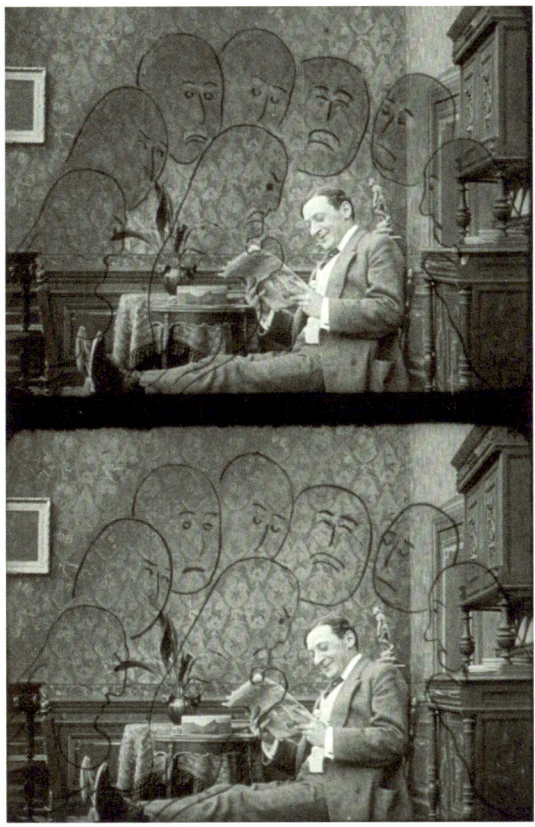

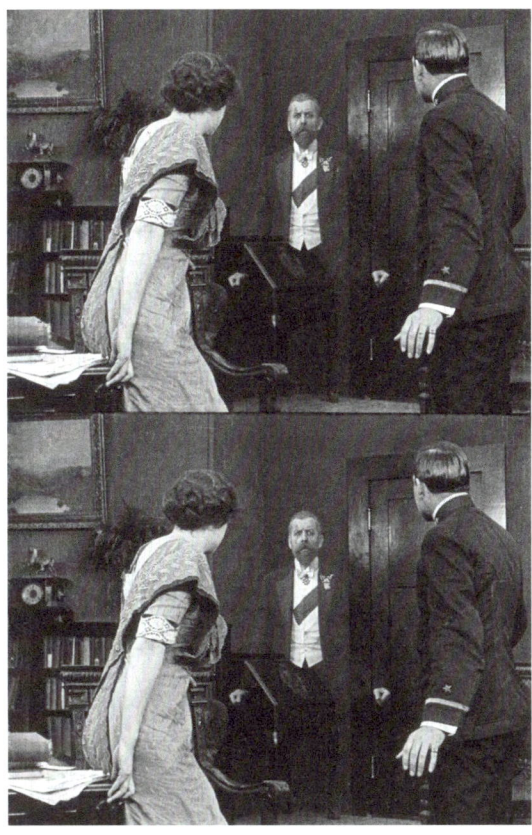

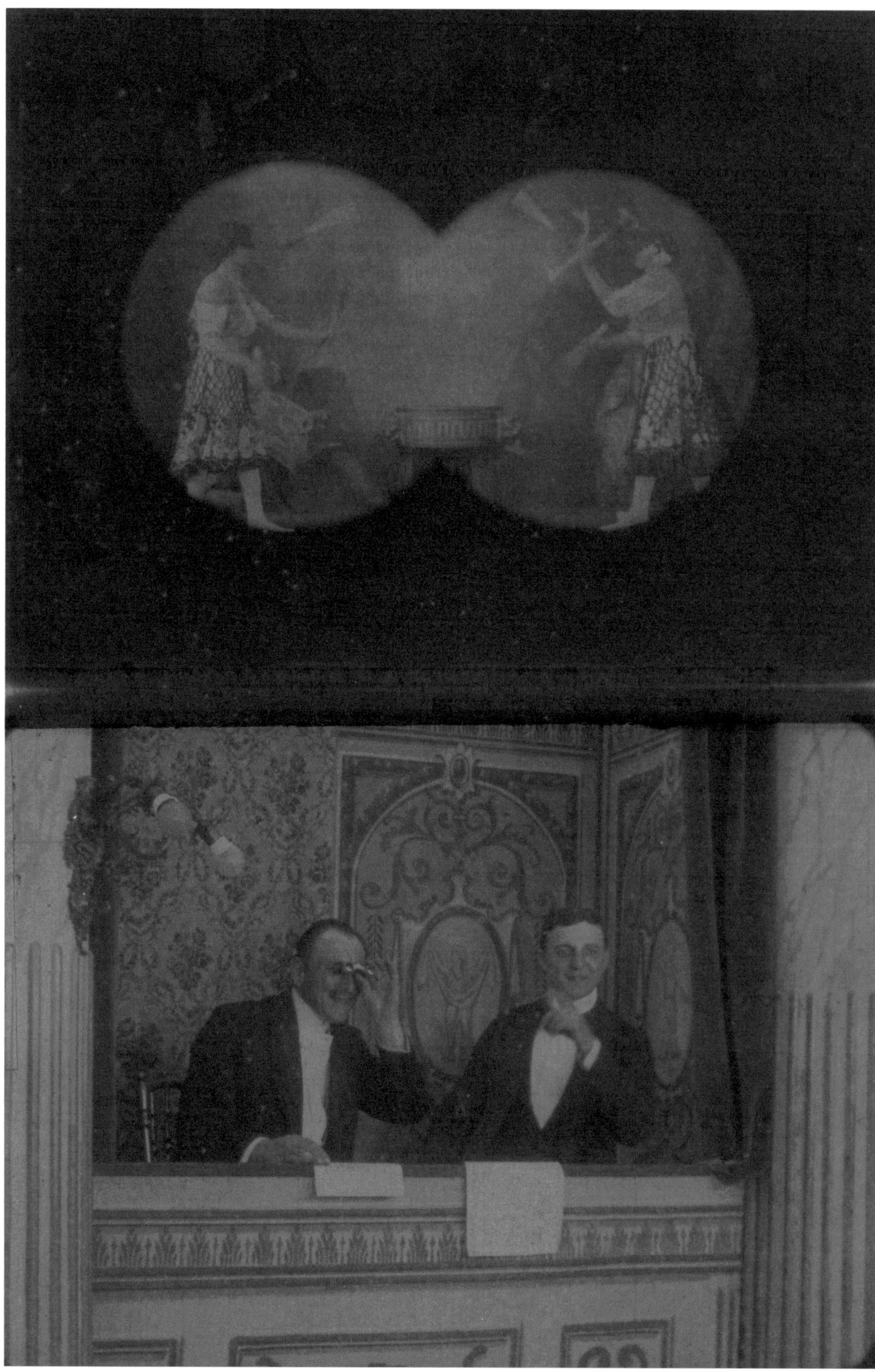

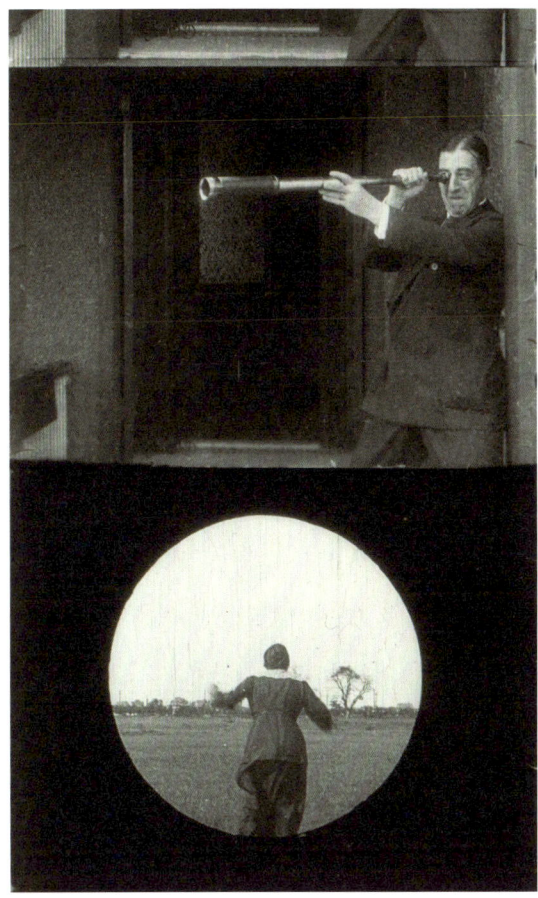

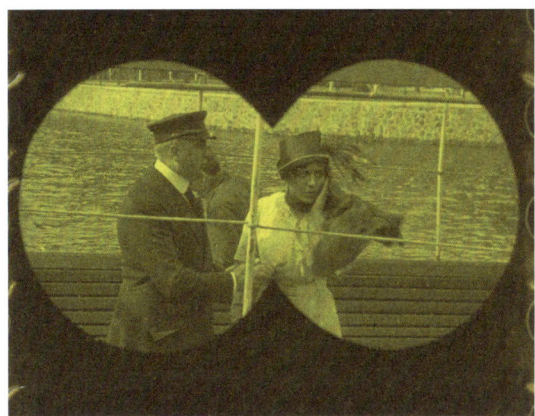

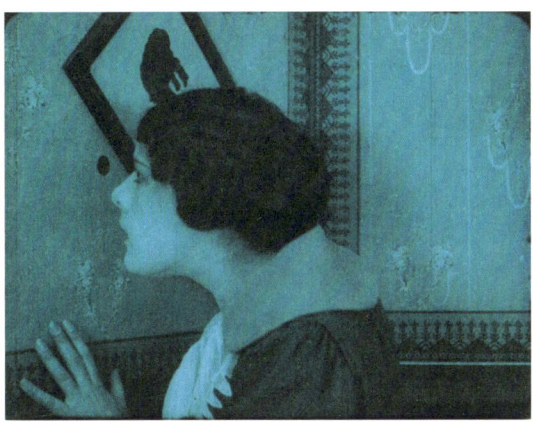

attempts to record electricity and magnetism, not to mention spirits, thoughts, and dreams, on photographic plates.[5] Terms such as 'spirit photography', 'aura photography' and 'thoughtography' were in vogue.

This fascination lived on in the world of film. 'Scientific films' brought microscopic worlds to the film screen, or showed silkworms, X-ray images or the growth of plants in time-lapse photography. Spiritism and séances were also the butt of jokes in many films, such as *La vengeance des esprits* (1911) by Emile Cohl, pioneer of the animated film. But many fictional films made eager use of the 'spirit photography' technique to depict dreams or memories, bring visions to life and resurrect the dead. The photographic technique used was simple but ingenious. Through double exposure of the film, two images were superimposed. The result was a vague and ghostly apparition with the power to drive the main character to despair. There are few more moving cinematic portrayals of remorse (*The District Attorney's Conscience*, 1913) or despair over lost love (*Eine Herzenseroberung*, 1911) than in these unknown classics from the 1910s.

The Eye and the Camera

One fascinating stylistic device in many films from before 1916 is the equation of the camera lens with the human eye. What the camera sees is then identical to what one of the characters sees. The clearest examples of this technique involve a character looking through binoculars or a telescope. The device is remarkably simple and effective; a mask is placed in front of the camera lens with one hole for a monocular instrument and two round holes, partly overlapping, for binoculars. This is the cinematic representation of the analogy

p. 66
Franz Hofer, *Die Schwarze Kugel oder die geheimnisvollen Schwestern*, 1913

p. 67
James Young, *Jerry's Mother-In-Law*, 1913

Charles Decroix, *Die Czernowska*, 1913

Franz Hofer, *Der Steckbrief*, 1913

p. 68
Marcel Fabre, *Robinet in vacanza*, 1912

Léonce Perret, *Léonce flirte*, 1913

between the optical instrument and the human eye, which had become a common trope in the nineteenth century.[6] In many other films, the camera's point of view coincides with that of a character, but without any optical instrument involved. The spectator sees what the character sees, not through the lens of an instrument such as a telescope, but through a peephole. The most intriguing of these peepholes are the keyholes, in which the hole cut out of the camera mask likewise takes the form of a keyhole.

By representing the view through a telescope or keyhole in this fashion, early films emphasized the activity of looking and the way it was mediated by the apparatus of film. What gives early films their modern quality is that viewers are repeatedly reminded of the presence and artificial nature of the cinematic construct. This strategy differs starkly from that of the now-classic later films that tried to make the screen a transparent window onto another reality. In these classic films, the medium strives to remain invisible so that the audience can lose itself in an illusionistic world. Film is always a kind of peep box, but while classic films can be said to make the box imperceptible and to draw the spectator into the box, the viewers of early films remain outside the box, peering in through the hole.

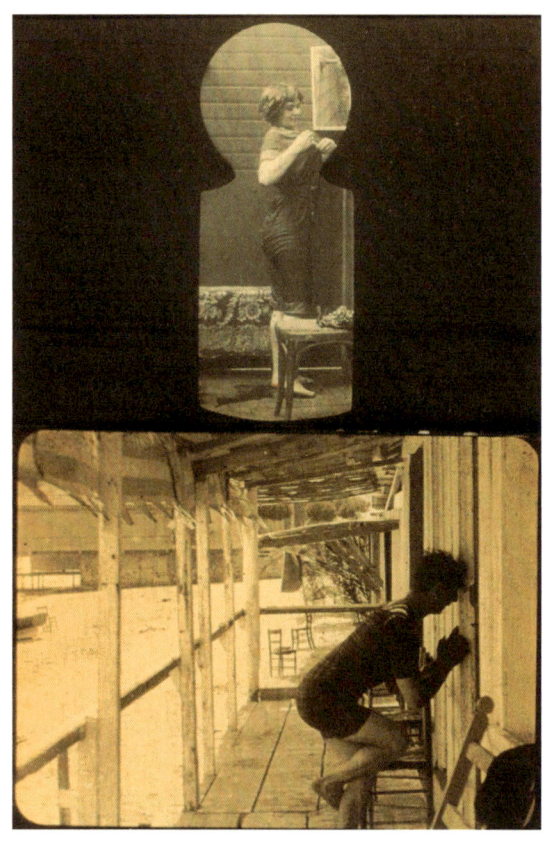

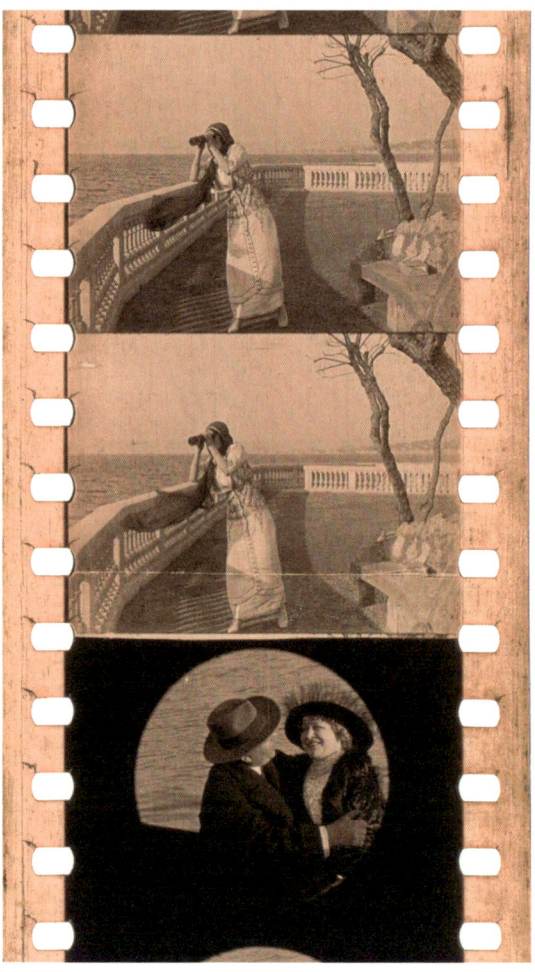

1
See also A. van Beusekom, *Film als Kunst. Reacties op een nieuw medium in Nederland, 1895–1940* (n.p., 1998), 51.

2
The first films preserved in colour in the 1980s were films from the Desmet Collection, and in 1995, the then Netherlands Filmmuseum organized an international workshop on 'colour in early film'.

3
For a concise overview, see the entry on this subject written by C. Dupré la Tour in: R. Abel, *Encyclopedia of Early Cinema* (London/New York, 2005).

4
Van Beusekom, *Film als Kunst*, op. cit. (note 1), 13.

5
'Photography became a Spiritist tool, a means of penetrating and revealing the invisible aspect of the visible world.' T. Gunning, 'Invisible Worlds, Visible Media', in: C. Keller (ed.), *Brought to Light: Photography and the Invisible* (San Francisco, 2009), 51-63, quote on 61.

6
'Beginning in the nineteenth century, the relation between eye and optical apparatus becomes one of metonymy: both were now contiguous instruments on the same plane of operation.' J. Crary, 'Techniques of the Observer: On Vision and Modernity in the 19th Century', *October* 45 (1988), 3–35, quote on 31.

Exoticism

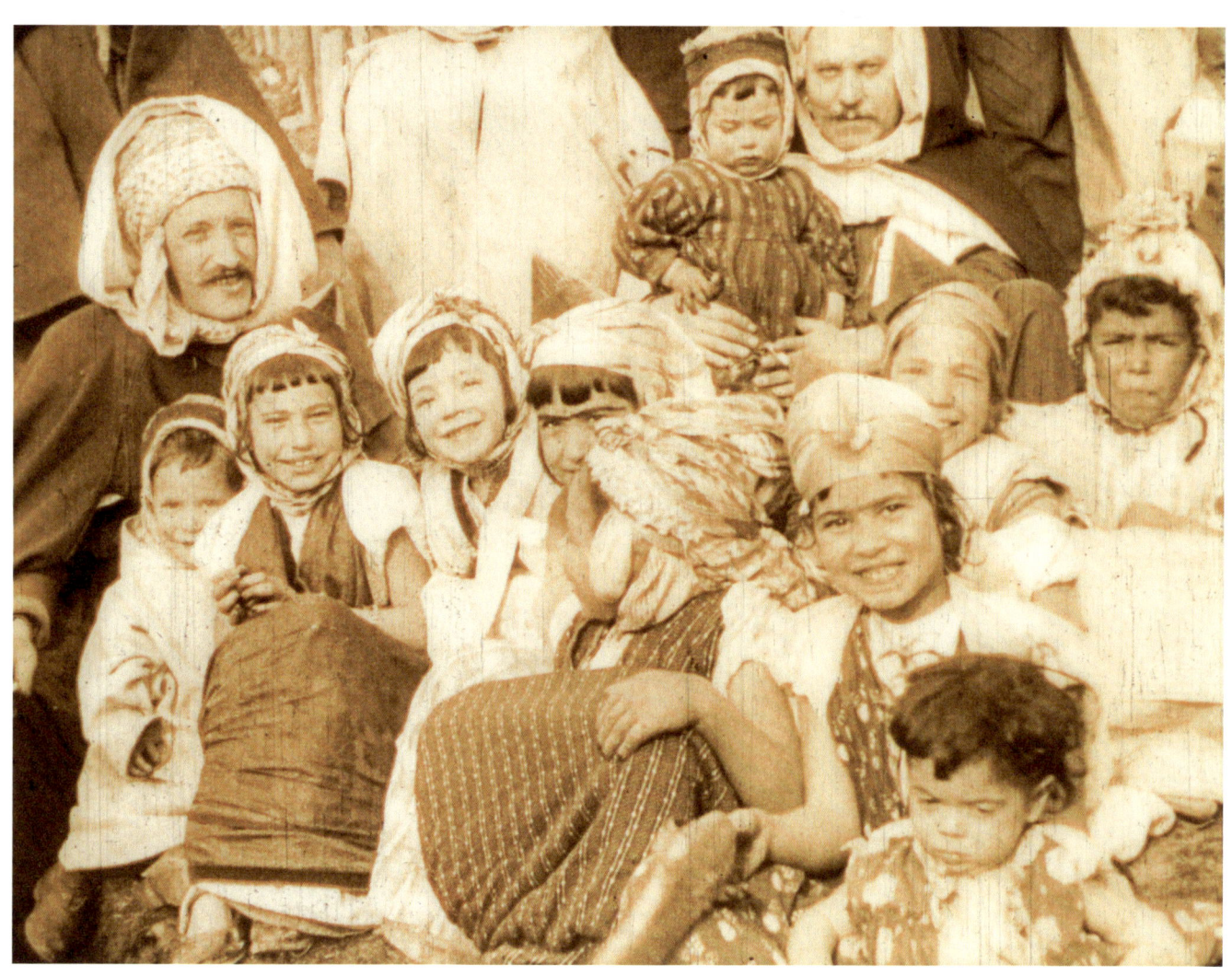

p. 70
Constantine, 1913

p. 71
La mousmée et le brigand, 1911

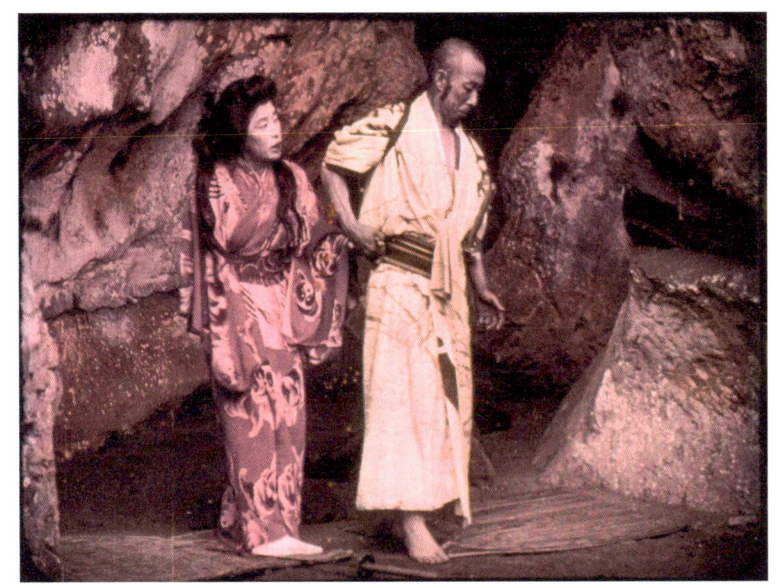

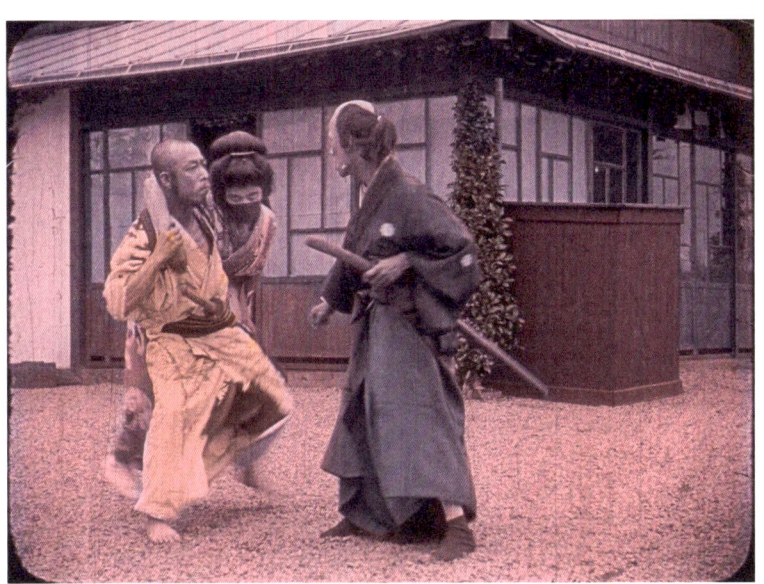

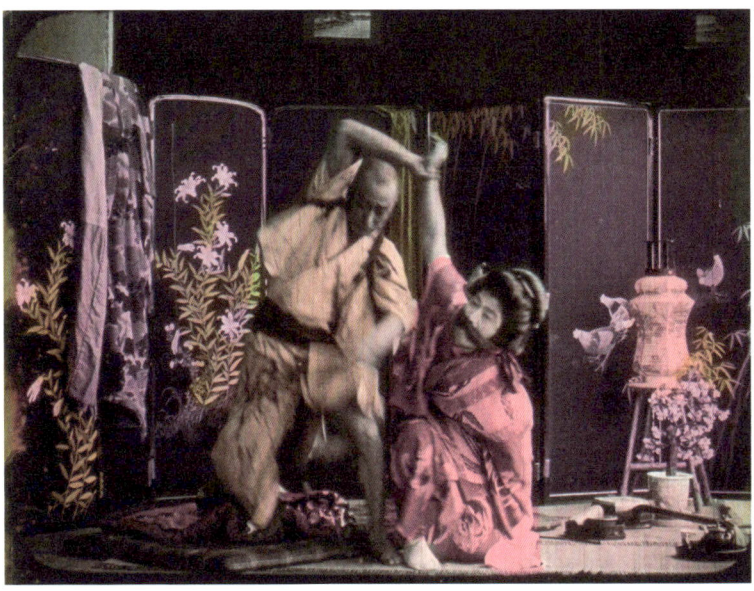

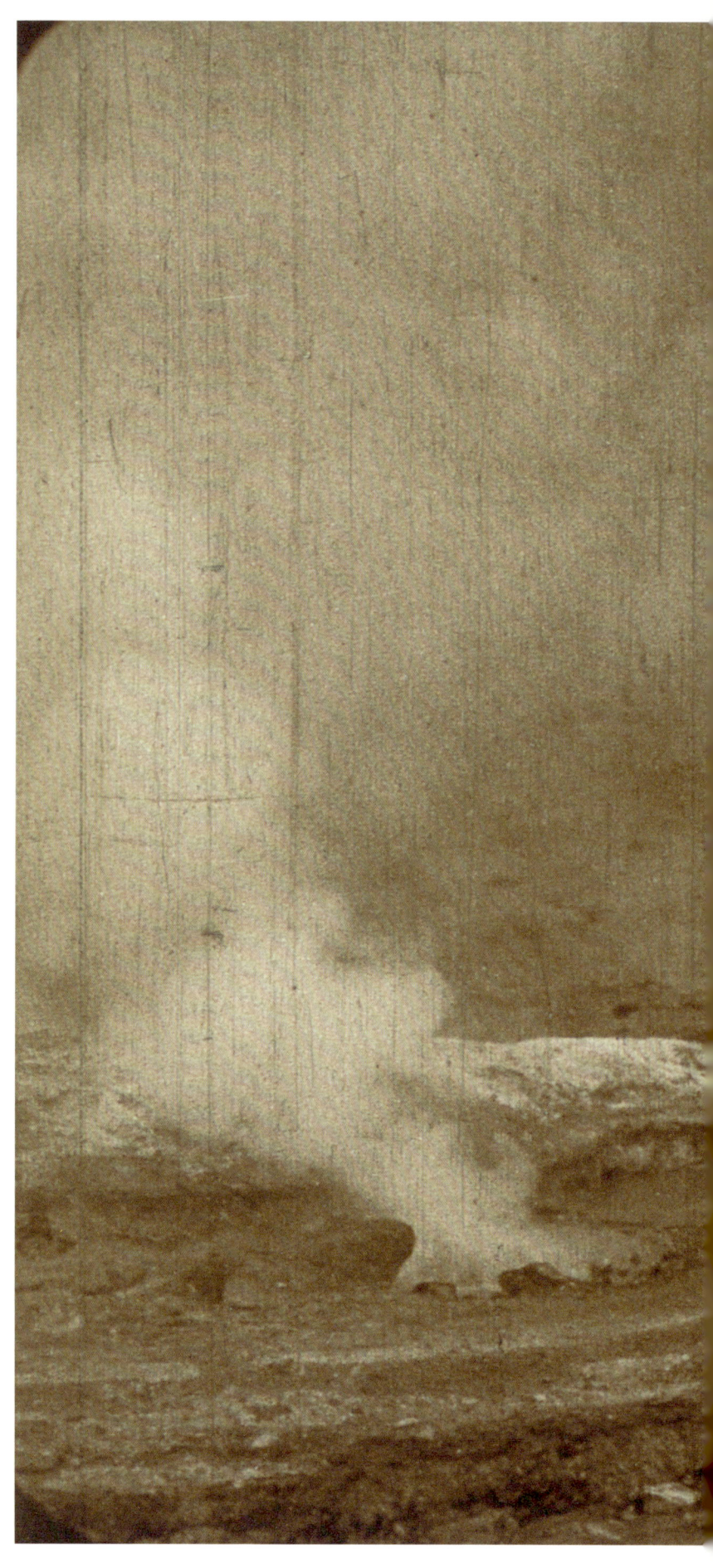

Paysages du Japon, 1911

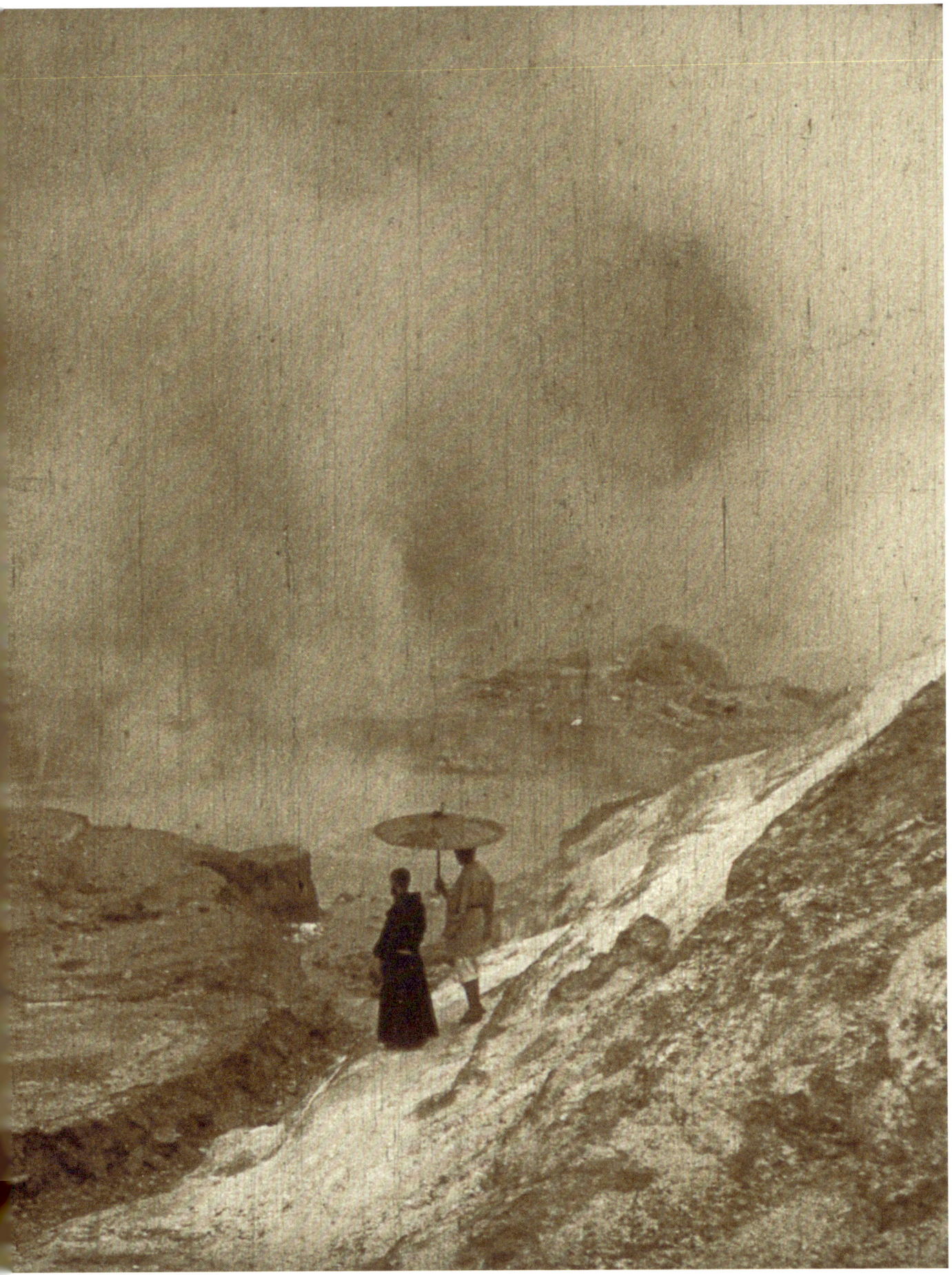

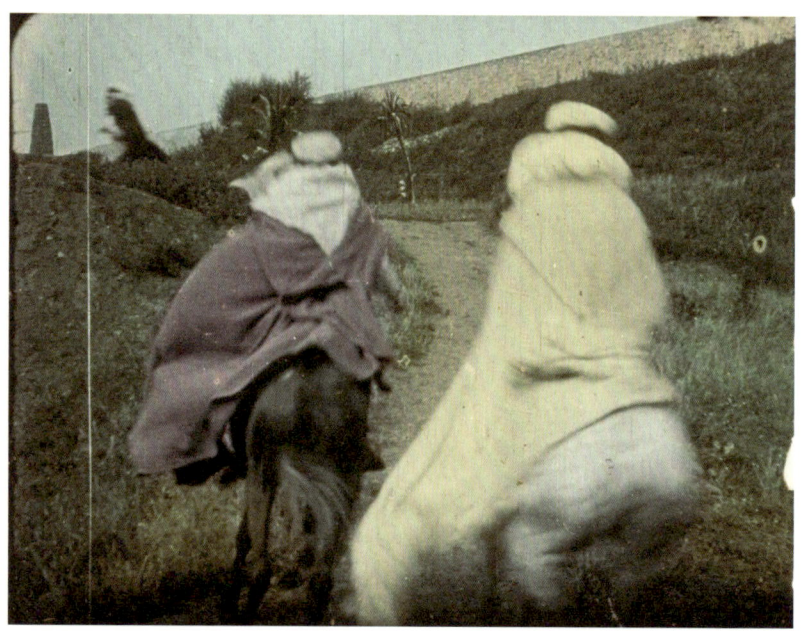

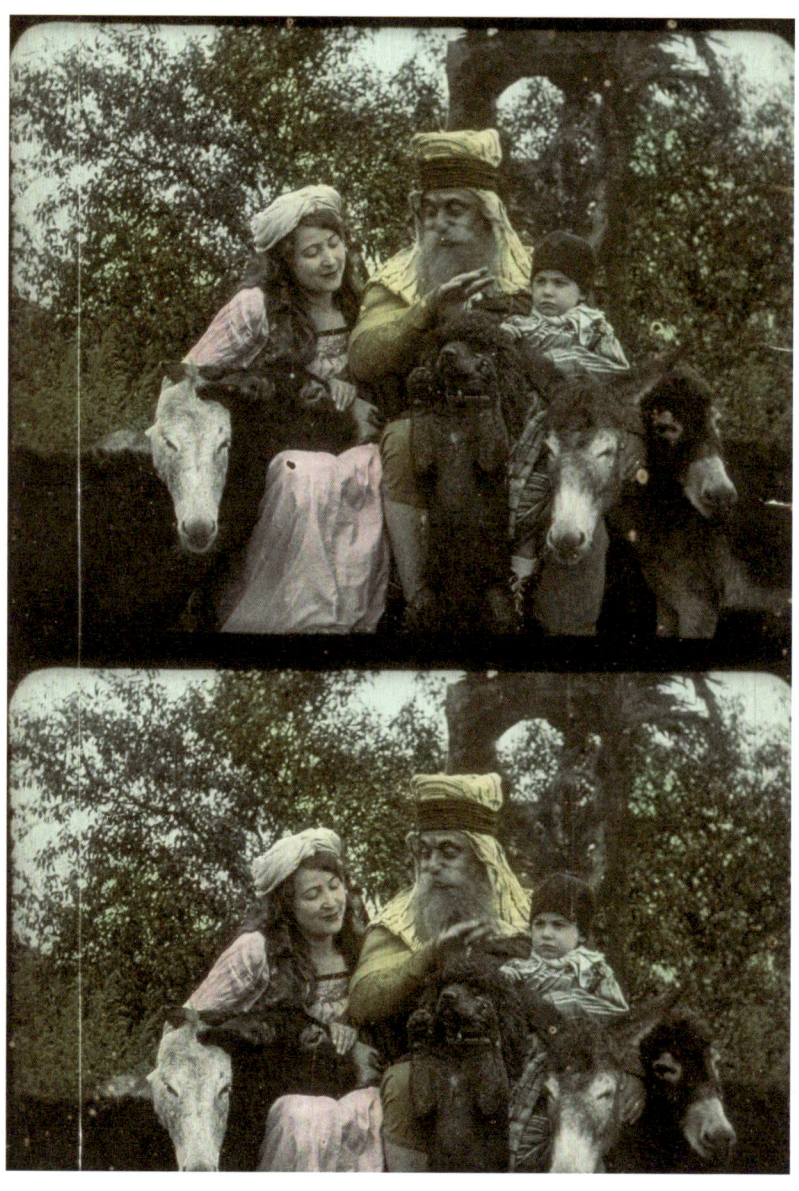

p. 73
Oliver G. Pike, *Les rapaces*, 1912

p. 74
Een uitstapje door China (A trip through China), 1911

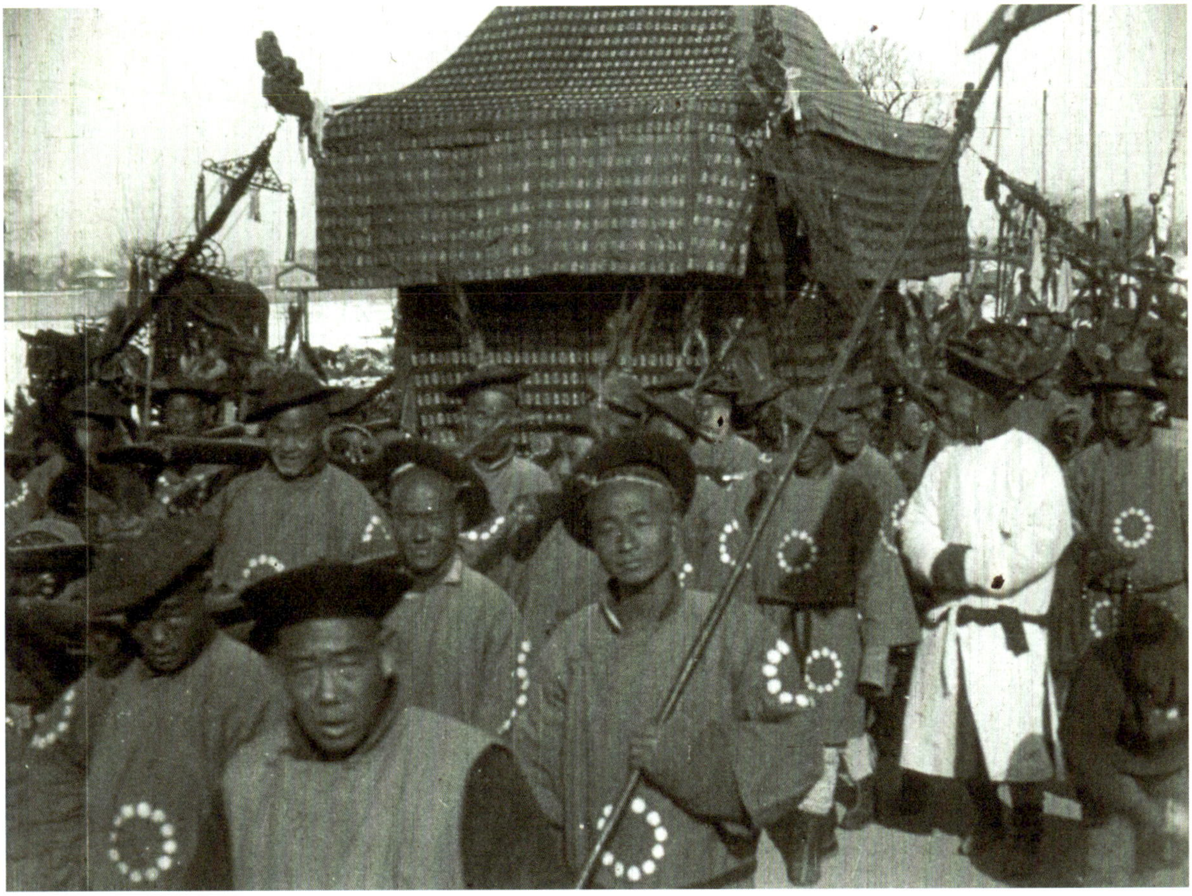

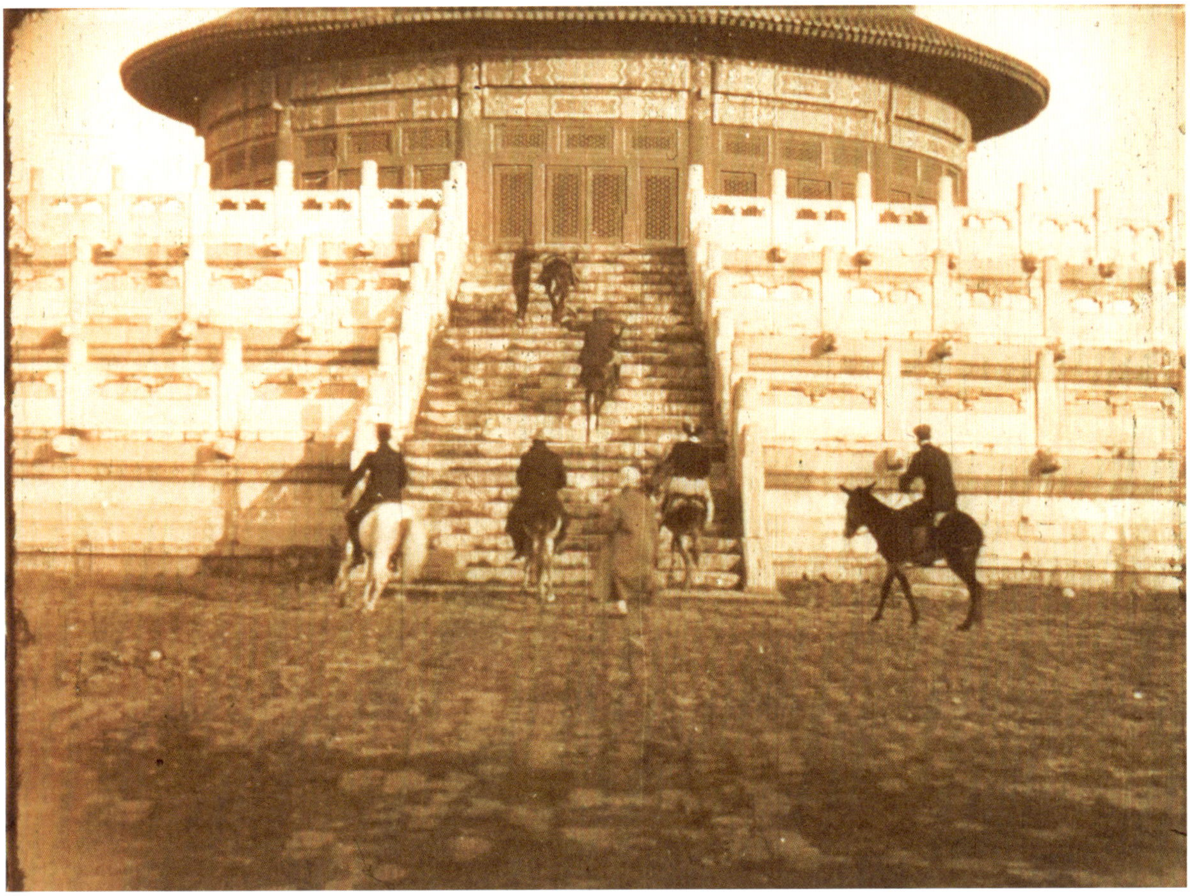

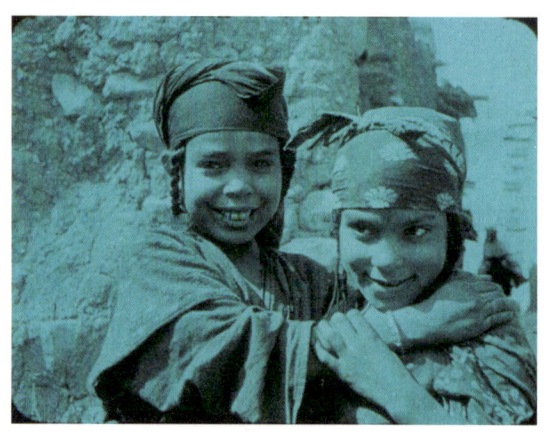

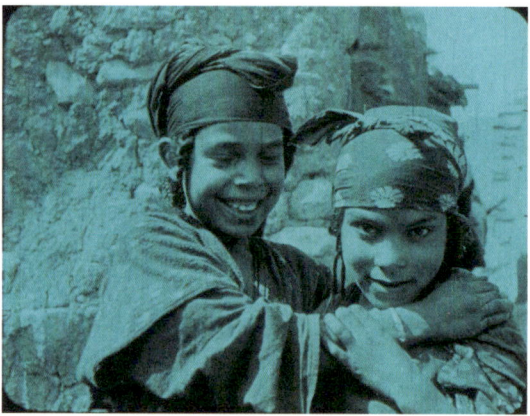

p. 76
L'oasis d'El-Kantara, 1913

Binnenland van Afrika (The interior of Africa), 1910

p. 77
Oogst van cocosnoten in Amerika (Harvest of coconuts in America), 1912

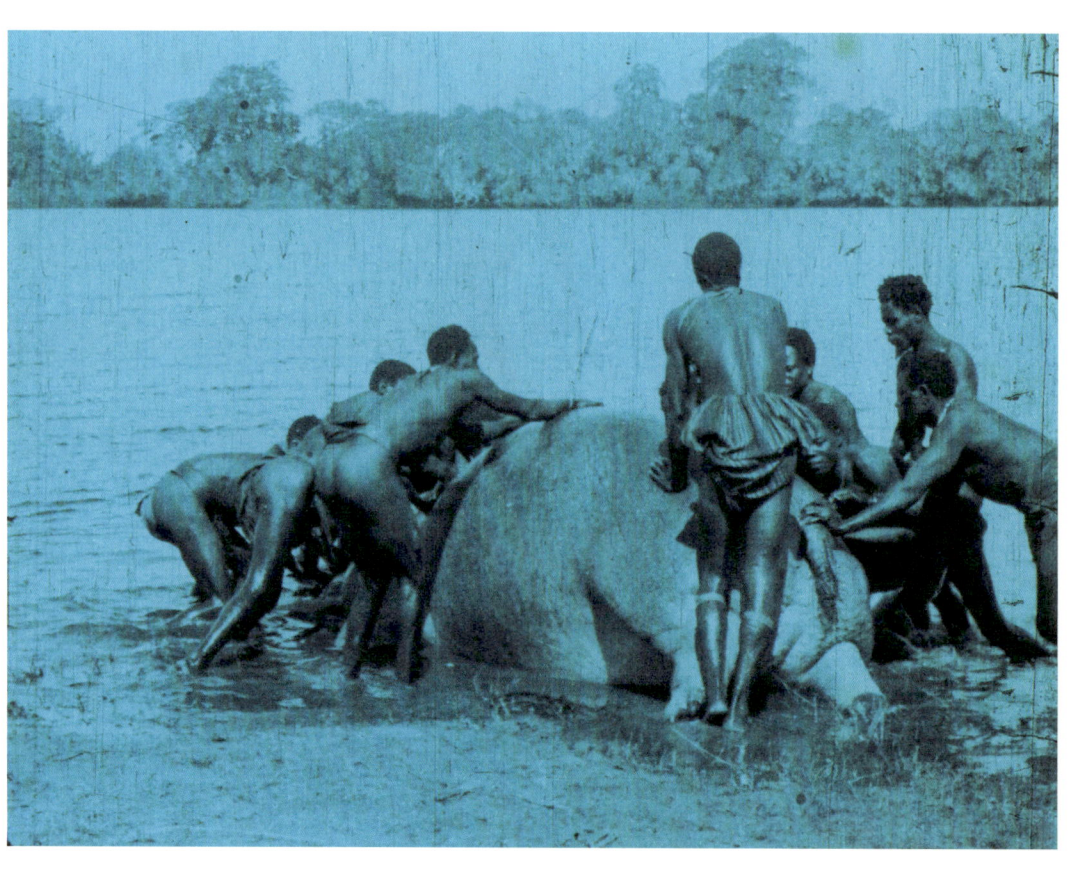

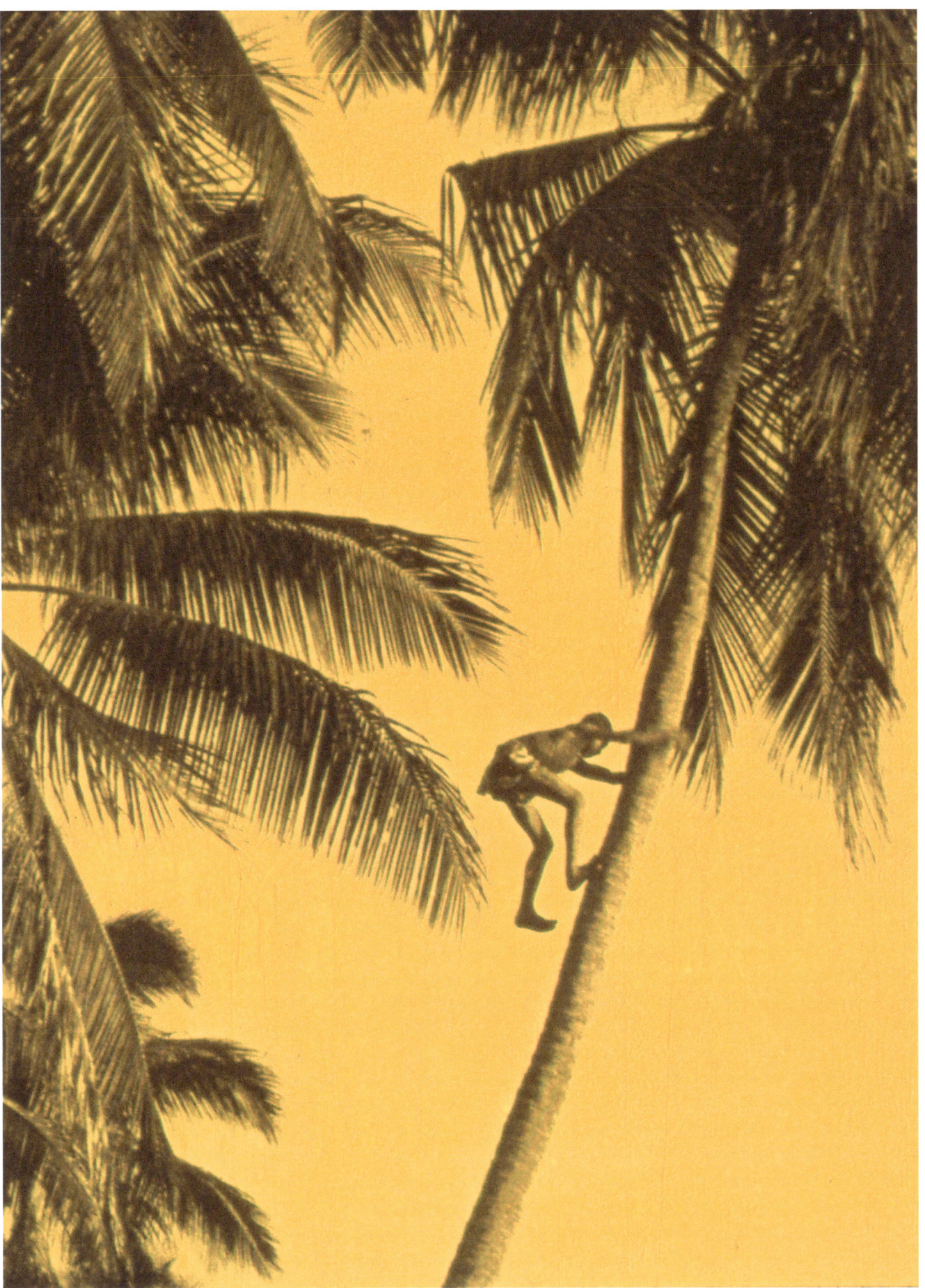

Les merveilles de l'Hindustan,
1914

Les tirailleurs anamites, 1913

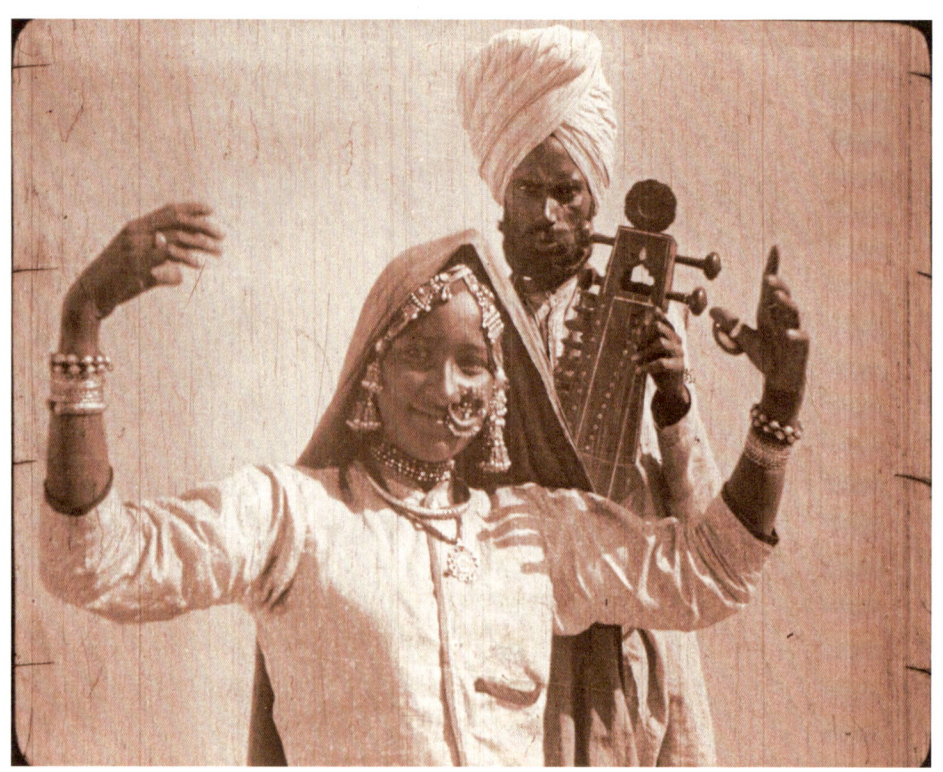

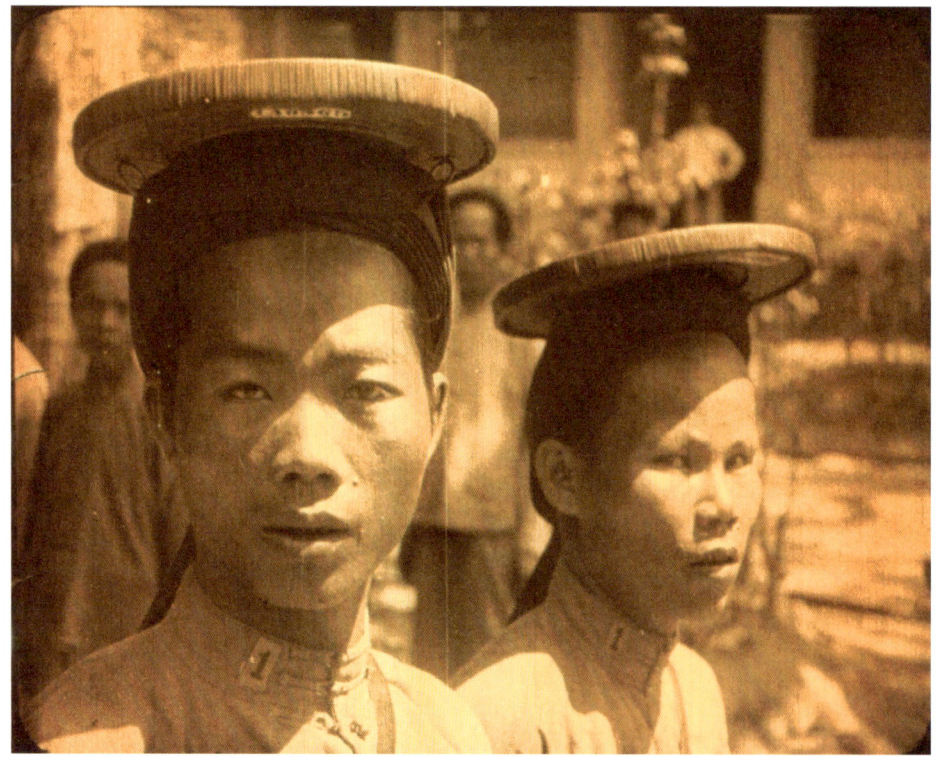

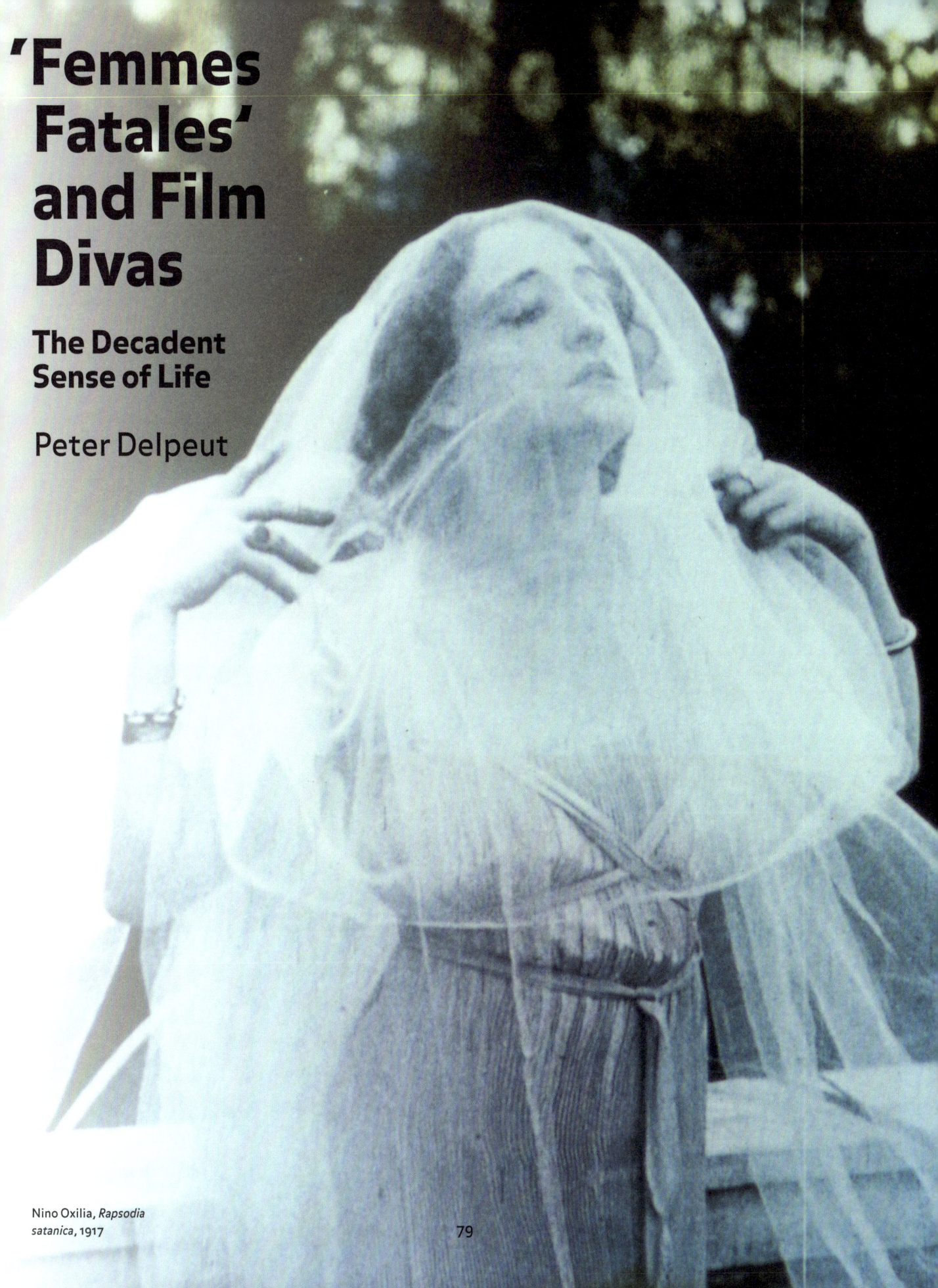

'Femmes Fatales' and Film Divas

The Decadent Sense of Life

Peter Delpeut

Nino Oxilia, *Rapsodia satanica*, 1917

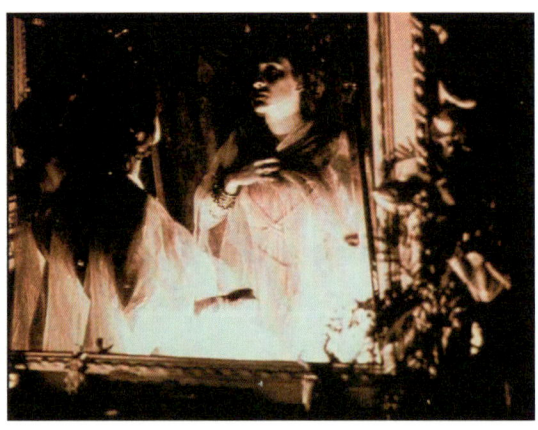

Flashes of insight tend to come at unexpected times. On the stage of the Carré theatre in Amsterdam, swathed in angelic robes, stood American singer Antony Hegarty, his long, straight black hair tumbling down over his pale face and red lipstick. He announced each song in a childlike whisper. Was this a man or a woman? It was anybody's guess. When he sang, his voice quavered as if he might burst into sobs at any moment. Was it genuine emotion, or mere theatrics? That too was anybody's guess.

Then the moment arrived. In a grave tone, with just a touch of irony, he described an accident that had once happened right in front of his home. A boy was hit by a car, and Antony ran outside to help. When he arrived on the scene, he froze. The boy was dead, but for Antony, it was love at first sight, a *coup de foudre*. He imagined curling up next to the beautiful dead boy, embracing him, kissing him, adoring him. 'I fell in love with a dead boy, oh, such a beautiful boy.'

What an odd mixture of seemingly irreconcilable concepts: love and death, irony and sincerity, sentiment and art, falling helplessly in love with a dead boy and singing a heartbreaking song about it. That was when I realized: *this* is the decadent sense of life.

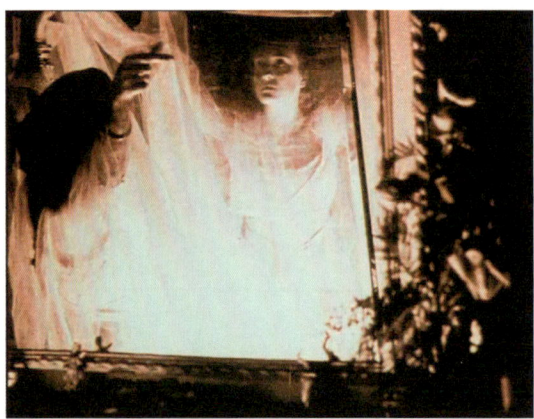

The decadent sense of life is usually associated with the decades around 1900, the celebrated *fin de siècle* (as if only one century had ever come to an end), but it took an androgynous American singer performing in Carré to drive home to me, at last, what inspired such diverse nineteenth-century painters as Rossetti, Waterhouse, Collier, Segantini, Von Stuck, Khnopff, Rops, Böcklin, Leighton and so on and so forth. This was what they sought: to fall in love with a dead boy, and proclaim their love in a voice choked with emotion.

The decadent sense of life feeds on paradoxical emotions, which can be captured only in extreme images or metaphors. Take the twofold fascination with lust and the death wish, for instance, or with Satanism and knowledge of God, the woman as both vengeful goddess and love object. The combination of the two should not really be possible or permissible, and yet it works, it happens. Because these emotions are contradictory, the images are not only unsettling but also amusing – or more precisely, sardonic. The decadent sense of life is the ultimate attempt to overcome a deeply felt powerlessness in the face of life's irrationality in a world abandoned by God, by means of impossible images.

The double meanings – and perhaps even double dealings – inherent to the decadent sense of life are found not only in nineteenth-century painting. In literature, there are D'Annunzio's fragile and Swinburne's fatal women, representatives of the late Romantic

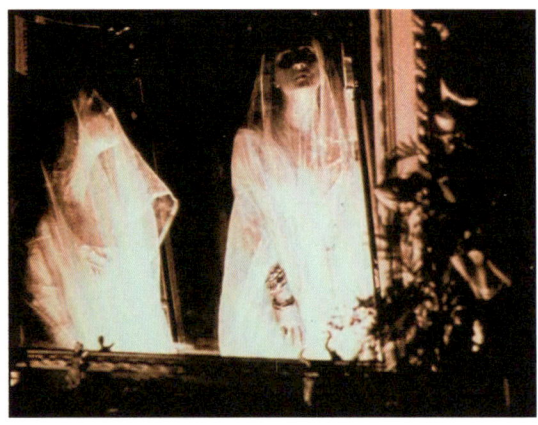

p. 80
Nino Oxilia, *Rapsodia satanica*, 1917

p. 81
Nino Oxilia, *Rapsodia satanica*, 1917

p. 81 top right
John Collier, *Clytemnestra after the Murder*, 1882
Oil on canvas, height 239 cm
Guildhall Art Gallery, London

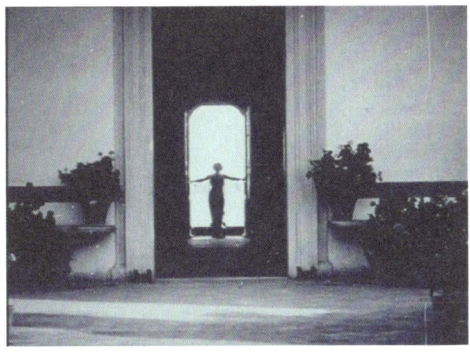

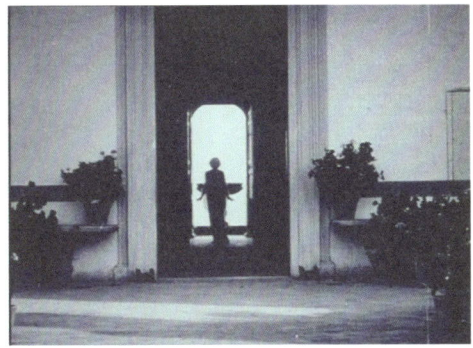

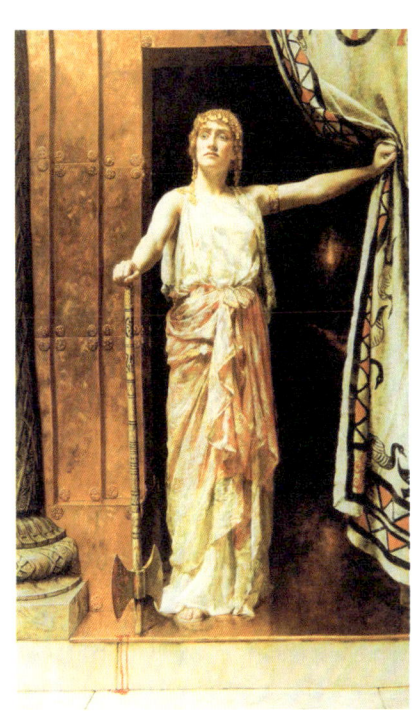

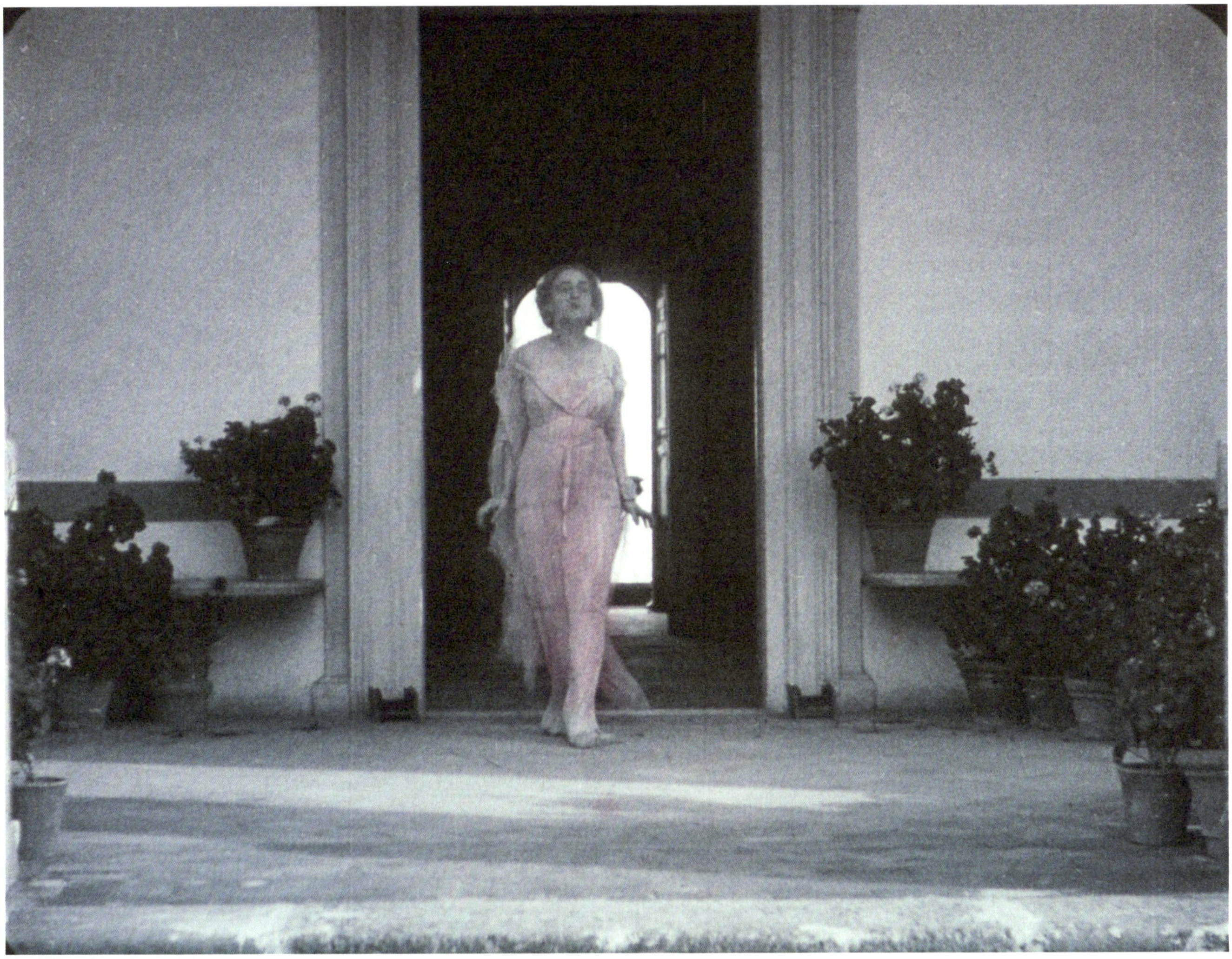

decadence so brilliantly chronicled by Mario Praz in *The Romantic Agony* (1930). In the theatre, Oscar Wilde, Von Hofmannsthal and Maeterlinck consistently presented women as unfathomable goddesses of retribution, all variations on Salomé of the seven veils, who cannot rest until she kisses the severed head of John the Baptist. In Richard Strauss's opera *Elektra* (1910), the hysteria of the female protagonist transforms the musical idiom into a maddening cascade of sound that does not permit the listener a single measure of rest. The operagoers are completely immersed in the musical pathology of female hysteria.

What a strange historical period it must have been, when artists had no qualms about putting the audience through such ordeals.

The same decades when all these intense emotions were being unloaded onto readers, listeners and viewers saw the emergence of a new art form: the film. In the early years, just after 1895, the first filmmakers enthusiastically borrowed from both the high culture (theatre and literature) and popular culture (vaudeville, dime novels and dioramas) of the nineteenth century. But strangely enough, only a handful of Italian filmmakers were daring enough to bring the decadent sense of life into film narrative. This short-lived and utterly unique movement relied, to no small extent, on the unparalleled cinematic presence of several remarkable actresses. They were known as divas, a title that lent them a divine quality, a hint of the sublime and of course linked them to the cult of Italian opera stars.

The three who dominated the world of Italian film from 1913 to 1920 were Lyda Borelli, Francesca Bertini and Pina Menichelli. All three were trained in the Italian theatre (and Borelli had shared the stage with the legendary Eleonora Duse), but it was the silver screen that made them stars, the first in that young medium.

The Italian divas invariably performed as if their lives depended on it. Their gestures were broad and forceful – grotesque and exaggerated, perhaps, by present-day standards. But if you look closely, you can see how precisely they composed their gestures and how little heed they paid to the laws of realism. Emotions are expressed in outbursts of physical display, grandiose sweeps of the arm and long-sustained melodramatic poses. They sing arias with their bodies and when they die, they draw it out almost as long as in an opera – drama queens in overdrive.

It requires very little art-historical research to conclude that the filmmakers were familiar with the visual culture of late Romanticism. They take a conspicuous interest in veiled women, serpentine and animalistic poses, and ecstatic facial expressions. The divas wear dresses by Mariano Fortuny, and when the

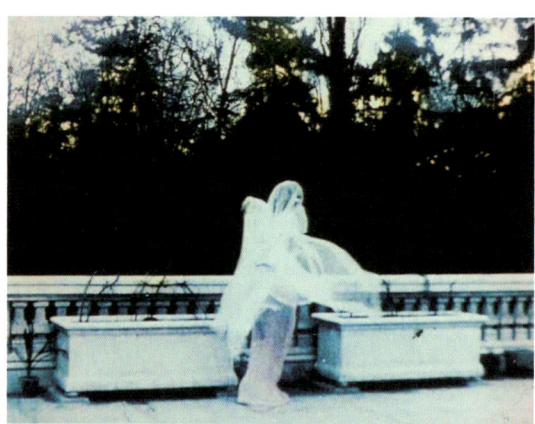

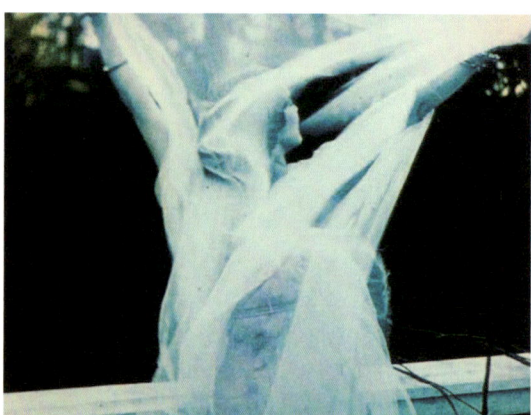

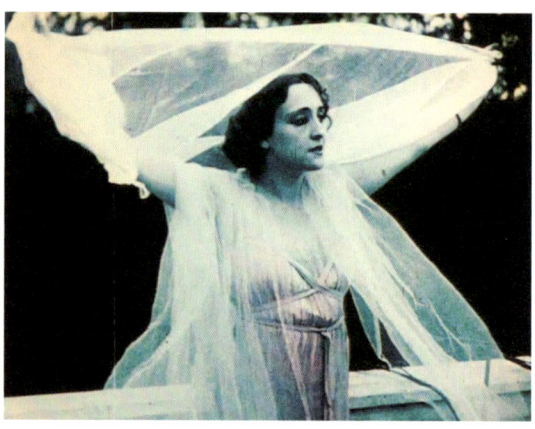

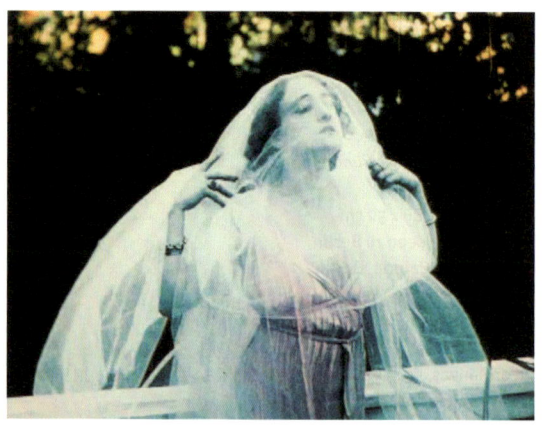

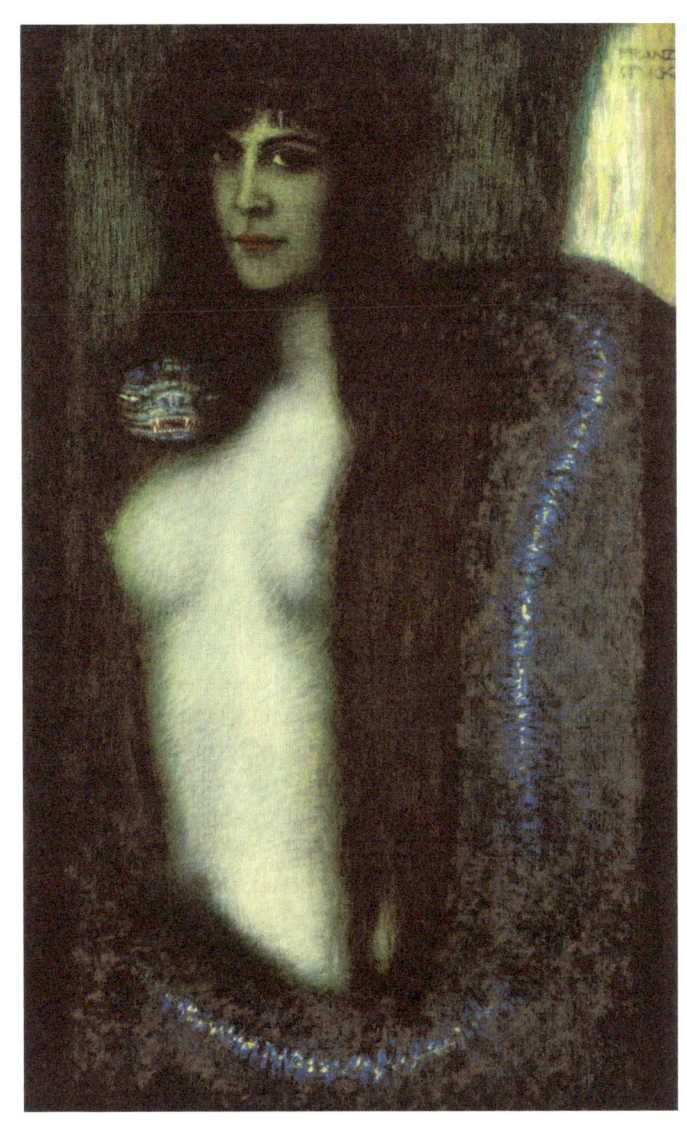

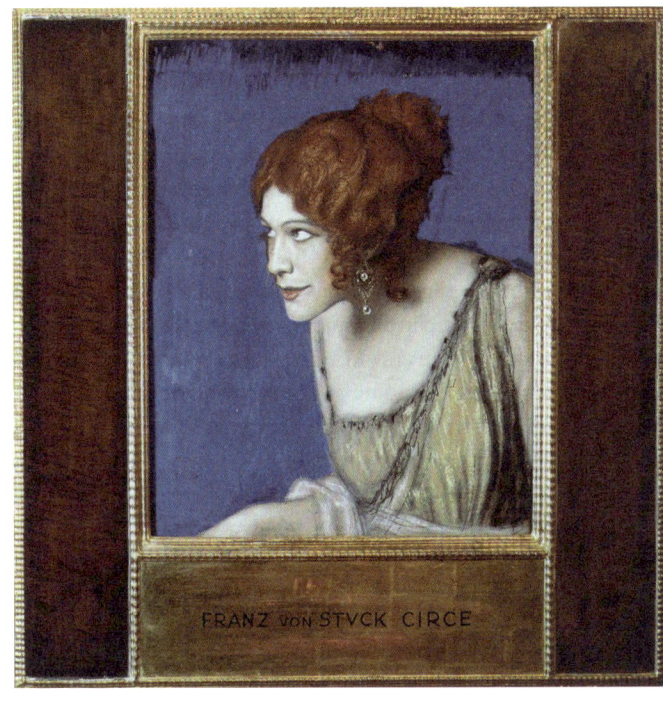

p. 82
Nino Oxilia, *Rapsodia satanica*, 1917

p. 83
Franz von Stuck, *Die Sünde*, c. 1912
Oil on canvas, 88 x 52 cm
Staatliche Museen zu Berlin, Alte Nationalgalerie, Berlin

Franz von Stuck, *Tilla Durieux as Circe*, c. 1912
Oil on canvas, 53.5 x 46.5 cm
Private collection

story calls for a masked ball they show up as Salomé. Their characters retreat to islands reminiscent of Arnold Böcklin's *Toteninsel* or wander down the long, dimly lit corridors of deserted palazzi in search of eternal youth.

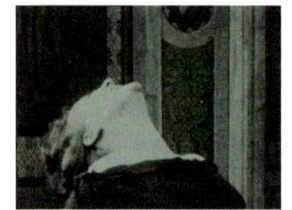 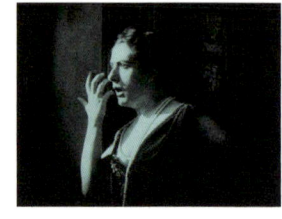

The figures portrayed by these divas are reminiscent of the pale and wan *femmes fragiles* of D'Annunzio (whose novel *Il fuoco* was adapted into a film starring Pina Menichelli) or the voluptuous, ruthless *femmes fatales* of Félicien Rops. Strikingly, many of them are Anna Karenina-like characters, women who choose love and so lose everything. Other women end up as prostitutes or, perhaps less tragically, as actresses earning a living on the stage. They are modern women who fly planes, parade past roulette tables or slip into a laudanum-induced stupor. Women on the brink of doom, with men who kiss their feet.

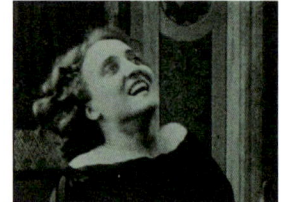 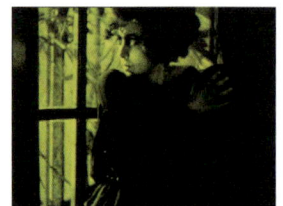

The brochures for their films included new Italian words like *lussuria* (lust), *isterico* (hysterical) and *nevrosico* (neurotic) – which together make a fine summary of the decadent sense of life. And this outpouring of decadence washed over the bourgeois and working-class audiences that flocked to the cinema, the women dreaming of someday gliding through life like a diva, and the men of someday holding such a woman in their arms. The diva films were decadent blockbusters.

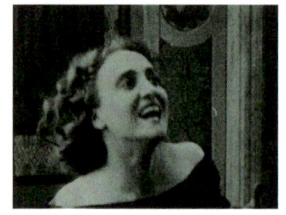 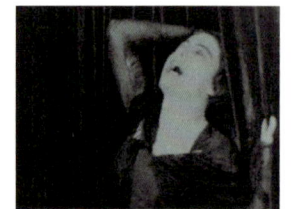

But there was a catch. Every diva story ended in guilt and repentance, if not outright punishment. However modern and liberated the female characters may seem as they glide across the screen, life ultimately gets the better of them: their children are kidnapped by a sadistic father, their old flames forget them, old age destroys their beauty, or they go hysterical and are sent to an asylum or locked away on an isle of the dead. In these film narratives, the lives of the divas always end in *dolore*, overwhelming pain and sorrow.

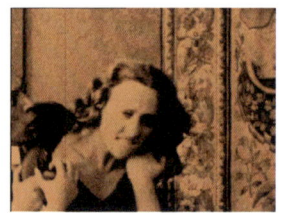 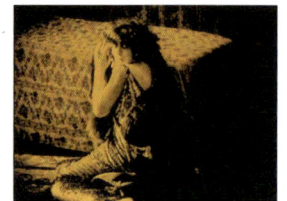

That's surprising, if you compare these stories to the literary, theatrical and painterly models that clearly inspired them. It would be facile to attribute the brutal ordeals with which these films invariably end to the moralism of their makers, or to see them as capitulations to commerce, confirming the bourgeois audience's sense of moral superiority. I believe there was something else that frightened the filmmakers, as if the cinema could not handle the ultimate consequences of the decadent sense of life – its irresolvable ambiguity, its ecstasy of contradictions.

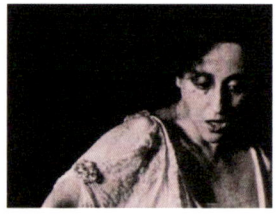 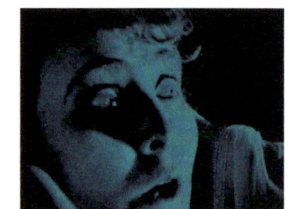

There is always a glimmer of reality in film – certainly more than in painting, but also more than in theatre or opera, despite the flesh-and-blood presence of the actors in front of the audience. Even the shakiest old black-and-white footage makes you feel like an eyewitness. In the cinema, you lose your sense of the stage and enter the world conjured up on the screen.

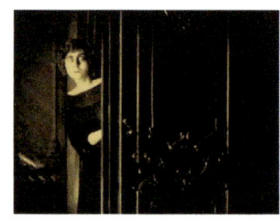 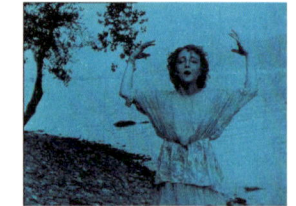

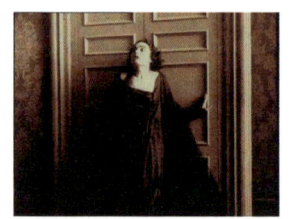 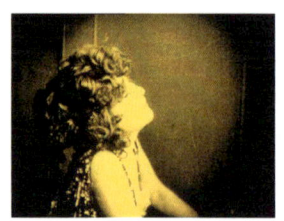

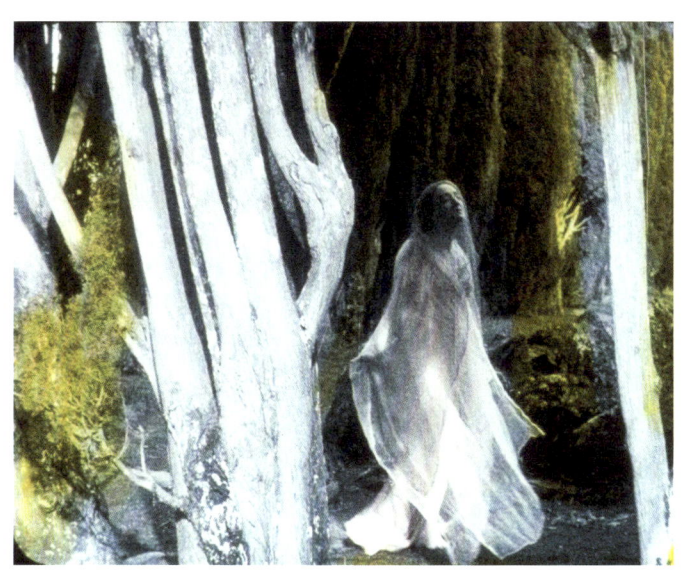

p. 84
Moments of hysteria from diva films, compiled in *Diva Dolorosa* (Peter Delpeut, 1999)

p. 85
Nino Oxilia, *Rapsodia satanica*, 1917

No longer conscious of the magic involved, you are literally lost, at the mercy of the film. The cinema lacks the safe distance of literature or painting, or even the footlights of the theatre. The cinematic image leaves no room for irony on the viewer's part, the step backward permitted by a painting or the pages of a novel. There is no escape. Could it be that the decadent sense of life is intolerable in this context? Does decadence bear watching only when it is finally neutralized through the imposition of a moral order?

It would seem so. Film is simply too confrontational to permit an unadulterated experience of the decadent sense of life. Film is too realistic, too close to the bone.

This became clear to me after I saw the photographs of hysterical patients taken by early French neurologist J.M. Charcot. In the final decades of the nineteenth century, Charcot would put on a kind of hysteria show during his famous Friday lectures at La Salpêtrière (where the audience included both his student Sigmund Freud and Sarah Bernhardt). His analysis had led him to the conclusion that 'classical' hysterical attacks showed an almost cinematographic storyline, with a beginning, a middle and an end. He schematically represented this sequence of events in series of photographs like Eadweard Muybridge's, using his own camera to document the primary stages.

Attacks of hysteria were a well-known phenomenon at the time. They could take place anywhere, even among 'the very best people'. They broke through the façade of bourgeois life, revealing the suppressed eroticism that ran wild, the unbridled sexual aberration. Families desperate for a solution would bring their girls to Charcot, who would photograph them. *Voilà la vérité*, he commented.

Looking at the photographs, it is striking how closely the hysterical convulsions resemble the poses of the gesticulating divas. There is more than a faint resemblance; it seems almost as if the divas had taken these girls as their mentors. How much more real can it get?

In *La donna nuda* (1914), Lyda Borelli plays a painter's illiterate muse. When she discovers he has a new mistress, she explodes. Borelli performs the longest attack of hysteria in film history. It is horrifyingly authentic, as if Charcot's girls had coached her.

This scene must have struck terror into the hearts of audiences in the 1910s. It depicts every right-thinking bourgeois family's greatest fear: an outburst of suppressed female emotion, the beast that could break loose at any moment. The divas were not simply playing a harmless, decadent game for cinemagoers. The late romantic iconography could not conceal a disturbing reality: this was no game or pose, but a genuine psychodrama that could break out in your home at any moment.

The diva films of the 1910s demonstrate the unbearable nature of decadence. Rather than an artistic adaptation, such as we find in literature, visual art or opera, they present an anatomy of the decadent, its medical history.

The psychoanalyst Félix Guattari once wrote: 'Film is the divan of the poor.' In their flirtation with decadence, the divas showed their audience that it was untenable as a sense of life. The viewers went home reassured. But were they also cured? Doesn't a typical course of psychoanalysis take seven years, with sessions at least twice a week, if not daily?

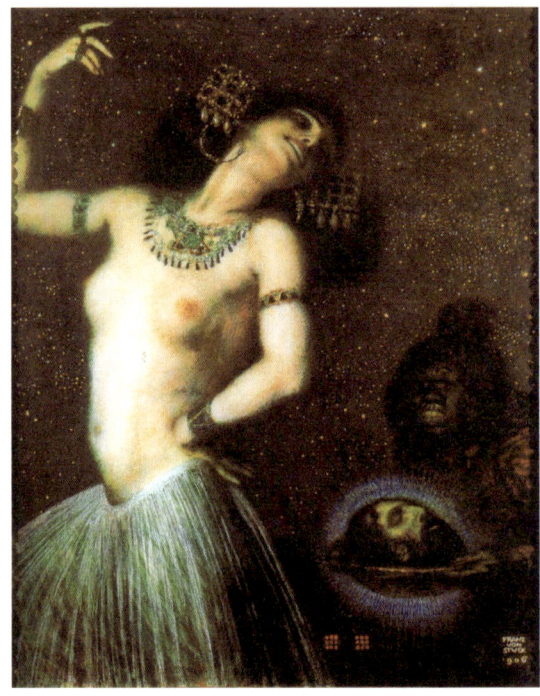

Sources

Diva Dolorosa (1999), a film by Peter Delpeut, released on DVD by Zeitgeist Films (USA)
Angela Dalle Vacche, *Diva: Defiance and Passion in Early Italian Cinema* (Austin, 2008), which includes a DVD of *Diva Dolorosa*
Mario Praz, *The Romantic Agony*, trans. Angus Davidson (Oxford, 1978)
Nelly Voorhuis and Ivo Blom (eds.), *De vroege Italiaanse speelfilm: Hartstocht en Heldendom* (Amsterdam, 1988)
Georges Didi-Huberman, *Invention de l'Hysterie* (Paris, 1982)
Bram Dijkstra, *Idols of Perversity. Fantasies of Feminine Evil in Fin-de-Siècle Culture* (New York, 1986)
Peter Delpeut, *Diva Dolorosa. Reis naar het einde van een eeuw* (Amsterdam, 1999)

Franz von Stuck, *Salome*, 1906
Oil on canvas, 115.5 x 62.5 cm
Städtische Galerie im Lenbachhaus, Munich

Arnold Böcklin,
The Death of Cleopatra, 1872
Oil on canvas, 76 x 61.5 cm
Kunstmuseum Basel

Historical Stories

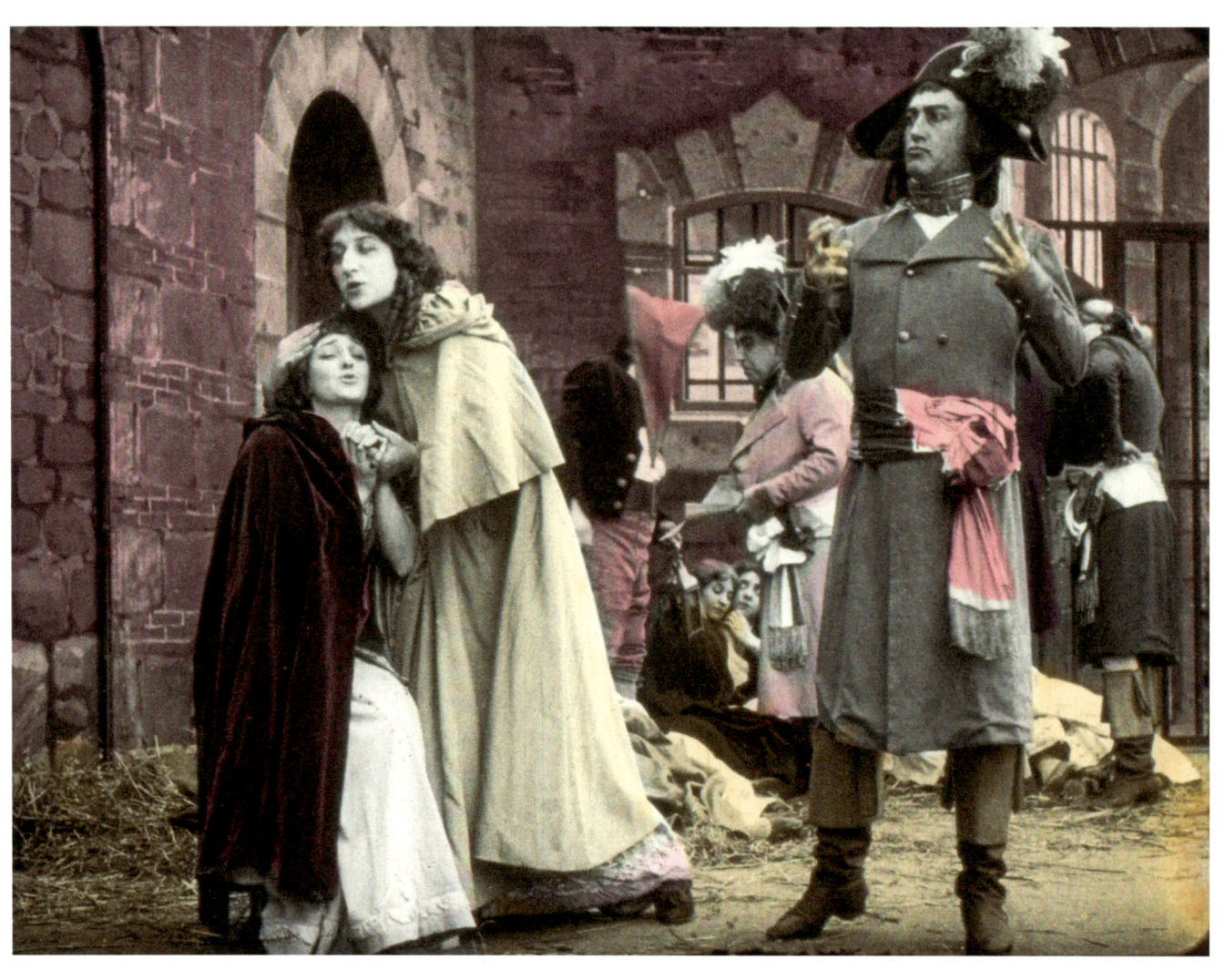

p. 88
Camille de Morlhon, *Madame Tallien, 1794*, 1911

p. 89
Ugo Falena, *Tristano e Isotta (Tristan und Isolde)*, 1911

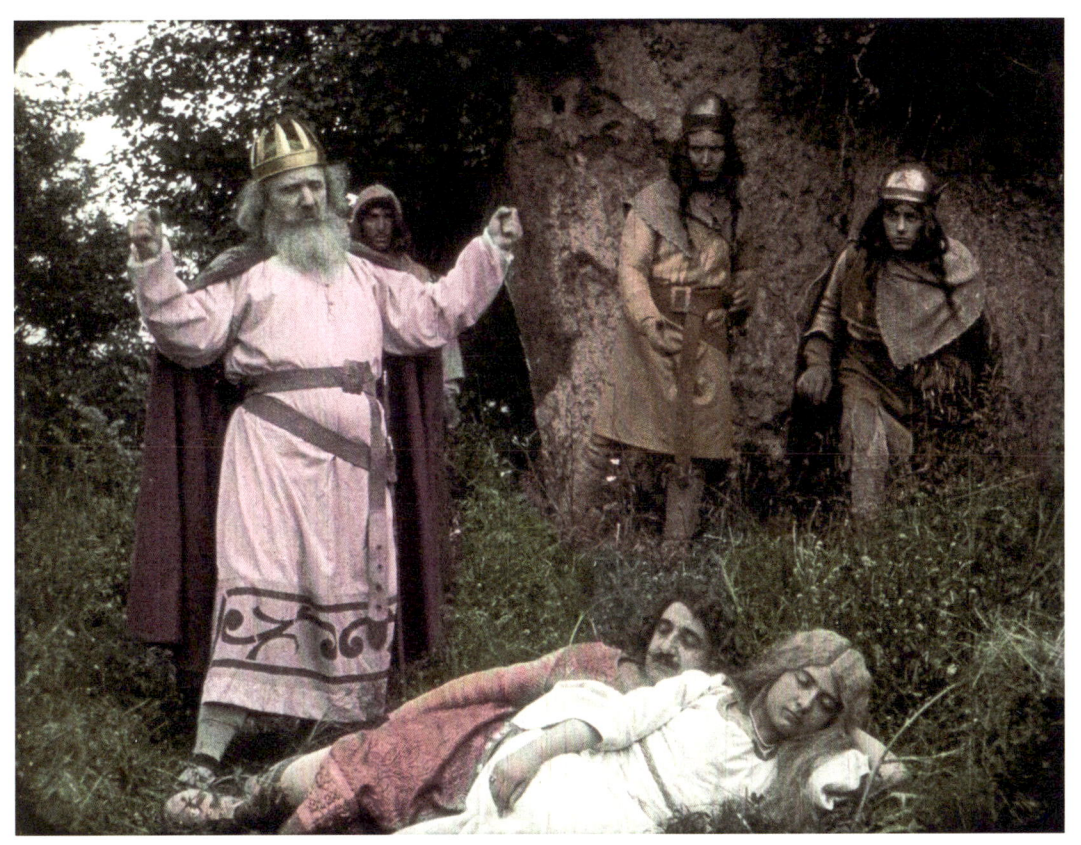

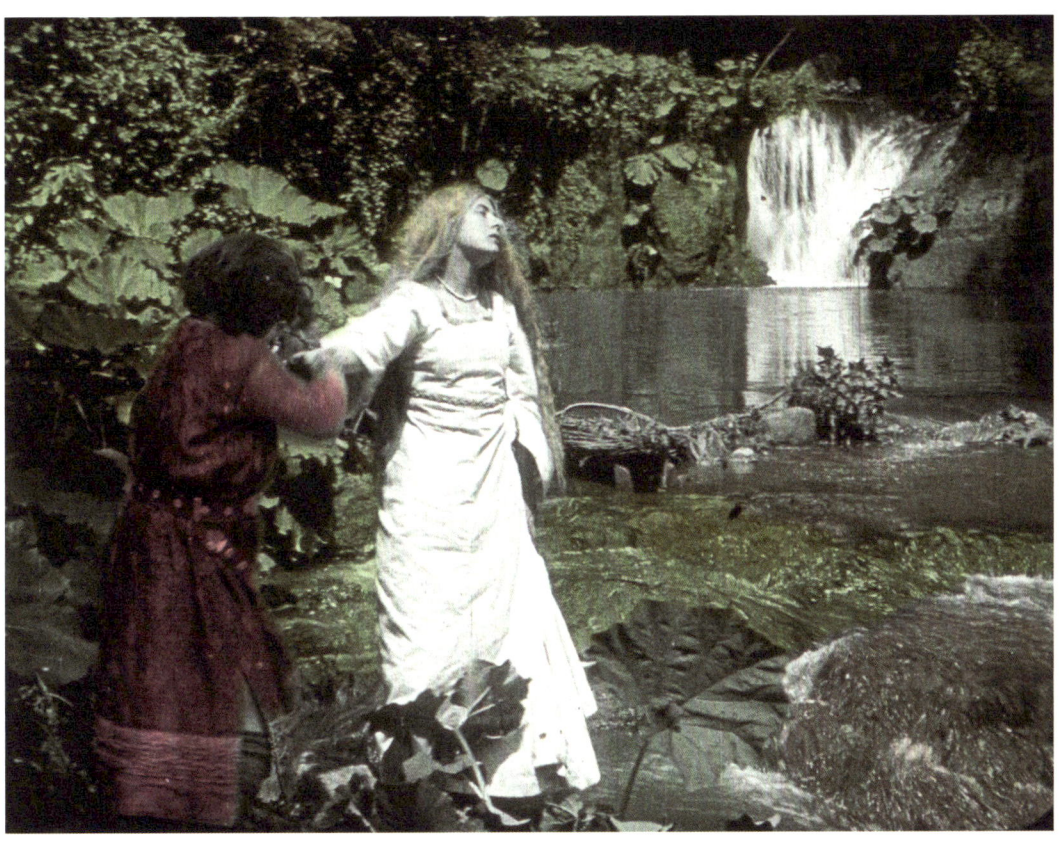

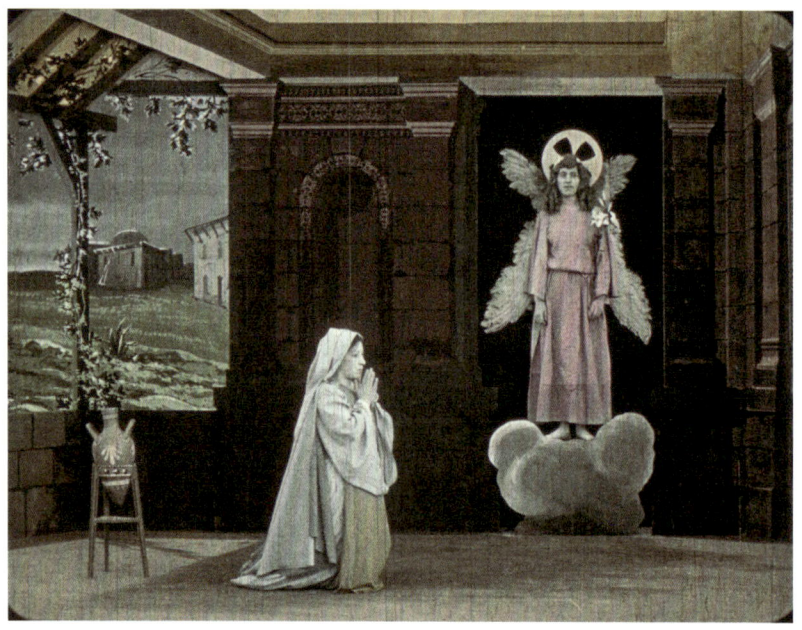
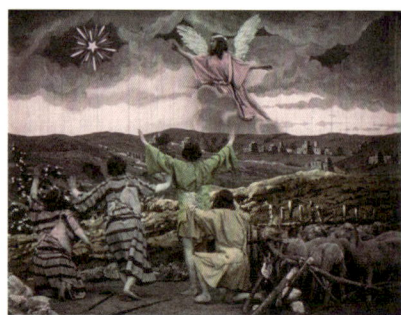
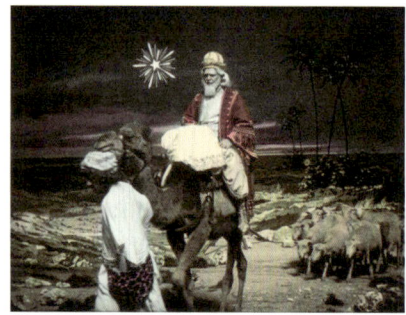
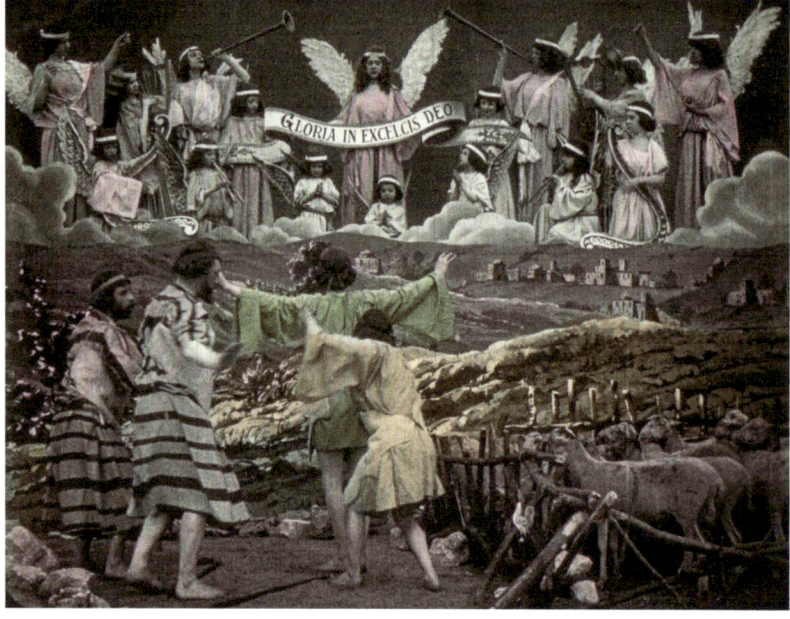
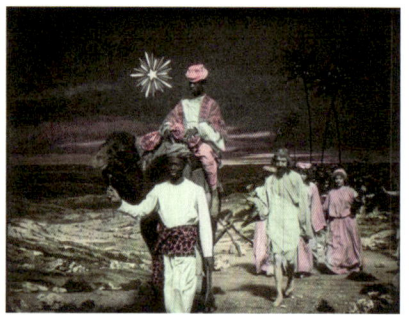
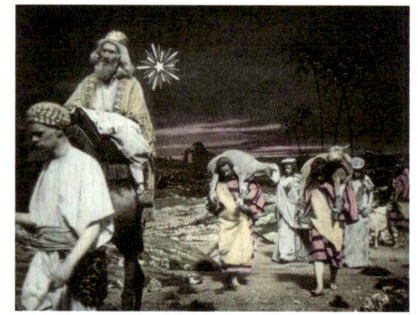
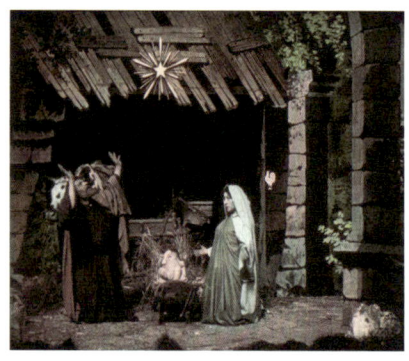

pp. 90-91
Ferdinand Zecca, *La vie et la passion de Notre Seigneur Jésus Christ*, 1907

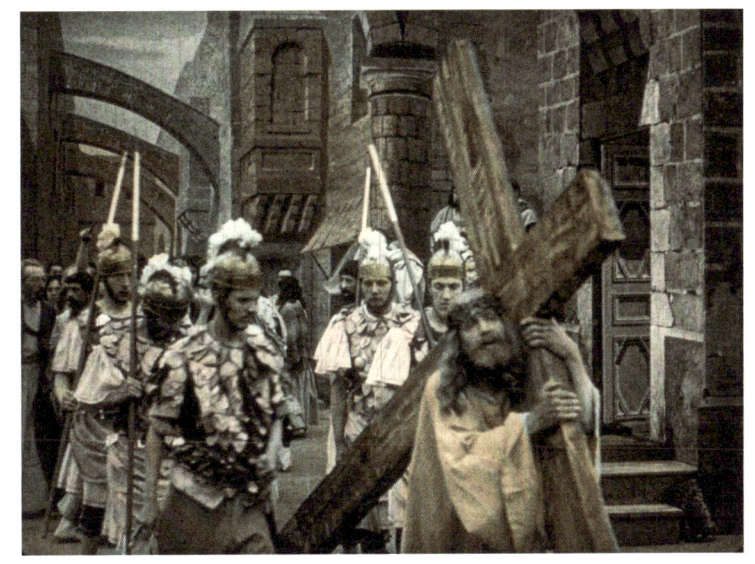

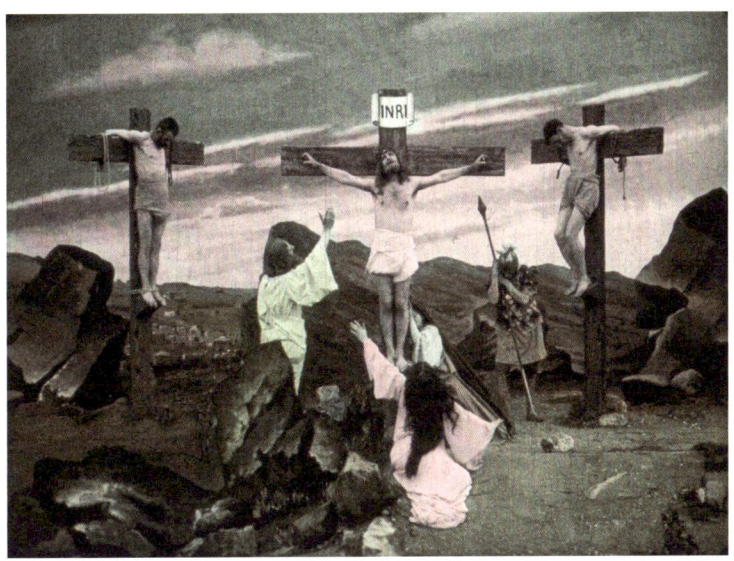

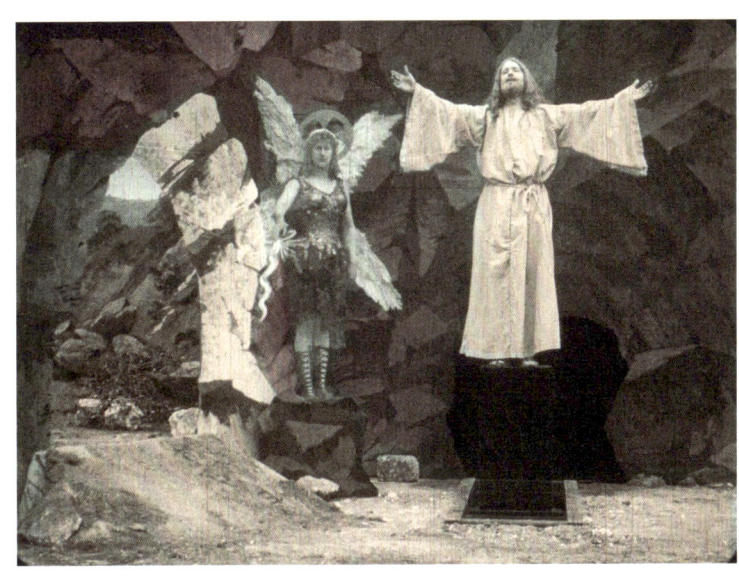

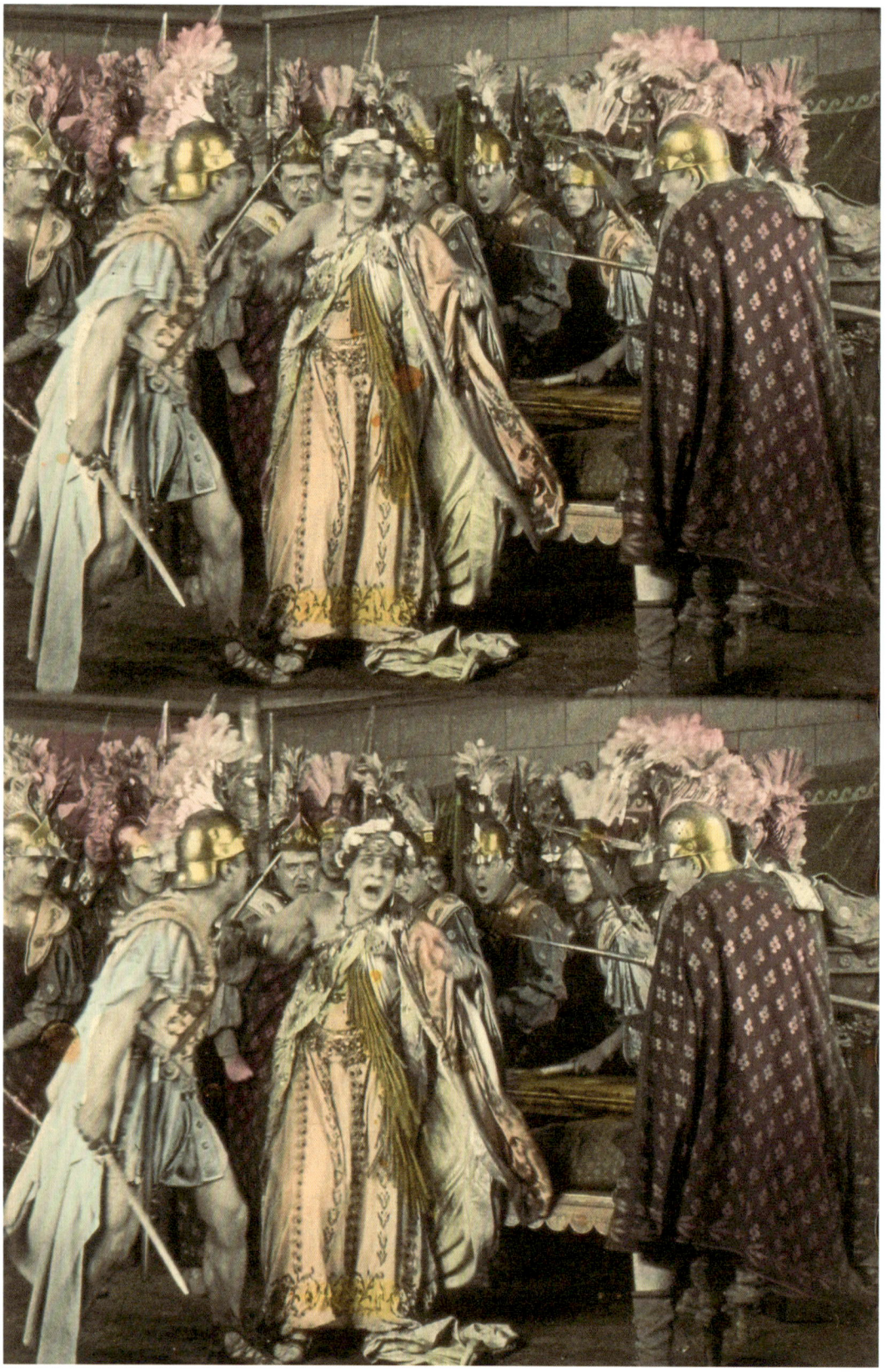

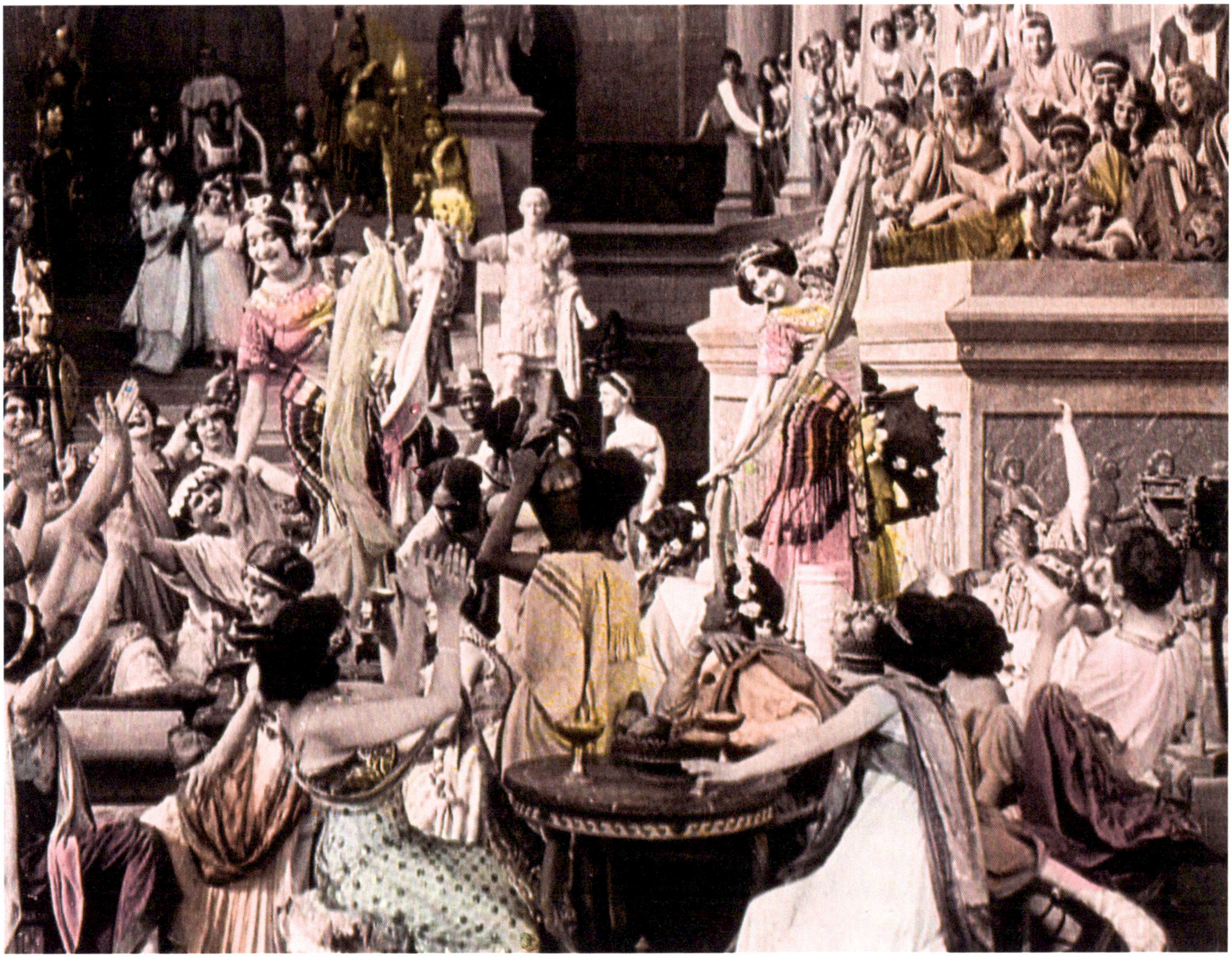

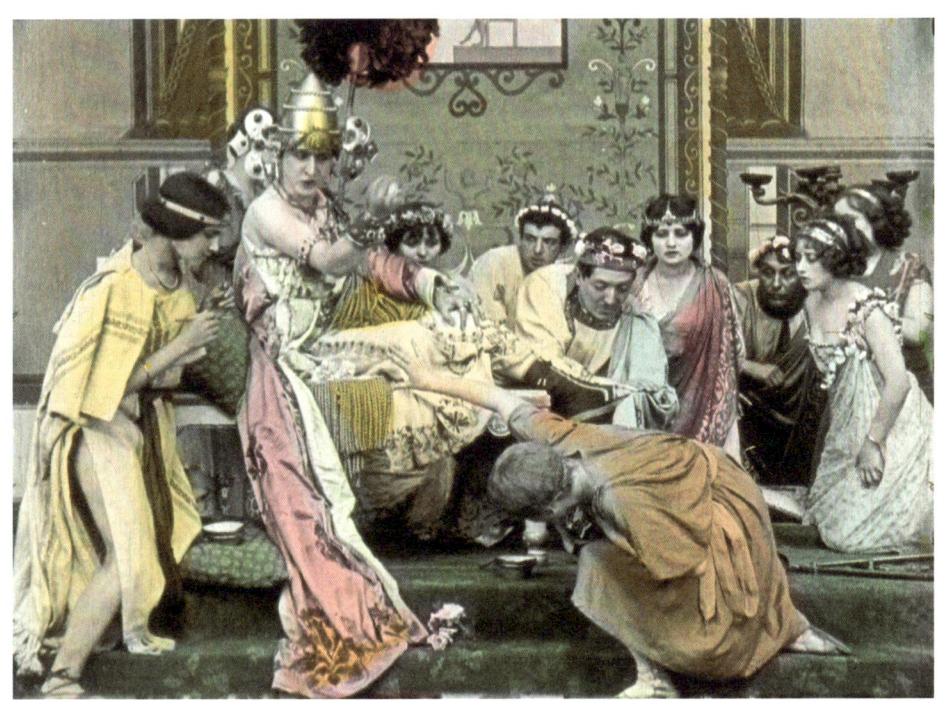

pp. 92-93
Louis Feuillade, *L'orgie romaine*
(*Die Löwen des Tyrannen*), 1911

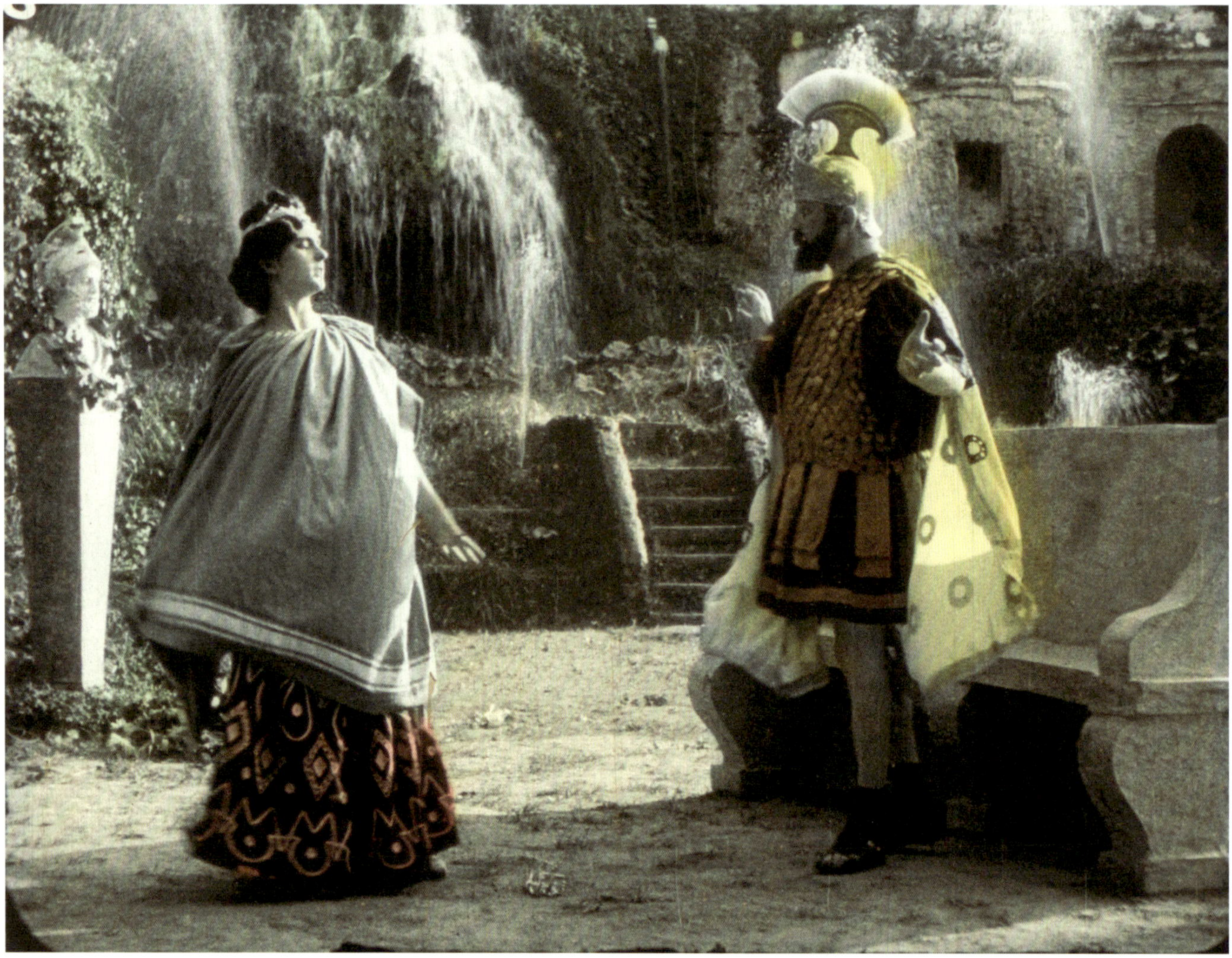

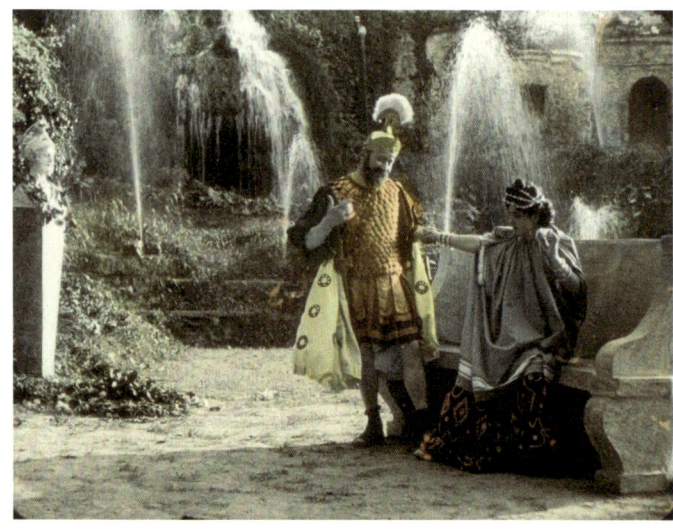

p. 94
Ugo Falena, *Il ratto delle Sabine*, 1910

p. 95
Enrico Guazzoni, *Cajus Julius Caesar*, 1914

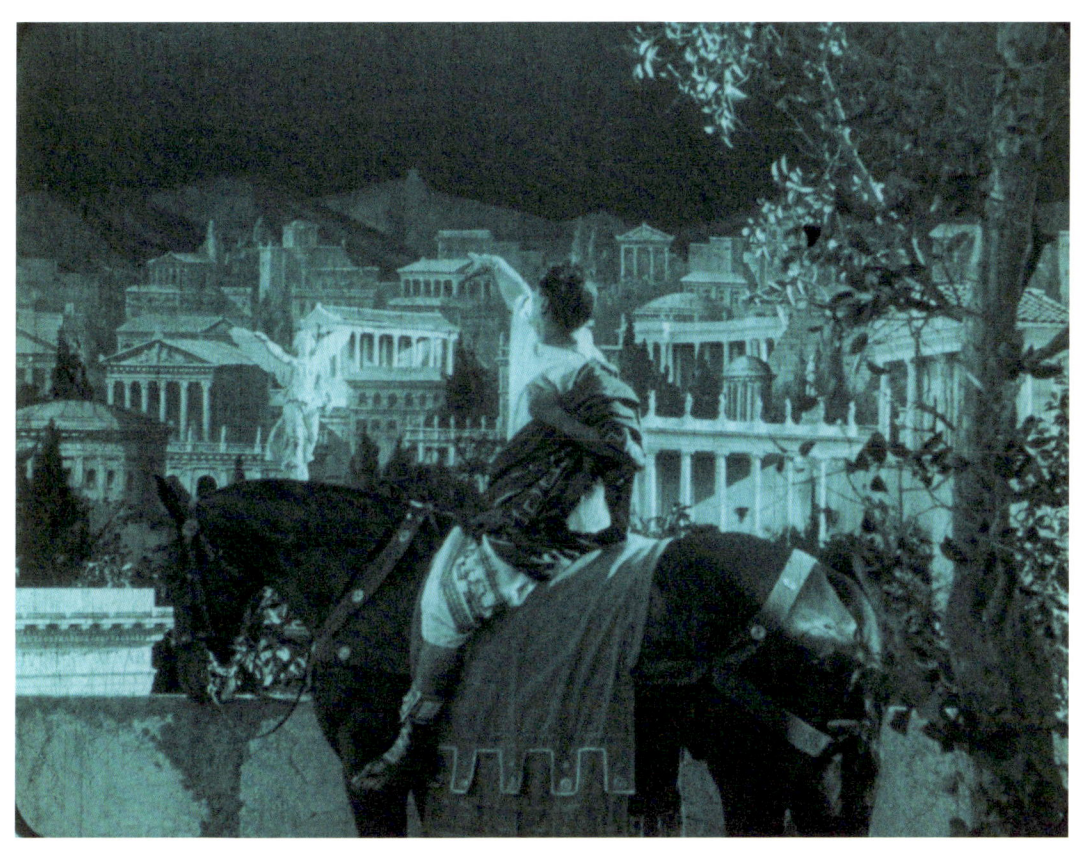
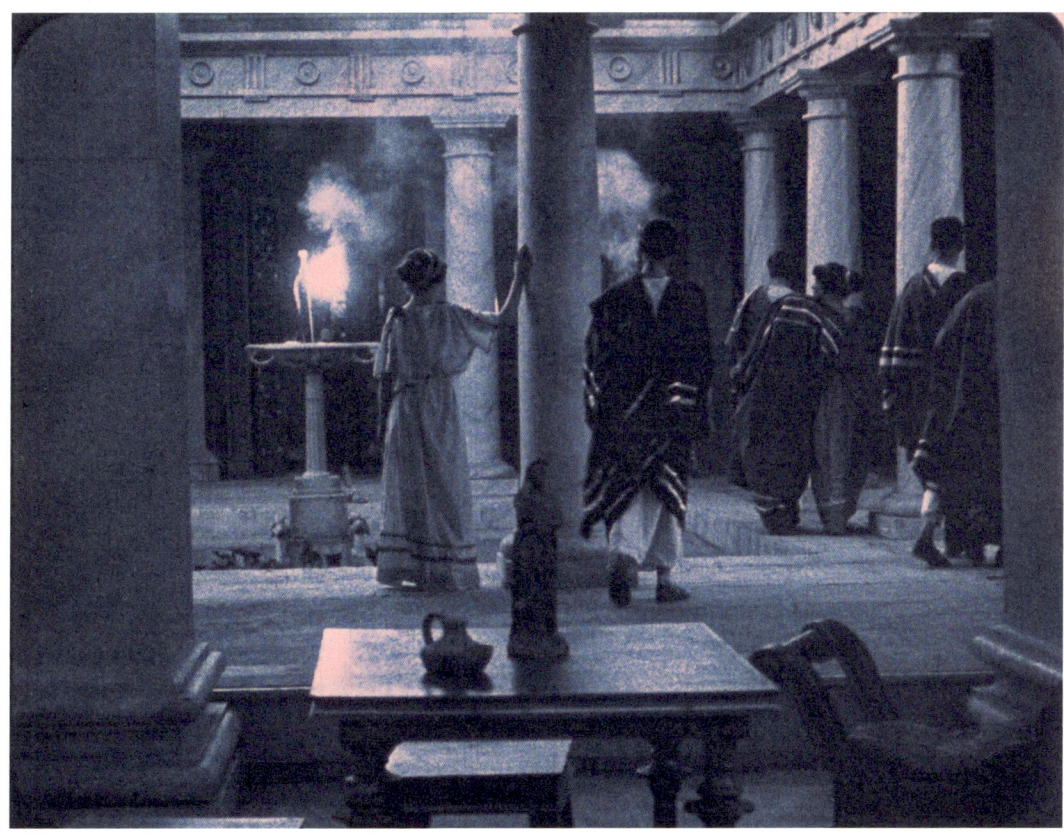

Georges Denola, *La légende des ondines*, 1911

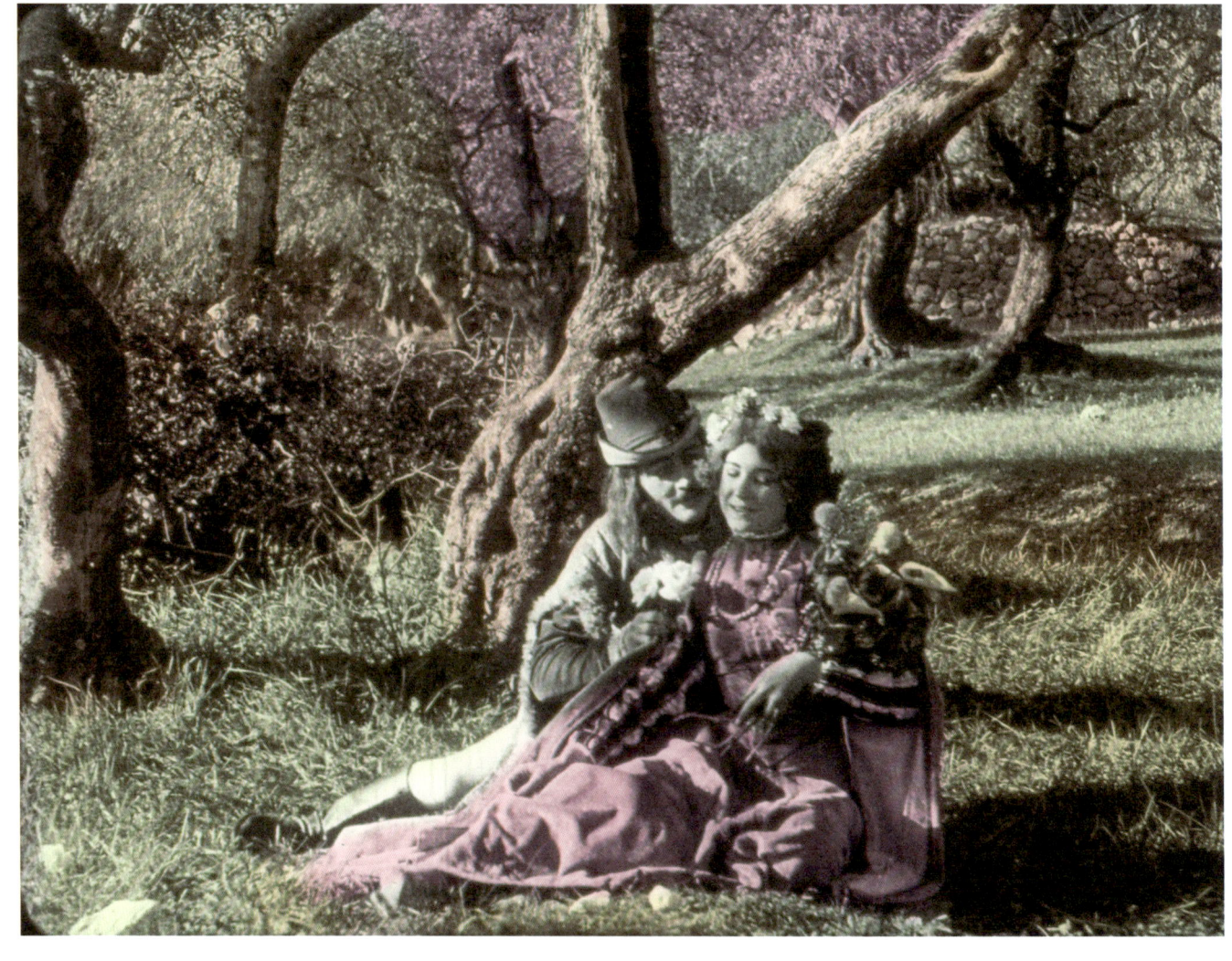

Terrifying, Modern and Artistic

The Film Posters in the Desmet Collection

Ivo Blom

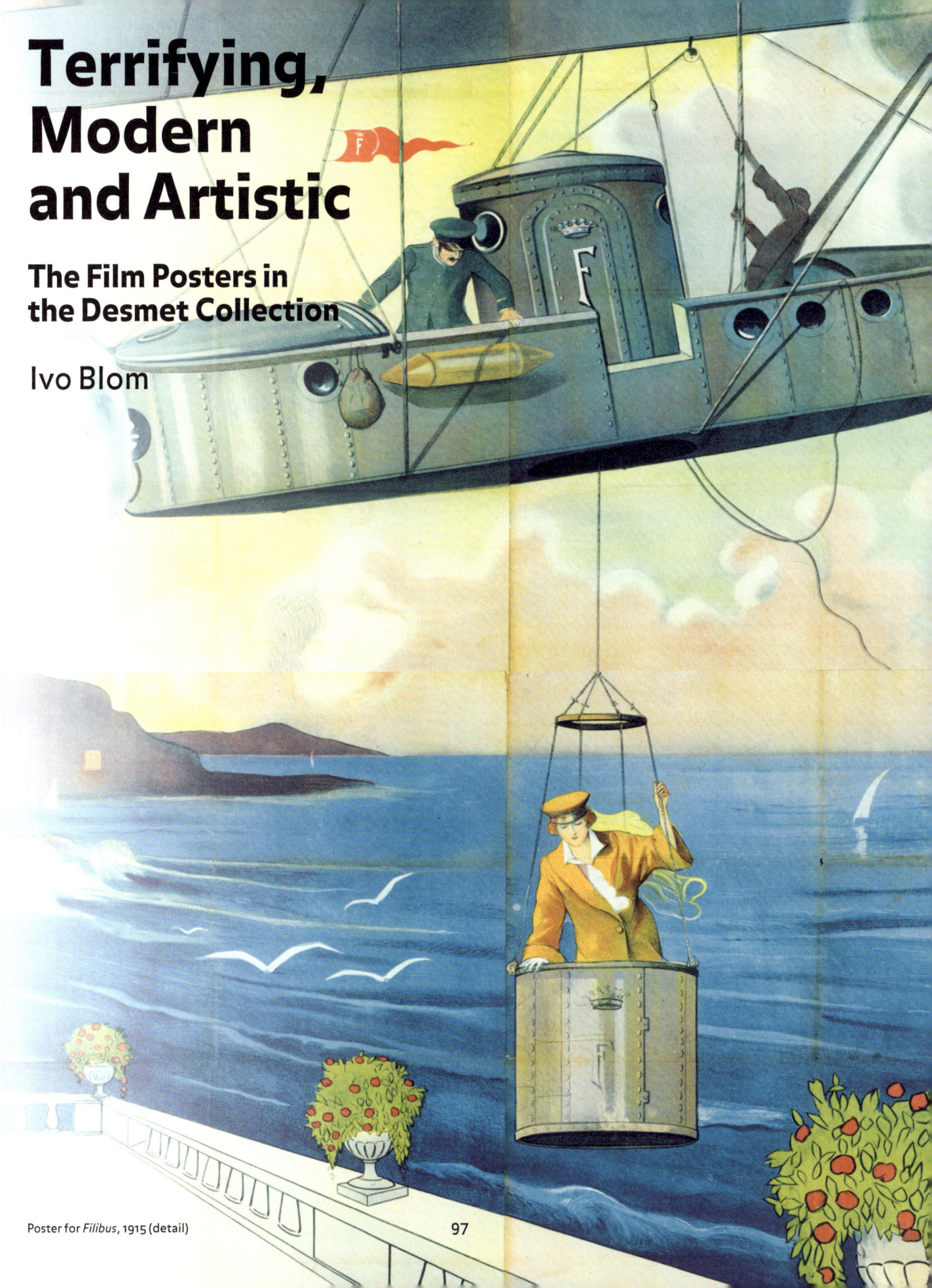

Poster for *Filibus*, 1915 (detail)

The posters in the Desmet Collection are packed with sensational images. Revolutionary inventions like the automobile, the train, the aeroplane and the ocean steamer charge towards the viewer with terrifying speed. The posters show in detail how these modern modes of transport caused accidents 100 years ago. The poster for *Auf einsamer Insel* (1913) depicts a fishing boat in flames out at sea, evidently struck by lightning.[1] The fire is so intense that it not only turns the sea red, but also illuminates the Dutch fishermen on shore. We find the same aesthetically pleasing effect on a poster for the Italian adventure film *Vittoria o morte!* (1913). The designer, Pier Luigi Caldanzano, created a blazing ocean steamer on the high seas.[2] The ship has already capsized and is sinking, and the towering waves bat the lifeboats about like toys. The highly emphatic brushstrokes of the fierce yellow and red flames contrast starkly with the deep blue of the sea, but the water also vividly reflects the glow of the fire, with streaks of yellow and red paint reminiscent of Van Gogh. Another poster for the same film, by famous commercial designer Leopoldo Metlicovitz, shows an earlier scene.[3] It is an aerial view of the main character, a woman detective played by Berta Nelson, swooping towards the ship in an aeroplane. Soon afterwards, the heroine boards the vessel and is caught in the shipwreck.[4] In the 1910s, cinemagoers were crazy about chase scenes involving more than one type of vehicle. On the poster for the British film *The Jewel Thieves Outwitted* (1913), an aeroplane pursues an automobile, and on a poster for *L'amazzone mascherata* (1914), a racing car speeds after a train, two years before the famous car-train chase in D.W. Griffith's *Intolerance* (1916).

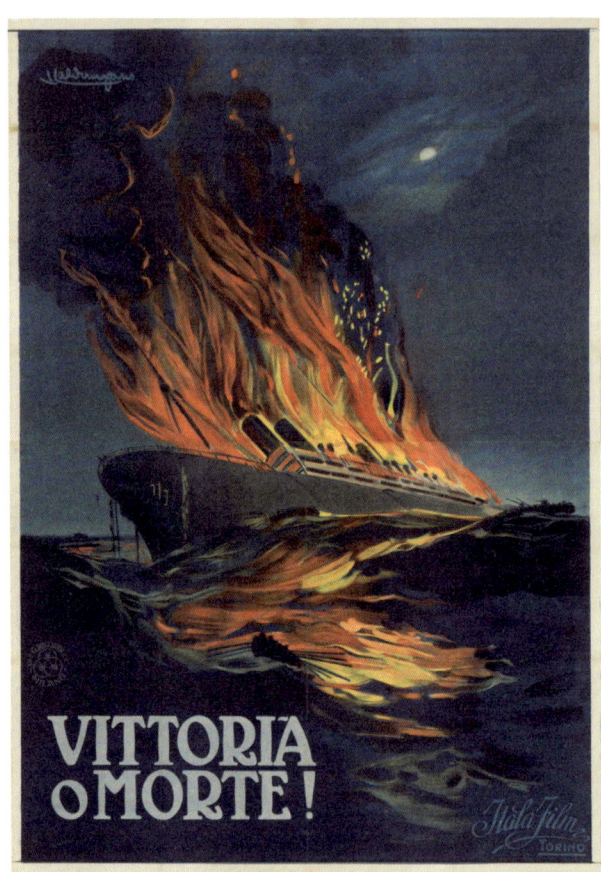

Some posters make a three-dimensional impression on the viewer without any need for 3D glasses. On the poster for *L'automobile della morte* (1912), for example, a car drives straight towards us – and towards the edge of a cliff. Likewise, in *Robinet automobilista miope* (1914), comedian Robinet drives a car straight towards the viewer. This was a popular theme; on the poster for *Das Recht aufs Dasein* (1913), a man and an engine driver wrestle on top of a locomotive that is hurtling over a railway bridge towards us in the night. Another train charges towards the unfortunate Anna Karenina – and us – from the same perspective in Vincent Lorant-Heilbronn's exotic poster for the Pathé film from 1911 of Tolstoy's novel. The train casts bright beams of yellow and green light out ahead, and this seems to catch Anna by surprise, despite the fact that in both the novel and the film she throws herself in front of the train deliberately. The train is at an angle to the viewer. This may be an allusion to the train in the Lumière brothers' *L'Arrivée d'un train en gare de La Ciotat* (1895) – the archetypal cinematic train, approaching

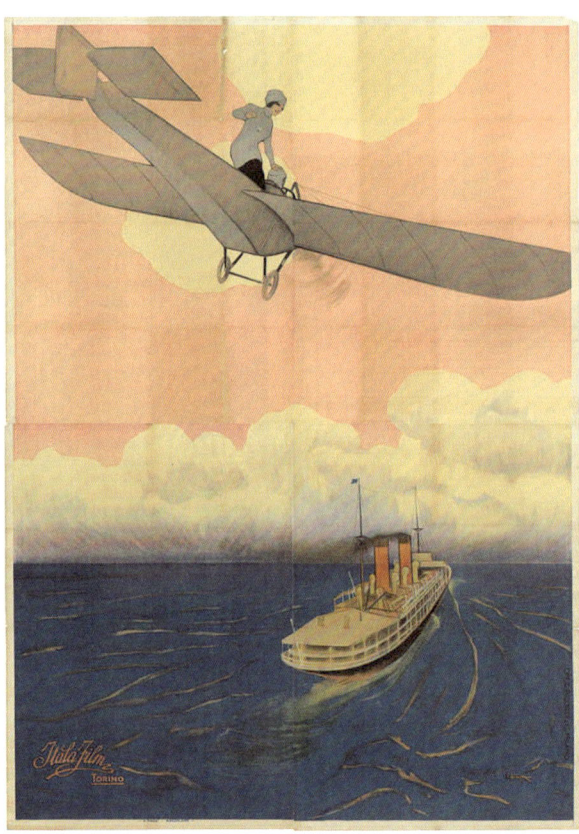

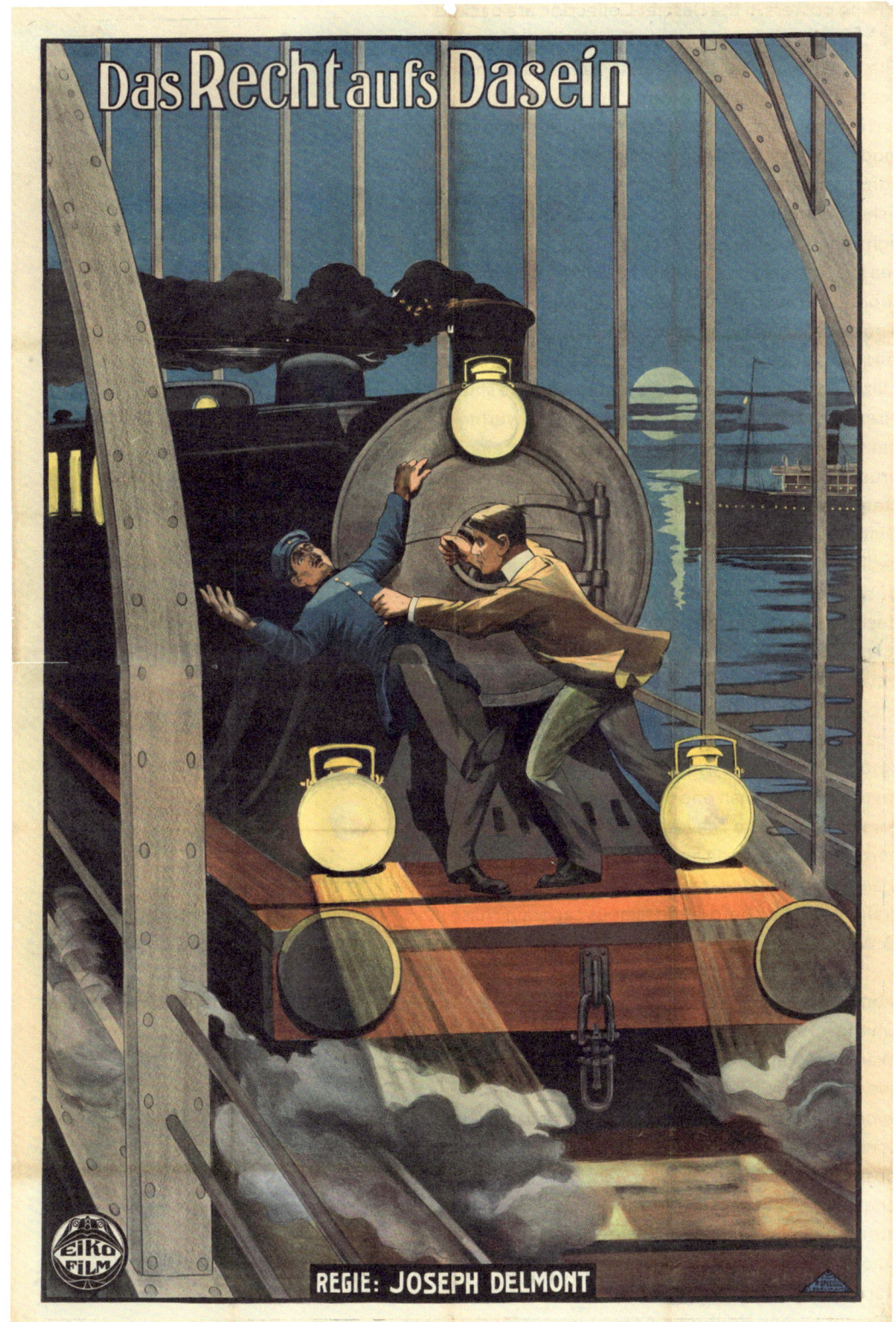

much more placidly and from the right rather than the left, unlike its fast and dangerous cousin in *Anna Karenina*.

Modernity, Hyperstimulus and Modern Dangers

In his article 'Modernity, Hyperstimulus, and the Rise of Popular Sensationalism' (1995), American film theorist Ben Singer argues that we should interpret the concept of modernity as not only socioeconomic, political and cognitive, but also neurological.[5] Building on the work of Georg Simmel, Walter Benjamin and Siegfried Kracauer, he claims that one way of seeing modernity is as a totally new variety of subjective experience, characterized by physical and perceptual shocks caused by the modern urban setting. Around 1900, city life became more chaotic, fragmented and disorienting than ever before.

Amid the unprecedented turbulence of the big city's traffic, noise, billboards, street signs, jostling crowds, window displays, and advertisements, the individual faced a new intensity of sensory stimulation. The metropolis subjected the individual to a barrage of impressions, shocks, and jolts. The tempo of life also became more frenzied, sped up by new forms of rapid transportation, the pressing schedules of modern capitalism, and the ever-accelerating pace of the assembly line.[6]

Not only in the arts, but also in popular science (in debates about the nervous disorder known as neurasthenia) and the popular press, there was a widespread belief that the modern world caused physical and nervous stimulation. The modern city offered an overkill of visual impressions and the popular press often emphasized the terrors of the big city and played on the fears of its inhabitants – whatever it took to sell more newspapers. Other sensationalistic themes that fuelled these fears included accidents in factories and dramatic conflicts between neighbours. Falls from a great height were an especially popular subject in the press. This illustrates both the nostalgia for simpler times and a morbid preoccupation with the grisly, the grotesque and the extreme.

Singer contrasts this with our familiarity with the metropolis today, more than a century later. Around 1900, city-dwellers had not yet grown used to their new environment. The rapid pace of urban development led to a hunger for more intense experiences, and this demand was met by commercial entertainment – not only the popular press, but also theatre and variety acts. Thrills – stunts, explosions and recreated disasters – became an ever more important part of such shows. This was the context in which the cinema was born. It is not

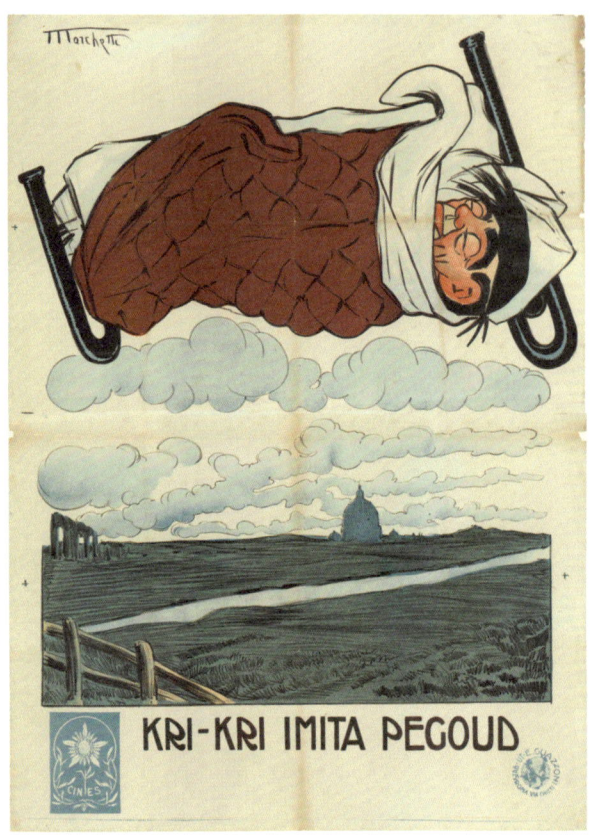

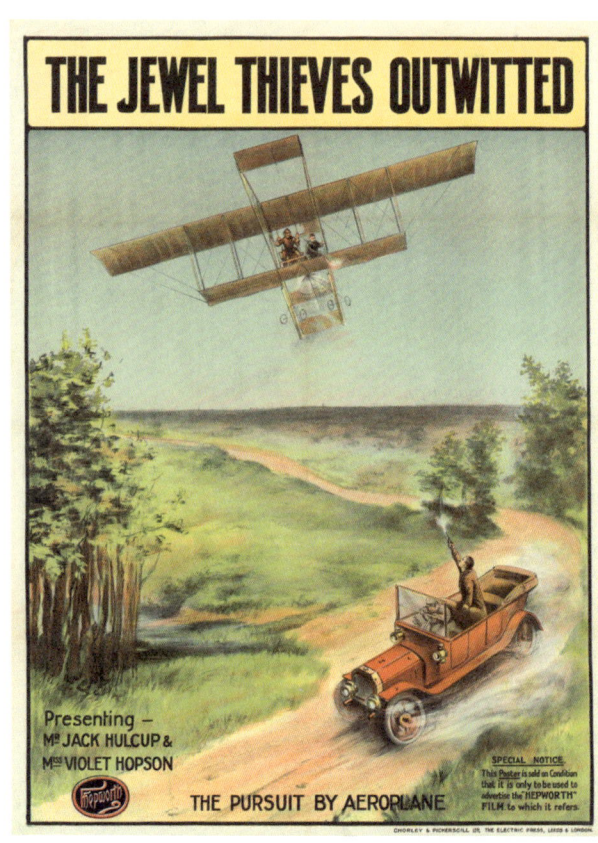

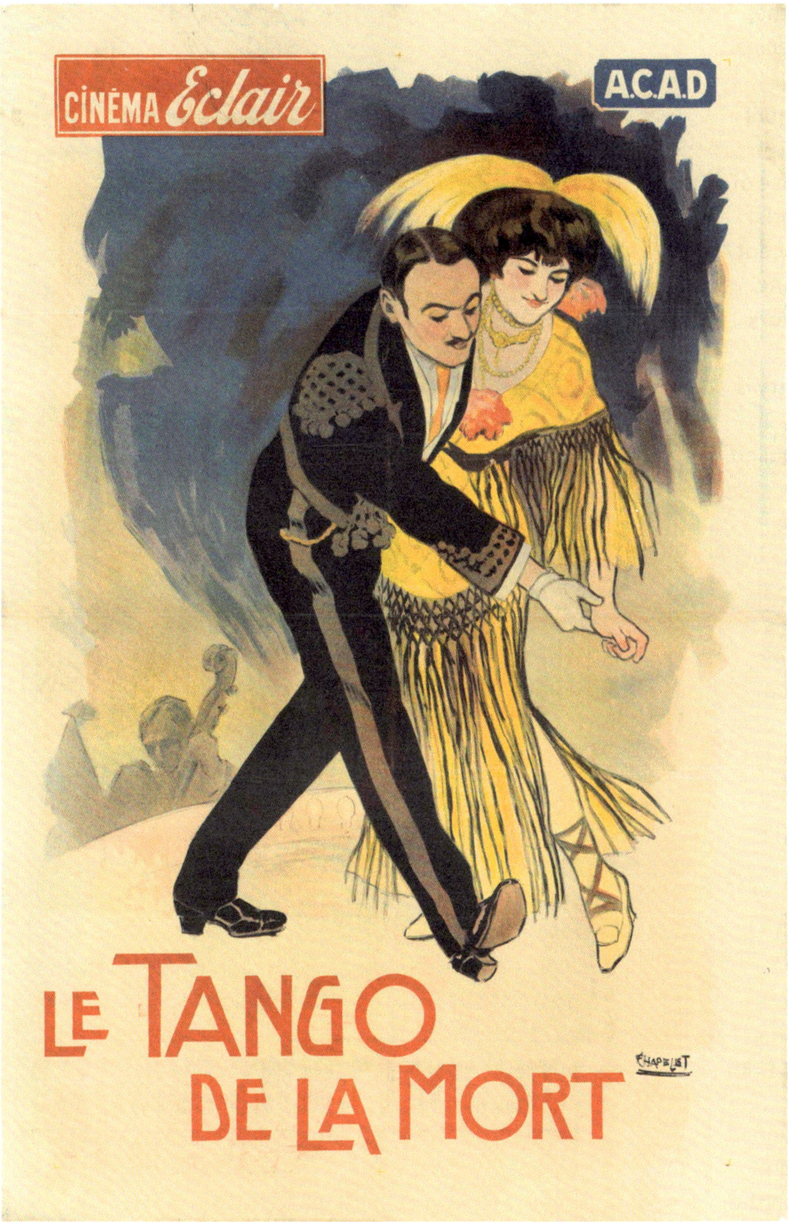

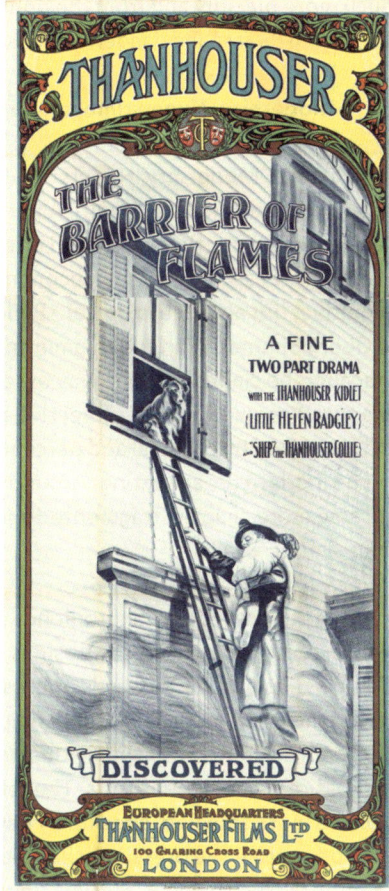

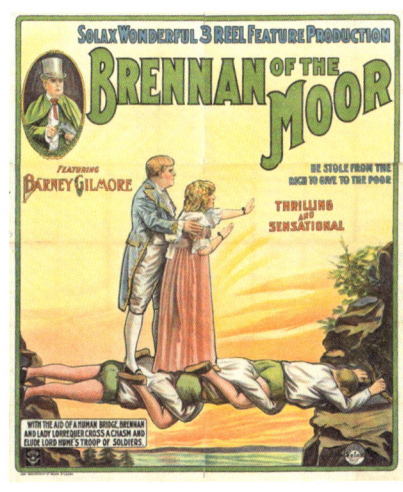

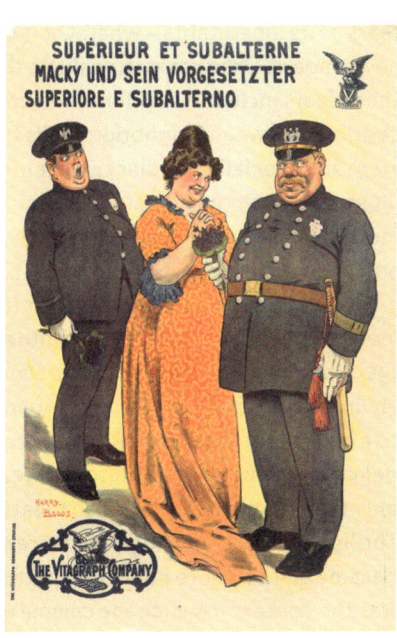

p. 100
Posters for
Kri Kri imita Pegoud, 1914
138 x 100 cm
The Jewel Thieves Outwitted,
1913
101 x 76 cm

p. 101
Posters for
Le tango de la mort, 1914
150 x 100 cm
Brennan of the Moor, 1913
228 x 204 cm
The Barrier of Flames, 1914
225 x 102 cm
Supérieur et subalterne
(*The Man Higher Up*), 1913
140 x 100 cm

surprising, therefore, that filmmakers were quick to cater to the hunger for the sensational, for tempestuous melodramas, explosions and collisions between fast-moving vehicles. Tellingly, the 1910s saw the emergence of the action serial genre, with cliffhangers in which the heroine literally hung from a cliff. Audiences had to wait in suspense for a week to find out whether she would survive. Sensational films served a genuine purpose. As Singer writes: 'Popular sensationalism both compensated for and mimicked the frenzied, disjointed texture of modern life.'[7] By analogy with Freud's concept of fear as a self-defensive reaction, Benjamin wrote that the shocks sustained in the cinema taught people how to cope with stimuli in the modern urban environment.[8]

In short, the posters of Desmet's film distribution company played two different roles; they were part of the overcrowded street scene in which modern people had to lead their lives, but at the same time they advertised the films that could teach city dwellers to cope with this hyperstimulus. This sheds light on posters in which the Italian comedian Kri Kri dreams he is the stunt pilot Pégoud (*Kri Kri imita Pegoud*, 1914), his compatriot Robinet zips about on motorized roller skates (*Gli auto-scat di Robinet*, 1911), a man performs a stunt on a tightrope between two chimneys over a burning factory (*Das Teufelsauge*, Vay & Hubert 1914), another man dangles from an electricity pylon (*Hochspannung*, 1913), yet another commits suicide by jumping from a high bridge into a river (*Erblich belastet?*, 1913), a family in the big city is rescued from a burning house at the last minute (*The Barrier of Flames*, 1914), and a woman in a zeppelin leads a gang of thieves (*Filibus*, 1915). Experienced filmgoers were not scared off but drawn to the cinema by these sensational images; for other viewers this may not yet have been the case.

Romance and Recognisability

Apparently, what modern urban life demanded of the film poster and the film was not only the representation of the terrors of the modern age, but also a flight into the past (*Brennan of the Moor*, 1913) or the sentimental portrayal of a rural world aglow with nostalgia and romance (*Léonce à la campagne*, 1913). Yet in other cases, the countryside is less idyllic, and its inhabitants are feudal and narrow-minded (*Alexandra*, 1914). The poster shows the rural villagers staring menacingly at Alexandra, who through no fault of her own has become an unwed mother.

Some of the films take place indoors, almost as if the outdoors did not exist. In domestic comedies and dramas, we mainly see salons, kitchens and bedrooms. Rather than crowds or spectacles in the streets, these films revolve around love triangles, daughters whose suitors are rejected because the class difference is too great (*Heisses Blut*, 1911), or men who sneak into the house disguised as maids (*Aus eines Mannes Mädchenzeit*, 1913) and of course are soon found out (*Der Schein trügt*, 1914; *Gontran dans la gueule du loup*, 1913). Besides the home, other popular locations include the café and restaurant, and sometimes places of entertainment such as the theatre, circus and cinema. These locations are usually simulated in the studio. The tango, which was all the rage in 1913, also figures in many posters (*Casimir tangue*, 1914; *Le tango de la mort*, 1914). One striking feature is the growing importance of women as commanding figures who take the lead and dominate men (*Das rosa Pantöffelchen*, 1913; *Die Welt ohne Männer*, 1913; *L'amazzone mascherata*, 1914) or at least play the leading role in the film, as we see in *Nordlandsrose* (1914) with Henny Porten, *Il focolare domestico* (1914) and *Tragico convegno* (1915) with Maria Jacobini, *Sangue bleu* (1914) with Francesca Bertini, and *Fior di male* (1915) with Lyda Borelli.

In the early 1910s, a vast number of short films centred on stock comic characters such as Max Linder, Gavroche and Patouillard in France; Cretinetti, Kri Kri and Polidor in Italy; and John Bunny, Maurice Costello and Charlie Chaplin in the USA. The makers of these farces strove to create continuity not only by giving the comic characters the same name in every film, through the use of stereotypes and through recurring costumes, hats and hairstyles, but also through the genre-specific use of caricature on the posters for these films. A number of production companies worked with regular poster designers, such as Romeo Marchetti, who made the Kri Kri posters for Cines. Nevertheless, over the years certain star comedians were clearly recognizable on posters for comedies. French designer Harry Bedos, who designed the Vitagraph posters printed in Paris, made sure that the face of Vitagraph comedian John Bunny was always identifiable, however caricatural the rest of his body and the rest of the poster might be. Maurice Costello, Vitagraph's other leading man, was also consistently depicted in a recognizable way on posters for both his dramas and his comedies. The demand for recognisability apparently did not extend to comic actresses, however; the caricatures of Flora Finch, who played opposite Bunny for Vitagraph, are not identifiable, and the same is true of posters showing French comic female characters such as Cunégonde and Petronille.

The emergence and popularity of film stars prompted star-centred publicity campaigns. In addition to posters emphasizing the film's title and storyline, there were others that simply advertised the star. The star became a brand, and star power was enough to

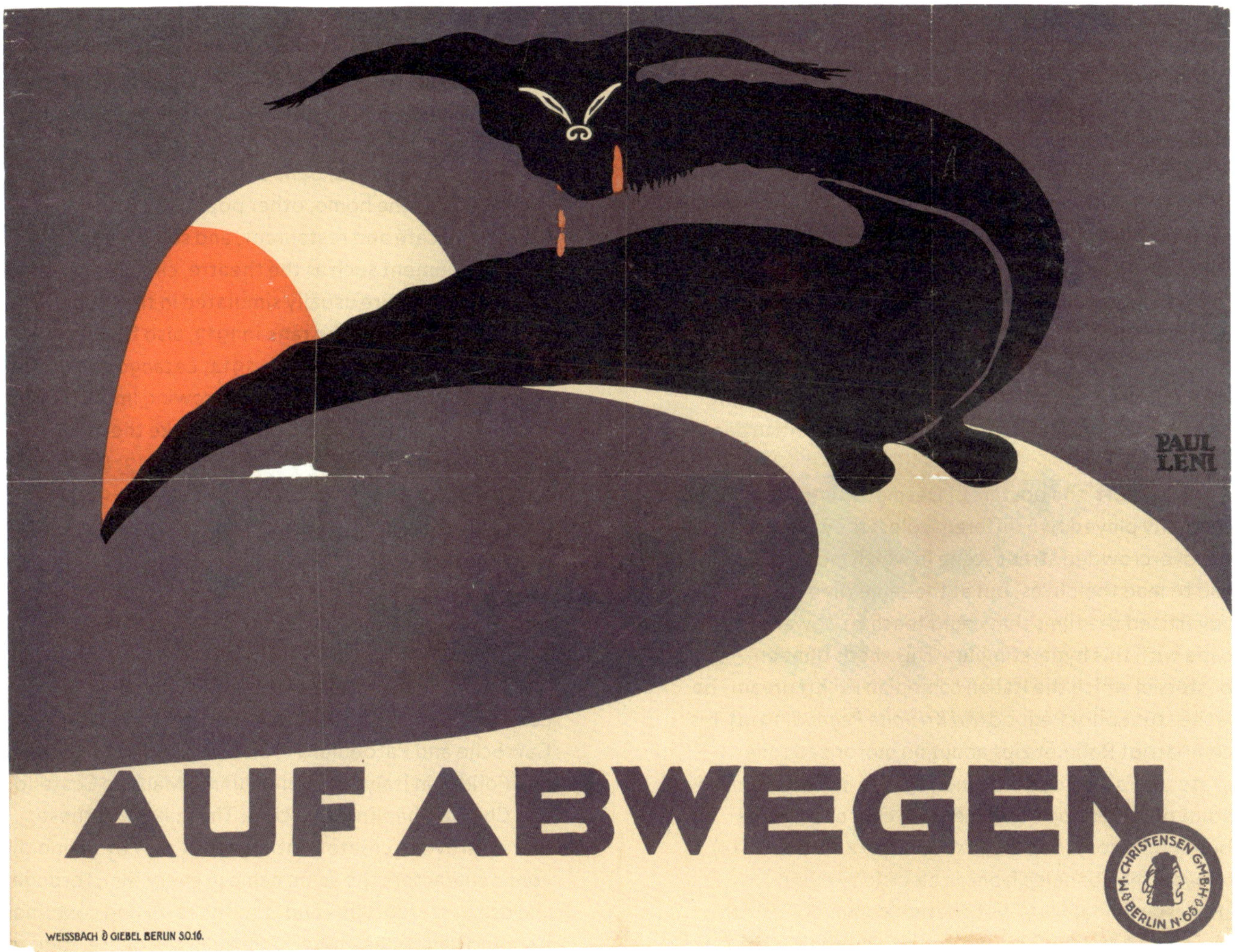

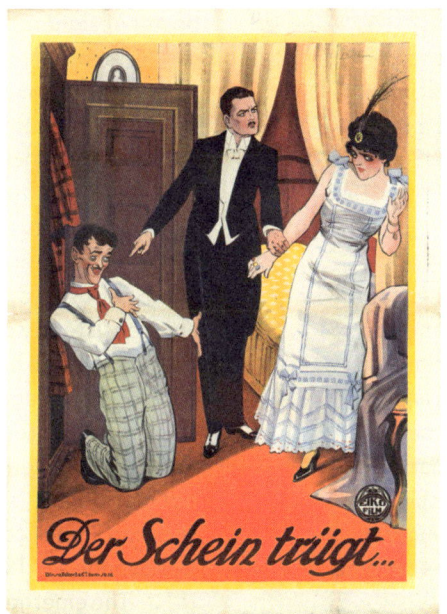
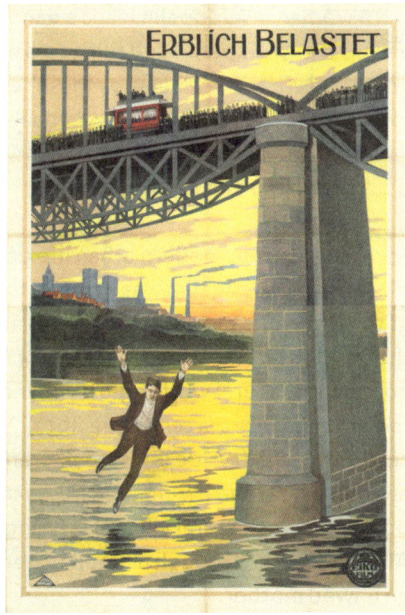

Posters for
Auf Abwegen, 1911
70 x 95 cm
Der Schein trügt, 1914
149 x 110 cm
Erblich belastet?, 1913
218 x 150 cm

draw spectators to the cinema. But in this area too, we find diversity. In dramas, the resemblance between the star and the figure on the poster became increasingly important, as is illustrated by posters for popular Italian divas Lyda Borelli, Francesca Bertini and Maria Jacobini and the Danish leading man Valdemar Psilander. In contrast, a good likeness was less important on posters for German films. Danish film actress Asta Nielsen is barely recognizable on the poster for *Heisses Blut*, and her German colleague Henny Porten likewise shows little resemblance to the women on Hans Kalmar's posters for *Alexandra* and *Das Ende vom Liede* (1915) or Erich Wohlfahrt's poster for *Nordlandsrose.* Posters with film stars do not always include the name of the star in large type; posters of Psilander, Borelli and Costello illustrate this point. In contrast, Porten and Nielsen were often named prominently on their posters. French stage actors who appeared in films were often mentioned by name, as was the American Western hero G.M. Anderson, better known as Broncho Billy. The name of American star King Baggot was printed on posters in particularly large type, for instance on the British posters for the American films *Ivanhoe* (1913) and *Absinthe* (1914).

Innovation and the Mainstream

The posters in the Desmet Collection offer a rich and many-faceted image of the development of the film poster in the early 1910s, the period that German media scholar Johannes Kamps described in his doctoral thesis as the first great artistic period of German film poster design.[9] German and Italian posters had more distinct national styles than posters from other countries. They were influenced more quickly and deeply by art movements ranging from traditionalism to symbolism and from Art Nouveau to expressionism. Tendencies in graphic design, such as the German *Sachplakat*, were also influential, as demonstrated by Hans Rudi Erdt's poster for *Europäisches Sklavenleben* (1912), Paul Leni's for *Auf Abwegen* (1911), John Dape's for *Treff-Bube* (1912) and Aleardo Terzi's for *L'amazzone mascherata*. These designers made a radical break with the lavishly ornamented women and frivolous framing elements of Art Nouveau; the subject stood proud and independent against a plain, flat background. The typography, too, is very straightforward. The Desmet Collection includes a remarkable number of posters by innovative leading European designers such as Pier Luigi Caldanzano, Leopoldo Metlicovitz, Achille Mauzan, Aleardo Terzi, Tito Corbella and Emilio Vacchetti in Italy; Robert Bell, Hans Rudi Erdt, Paul Leni and Tjerk Bottema in Germany; and Adrien Barrère, Vincent Lorant-Heilbronn, Roger Chapelet, Auguste Leymarie and Louis Charbonnier in

p. 104
Posters for
Ivanhoe, 1913
225 x 102 cm
L'amazzone mascherata, 1914
208 x 100 cm
The District Attorney's Conscience, 1913
102 x 75 cm

p. 105
Poster for *Europäisches Sklavenleben*, 1912
125 x 94 cm

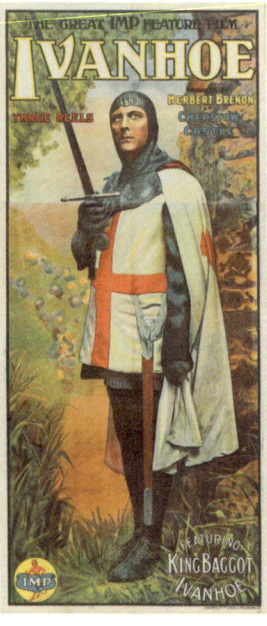
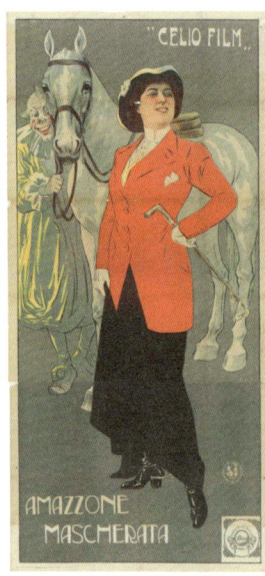
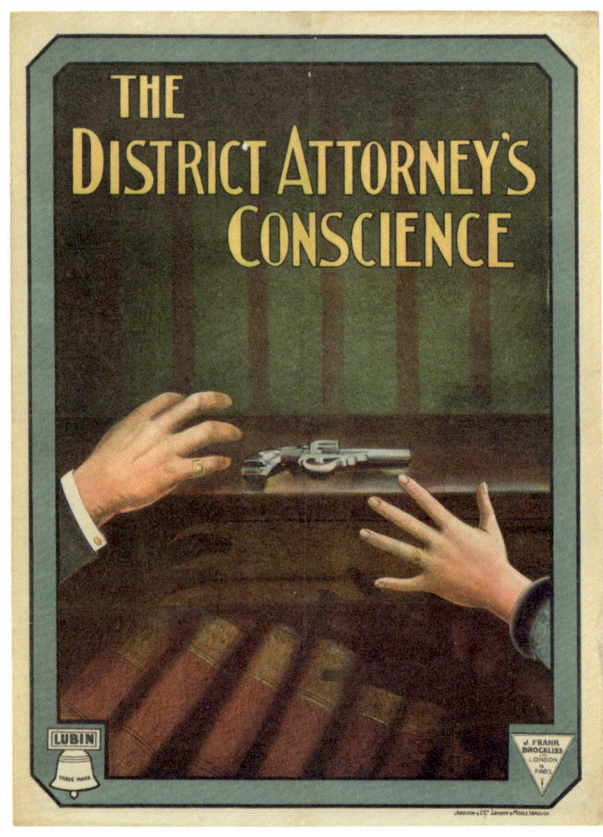

Europäisches Sklavenleben

Austria Film Vertrieb
G.m.b.H.
Berlin S.W. 48. Friedrichstr. 5·6

H R ERDT

France. The lithographs for Desmet's customers were also expertly printed, by firms such as Dinse & Eckert and Spiegel in Berlin; Guazzoni in Rome; Jordison & Co., Waterlow & Layton, Allen & Sons and Stafford Co. in London and Nottingham; the ABC Co. in Cleveland; and the printing departments of film studios like Gaumont, Pathé and Eclair.

Strikingly, American poster designers tended to work in a naturalistic style, both before and after the First World War, while their European counterparts frequently departed from this style. Nevertheless, not all the posters are artistically innovative. Both artistic and mainstream film posters are well represented in the large Desmet Collection. British and American posters show the greatest uniformity; this is true of both painted posters and those consisting solely of a richly decorated frame around a series of stills. One clear example of standardization is the poster for Chaplin's Keystone comedy *His New Profession* (1914); the title of the film and the name of the production company are consistently the central element, and these posters were not signed by their designer. This resulted in part from the need for control at studios where mass production and cost management were essential. But there was another reason for designers not to sign their work: namely, the low status of film posters, which for many years were regarded as a lesser art form, especially in France. Furthermore, designers were paid less for film posters and therefore could not spend as much time on them as on advertising posters for brands or products. Anonymity camouflaged a line of work that held little prestige.

Only after the First World War did avant-garde artists show a growing interest in the film poster. During the 1920s, they promoted a teleological narrative in which their own work was the pinnacle of the film poster's development. Consequently, posters from the early 1910s were underappreciated for many years, relative to those produced in the following decade. But the Desmet posters, with their images of modernity, romance and stardom, not to mention their combination of popular culture and artistic influences, richly deserve to be studied and enjoyed. As Mauzan's later biographer Arturo Lancellotti put it in 1912:

> The poster is the aristocracy of advertising, because it is one of the few forms of expression that can truly rise to the status of art. It is like a painting that anyone can admire without paying admission or leaving his walking stick or umbrella in the exhibition cloakroom. The wind caresses it, the sun illuminates it, and even the most hurried of men can peer at it in contentment.[10]

1
For a visual and textual overview of most of the posters in the Desmet Collection, see the website EFG1914, www.europeanfilmgateway.eu/content/efg1914-project. On Eiko's sensational films, especially those directed by Joseph Delmont, see H. Schlüpmann, *Unheimlichkeit des Blicks. Das Drama des frühen deutschen Kinos* (Basel/Frankfurt am Main, 1990).

2
On Caldanzano, see R. Della Torre, *Invito al cinema. Le origini del manifesto cinematografico italiano (1895-1930)* (Milan, 2014), 92-94.

3
Metlicovitz designed the famous poster for the cinematic spectacle *Cabiria* (Giovanni Pastrone 1914), in which a young, naked girl is offered up to the flames by unidentified hands. Ibid., 82-83.

4
The Desmet Collection includes a second Metlicovitz poster for *Vittoria o morte*, in which the woman detective is shown in full figure holding a pistol.

5
B. Singer, 'Modernity, Hyperstimulus, and the Rise of Popular Sensationalism', in: L. Charney and V.R. Schwartz (eds.), *Cinema and the Invention of Modern Life* (Berkeley etc., 1995), 72-99.

6
Ibid., 73.

7
Ibid., 93.

8
Ibid., 94.

9
J. Kamps, *Studien zur Geschichte des deutschen Filmplakats von den Anfängen bis 1945*, Johannes Gutenberg-Universität (Mainz, 2004), available online at: http://ubm.opus.hbz-nrw.de/volltexte/2004/512/pdf/diss.pdf.

10
Della Torre, *Invito al cinema*, op. cit. (note 2), 77.

Sources

I. Blom, *Jean Desmet and the Early Dutch Film Trade* (Amsterdam, 2003)

J. Kamps, *Studien zur Geschichte des deutschen Filmplakats von den Anfängen bis 1945*, Johannes Gutenberg-Universität (Mainz, 2004), available online at: http://ubm.opus.hbz-nrw.de/volltexte/2004/512/pdf/diss.pdf

C. Keil and S. Stamp (eds.), *American Cinema's Transitional Era. Audiences, Institutions, Practices* (Berkeley/Los Angeles, 2004)

H. Schlüpmann, *Unheimlichkeit des Blicks. Das Drama des frühen deutschen Kinos* (Basel/Frankfurt am Main, 1990)

B. Singer, 'Modernity, Hyperstimulus, and the Rise of Popular Sensationalism', in: L. Charney and V.R. Schwartz (eds.), *Cinema and the Invention of Modern Life* (Berkeley etc., 1995), 72-99

R. Della Torre, *Invito al cinema. Le origini del manifesto cinematografico italiano (1895-1930)* (Milan, 2014)

Other sources:
EFG1914, http://www.europeanfilmgateway.eu/content/efg1914-project

Morality

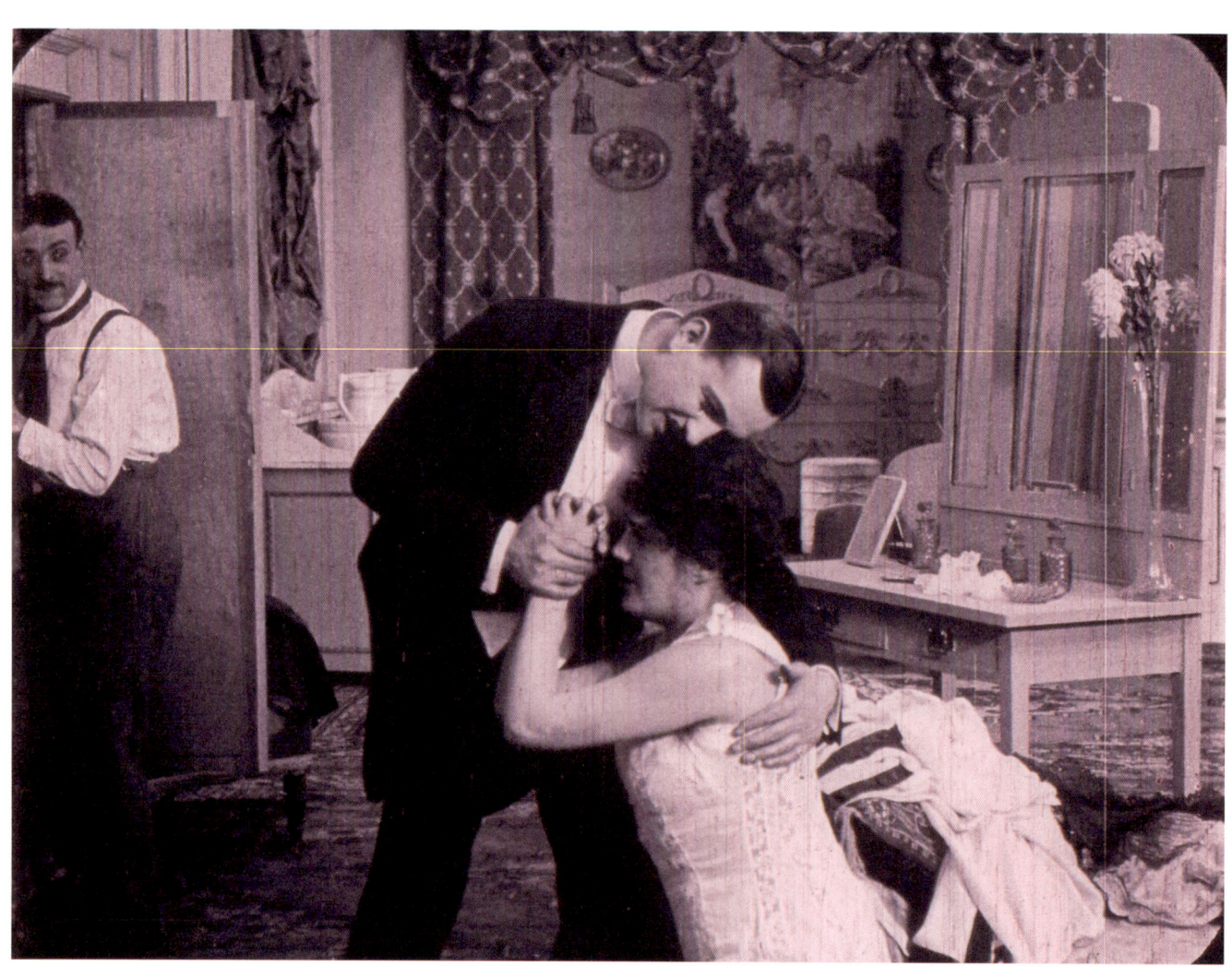

p. 108
Der Schein trügt, 1914

p. 109
The Red Barrier, 1912

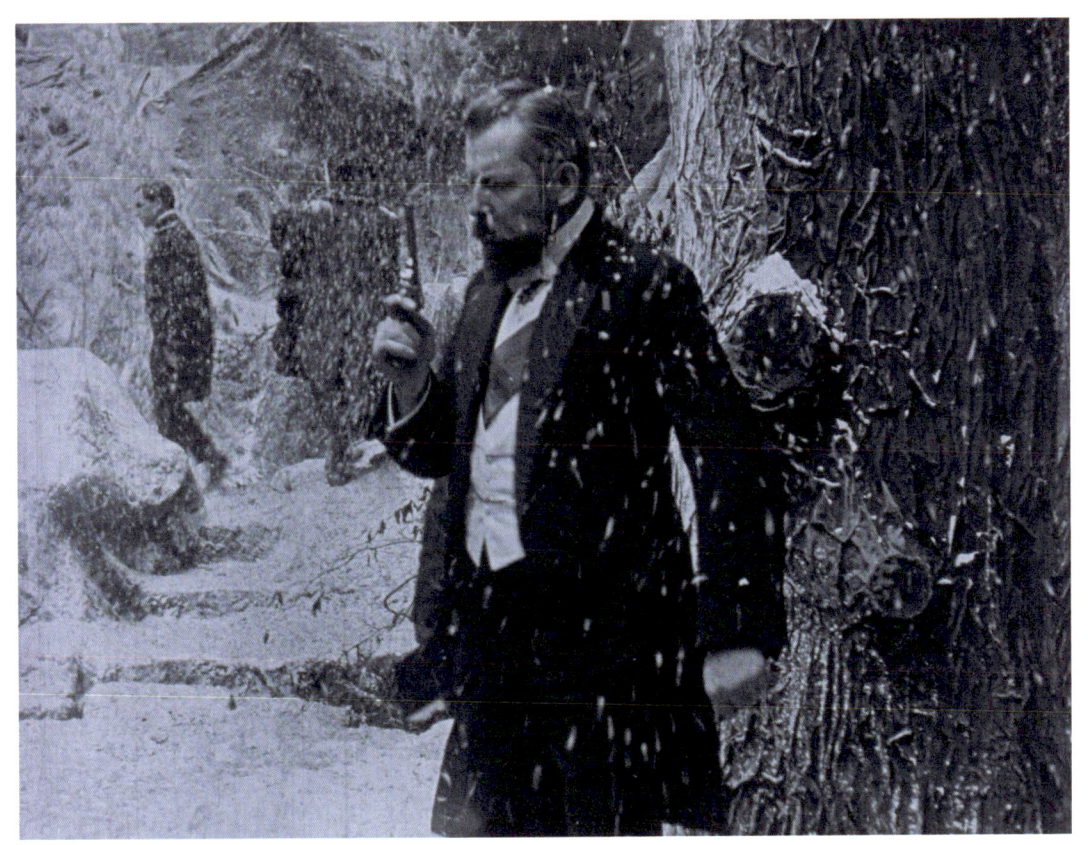
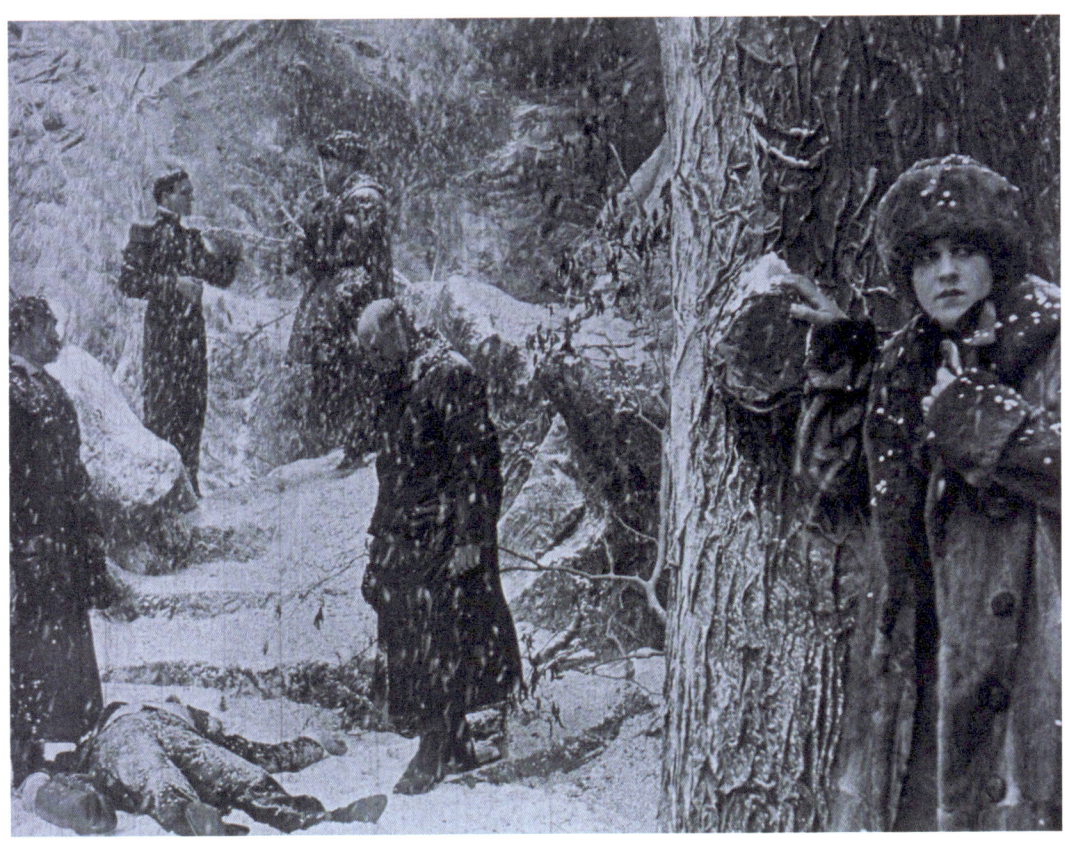

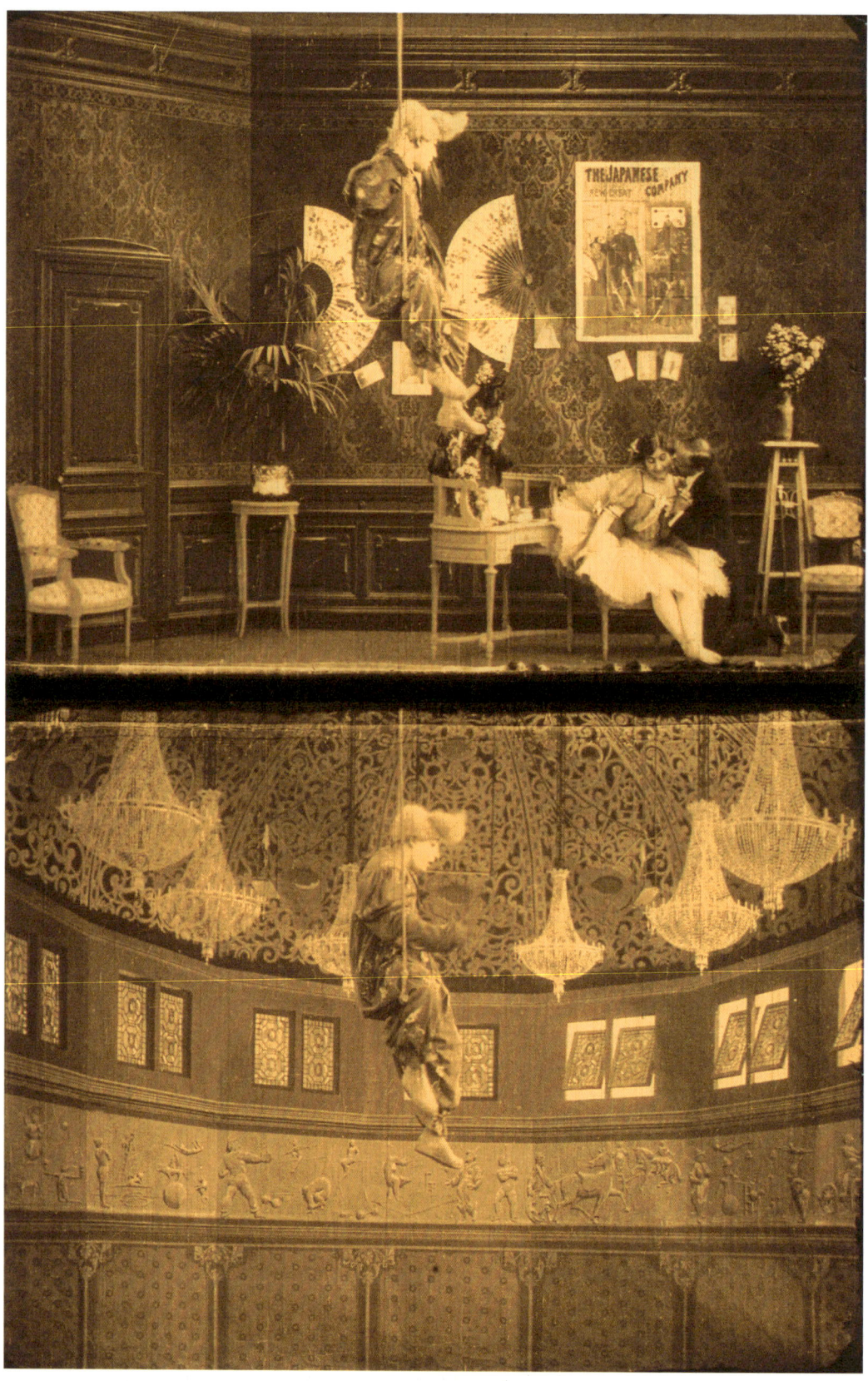

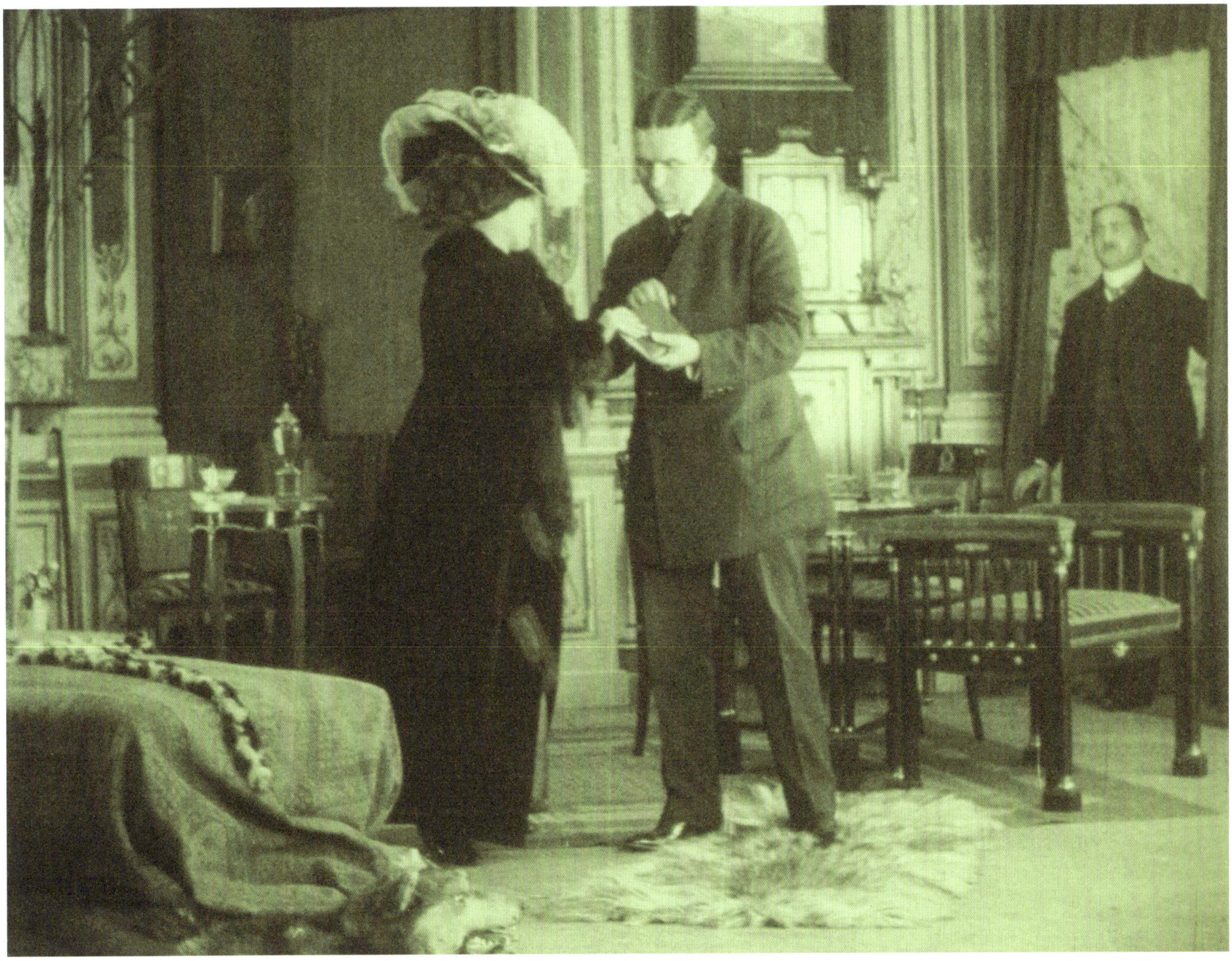

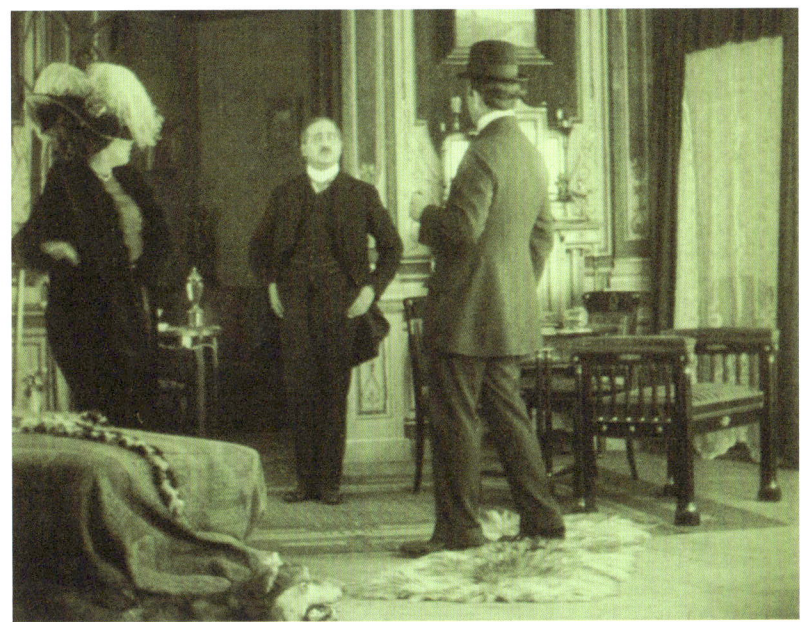

p. 110
Camille de Morlhon, *Le Roman de l'écuyère* (*Der abgewiesene Verehrer*), 1909

p. 111
Walter Schmidthässler, *Vergebens*, 1911

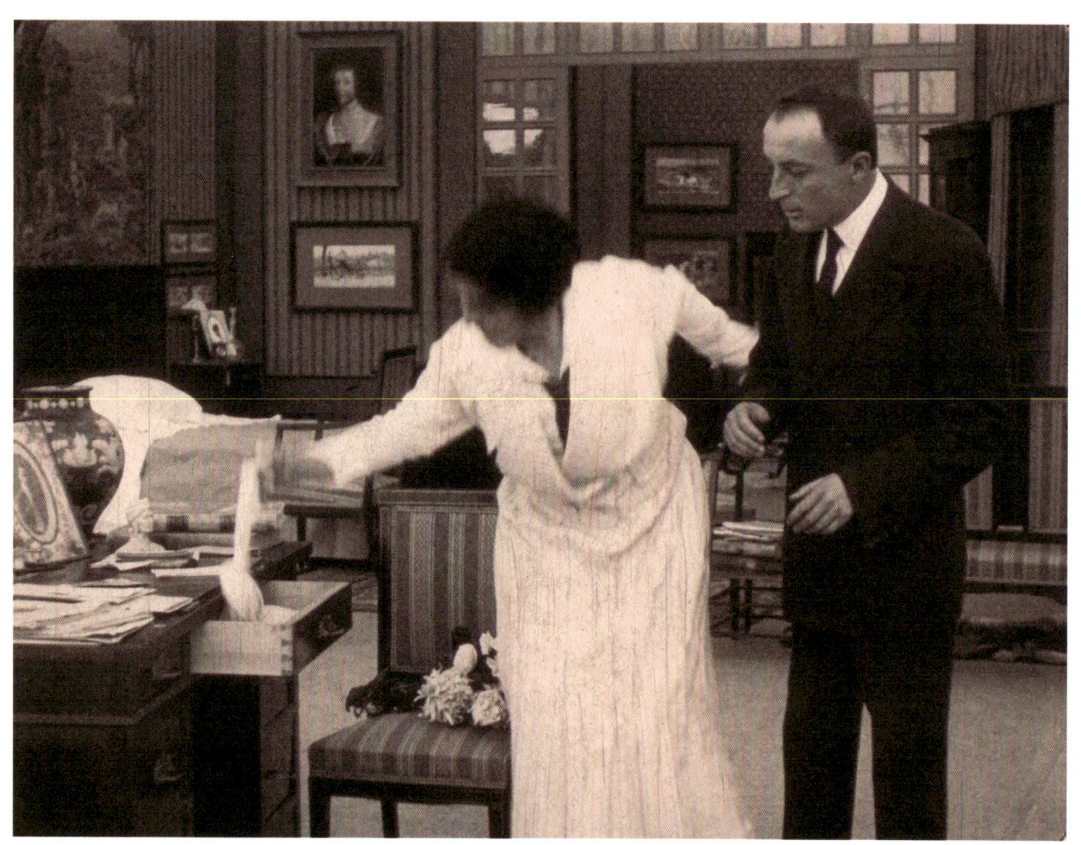
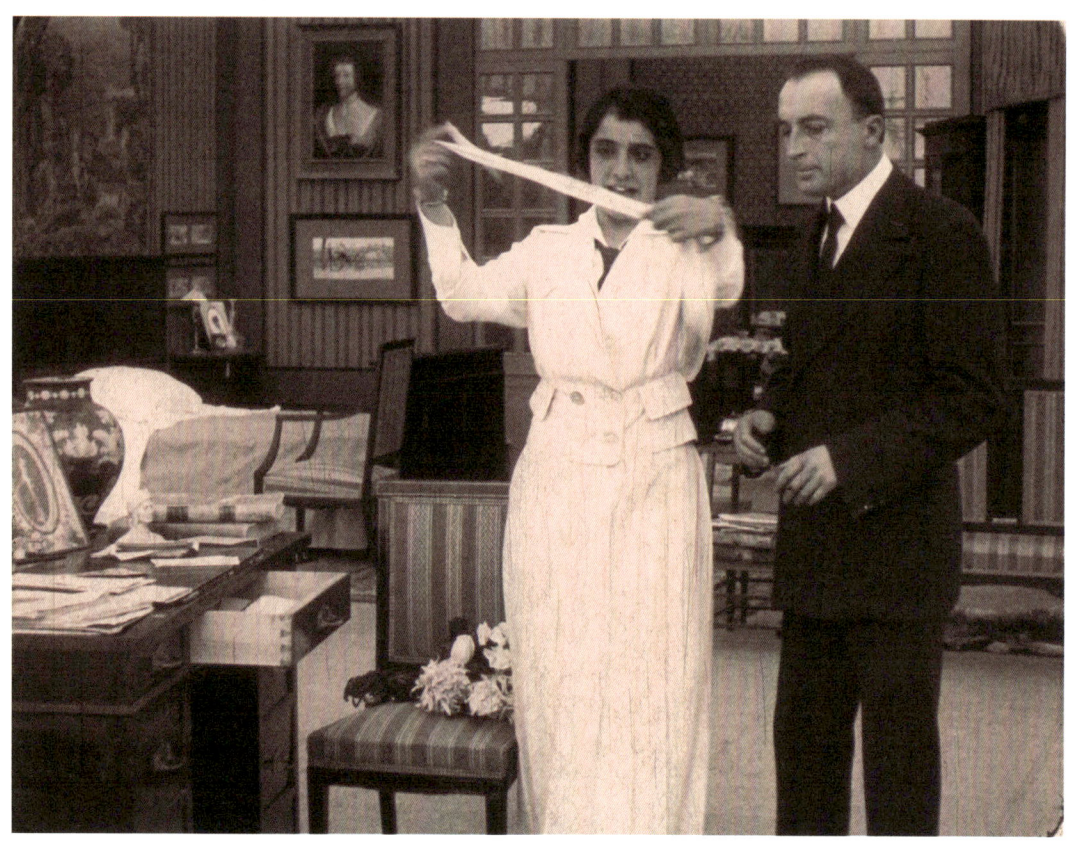

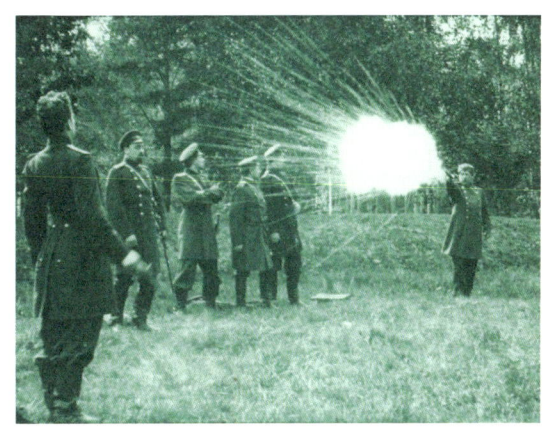

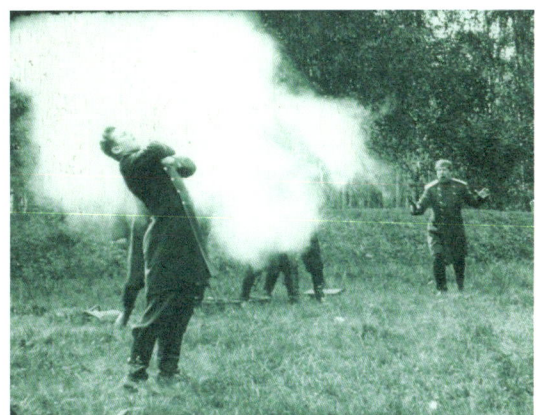

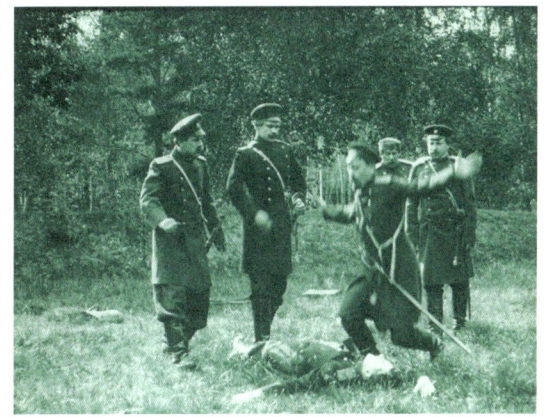

p. 112
Ivo Illuminati, *Tragico convegno*, 1915

p. 113
Maurice André Maître, *Poedinok*, 1910

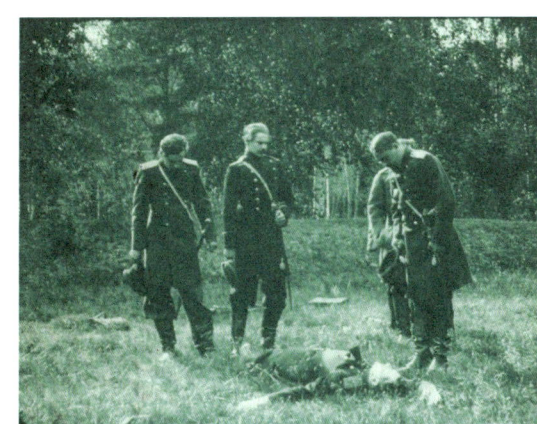

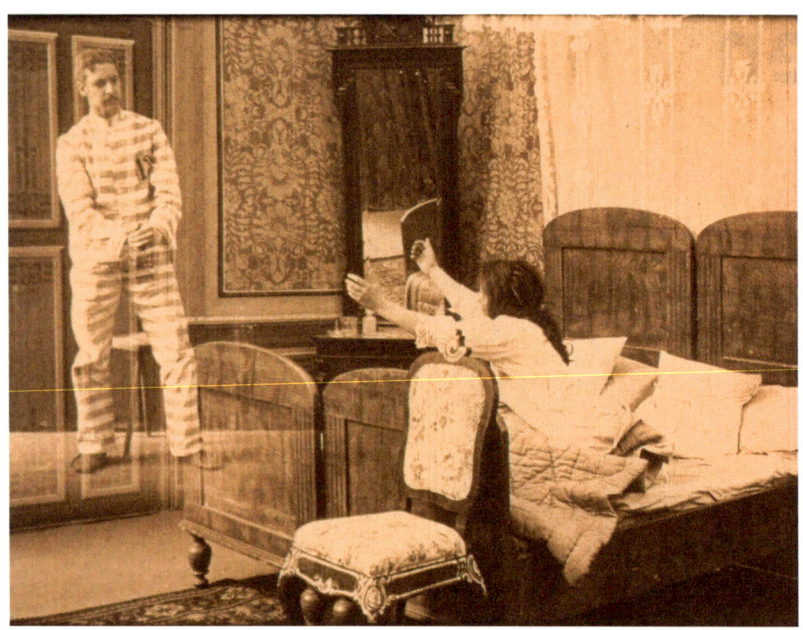

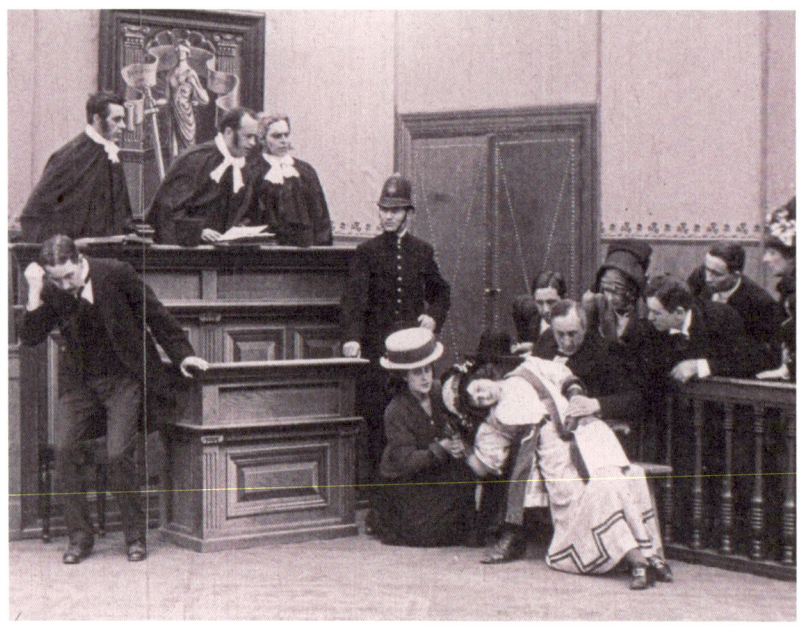

Willam Augustinus, *Dyrekobt aere*, 1911

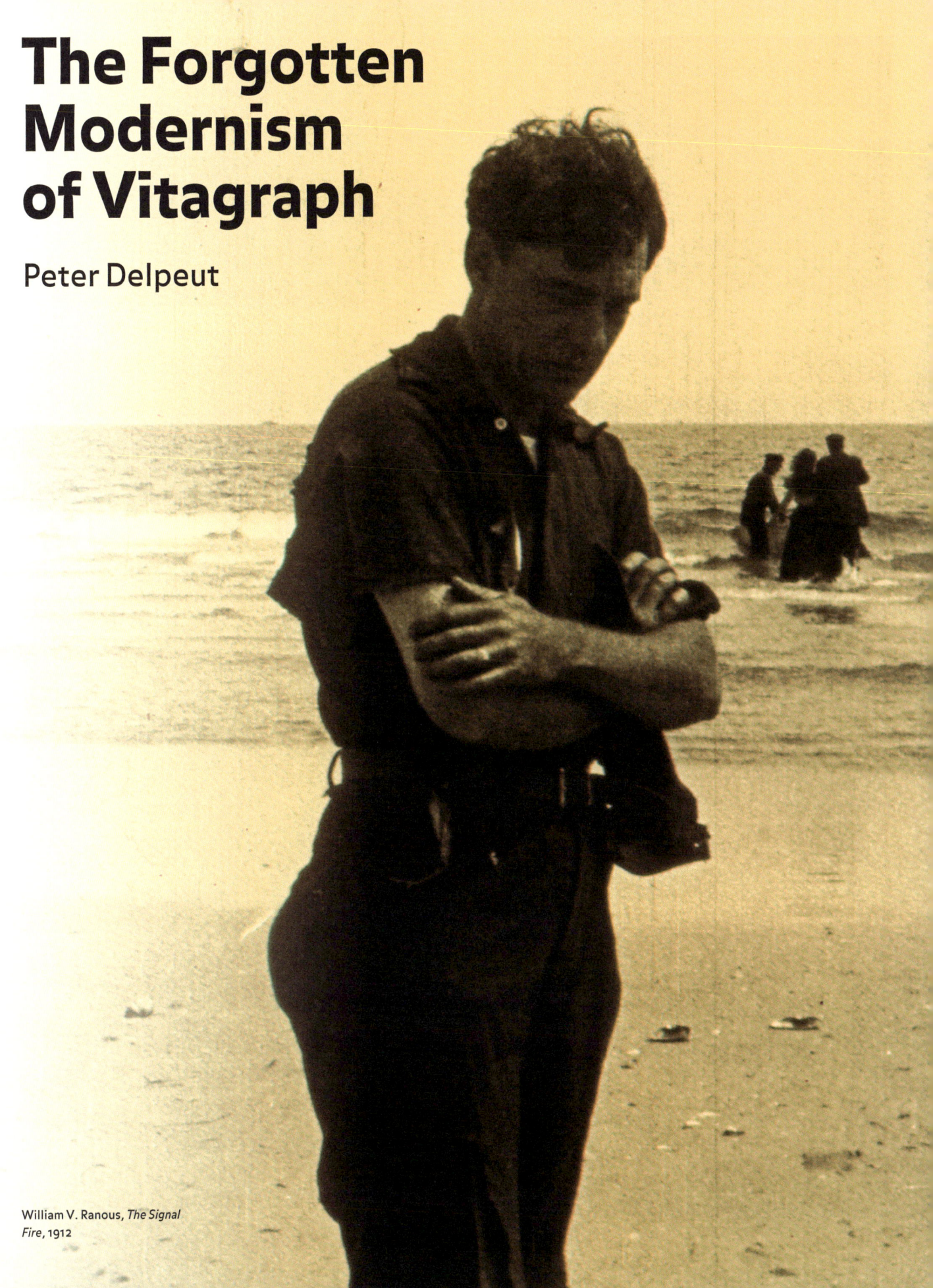

The Forgotten Modernism of Vitagraph

Peter Delpeut

William V. Ranous, *The Signal Fire*, 1912

Jean Desmet's Dutch distribution catalogue, preserved in such miraculously pristine condition, is an arbitrary time capsule. Both experts and film buffs have a fairly stable image of film history, but a collection like Jean Desmet's puts the long-term narratives of historical writing under pressure, offering pieces that do not seem to fit into the mosaic of film history.

When I first encountered the Desmet Collection in the late 1980s, the films of the American Vitagraph studio included in it were one such mosaic tile that puzzled me no end. At first glance, Vitagraph seems to fit neatly into film history; it played a pioneering role out of New York City even before 1900, shooting films on a rooftop in Brooklyn, experimenting with animation and special effects, acquiring a stable of movie stars (including the divine Florence Turner) at an early stage, producing 'quality films' comparable to European *film d'art*, moving to the West Coast in 1910 (when Hollywood began), and opening European offices in London, Paris and Berlin (which explains the large number of Vitagraph films in Jean Desmet's distribution catalogue), but later falling into decline because of changing American distribution practices (studios with their own chains of movie theatres) and the loss of the European market (when the First World War broke out), being acquired by Warner Brothers in the 1920s, and eventually vanishing from the memory of the general public. A straightforward story of a studio's rise and fall, offering plenty of opportunities to sketch the origins of the US movie industry.

But this history is hardly visible in the 90 Vitagraph films in the Desmet Collection. All but two were produced between 1911 and 1914 – a very narrow time capsule indeed, considering both the studio's 25 productive years and the more than 100-year span of film history. But what a capsule, what a buried treasure!

What astonished me most was the formal power of the Vitagraph films. They showed a phenomenal consistency of style, as if all produced by a single filmmaker with a predilection for rock-solid frames within which carefully positioned actors acted out the stories in clear dramatic statements.

These shots resemble what is now known as a *plan américain*: the characters are visible from approximately the knee up, a classic camera position in Hollywood films, in which the alternation between long shots, mediums and close-ups is central to the dramaturgy of the narrative. But the Vitagraph films did not bother with alternation between shots; each scene is a single, stationary take. The Vitagraph *plan américain* was not part of an edited sequence of shots, but was a fixed frame within which an entire scene took place.

There was more to this than simply the standardized assembly-line working method of a company that

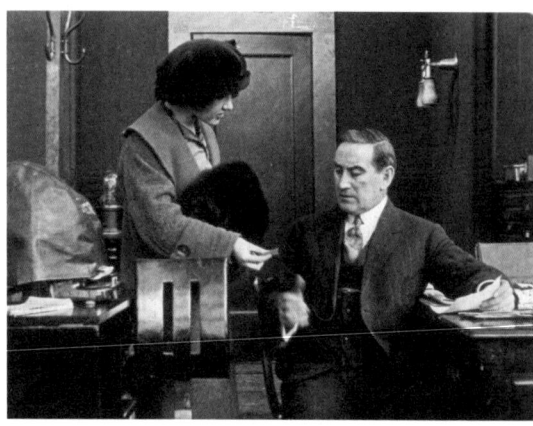

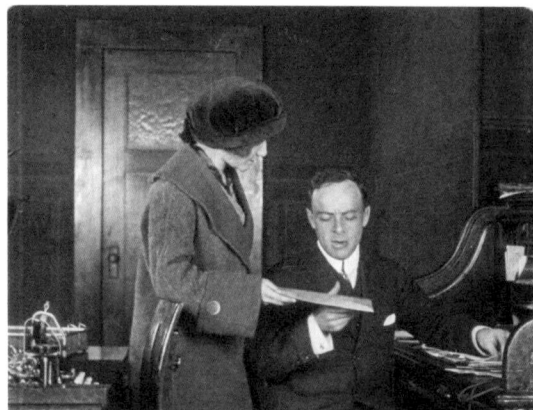

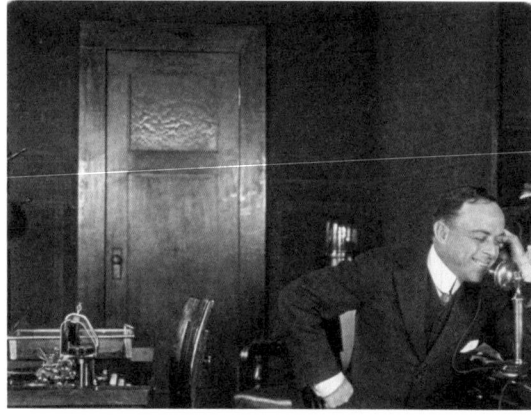

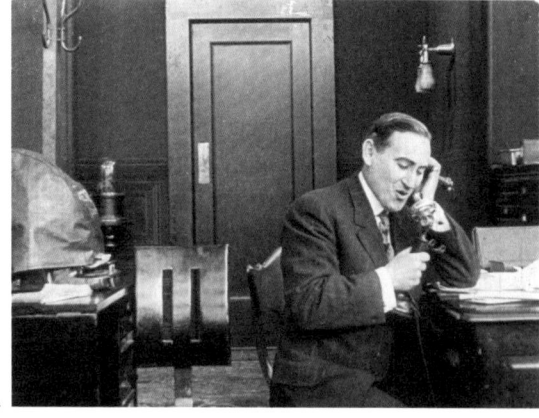

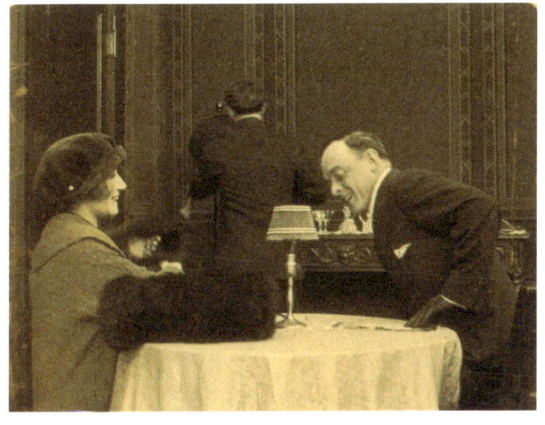
5

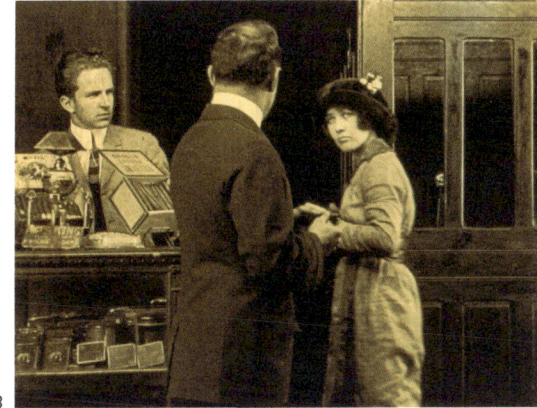
8

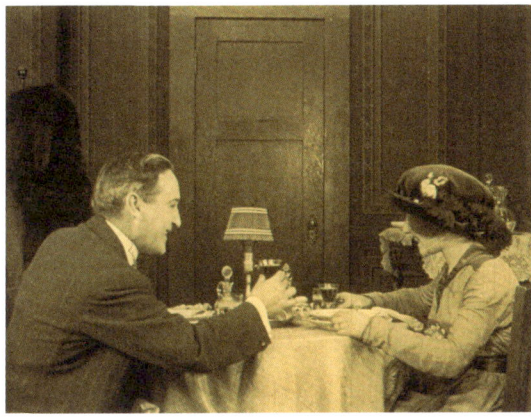
6

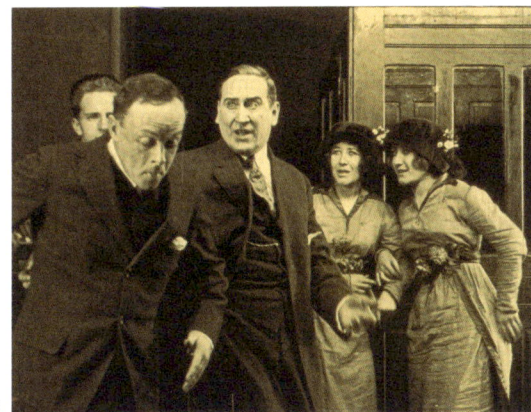
9

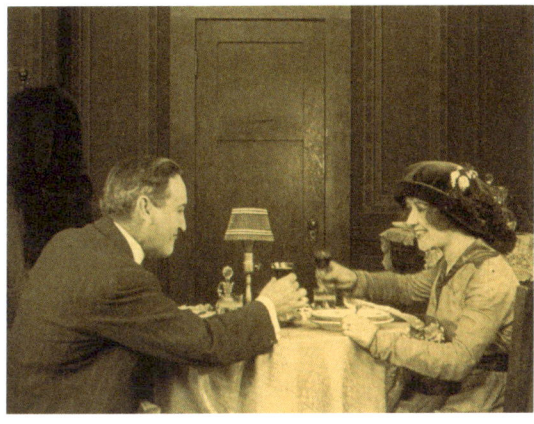
7

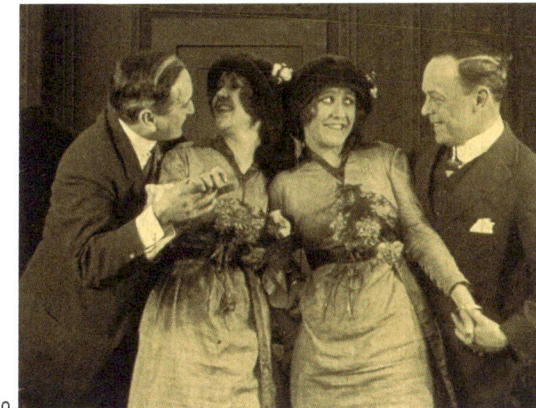
10

Vitagraph's formal basis

At some point, the Vitagraph studio must have become aware of the potential for exploiting the formal rigidity of its system in its storylines. One fine illustration is the sequence shown here from *Mixed Identities* (1913), in which the confusion that a pair of twins cause their bosses and suitors is deftly exploited in a system of mirror-image framing and mise-en-scène.

1. twin 1/boss 1
2. twin 2/boss 2
3. boss 2 calls
4. boss 1
5. boss 2 goes out to eat with twin 2
6,7. boss 1 goes out to eat with twin 1
8. boss 2 runs into twin 1 in the lounge
9. confusion
10. reconciliation

produced up to eight films a week. Vitagraph's strict procedure was in no sense a concession made in order to churn out films more quickly. Instead, it proved to be an artistic virtue. It inspired a creative approach to mise-en-scène, in which the relationships between actors were expressed in an intimate and crystal-clear interplay of lines. The use of a single persistent frame encouraged blocking that involved one character's back or lent extra weight to the position of the protagonist in the deep space of the image. Unlike the much wider tableau shot, it required precise choreography and permitted actors to take advantage of the relative proximity of the camera.

This strict aesthetic constraint was applied with miraculous ease to the whole gamut of genres from farce to melodrama, from Western to social drama, from light-hearted comedy to historical spectacle, indoors and out, and in both urban and natural settings.

The explanation for my astonishment was undoubtedly that I had sat down to watch with particular expectations. The general contours of film history had taught me that D.W. Griffith had invented classical *découpage* (the activity of dividing a scene into shots) around 1910. But now I was seeing a style of filmmaking that reminded me more of modernist films such as *Gertrud* (1964) by Carl Theodor Dreyer or, in a different generation, Chantal Akerman's *Jeanne Dielman, 23, quai du Commerce, 1080 Bruxelles* (1975). These two filmmakers tried to escape the dominance of standardized Hollywood *découpage*. Both Dreyer and Akerman had made use of the same immovable frames and sophisticated mise-en-scène that I now saw used so naturally in the industrially produced Vitagraph films. My straightforward mosaic of film history was profoundly shaken.

Of course, the question is whether I would have admired the Vitagraph films as much if I had been unaware of Dreyer and Akerman. Isn't it possible that the Vitagraph films were simply old-fashioned, not yet touched by Griffith's genius?

That suggestion overlooks one crucial aspect of what the Desmet time capsule offers us: a welcome opportunity to sidestep the teleological pitfalls involved in writing film history, an invitation not to succumb to the reflex of 'before' and 'after', not to assume a line of development from primitive to sophisticated with relationships of influence and foreshadowing, but to construe the artistic process as a domain of possibilities that opens or closes depending on the objectives of the filmic storytellers.

This places the 1911-1914 Vitagraph films in the Desmet Collection in a very different light. They are not primitive, nor old-fashioned, nor the products of a clever mass-production method, but reflections of an approach to storytelling that was tried out – given a

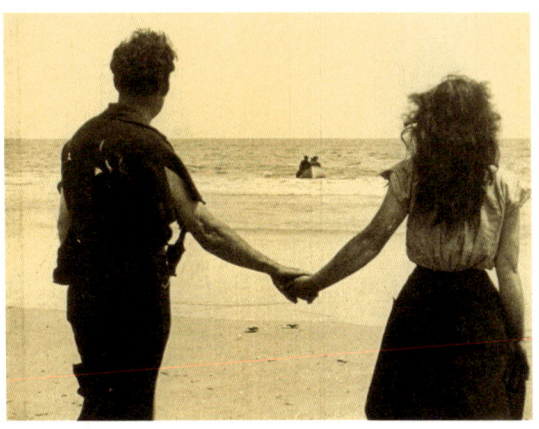

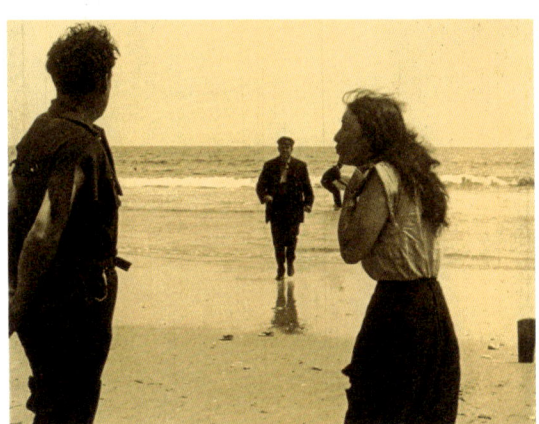

Mise-en-scène

The brilliant mise-en-scène in the final scene of *The Signal Fire* (1912) shows how Vitagraph managed to tell stories. After a shipwreck, a captain's wife and a sailor wash up on a desert island and fall in love. By sheer coincidence, their signal fire is spotted by the woman's husband. The moment they are saved is thus the moment their romance ends – all this in a single shot, in which the sailor finally decides to remain on the desert island, without his love, rather than return to civilization.
Notice, also, that the *plan américain* is maintained in the foreground.

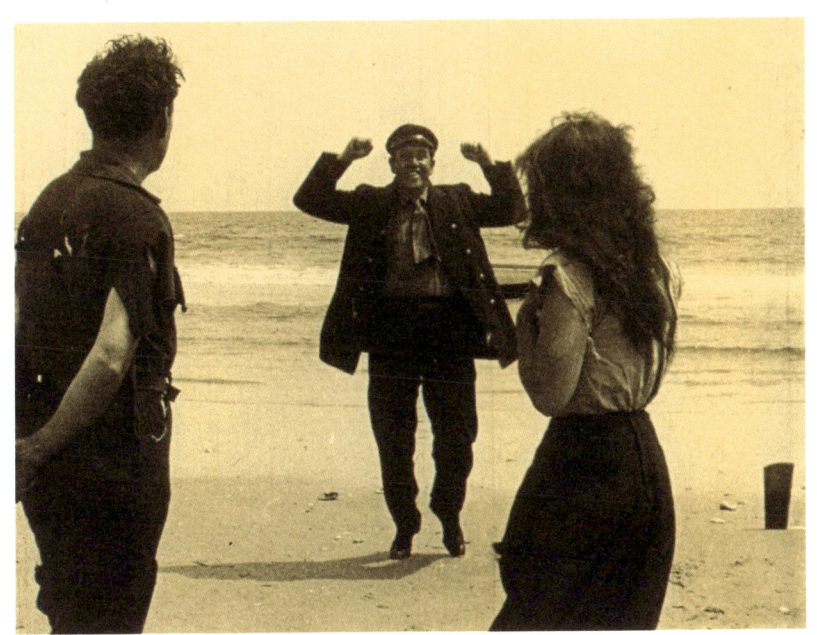
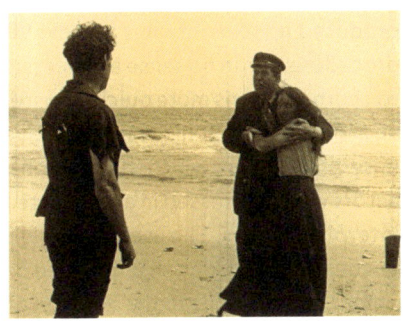
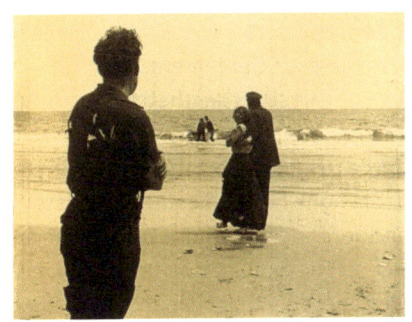
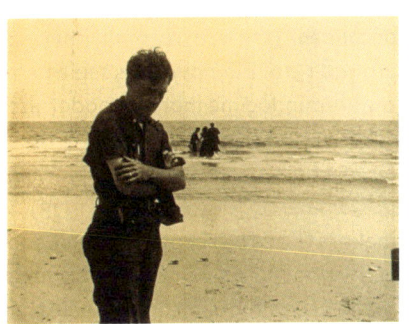
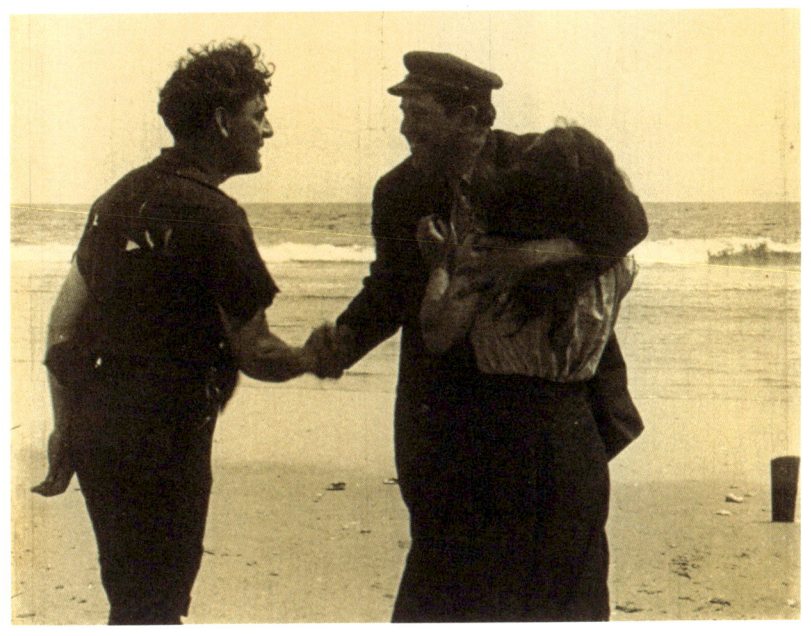

test run, you might say – in the medium of film with its unique range of possibilities. Yes, this approach was ultimately overshadowed by the classic *découpage* paradigm, but that in no way diminishes its virtues. In fact, it went underground, resurfacing decades later in the modernist idiom of cineastes such as Dreyer and Akerman. That places not only Vitagraph in a new light, but also those filmmakers.

Interestingly, the Vitagraph productions have a more rough-hewn style than their modern counterparts, but that actually makes it easier to gain insight into them. In both the dramas and the comedies, emotions and moral dilemmas are depicted in an almost rebus-like way. Within the rock-solid *plan américain*, there flourishes a style of narrative that you might call 'performative', as if every shot (and one shot often equals one scene) can be understood as a statement. This gives the storytelling a rigid, almost doctrinaire, quality.

Every one of the Vitagraph films can be read as a *Lehrstück* (Brecht's term, which he translated as 'learning-play') in which the depiction of an emotional process fades into the background, while the spotlight is stolen by a 'moral lesson'. I see a connection to the tradition of emblem books, collections of images illustrating a pithy saying, which were especially popular from the sixteenth to the eighteenth century. They are short stories that serve as proverbs, often with a moral undertone or an explicit life lesson. One well-known example is the *Book of Emblems* published in 1531 by Italian jurist Andrea Alciato. In the Netherlands, there was a long tradition, enduring well into the nineteenth century, of 'love emblem books' – lessons in the perils of love.

Many titles of Vitagraph films appear to have come straight from emblem books: for example, *Destiny is Changeless* (1911), *The Bond of Music* (1912), *The Triumph of Right* (1912), *The Whimsical Threads of Destiny* (1913), or *Fortune's Turn* (1913). In the Dutch titles – which are often summaries of the movies rather than direct translations from the English – this quality is even more pronounced, as if Vitagraph's Dutch agents sensed how neatly these films fit into the strong Dutch tradition of love emblem books: *Liefde maakt vindingrijk* (Love leads to ingenuity), *Geduld overwint alles* (Patience conquers all), *Barmhartigheid en naastenliefde* (Mercy and charity), *Overwinning van het recht* (Triumph of justice), *Een lesje in de liefde* (A lesson in love), *Goede zijde van de bioscoop* (Good side of the cinema).

Performative storytelling and a moralistic undertone go well together in Vitagraph films, but are they intrinsically linked? Or to put it differently: When modernist cineastes such as Dreyer and Akerman work in the same tradition of framing and mise-en-scène as

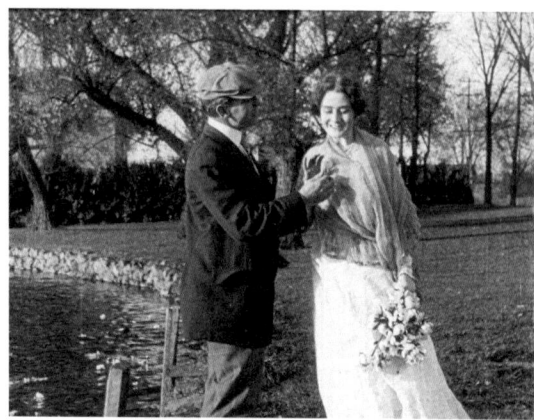

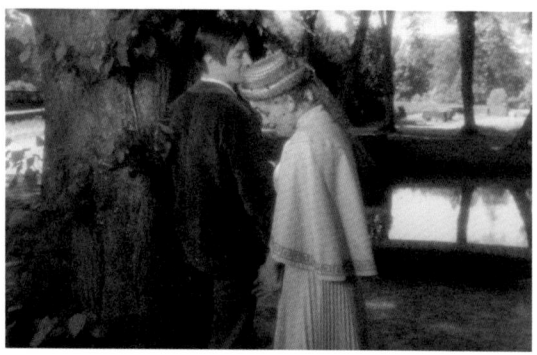

Vitagraph's modernism
Water Lilies and *Gertrud*

In *Water Lilies* (1911), a budding romance between a dancer and a young man is cut short when he suddenly goes blind and then pretends no longer to love her. The framing and mise-en-scène of this consummate masterpiece from the Vitagraph studio seems almost to duplicate a number of crucial scenes from the modernist masterpiece *Gertrud* (Carl Theodor Dryer, 1964), at least if we follow the chronology of most film lovers and not the actual dates. In *Gertrud*, a former opera singer falls in love with a much younger writer. She is prepared to give up her passionless marriage for him, until she finds out he has bragged about his affair with her. The cinematography in *Gertrud* is more dynamic than that in *Water Lilies*, but the relationship between the actors and the frame and the use of depth and proximity within a single shot are remarkably similar.

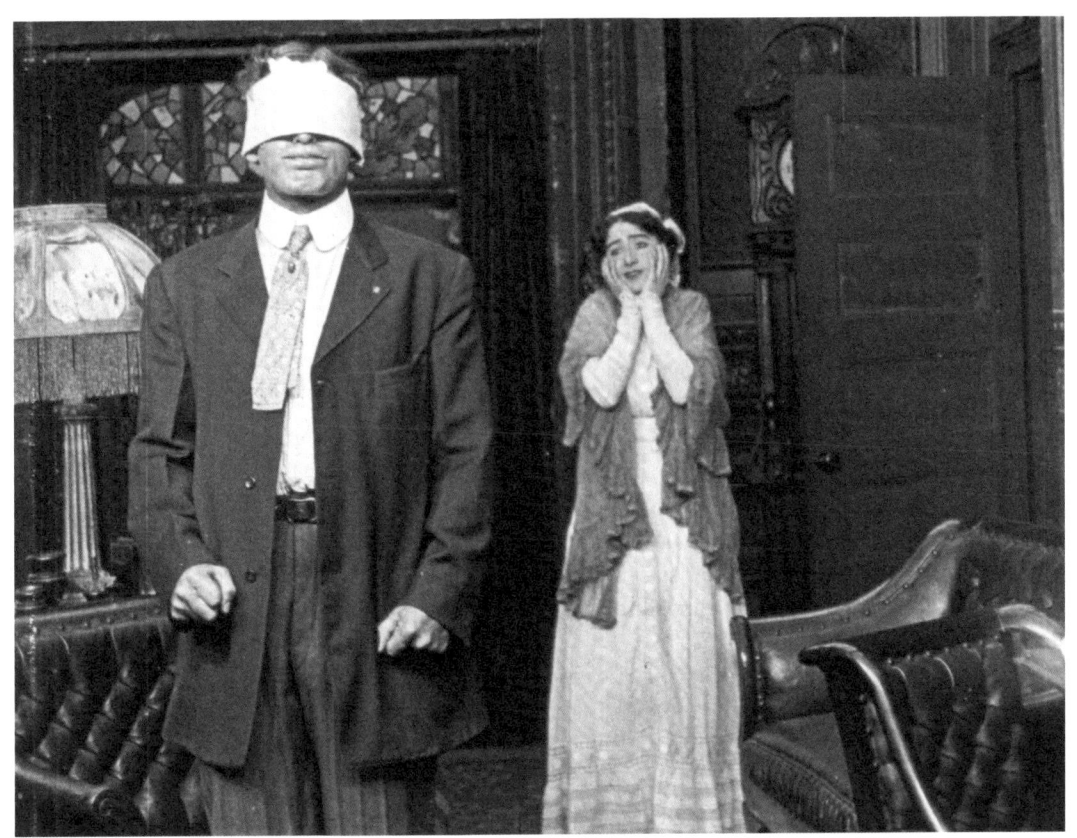

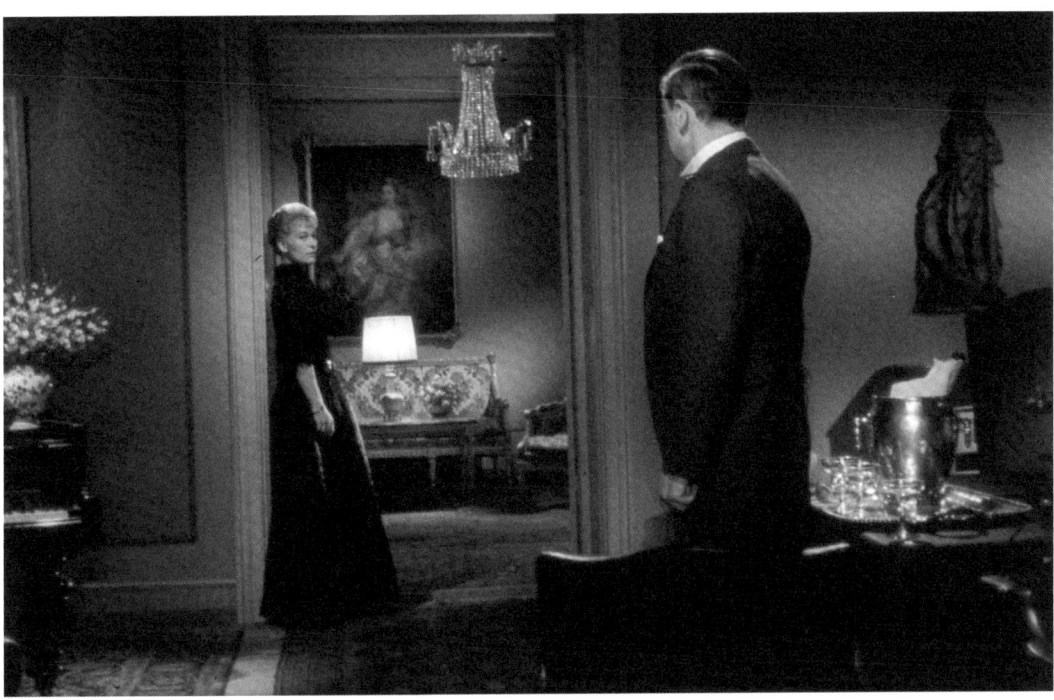

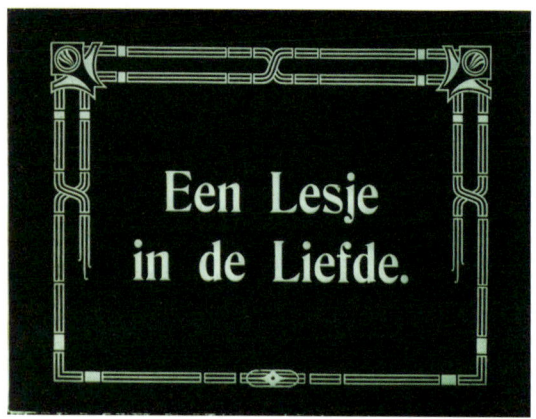

the Vitagraph studio, can their films or individual scenes, too, be read as emblematic?

Discussions of the work of these filmmakers certainly do not tend to draw a link between formal properties and the moralistic tone of emblem books, since that would clash with the directors' status as avant-garde icons. They are characterized as 'severe', but not as 'moralistic'. But don't the heroines of Dreyer's *Gertrud* and Akerman's *Jeanne Dielman* meet their fate with a stiff-necked quality that betrays a moralistic, emblematic undercurrent? In any event, learning about Vitagraph made me look at these films differently. All at once, I saw a connection between their formal rigidity and their moral standpoint.

Perhaps there are not as many ways of telling a story as the 'innovators' in any narrative form would have us believe, and instead, age-old traditions are resuscitated as the need arises. The Jean Desmet Collection gives rise to ideas like this, a virtue that should not be underestimated, let alone overlooked.

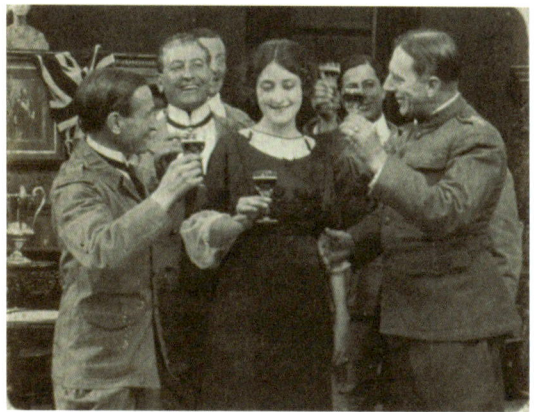

Emblematic storytelling

One clear illustration of emblematic storytelling is *A Lesson in Jealousy* (Harry Lambart, 1913), a comedy in which the husband makes up a tale of jealousy to impress his wife. The plot could come directly from Alciato's *Book of Emblems* or a Dutch love emblem book.

Andrea Alciato, *Book of Emblems* – Emblem 192

That respect is to be sought in marriage
When the viper is sexually aroused, it stations itself on the seashore and ejects the dread poisons from its gut. To summon the moray eel, it raises a loud hissing, and suddenly she comes to the embrace of her mate.
– Great reverence is owed to the marriage bed, and the partners owe each other mutual respect.

Mind-Expanding

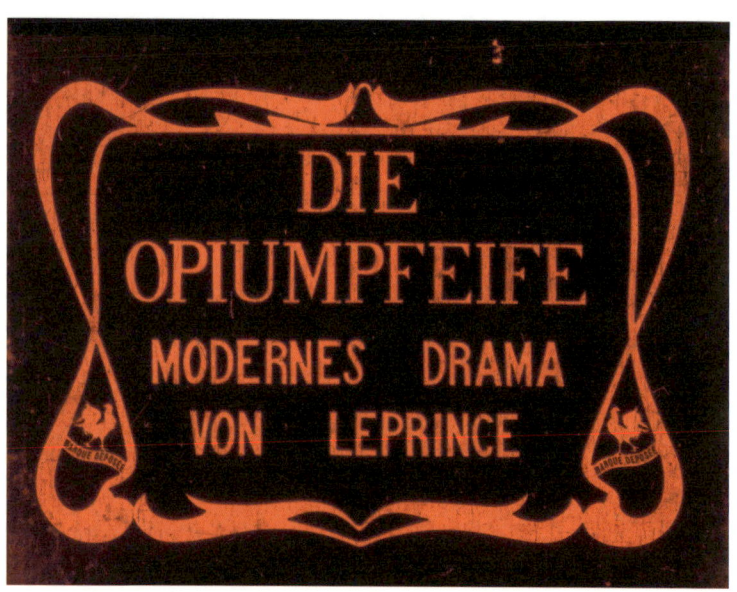
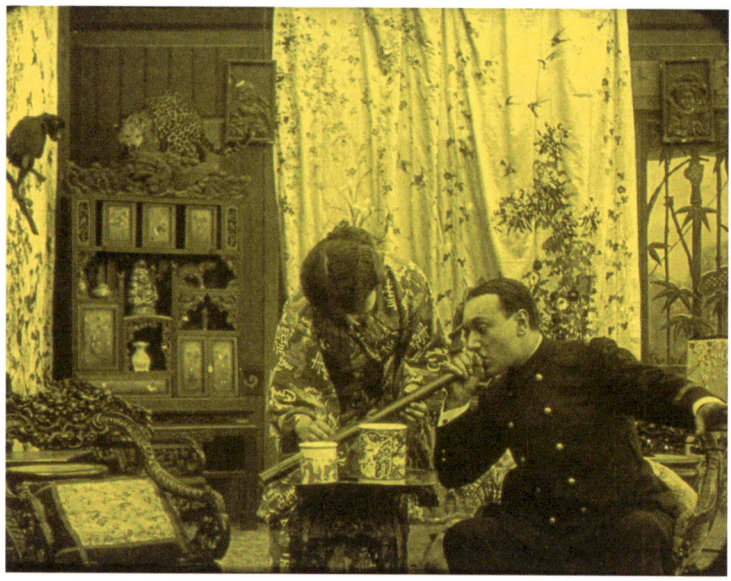
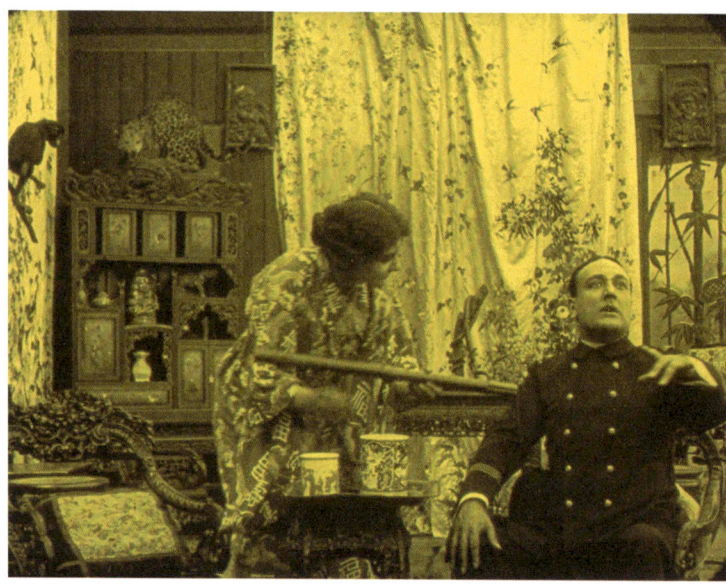

pp. 124-125
René Leprince, *La pipe d'opium*
(*Die Opiumpfeife*), 1912

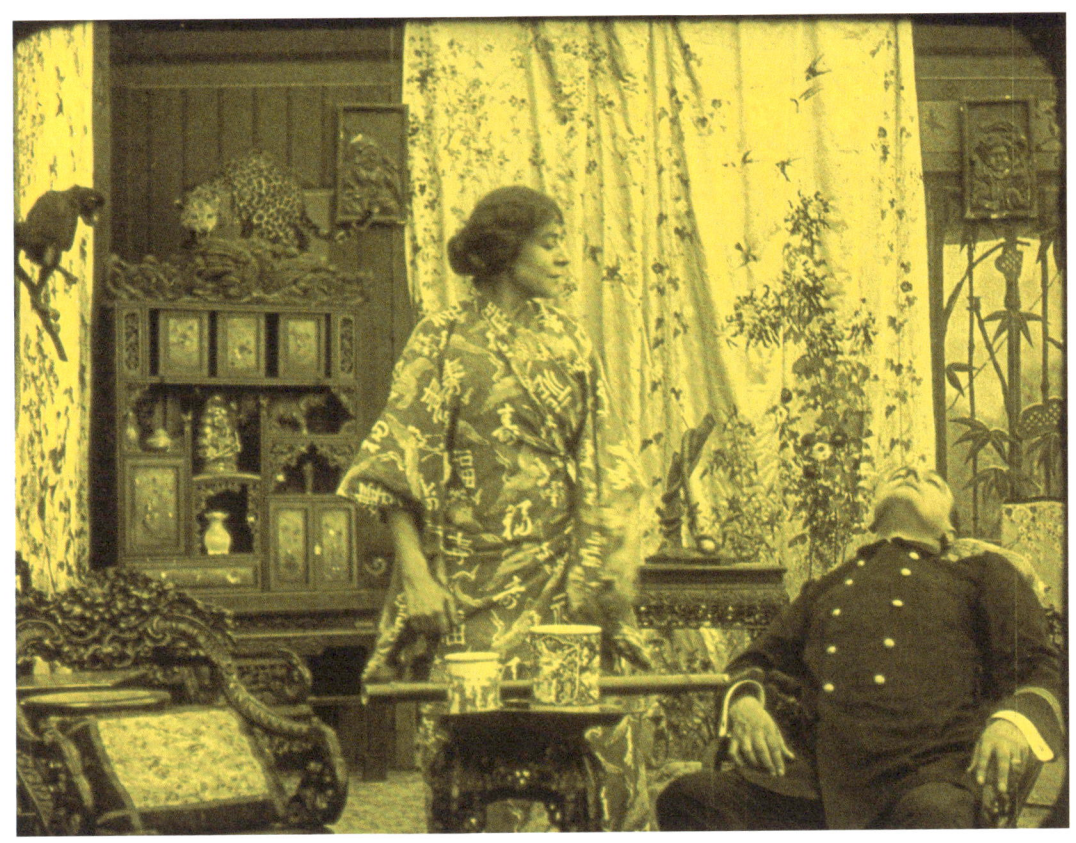
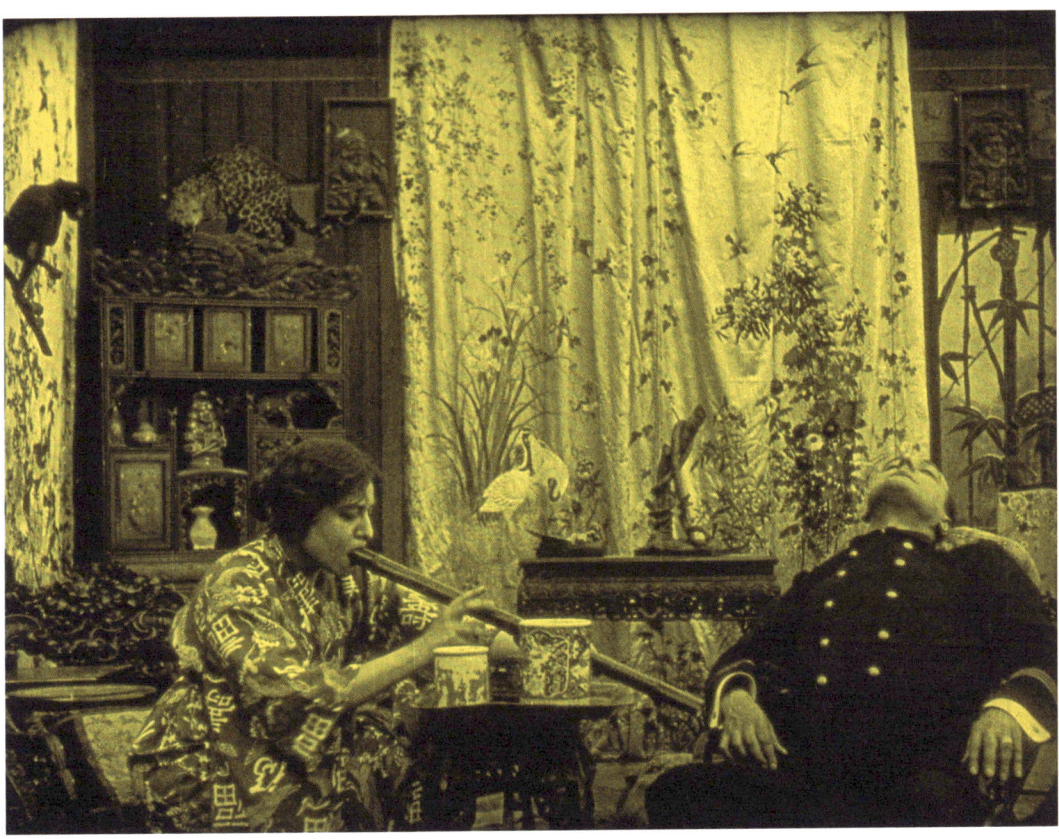

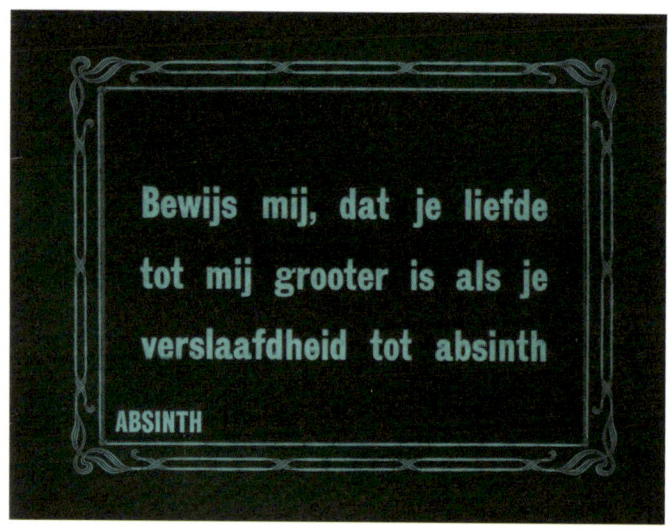

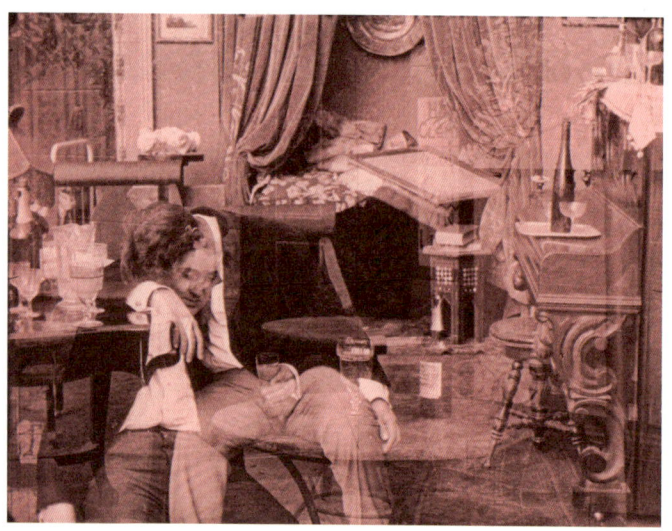

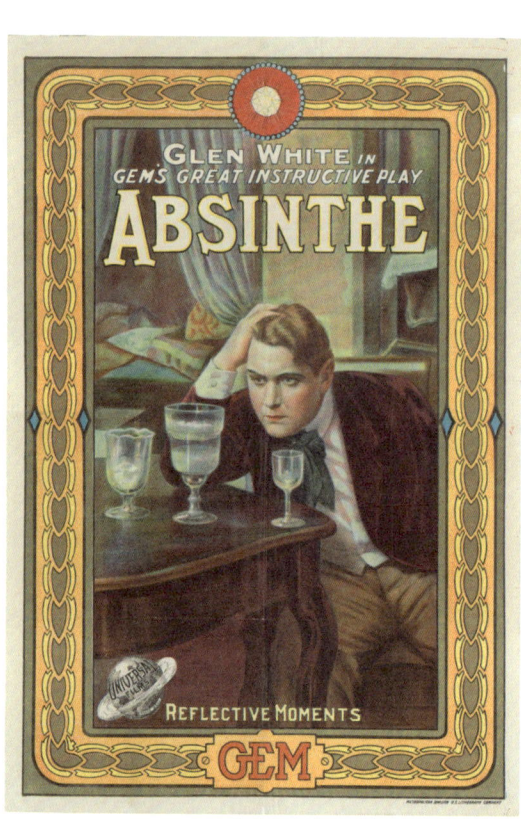

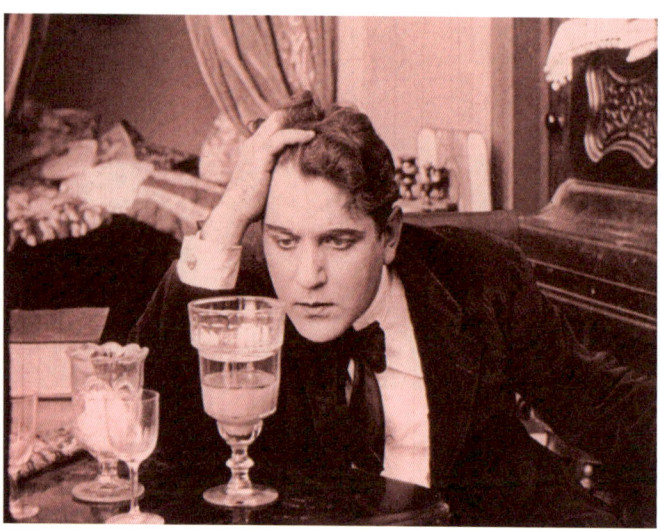

p. 126
Herbert Brenon, *Absinthe*, 1913, intertitle and two frame enlargements

Poster for *Absinthe*, 1913
104 x 72 cm

p. 127
Mario Morais, *Pik Nik veste la jupe-culotte*, 1911

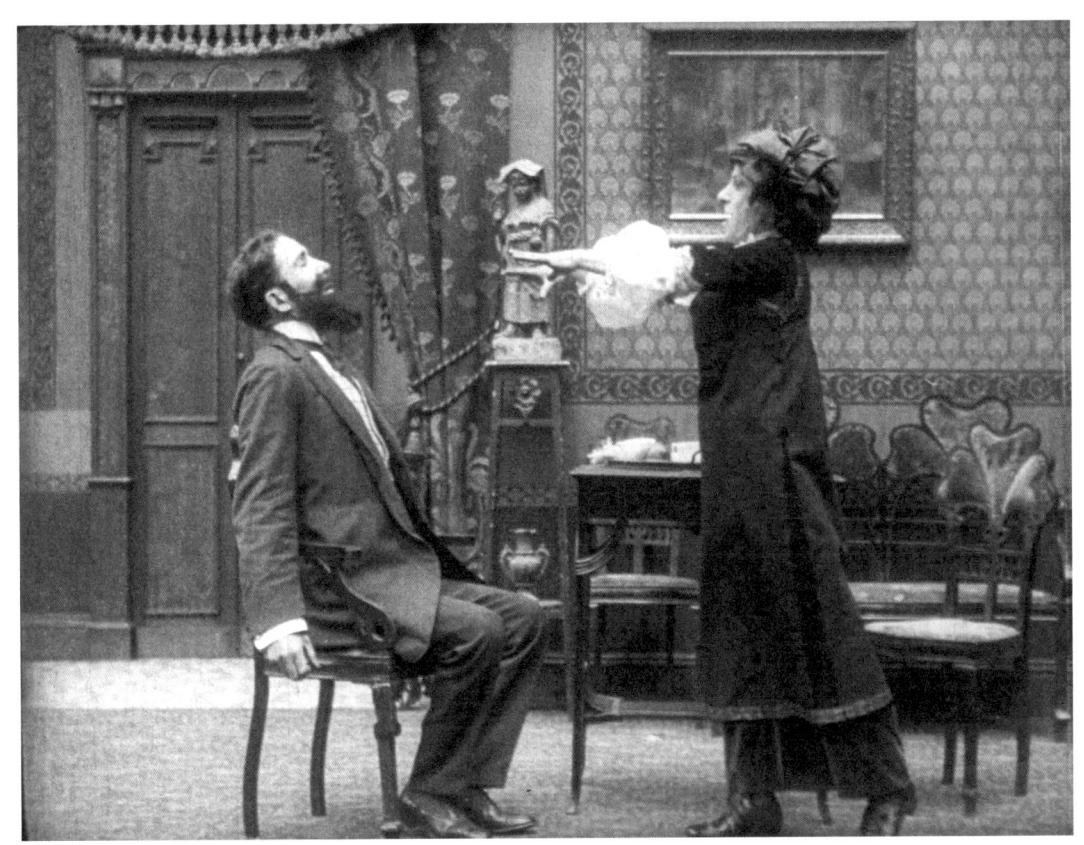
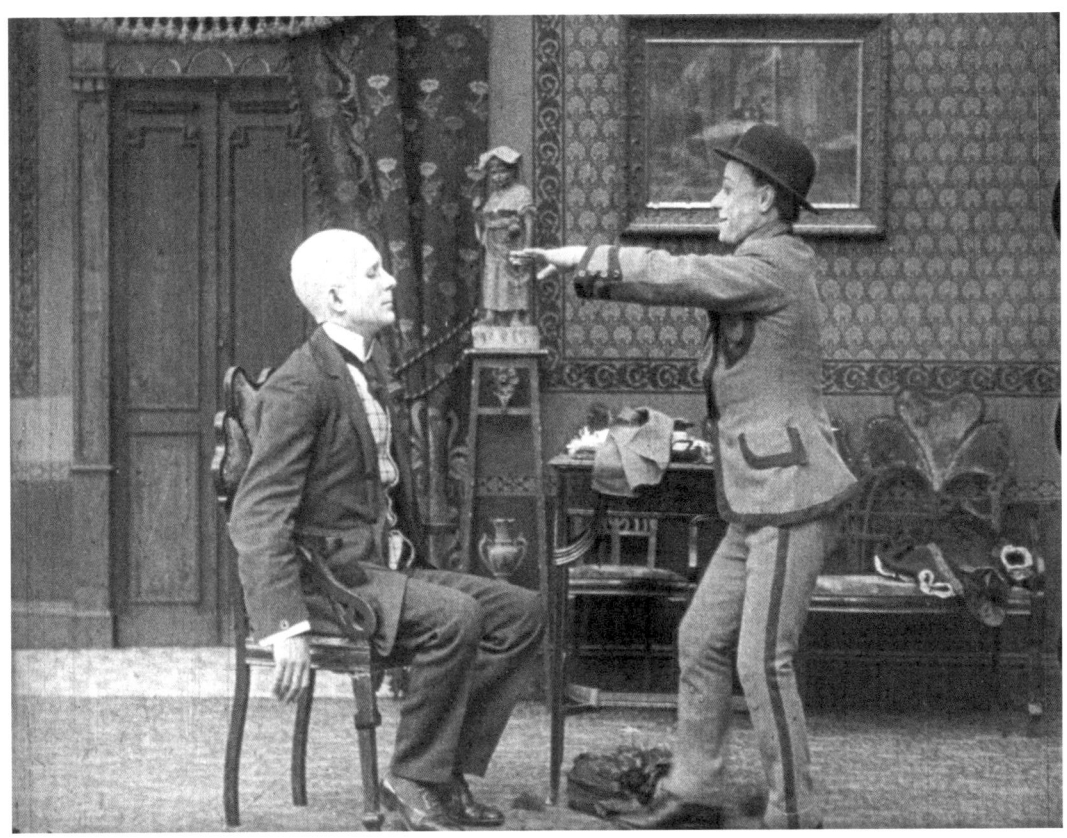

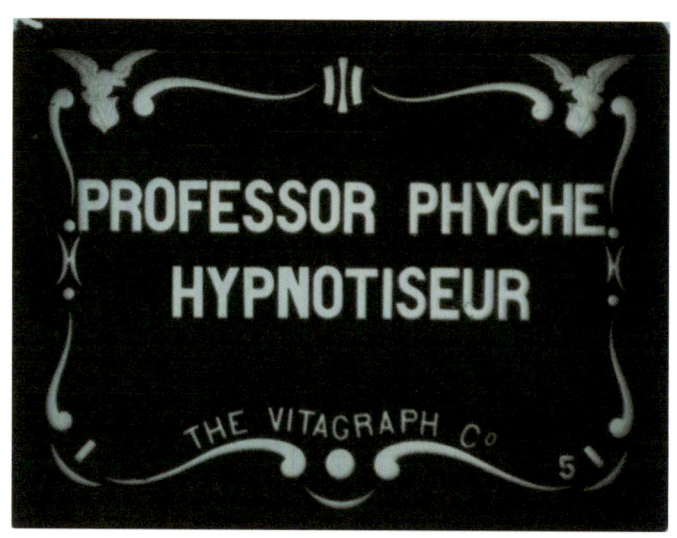

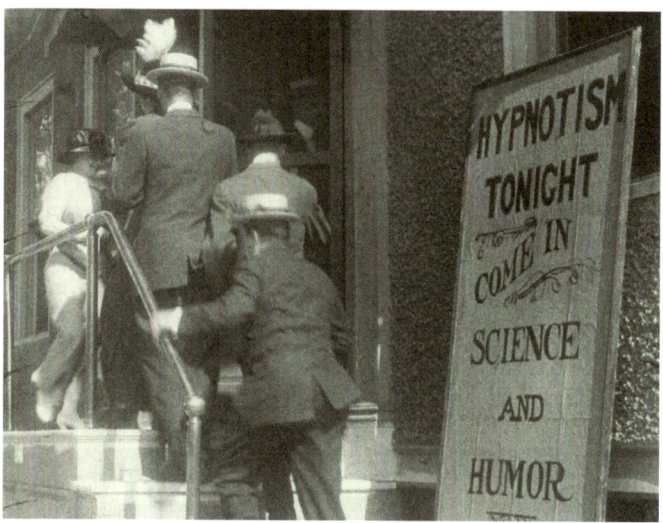

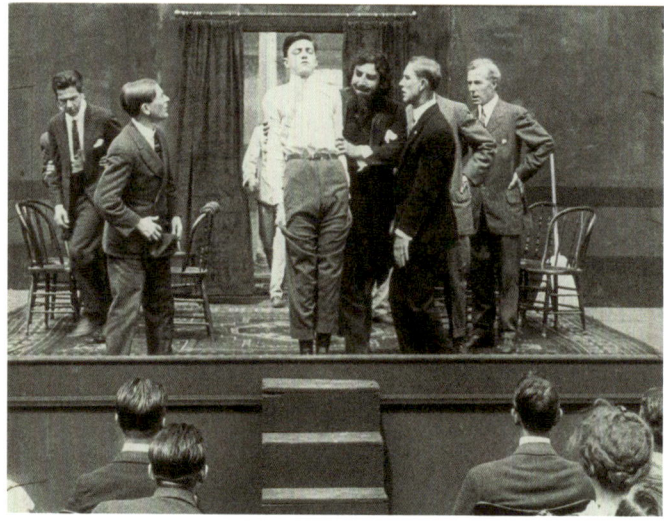

James Young, *Jerry's Mother-In-Law*, 1913, intertitle and two frame enlargements

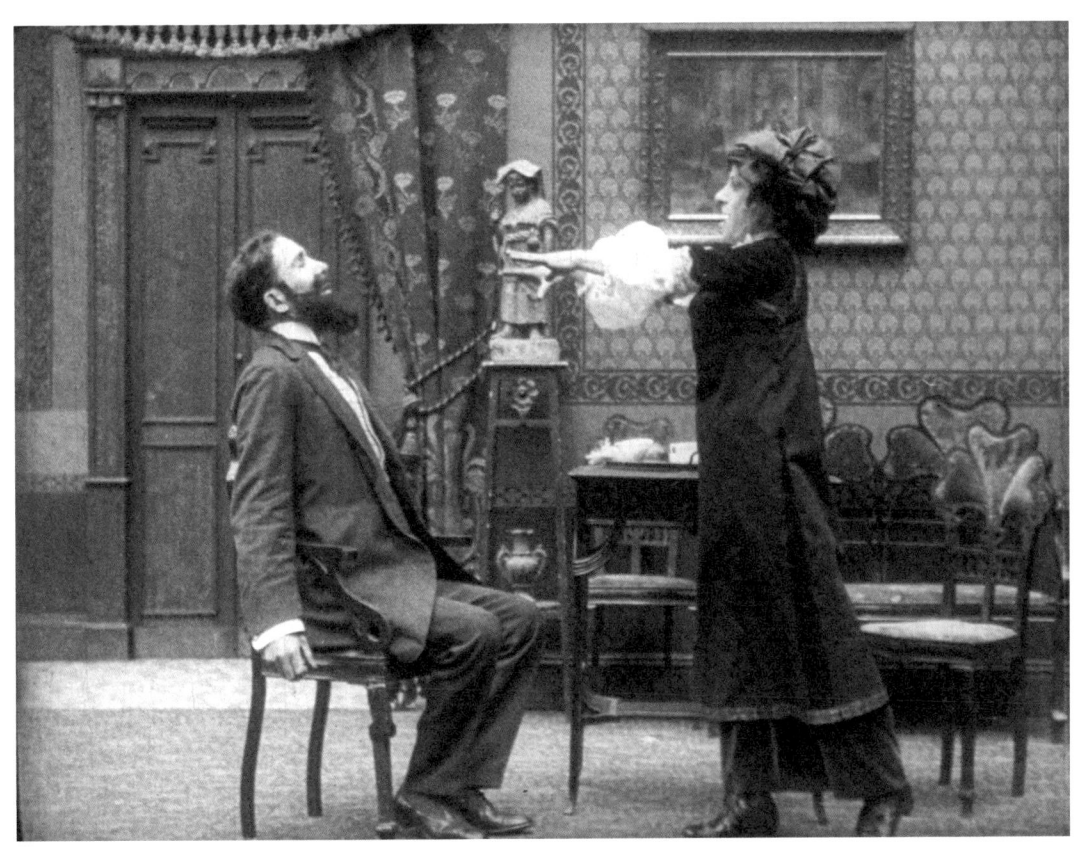

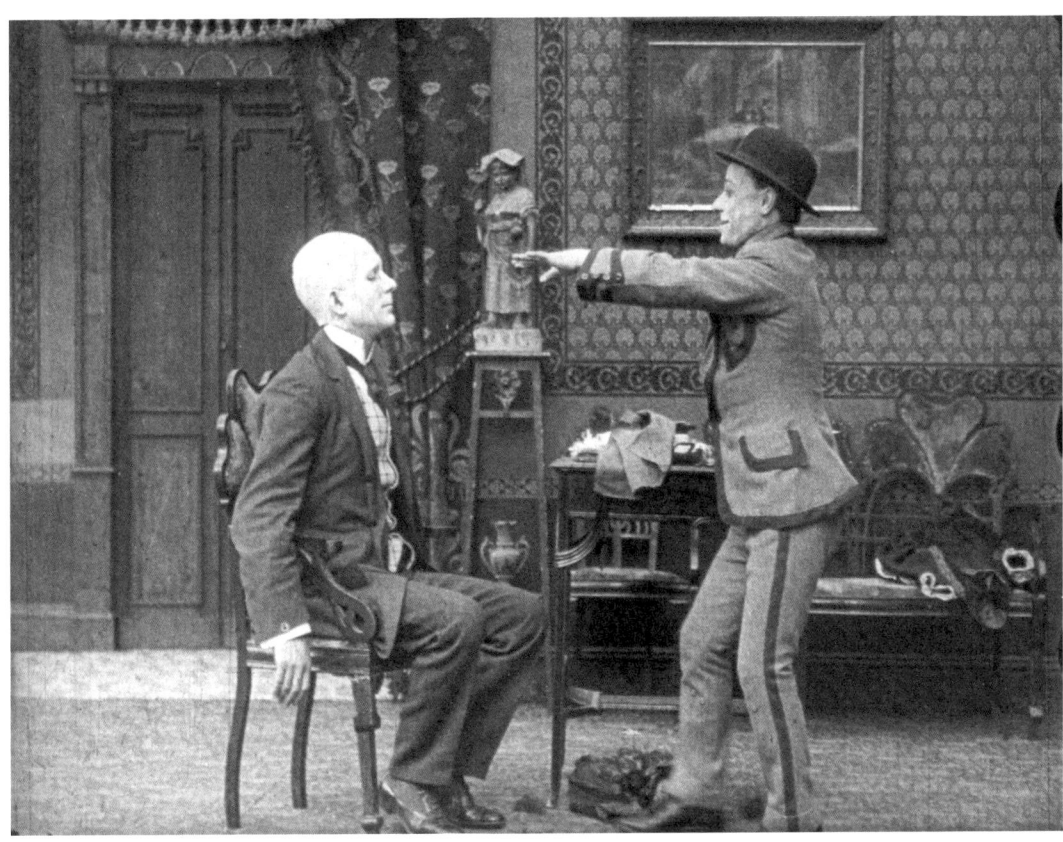

127

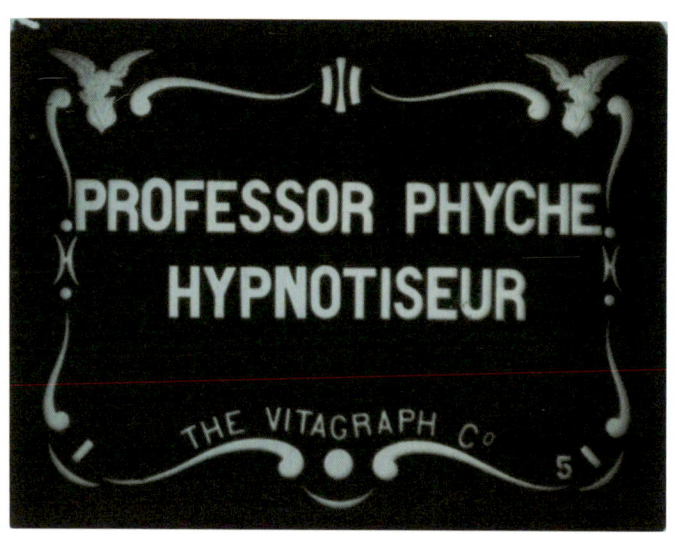

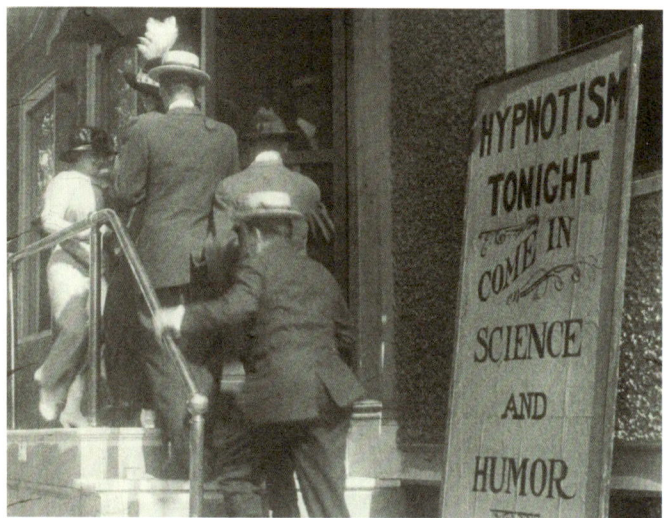

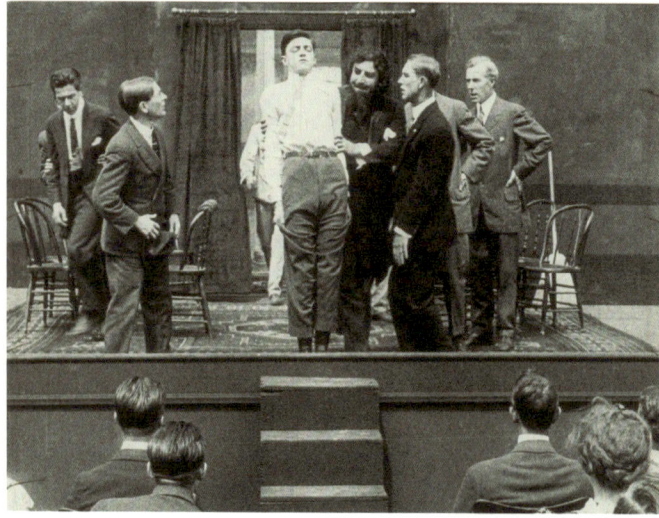

James Young, *Jerry's Mother-In-Law*, 1913, intertitle and two frame enlargements

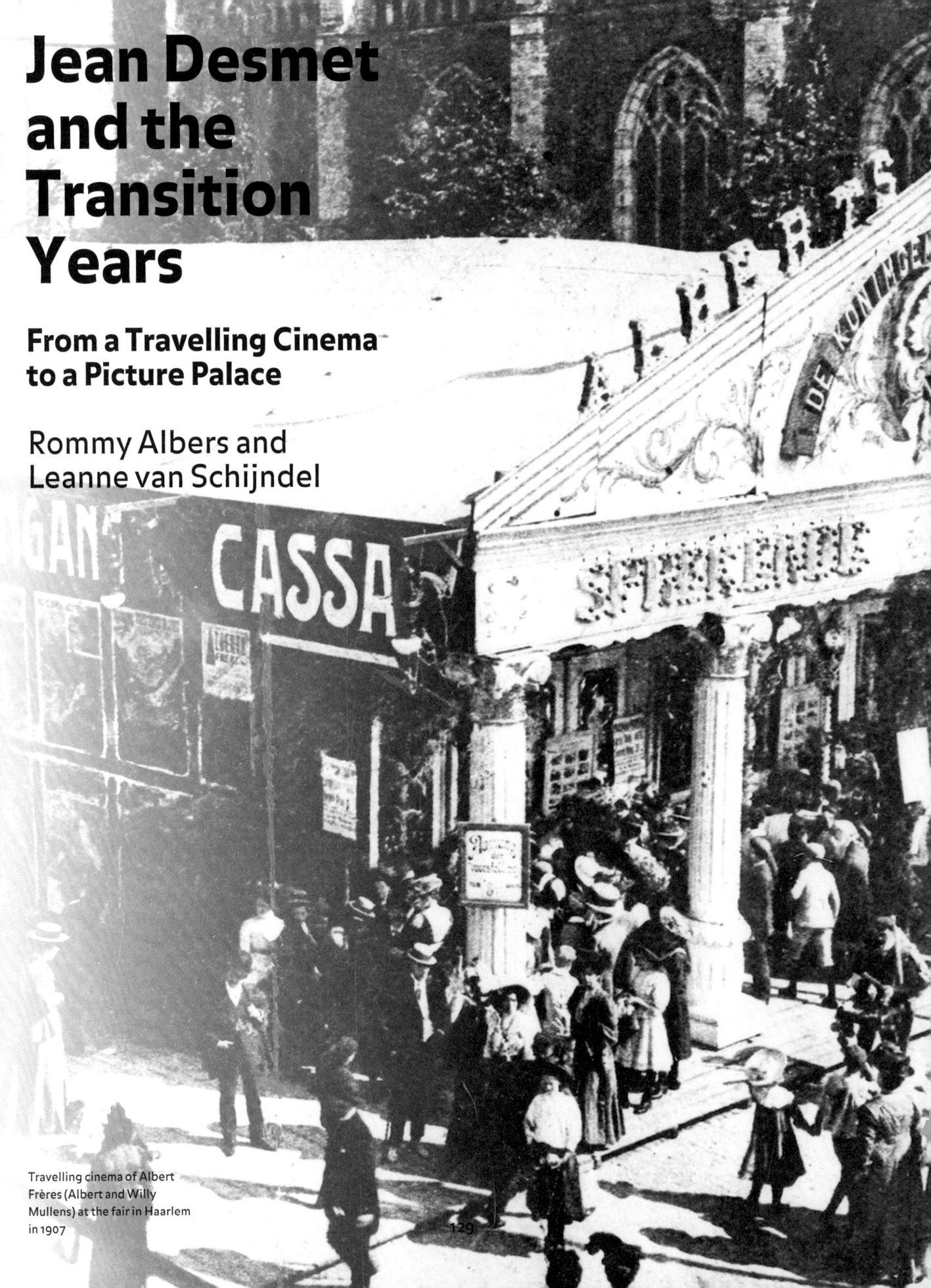

Jean Desmet and the Transition Years

From a Travelling Cinema to a Picture Palace

Rommy Albers and
Leanne van Schijndel

Travelling cinema of Albert Frères (Albert and Willy Mullens) at the fair in Haarlem in 1907

On 19 February 1907, the Amsterdam newspaper *Het Nieuws van den Dag* published the following item:

> A Cinematographic Theatre
>
> There are plans to build a theatre for cinematographic shows on Reguliersbreestraat here [in Amsterdam]. For this purpose, the housing complex measuring about 500 square metres . . . will be demolished, after which the new theatre will be built on the cleared site . . .

The driving force behind the construction of this theatre was F.A. Nöggerath, Sr., director of the Variété Flora and one of the first Dutch film producers and exhibitors. The opening of the theatre would be a turning point in the still brief history of film screenings in the Netherlands. The location of this new theatre – which was named *Bioscope-Theater* ('Cinema-Theatre') – in the heart of Amsterdam's entertainment district made it clear to the general public, for the first time, that serious changes were under way in the Dutch film world. Until then, films had been screened by travelling showmen who went from fairground to fairground with their equipment, or as novelty acts in variety theatres such as Nöggerath's Variété Flora or his leading Amsterdam rival Carré.

With the advent of the cinema, films – or, more precisely, film screenings – acquired a home, a place of their own, where viewers could attend an autonomous film screening any day of the week. No longer would they have to wait until a travelling exhibitor came to town or be content with a short film in the middle of a theatrical revue, sandwiched between wresting Icelanders, trained dogs and jugglers. They could henceforth go to a permanent theatre, night after night, where films were the main attraction and all other forms of entertainment were strictly secondary.

The arrival of the cinema in the Netherlands followed its earlier introduction in the United States and the countries around the Netherlands, where the cinema had already made its debut by 1905. The first signs of this profound shift came to the Netherlands in the winter of 1905-1906, when the French film production company Pathé Frères opened its Dutch branch in Amsterdam, as part of a strategy to build up a worldwide network of sales outlets. It was important to the new cinema owners to offer new films on a regular basis. Travelling cinemas had a new audience at every stop on their route and so could screen the same films many times, but permanent cinemas had returning audiences that required a steady supply of new films. This led to a lively trade in used copies. When Pathé realized that other parties were profiting from the trade in films that it had originally sold, it decided to begin renting out its own films. Renting out the same films many times proved more profitable than selling them just once. At the same time, the rental business enabled Pathé to exercise more control over the exhibition of its films and to guarantee their exclusivity.

In the summer of 1907, as part of these activities, Pathé organized a number of full-evening film programmes in Amsterdam's Grand Théâtre. These programmes were described in the press as a foretaste of what Amsterdam audiences could expect in September 1907, once Nöggerath had completed his permanent cinema.

It took a few more years for the permanent cinema to become a firmly established institution in the Netherlands, but the first steps had been taken down the road to the sweeping reorganization of Dutch screening practice – a process in which Jean Desmet would play an important role. This former fair manager and travelling cinema showman was one of the first to switch to a permanent cinema and he became a leading film renter in the early 1910s, the transition years. In the new structure of the film world, production, rental and exhibition would be prised apart into three largely independent lines of business.

The Travelling Cinema

In the early years of the twentieth century, films were shown primarily by travelling exhibitors. These were generally fair operators who went from fairground to fairground with their equipment, showing their films at every stop. In the first decade after the introduction of film in the Netherlands in March 1896, the travelling cinema shows grew into one of the most popular fairground attractions.

The best-known Dutch exhibitors were the brothers Albert and Willy Mullens (also known as Alberts Frères). In a luxurious tent, they showed cinema programmes that included the latest hand-coloured Pathé films, with musical accompaniment and enthusiastic narration. Their ever-changing, increasingly spectacular programmes lured visitors into their tent several times during the several-week run of the fair. The film series often concluded with an exclusive closing event on the last evening. The highlight of this event was generally a long film such as Ferdinand Zecca's *La vie et la passion de Notre Seigneur Jésus Christ* (1907).

As noted above, travelling cinema exhibitors had a fixed set of films that they took from place to place. New films were used mainly for publicity purposes. Additional publicity was provided by a new genre of film characteristic of the travelling cinema: the local film. This was a type of short film produced by the travelling

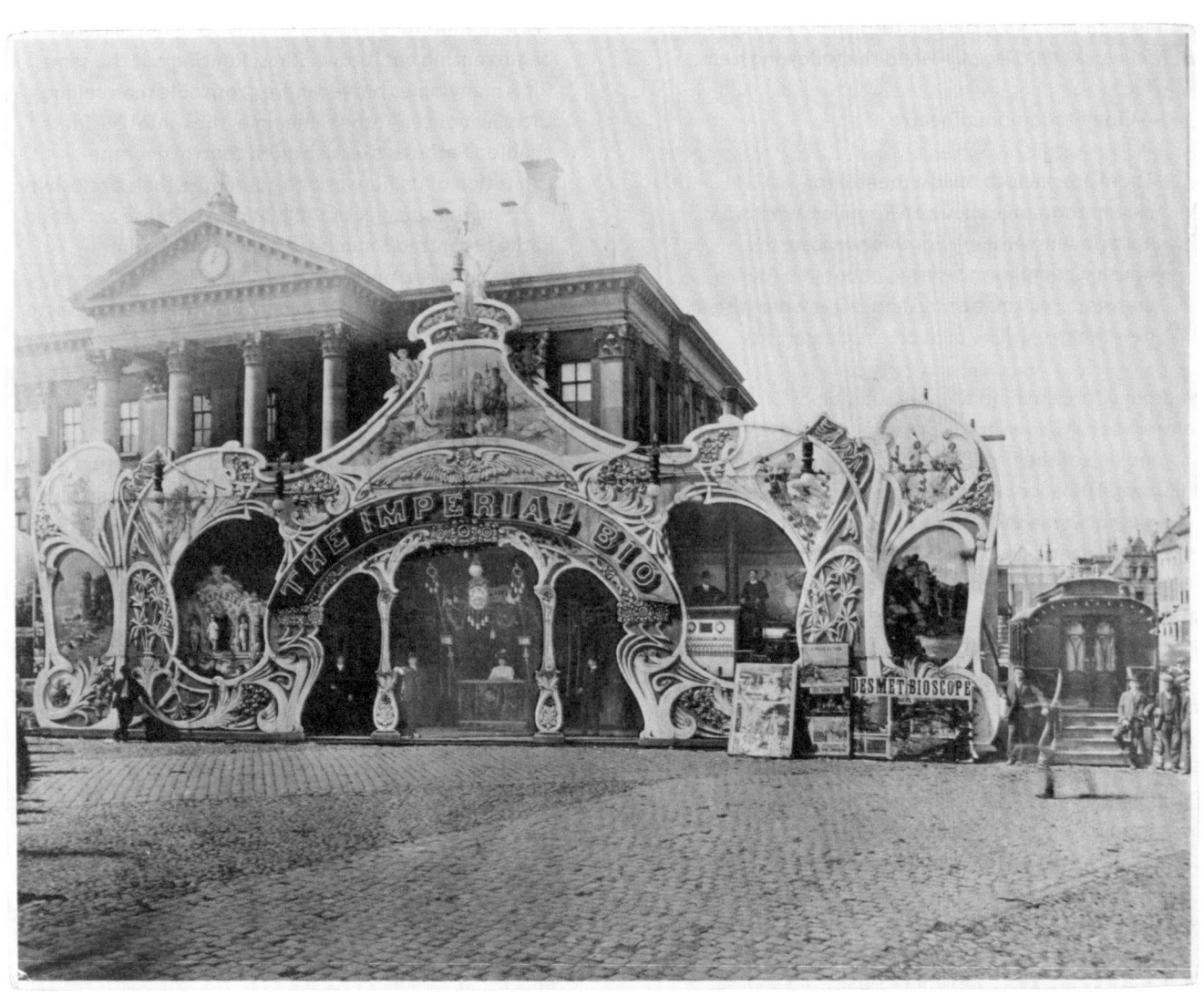

The Imperial Bio, Jean Desmet's travelling cinema, with his luxury caravan on the right, on the main square in Groningen, May 1908

showmen themselves, in which the host city and its inhabitants played the leading role. For example, there were films of the congregation leaving church after the Sunday mass, with plenty of screen time for individual churchgoers, as well as films of the most attractive or distinctive local squares and buildings. These films were hugely popular with local audiences, but also strongly tied to a particular place – many of them were one-off productions that were never shown again. One famous example is *De mésaventure van een Fransch heertje zonder pantalon aan het strand van Zandvoort* (The misadventure of a French dandy without trousers on the beach at Zandvoort; 1905) by the Mullens brothers.

In July 1907, when Jean Desmet decided to give up his other fairground attractions for a travelling cinema and appeared at the Leiden fair as the operator of the Imperial Bio, he was following in the footsteps of renowned travelling showmen such as Alberts Frères, Alex Benner and Henricus Hommerson. He had a large cinema tent with an Art Nouveau exterior and an opulent interior, which could accommodate a few hundred audience members. He hired a pianist to accompany the films and a narrator to provide commentary.

The programmes consisted of short films in various genres: comedy, drama, fantasy and actualities, one after another. He initially bought most of his films from Pathé, and titles such as *La vengeance du forgeron* (1907) and *La maison ensorcelée* (1907) can still be found in the Desmet Collection. At a later stage, he also purchased films from the above-mentioned F.A. Nöggerath. These films came from French production companies such as Eclair and Gaumont and Italian studios such as Cines, Lux and Ambrosio.

It was also Nöggerath who supplied Desmet with the latest development in cinema: *films d'art* (art films). These were longer films, generally based on historical events or well-known plays, with famous actors and actresses in the starring roles. The new genre was the film industry's response to mounting criticism that it was producing too many coarse, crude, indecent farces and comedies, each one indistinguishable from the last. The production of art films was an attempt to earn the cinema a legitimate place among other, more respected forms of art, and also to attract more cultivated audiences.

These art films came to occupy a central place in the programme. The standard format of the programme also involved regular slots for nature scenes, actualities, comedies and tragedies.

The arrival of the art film more or less coincided with the introduction of film distribution in the Netherlands. Around 1909, Pathé and Nöggerath began renting out films. Although there are no sources that describe this transition, we see clear indications of it in changing exhibition practices. For instance, the Mullens brothers (Alberts Frères) announced in an advertisement in July 1909 that they had acquired the right to show films by a number of major studios (including Pathé and Gaumont). From then on, we find many films by these studios mentioned exactly once in the Alberts Frères programmes. The rich variety of titles and their one-off appearance in the programme suggests that they were not sold to Alberts Frères (which typically showed the films it owned many times), but rented to the company temporarily.

Another sign of this shift is the fact that from 1909 forward, the number of cinemas increased rapidly and it became easier for them to survive. While the preceding years had seen many failed attempts to establish permanent locations for screening films, from 1909 onward cinemas were increasingly likely to succeed. It was also around this time that the major film exhibitors made the transition, one by one, to the permanent

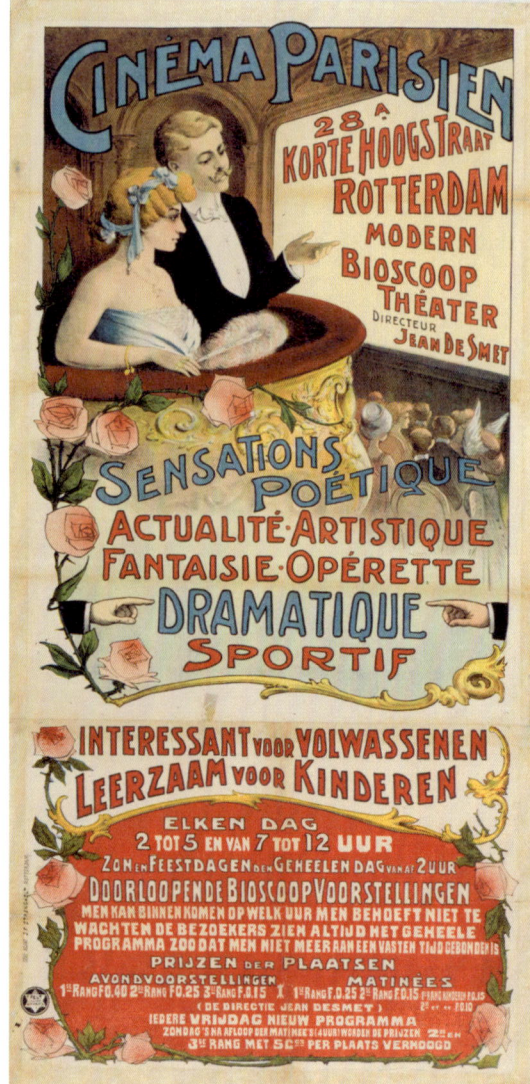

p. 132
Poster specially designed by Julien 't Felt for film screenings at Cinema Parisien in Rotterdam, 1909

p. 133
Handcart with advertisement for Cinema Parisien in Rotterdam, which was screening Eduard Schnedler-Sørensen's film *Dødsspring til hest fra cirkuskuplen* (1912)

Text strip to promote the film *V dni Getmanov*, 1911
31 x 84 cm

Text strip to promote the film *Streets of New York*, 1913
31 x 84 cm

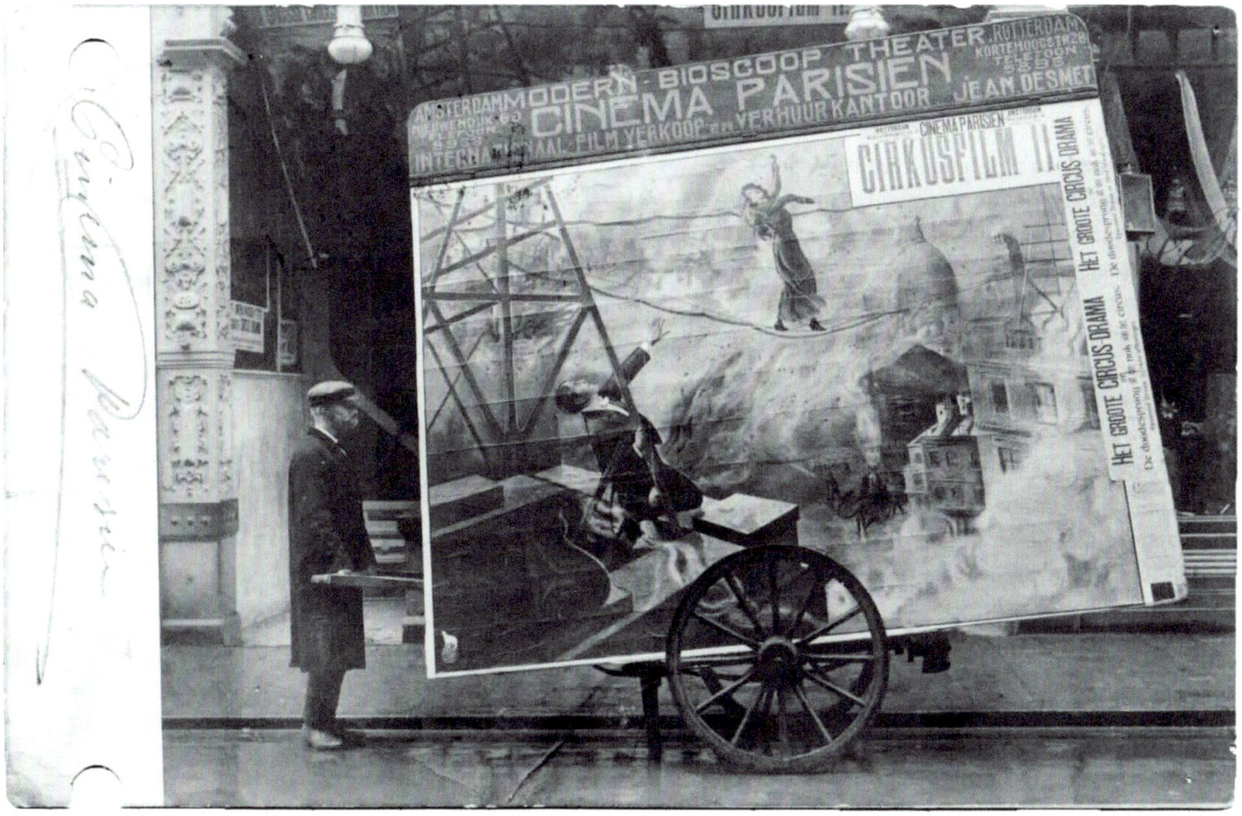

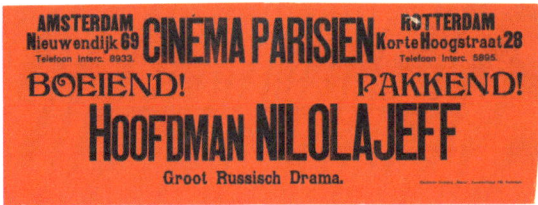

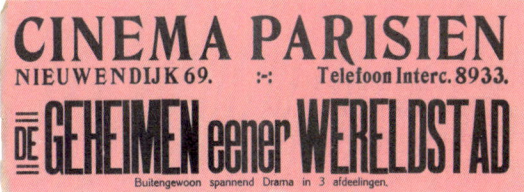

cinema. Nöggerath led the way in 1907, but he was followed by exhibitors such as Alberts Frères, Alex Benner and Jean Desmet around 1909. Even Pathé Frères joined the bandwagon. Without the arrival of film distribution, this transition could not have taken place.

The First Cinemas

The year 1907, when Desmet entered the film world, was the same year that the permanent cinema, as a place for screening films, made its first emphatic appearance in the Netherlands, with the construction of the Bioscope-Theater in Amsterdam. The first cinemas sprang up in Amsterdam and elsewhere. They were often small in scale and led a precarious, marginal existence. Many of them went belly up, and even the Bioscope-Theater went through difficult times and more than once had to resort to hosting theatrical performances.

But it was too late to turn the tide, and from 1909 onwards, the cinema became a permanent fixture of the entertainment world. Like the Mullens brothers – who established their first cinemas in The Hague and Haarlem – Desmet too made the transition. On 13 March 1909, he opened his first cinema on Rotterdam's Korte Hoogstraat: the Cinema Parisien.

Desmet was one of the first cinema owners in Rotterdam, but others would quickly follow. Rotterdam is reported to have caught 'cinema fever' in the years 1910-1911, and many new cinemas popped up in the centre of the city.

Desmet himself also expanded beyond his first cinema. A bit more than a year later, on 26 March 1910, he opened his second cinema, this one in Amsterdam, also called the Cinema Parisien. It was located on Nieuwendijk, in the city centre and close to Central Station. Desmet was one of the first cinema owners in Amsterdam, as he had been in Rotterdam, although he did have an early competitor – Nöggerath, Jr, who had taken over from his father in 1908. But in 1911-1912, the 'fever' hit Amsterdam. By the outbreak of the First World War in 1914, the city had some 40 cinemas, including a few small ones that did not last long – usually less than a year.

The explosive increase in the number of cinemas – which many a newspaper article described as 'springing from the ground like mushrooms' – eventually precipitated a radical change in the Dutch entertainment world. Within three years, the cinemas spread across the country, and in the major cities, entertainment outside the home was dominated by the cinemas, to the serious detriment of traditional forms of entertainment such as music, theatre and other performing arts.

In 1916, in the middle of the First World War, the 170 cinemas in the Netherlands attracted 15 million visitors, 3.7 million of them in Amsterdam alone. In 1930, these figures doubled: there were 300 cinemas and 30 million visitors. In this period, the Dutch population grew from 6 to 8 million.

The rise of the cinema also brought an end to the travelling cinema. Travelling exhibitors persisted until well into the second half of the twentieth century, but only on the margins of the film world. Desmet followed the trend, calling a halt to his travelling cinema shows. His last one was at the annual fair in Tiel in October 1910.

Elite Cinemas and Family Businesses

In 1912 and 1913, Desmet opened two more cinemas: the Cinema Palace in Amsterdam and Cinema Royal in Rotterdam. They both fall into the category of the *Elite-bioscoop* ('Elite cinema'): a luxury cinema in the centre of town, with its own orchestra to give the showings a lavish, exclusive character.

As when he had built his first two cinemas, Desmet once again proved to have a good eye for new developments in film screening. The Elite cinemas were part of a tendency towards differentiation in the cinema market. In the major Dutch cities, cinemagoers could choose from several kinds of cinemas: large, luxurious ones where the surroundings and accompaniment added

p. 134
Dutch leaflet with a description of the film *Il veleno delle parole*, 1913

p. 135
Dutch leaflet with a description of the film *Dødsspring til hest fra cirkuskuplen*, 1912

Admission ticket for Cinema Royal in Rotterdam

extra lustre to the film programme, smaller ones in the city centre, and neighbourhood cinemas in the areas surrounding the centre.

The first Dutch cinema to be labelled an *Elite-bioscoop* was the Theater Union on Heiligeweg, Amsterdam. The director of this cinema was Desmet's fellow distributor and competitor Johan Gildemeijer. At the Theater Union, Gildemeijer presented the films of the wildly popular Danish actress Asta Nielsen; he possessed the exclusive rights in the Netherlands for all her films made for the German production company PAGU.

Acquiring exclusive exhibition rights became a common practice in the Netherlands around 1912-1913. This provided distributors with a guarantee that no competitors would bring the same film onto the market. High prices were charged for these 'monopoly films', as they were called – sometimes more than 10,000 guilders in the Netherlands – but the box-office takings could be correspondingly high.

Desmet, too, purchased and rented monopoly films, such as *Le rançon du bonheur* (The Ransom of Happiness, 1912) and *Richard Wagner* (1913). This latter title was shown for two weeks in August 1913 as the main film for the opening of Desmet's Elite Cinema Royal in Rotterdam. That was standard practice: expensive new feature films were first shown at Elite cinemas, and rented to other cinemas only afterwards.

So the selection of films was not the sole distinction between the Elite cinemas and the others; the setting, furnishings, decoration, musical accompaniment and premiere showings gave the Elite cinemas an aura of grandeur and exclusivity that set them apart.

Meanwhile, Desmet was opening still more cinemas. In addition to the four above-mentioned ones in Amsterdam and Rotterdam, there were six others. In Rotterdam, Desmet's sister Rosine ran a cinema called Gezelligheid. His brothers Theo and Mathijs were the directors of Bellamy in Vlissingen and the Cinema Parisien in Eindhoven, respectively. Jean Desmet himself opened the Cinema Palace in Bussum on 3 May 1913.

By that stage, the Bioscope-Theater in Amersfoort had also come into Desmet's possession, as did his final cinema, Delfia in Delft, in November 1915. All in all, Jean Desmet and his family had their own little cinematic empire.

Jean Desmet as a Film Distributor

At first, Jean Desmet's films came from Nöggerath and Pathé, but starting in early 1910, he began to rent programmes of short films from Gustav Hattingen at the West-Deutsche Film-Börse in Krefeld. Six months later, Desmet started buying film programmes and renting them to other parties. He thus joined the small group of film renters in the Netherlands, which in the early years was dominated by Nöggerath, Pathé, Desmet and Gildemeijer.

The first programmes that he bought from the West-Deutsche Film Börse, from October 1910 to July 1911, consisted mainly of fixed packages of short films ('one-reelers') that had already been showing in Germany for a couple of weeks. Desmet screened these programmes in his own cinemas and rented them initially in unchanged form to other cinema owners. The programmes were projected on a continuous loop; visitors could enter or leave the cinema whenever they wished. The screenings often began around noon and went on until midnight.

Around 1911, longer films gained in popularity. This was one reason that in July 1911 Desmet switched over to the Deutsche Film Gesellschaft, which sold more long films. In this period he bought about 14 films a week, enough for two film programmes. He also stopped showing and renting the pre-assembled packages in their entirety, instead selecting individual films from those programmes and combining them into programmes of his own. Desmet's programmes were highly diverse, with a variety of genres. The films came mostly from France, but also from America, Italy, Germany and Denmark. The genres were often presented in a standard sequence: nature footage, newsreels, comedies and tragedies, in that order.

In 1912, when Desmet's customers became more demanding and started requesting a more varied assortment of long films, Desmet stopped buying films from the Deutsche Film Gesellschaft and began purchasing them directly from the production companies and their agents. A number of companies provided him with publicity materials, from which he selected films based on stills or a short description. The company archive shows that he sometimes went abroad to view films, but in general, sales representatives from Brussels or Berlin came to him to show their films.

By making the switch to dealing with individual production companies, Desmet acquired much greater freedom in the composition of his film programmes. He could now not only decide on the order of the films, but also personally select each film to be shown. Of course, he was still dependent on the offerings of the production companies, but the publicity materials show that he could choose from a wide assortment. For example, the French film company Eclair offered six films a week, of which he ordered just one on average. From this time on, his programmes always included a long film, which was often a monopoly film. This was a response to his audiences' wishes.

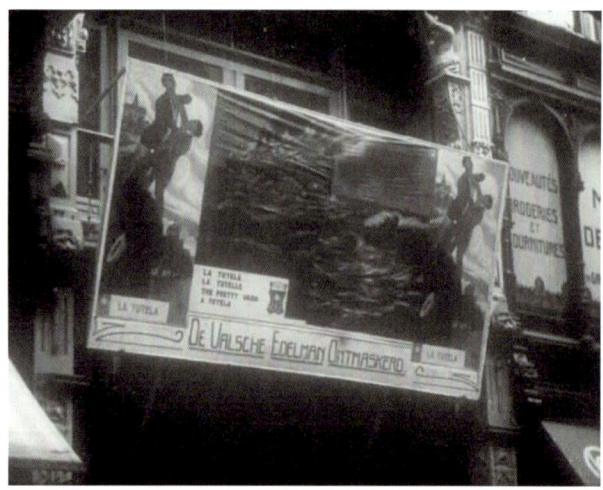

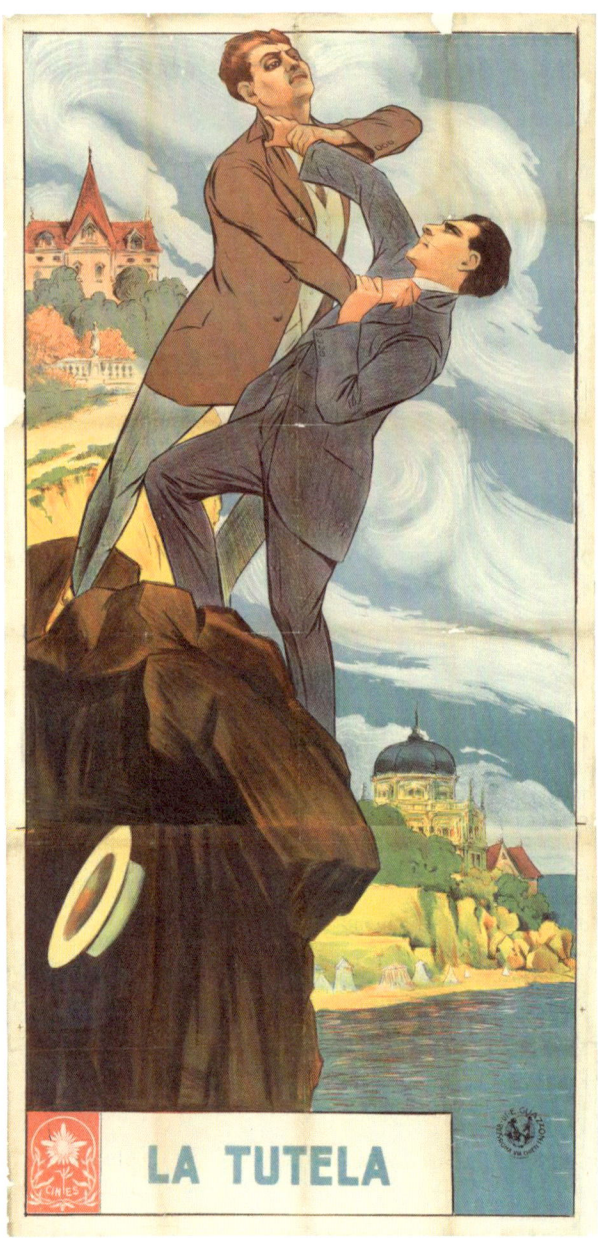

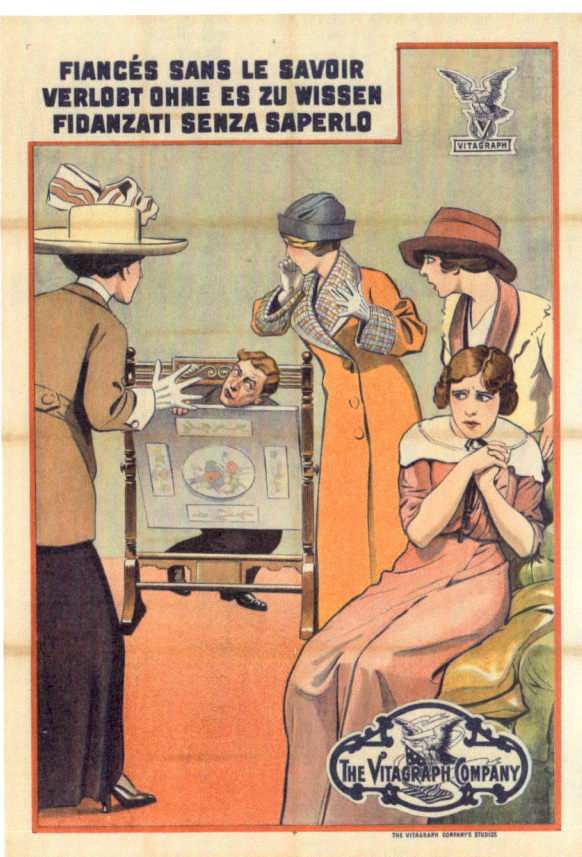

p. 136
Exterior of Cinema Parisien in Rotterdam. In September 1913 Jean Desmet commissioned a short report of the royal visit to Rotterdam (*Bezoek van de koninklijke familie te Rotterdam. Speciale opname voor de Cinema Royal. Eigenaar Jean Desmet*). Footage of Cinema Parisien and Cinema Royal was also shot. The film *La tutela* (1913) was playing at the time in Parisien.

Poster for *La tutela*, 1913
208 x 100 cm

p. 137
Poster for *La princesse solitaire*, 1913
140 x 100 cm

Jean Desmet's Film Programmes

In the years 1913 and 1914, Desmet's film programmes typically consisted of five to seven short films, with a combined length of about two hours. The main film, which was approximately 40 minutes long and often a drama, was combined with shorter films in various genres: non-fiction, comedy, farce and romance. The programme began with a non-fiction film, and the long film was in the middle, with comedies, farces or romantic films before and after. Great emphasis was placed on variety and the composition of the programme. For example, Desmet never concluded the programme with a drama that had an unhappy ending; such films were always followed by light comedies, so that the audience did not go home feeling gloomy. And when two comedies, or two films by the same production company, were shown one after the other, he always made sure that there was sufficient contrast between them.

The EYE collection includes not only more than 900 films shown by Desmet, but also newspaper articles and publicity materials. There are also a few film programmes in the collection, in the form in which they were shown by Desmet. The programme shown in the Cinema Royal from 29 August to 4 September 1913 began with a short non-fiction film, *Fleurs des champs* (1912), images of a variety of flowers and a brief dance by a woman in a butterfly costume. The second film, *Kasperl-Lotte* (1913) is about two children, Lotte and Hans. Lotte travels from place to place with a marionette theatre, and Hans lives with his grandmother and grandfather. When Hans rescues Lotte from boys who bully her after a performance, they become the best of friends, and in the end Hans's grandparents adopt Lotte too. The next film was *Il veleno delle parole* (1913), a long (40-minute) drama about a man who suspects his wife of adultery. He eventually shoots and kills her, but when he reads her diary afterwards, he discovers her innocence and is left alone and grieving. This dramatic film was followed by the lighter *Cutey Plays Detective* (1913), in which Freddy disguises himself as a housemaid to be close to the woman he loves. The programme concluded with *Broncho Billy's Narrow Escape* (1912), a Western about a man accused of horse theft, who is saved at the last moment by his sweetheart.

Artistically, these films do not show a strong resemblance to one another. Black-and-white films were combined with hand-coloured ones, and there were also large differences between their plots, themes and symbolism.

It seems that Desmet strove primarily for contrast in his programmes. Dramas were always alternated with lighter films and he never programmed two films in a row in the same genre, or with a shared theme.

Another example of a varied programme of this kind was shown in the cinema Gezelligheid in February 1914. In this case, the main film was the long drama *Gebrochene Schwingen* (1913), about a man named Fritz who has to leave his fiancée to earn money in America. After arriving there, he ends up down and out, and eventually tries to drown himself. The inventor of the parachute rescues him and Fritz returns to Germany. When he demonstrates the parachute there, he falls to his death before his fiancée's eyes. This drama was followed by *Solitaires* (1913), a comedy in which a writer's neighbour is mistaken for his fiancée when they pick up a ring for a friend together. She is spotted by a local gossip and showered with gifts and letters. In the end, the writer actually does ask her to marry him. Perhaps Desmet thought that after the long romantic drama *Gebrochene Schwingen*, the audience would be ready for a short romantic comedy such as *Solitaires*. He rented the film *Solitaires* to other exhibitors in combination with *Gebrochene Schwingen* a full nine times.

Another striking feature of Desmet's approach to programming was the lifespan of his films and their rental history. The film *Gebrochene Schwingen* can serve as a good illustration. Jean Desmet rented out this film a total of 43 times. After he purchased the film, on 19 October 1913, he first showed it in Amsterdam and then in Rotterdam. In both of these major cities, the film was screened in Desmet's Elite cinemas, the Cinema Palace and Cinema Royal, for the first week, and subsequently in his regular cinemas (the Parisien Amsterdam and Parisien Rotterdam). It took two months for this film to arrive at the Gezelligheid in Rotterdam, which was the eighteenth cinema to show *Gebrochene Schwingen*. After the first year, this film was no longer shown as regularly, but in general, Desmet went on renting out any given film for quite a while.

The End of an Era

Major changes occurred during and after the First World War. For one thing, the conflict knocked large holes in the pre-war infrastructure. Some of the routes by which films had come to the Netherlands were blocked, and production stagnated in some major film-producing countries, particularly France. At the same time, there were new competitors and new strategies. A novel practice came to Europe from the United States: in exchange for exclusive exhibition rights, distributors were forced to buy from just one company and give up a portion of their profits. This business method left no room for independent distributors who bought from various sellers. New entrants to the business, such as the wealthy Loet C. Barnstijn and Abraham Tuschinski, were willing to take much greater financial risks, and they developed expensive new publicity campaigns – for instance, they brought famous film stars from Hollywood or its German counterpart Babelsberg to the Netherlands.

A new transition period began, which was the end of the line for the first generation of distributors. Nöggerath, Gildemeijer and Desmet made way for their successors. Desmet left the film industry almost entirely. He stopped trading in films, sold almost all of his cinemas and focused on the property business. Only the Cinema Parisien in Amsterdam remained in his possession until his death.

This brought an end to Jean Desmet's substantial role in early Dutch cinema. As one of the earliest Dutch cinema owners and film renters, he had a profound influence on the groundbreaking changes that led, around 1910, to film's emergence as a mature industry and established a central place for the cinema in the world of Dutch entertainment.

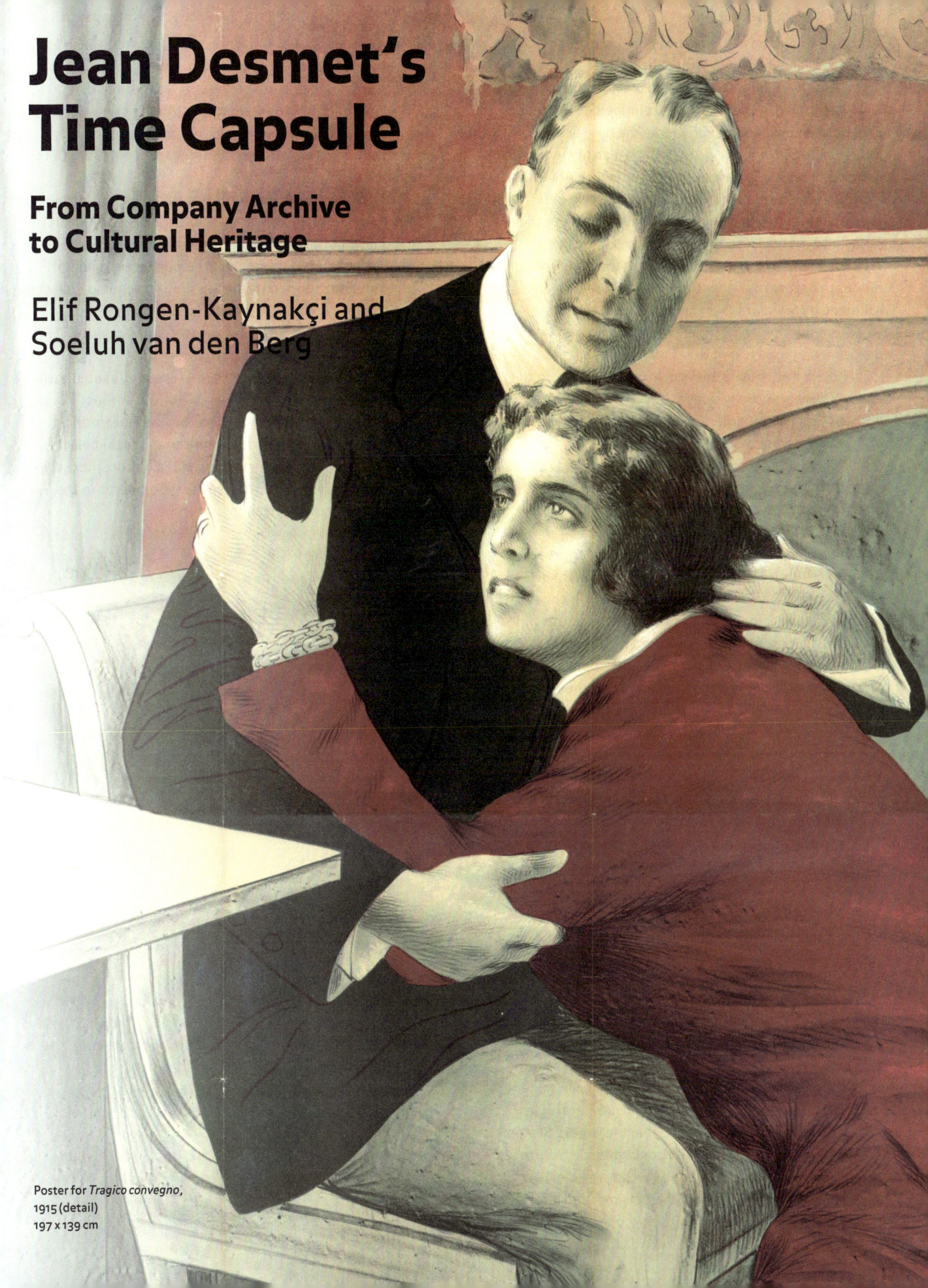

Jean Desmet's Time Capsule

From Company Archive to Cultural Heritage

Elif Rongen-Kaynakçi and
Soeluh van den Berg

Poster for *Tragico convegno*,
1915 (detail)
197 x 139 cm

The EYE Filmmuseum has established a formidable international reputation with its collection of early films. The Jean Desmet Collection is the unquestionable highlight of this collection and forms the basis for many of EYE's archival presentations today. The Desmet Collection, which does not consist solely of films, stands out as larger and more varied than most other collections of its kind. In 2010, EYE decided to nominate the Desmet Collection for UNESCO's Memory of the World Register, the world heritage list for documentary heritage considered of major significance to the collective memory of world history. The items inscribed on the register include the archives of the Dutch East India Company (VOC) and the diary of Anne Frank, as well as the films of pioneering French filmmakers Auguste and Louis Lumière and Fritz Lang's classic science fiction film *Metropolis* (1927).

EYE's goal in nominating the Desmet Collection was to underscore its international relevance. The institute wished to put the collection on the map as one of the richest sources of early film history and emphasize that its exceptional significance and richness lie in the combination of films, photographs, posters and paper documents, and not in one of its component parts. On the nomination form, EYE wrote:

> The collection consists not only of objects of artistic or film historical value, but also of non-artistic documents. The uniqueness of the collection is largely situated in the cohesion between the aesthetic and non-aesthetic parts. The detailed administration with correspondence, invoices, programmes, lists of acquisitions, sales and rentals is of enormous cultural and socio-historical value. The Desmet Collection conceals many stories about the 1910s that still need to be unveiled and that will give future generations a fascinating insight into a decade that proved to be fundamental for the development of modern culture and society . . . the strength of this collection is not so much that it contains several masterpieces, but on the contrary, that it gives a representation of daily programming, of supply and demand in both cultural and economic terms. The strength of the collection is therefore situated in the details; films and documents that are often marginalised gain enormous value within the relative context of a coherent collection.[1]

The announcement, in 2011, that the Desmet Collection would be inscribed on the Memory of the World Register represented an official acknowledgement of its universal value and raised the collection's international profile.[2]

The nomination process also influenced EYE's internal policy on the status and importance of the Desmet Collection, which is now seen not only as one of the museum's most valuable collections, but also as the one that most vividly illustrates the importance of the cohesion between the film collection and the film-related collections.

What we now call the Desmet Collection is the company archive of a businessman who was an extraordinarily successful film exhibitor and distributor from 1907 to 1916. The archive also covers the years before and after this period, up to the time of his death.[3] This provides us with a remarkably complete picture of Jean Desmet as an entrepreneur. The fact that he saved everything makes the collection a kind of time capsule. It is important both to conserve that time capsule and to make it accessible, so that it can be explored for purposes of exhibition and research.

Broadly speaking, the Desmet Collection has two parts, the film collection and the film-related collection. The film-related collection can be further broken down into photographs, posters, documents and objects. Because these components of the collection have to be stored under different conditions, they are physically separated from one another. Their separate registration systems always made it clear how each film or poster had entered the collection, but the link between them was not always immediately apparent. Furthermore, the emphasis for many years was on the parts of the collection most directly related to film history and the visual arts: films, stills and posters. Consequently, the company archive was relegated to a subordinate role during this time. Under those circumstances, there was no straightforward way to take a more integrated approach to the collection. But improved access strategies in recent decades have made it easier to access and work with the collection, thus changing the situation fundamentally.

The Film Collection

Jean Desmet purchased the films that he exhibited and distributed; they were his own property. He resold some of them to other parties, but the vast majority remained in his possession until his death. Interestingly, this led to the preservation not only of the feature films or generally recognized 'masterpieces', but also of dozens of comedies, newsreels, nature films, short romantic dramas, and so forth – films from the margins of film programming, which have not gained a prominent place in the standard accounts of film history and had, for the most part, been completely forgotten. These films provide an exceptionally rich picture of film culture in the period in question, and many of them can

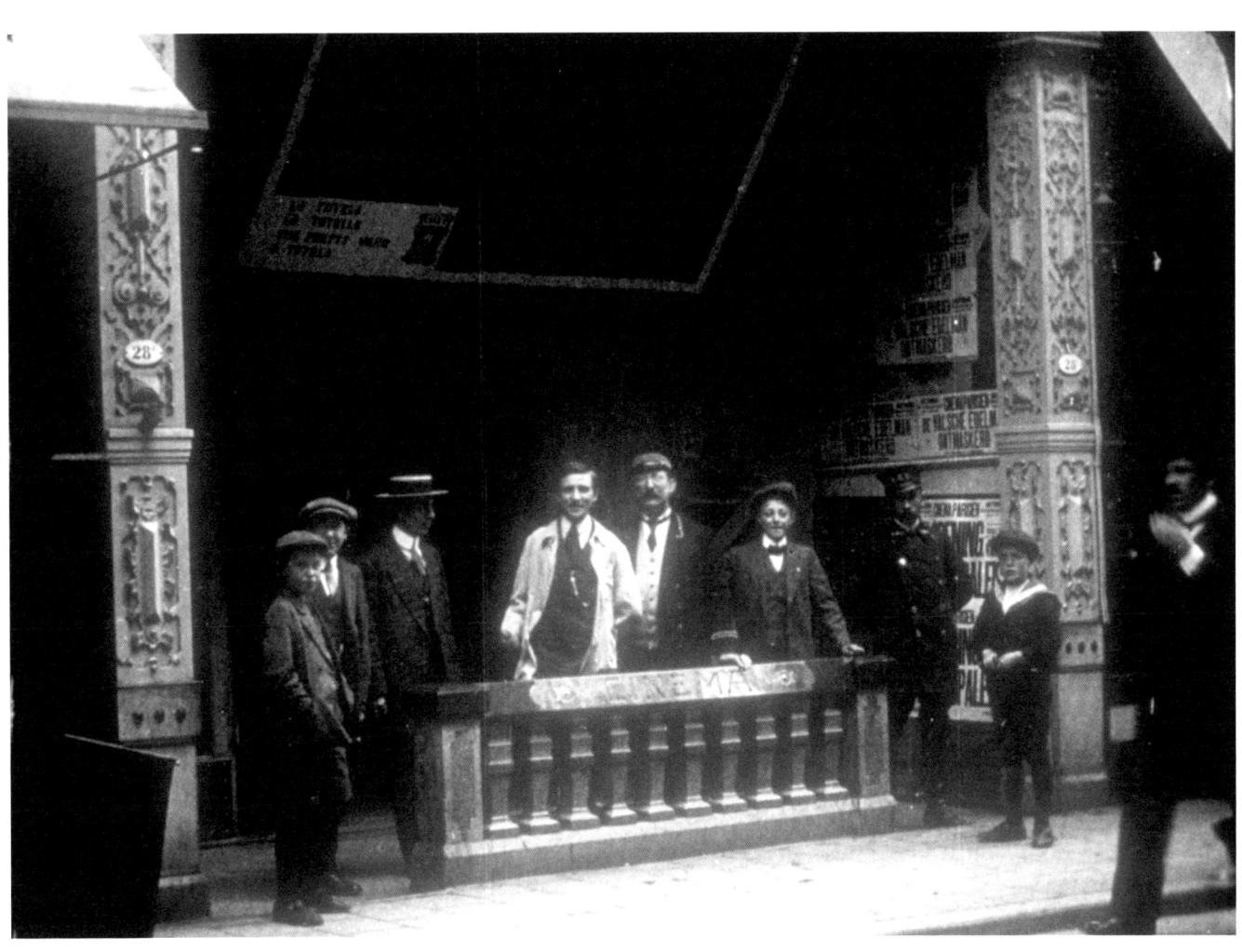

Entrance to Cinema Parisien (Rotterdam) with staff posing, 1913

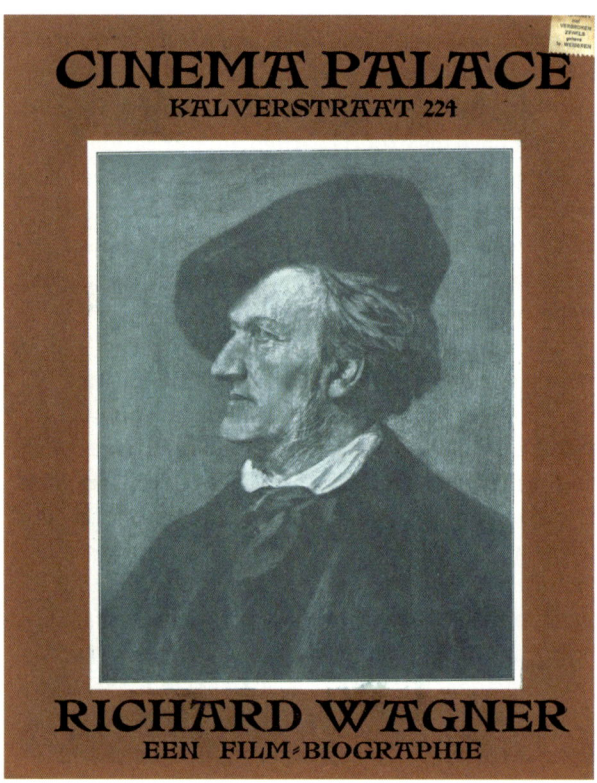

p. 142
Only very rarely did Desmet have a brochure printed in Dutch, as he did for the grand release of *Richard Wagner*, 1913

143
Brochure in Dutch published by Desmet for the historical film *Cajus Julius Caesar*, 1914

Still of *Cajus Julius Caesar*, 1914

now be found only in the Desmet Collection. Today at least 80 percent of all the silent films ever made are presumed lost. It is thus not surprising that so many of the films in the Desmet Collection are unique specimens; they are the only surviving copies in the world.

One important characteristic of the films in the Desmet Collection is that they are 'vintage' prints: original copies exhibited and distributed by Desmet at the time when the film was first released, rather than later reissues. This is important in that the colours are original, the intertitles date from the period and were often made specifically for the Dutch market, and the photographic quality is good. They are not the result of multiple generations of duplication, with the mediocre photographic quality that this would imply. In some cases, the negatives have survived in the original country of production, for instance in the case of the French Pathé studio or the Danish Nordisk Film. But these negatives do not include either colour or intertitles, and sometimes even the editing, the order of the scenes, is unclear. This is because the final versions of the films were assembled from the positive stock. The rationale for this method was that scenes from the film that were to be tinted the same colour in a dye bath were joined together on a single reel. This entire reel of film could then be tinted red or yellow, for instance, after which the scenes could be separated and then spliced together in the correct order, with the intertitles added. The intertitles were introduced during the final stages of production, especially if they had to be translated into other languages for international distribution. These 'vintage' prints are unique archival holdings and form a crucial source for scholars of world film history.

In 1957, when the hundreds of film cans arrived at the Nederlands Filmmuseum, they first had to be inspected and registered. Since cellulose nitrate, the base used in early films, is highly flammable, fire safety was a major concern in storing the films, and they were therefore placed in a special vault for nitrate films. In the 1950s, the exhibition of nitrate films came to a virtual halt for fire safety reasons, and non-flammable cellulose acetate became the preferred base for new productions. There were very occasional screenings of nitrate films, but in general, it is fair to say that the Filmmuseum stored the Desmet films like rare and costly wines, under safe and favourable conditions. This made it possible to keep all the films together, and so the time capsule survived in an integral form for a few more decades without being exposed to possible sources of damage.

Many films were difficult to identify at first. Most of them had Dutch titles, but the collection also includes American films with German titles, for instance, because

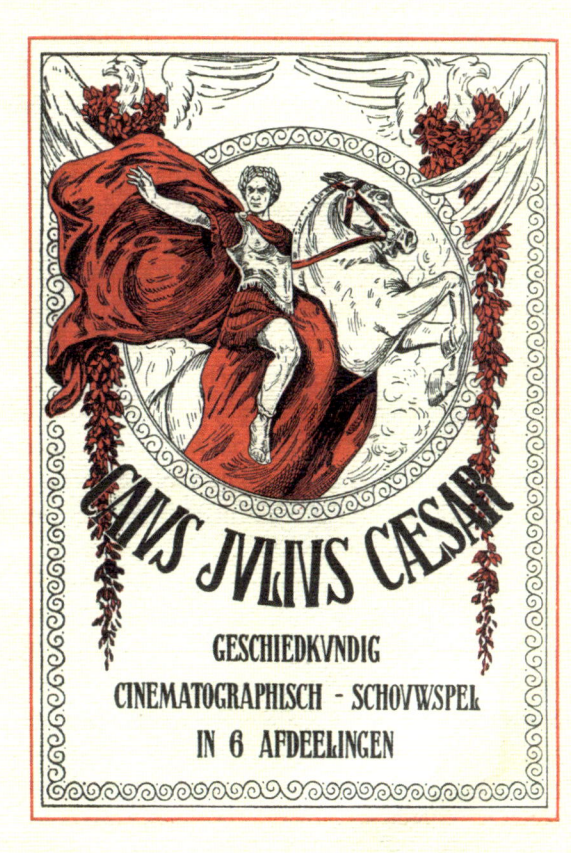

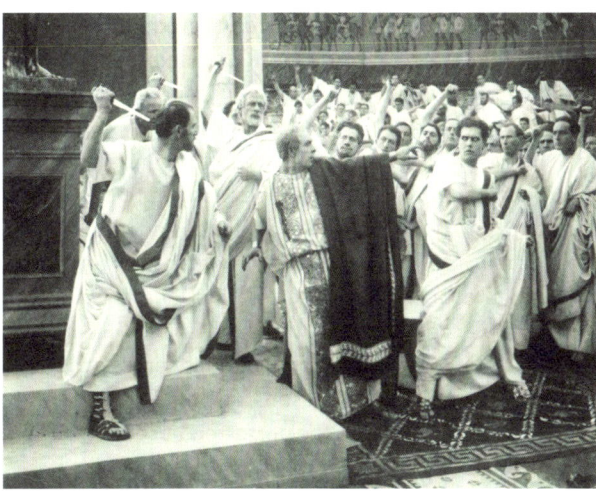

Desmet had bought the copies in Germany. The exact identity of many films was therefore not immediately apparent. Furthermore, the availability of source materials and documentation was still rather limited in the 1960s, and even in the 1980s and 1990s, identification was often a daunting challenge. By now, nearly all the films have been identified, although there are still a few that have the experts baffled. Identification is important not only for determining what we have in the collection, but also for deciding, in consultation with other archival institutions, just how exceptional a particular copy is and what the best strategy would be in the event of its restoration.

From the 1970s to the mid-1980s, the Filmmuseum's policy was to repatriate the foreign film material. This was standard practice among film archives at that time, not only because of the widespread belief that each country was responsible for the conservation of its own film heritage, but also due to the high costs of salvaging the film prints, some of which were in poor condition.[4] In the case of the Desmet Collection, this policy led the Filmmuseum to return a number of Danish, American, and German films to their countries of origin on a permanent basis. As a rule, it expected to receive one exhibition copy of each film in exchange. An initial selection of 35 films, which were considered urgent because they showed signs of serious nitrate decay, was sent to Denmark in 1972. Unfortunately, few exhibition copies were received in return. In 1990, when the Filmmuseum received additional funding and requested the return of the nitrate copies so that they could be restored in colour in the Netherlands, it transpired that at least half the material had already been destroyed due to decomposition. Archival institutions in the United States, such as the Library of Congress in Washington, the Museum of Modern Art in New York and the George Eastman House in Rochester, likewise received film materials from the Filmmuseum, but this exchange programme proved too complex to be viable, as it involved many institutions, each with different policies. In the case of Germany, the films were sent to the storage facilities of the West German film archives in Koblenz. Although most of these films were returned in the 1990s, a few of them were lost forever.

Until the mid-1980s it was not seen as a priority to make projection copies – let alone to restore the films. Because most of the films in the collection had not been made in the Netherlands and the Filmmuseum devoted its limited resources to the conservation of Dutch films, the Desmet films had to wait for better days. Those better days arrived in the mid-1980s, a time of growing appreciation for the collection's cultural heritage value. Frank van der Maden was appointed as the curator of the collection and started to accession the films. He kept up a prolific correspondence with other archival institutions and experts, also including the posters and publicity materials in his research programme.

Around that time, the first experiments with colour preservation of silent films were taking place, and the films in the Desmet Collection were starting to draw international attention through Van der Maden's research network. In 1990, the conservation of the Desmet films received a tremendous boost when the Filmmuseum was awarded additional funds for film preservation. Preserving the original colours of early cinema became a prime objective of the Filmmuseum, and this work was focused primarily on the prints in the Desmet Collection.[5]

By now, almost all the nitrate films in the Desmet Collection have been preserved on non-flammable acetate or polyester film. Besides the potential fire hazard, the chemical instability of the nitrate base is another major reason for making duplicates of such films on a more chemically stable base. Remarkably, in the case of the Desmet Collection, fairly little material has been lost to cellulose nitrate decomposition. We now know that over the past 50 years, only 3 per cent of the film material originally donated to the museum has had to be destroyed as a result of nitrate decay. A few films are regarded as 'not presentable', because they consist of mere fragments or are so incomplete that a viewer could no longer follow them if they were preserved in their current state. These reels are passively preserved in the EYE archives, particularly when elements in better condition are known to exist elsewhere.

To make the films more widely available, EYE initially transferred them to video and, starting in the mid-1990s, digitized them on DVD-quality Digital Betacam tapes. Because broadcasting companies and websites have recently begun to prefer high-definition scans, all 35mm preservation copies are now being scanned again at a much higher resolution, in keeping with present-day standards.

The Film-Related Collections

Film archives specialize in preserving film material. But every film archive knows that film history does not consist entirely of celluloid. The production, distribution and exhibition of films involves a wide variety of other materials, which vary from paper (letters, screenplays, design sketches, photographs and posters) to textile and wood (for costumes and set pieces) and even machines (cameras and projection equipment). The Desmet Collection proves this point. In addition to the reels of film, it includes an astonishing number of paper documents, as well as furniture from Amsterdam's Cinema Parisien.

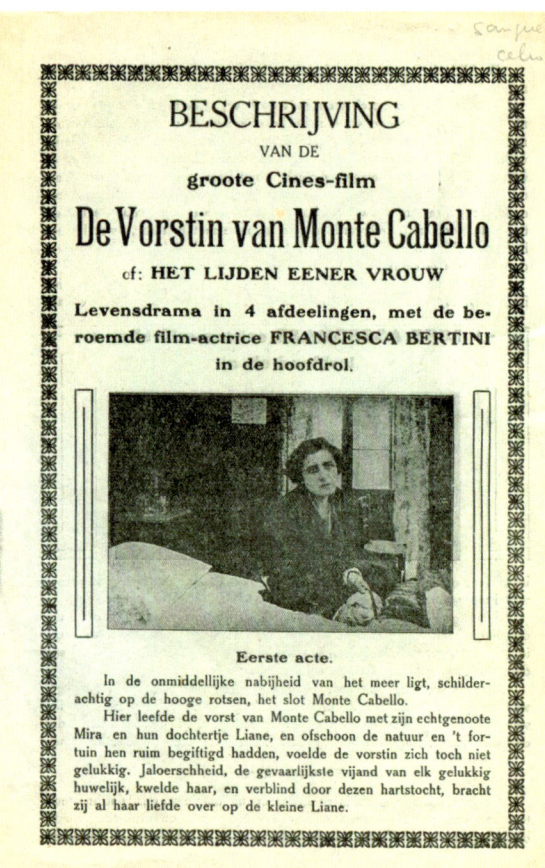

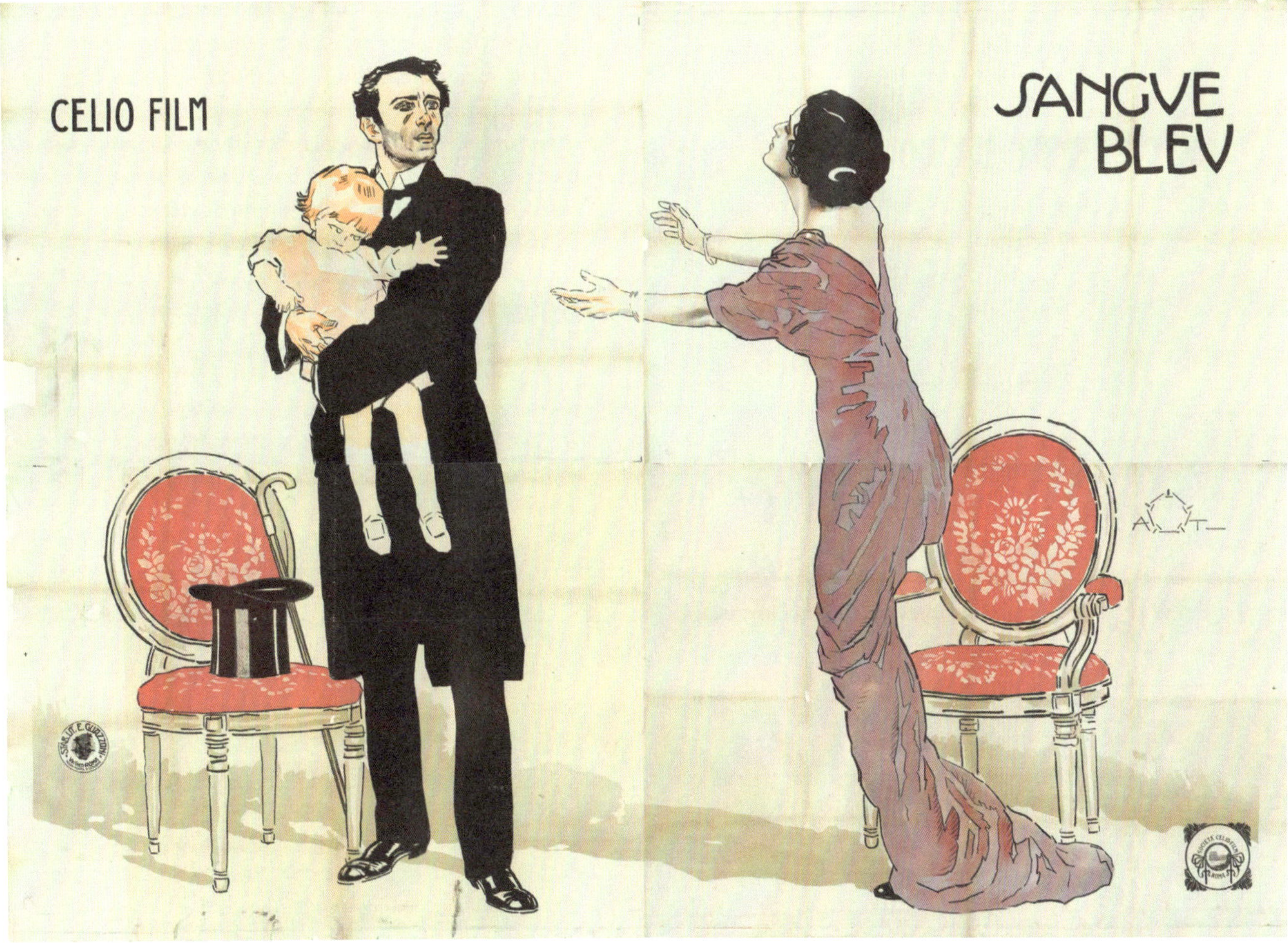

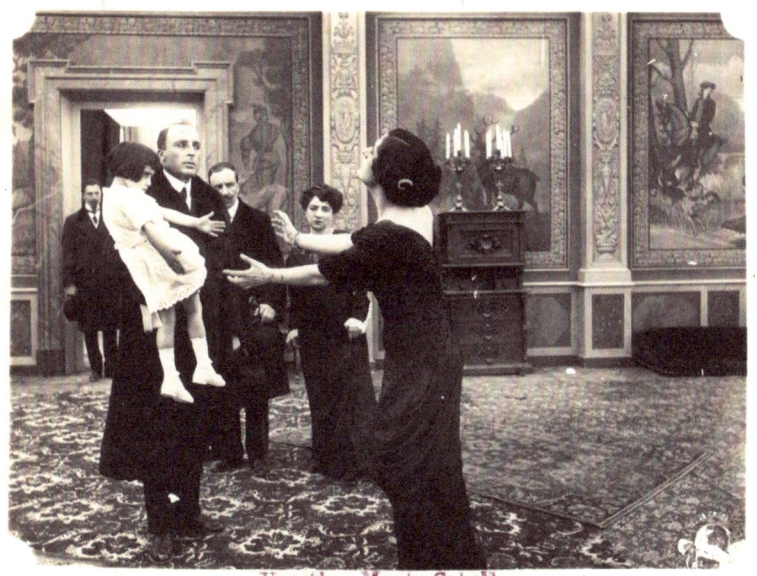

p. 144
In this Dutch brochure the film *Sangue bleu* is referred to as *De Vorstin van Monte Cabello of Het lijden eener vrouw*

p. 145
Original poster for *Sangue bleu*, 1914
280 x 200 cm

Still of *Sangue bleu* with the imprint of the Dutch title 'Vorstin – Monte Cabello'

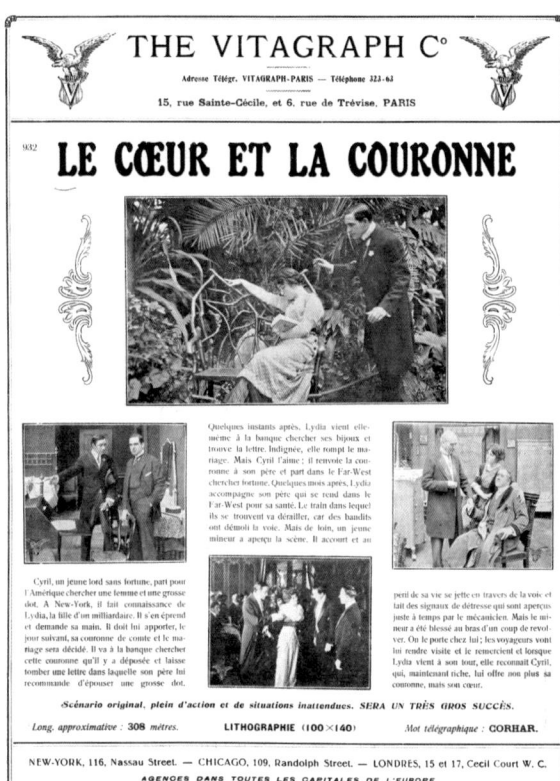

p. 146
Vitagraph produced fine publicity material with pictures and extensive film descriptions to advertise its wares among European film exhibitors

p. 147
Invoice from German camera producer Ernemann for machine parts, 1912

Acquisition letter from Dutch Advertisement Office to interest Jean Desmet in advertising in trams

Order form belonging to Desmet featuring the logos of 22 international film producers that he worked with, c. 1911

As early as 1957, the Filmmuseum included a clause in its collection policy relating to what are now called the 'film-related collections', for 'the acquisition of a permanent collection of screenplays, film photographs, literature on film, musical recordings, film set designs, posters and other production and development-related materials, press clippings, filming devices, etc., in order to make the film museum complete in technical, historic and aesthetic terms'.[6] Later that year, a very important step was taken: the acquisition of parts of Jean Desmet's archive that met this description.

The films, photographs and posters came into the museum's possession that first year, and the company archive followed in the course of the 1960s. In 1962, for example, the correspondence copy books and a few other volumes were handed over to the museum, followed by the business records of the Cinema Parisien in 1968. It was not until 1970 that the museum acquired the crucial core of the company archive: 60 office binders containing accounts, other records and correspondence. This essentially completed the transfer of the collection.[7]

There was, however, one noteworthy addition in the late 1980s: the Art Deco interior of Amsterdam's Cinema Parisien was offered to the Nederlands Filmmuseum in 1987, when the building was slated for demolition. After a few minor adjustments, the interior was installed in the Filmmuseum cinema, then located in the Vondelpark Pavilion. In 2010, the Filmmuseum became part of the new EYE Film Institute (now the EYE Filmmuseum). When EYE moved to its present location in 2012, the Cinema Parisien interior was removed from the pavilion to be installed in one of the theatres in the Amsterdam cinema De FilmHallen in 2014. In the new EYE building on the IJ, special light effects were installed in the small theatre to evoke the original 1920s interior of the Cinema Parisien.

Among the film-related parts of the Desmet Collection, the posters and photographs began to receive attention soon after 1957. The stills were incorporated into the Filmmuseum's stills collection, and in 1960 almost all the posters with dimensions up to 72 x 104 cm were registered. Larger posters required more space, which was not yet available. In 1962, work could begin on cataloguing the larger posters, but making them accessible was a slower process. The annual report for 1969 stated that almost 800 posters in the Desmet Collection had been catalogued. Until about 1980, the Filmmuseum's poster collection was actively managed and described, but after that it fell into neglect. Starting in 1988, under new management, the museum took charge of the situation and, for the first time, accessioned both the posters and the stills into a database.

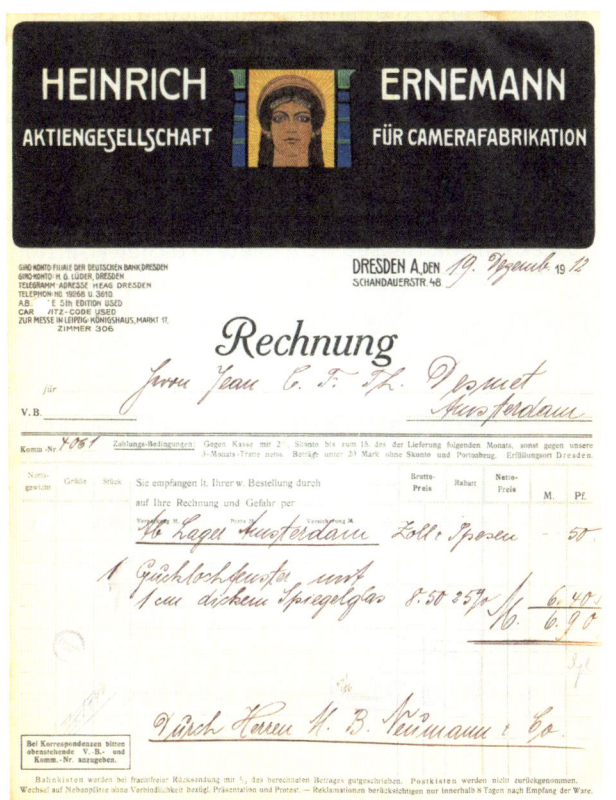
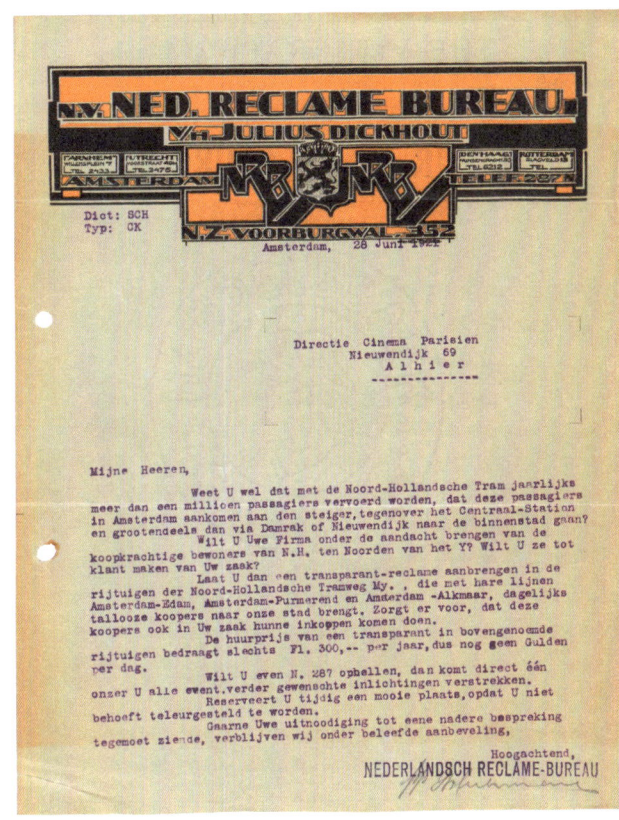
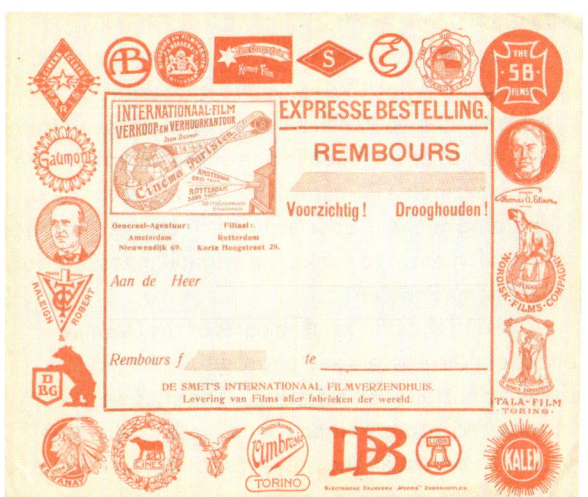

The publicity materials were added to the database and made accessible by title, mostly in the years 1992-1993. Most of the publicity flyers and brochures in the Desmet Collection are in foreign languages. Desmet had Dutch-language brochures printed only rarely, for instance as part of the large-scale publicity campaigns for *Richard Wagner* (1913) and the historical film *Cajus Julius Caesar* (1914). Given that much publicity material was clearly lost in a fire in the Parisien in 1938, this claim cannot be made with complete certainty. In any case, Desmet left behind a very large number of French and English-language flyers. Major studios such as Vitagraph supplied attractive materials for each film, with illustrations and descriptions of the storyline that are very helpful in identifying and describing the films. A few studios, such as Éclair in France, are represented mainly by flyers containing weekly programmes. These were intended partly as catalogues from which Desmet could place his orders, and partly to provide descriptions of storylines.

Desmet did often produce handbills with Dutch descriptions of the story, usually in bright colours, and with his own Dutch title replacing the original. Remarkably, some films were promoted several times, under a different Dutch title every time. For example, the Italian film *Sangue bleu* (1914) is known under the titles *Het lijden van een vrouw* (The suffering of a woman), *Het lijden eener vrouw* (A woman's suffering), and *De vorstin van Monte Cabello* (The Princess of Monte Cabello).

It took many years to accession the company archive. An initial list of the files was made in the 1980s, but the actual inventorying did not begin until 1994. Later, the inventory was improved and published on the Internet in connection with the Metamorfoze digitization project in the years 2008-2011.[8] The 120,000-page archive can now be consulted in digitized form in the EYE library.

For years, the stills were kept in office folders without any form of climate control. In the mid-1980s, they were moved to a storage facility that offered a stable climate, but it was not until 2009-2012, with the digitization project Beelden voor de Toekomst (Images for the Future), that ideal preservation conditions were achieved: the stills were individually packaged in special photo envelopes and stored under controlled conditions. Furthermore, almost all the stills are now available digitally in high resolution. There is thus hardly any need to examine the physical artefacts any longer, and potentially damaging physical contact with them can be kept to a minimum.

For many years, the posters were the only part of the film-related collections to be actively preserved or restored. In the 1960s, current preservation methods were applied to the Desmet posters. The Filmmuseum and the Stedelijk Museum Amsterdam had jointly developed a new method that was adopted by the International Federation of Film Archives (FIAF) and described in the brochure 'Preservation of Film Posters', published in 1967. The most important step in this method was to reinforce the edges of the posters with adhesive tape. Folds were also reinforced on the back of the poster if they started to tear. The posters thus treated, which were considerably sturdier, were then hung vertically on special racks from a cardboard hanger attached to the back of the upper edge with adhesive tape. This made it possible to store a large number of posters with a limited surface area. It was also a reasonably user-friendly method, since it was possible to leaf through the posters.

But after a few years, the disadvantages of this solution became clear: the tape hardened and the glue showed through on the front side in the form of brown stains. The new manager of the poster collection issued a correction to the aforementioned brochure in 1971, stating that the use of adhesive tape was no longer recommended. The storage method also created problems: many posters fell off the hangers sooner or later, piling up underneath the racks. Obviously, this led to further damage.

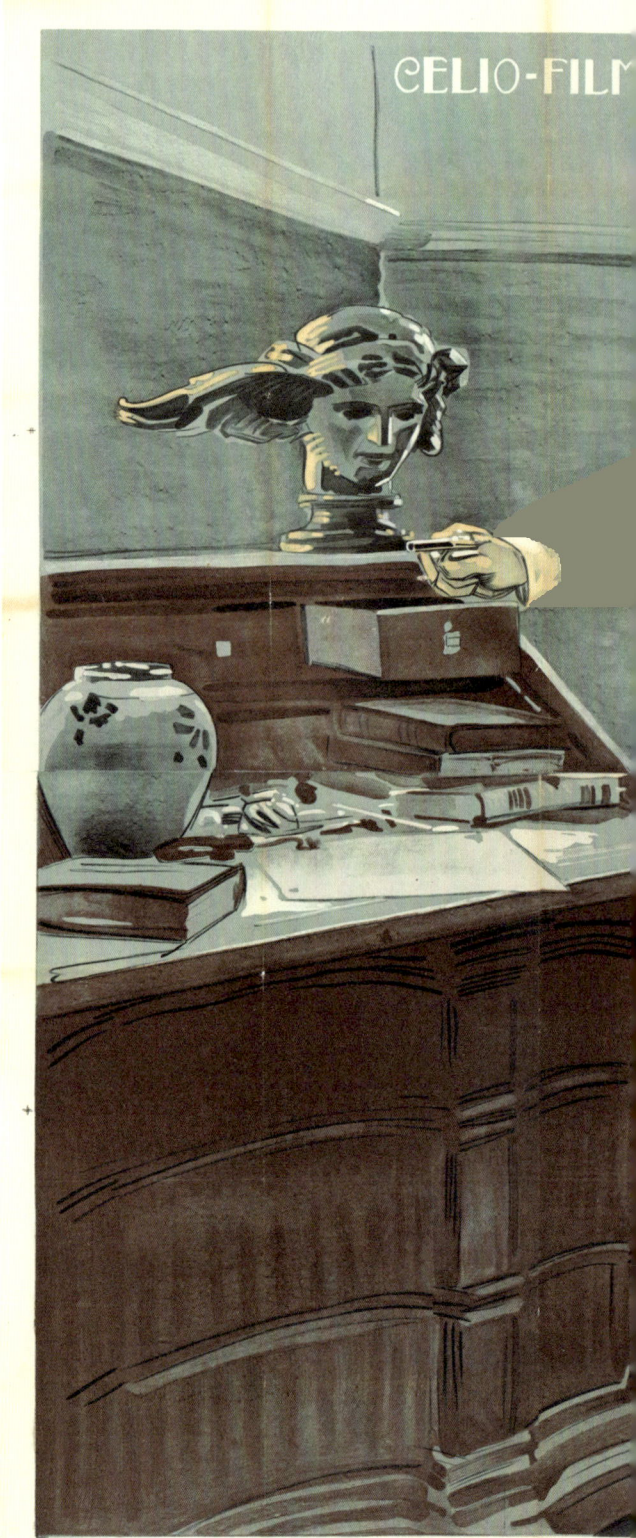

Poster for *Tragico convegno*,
1915
200 x 279 cm

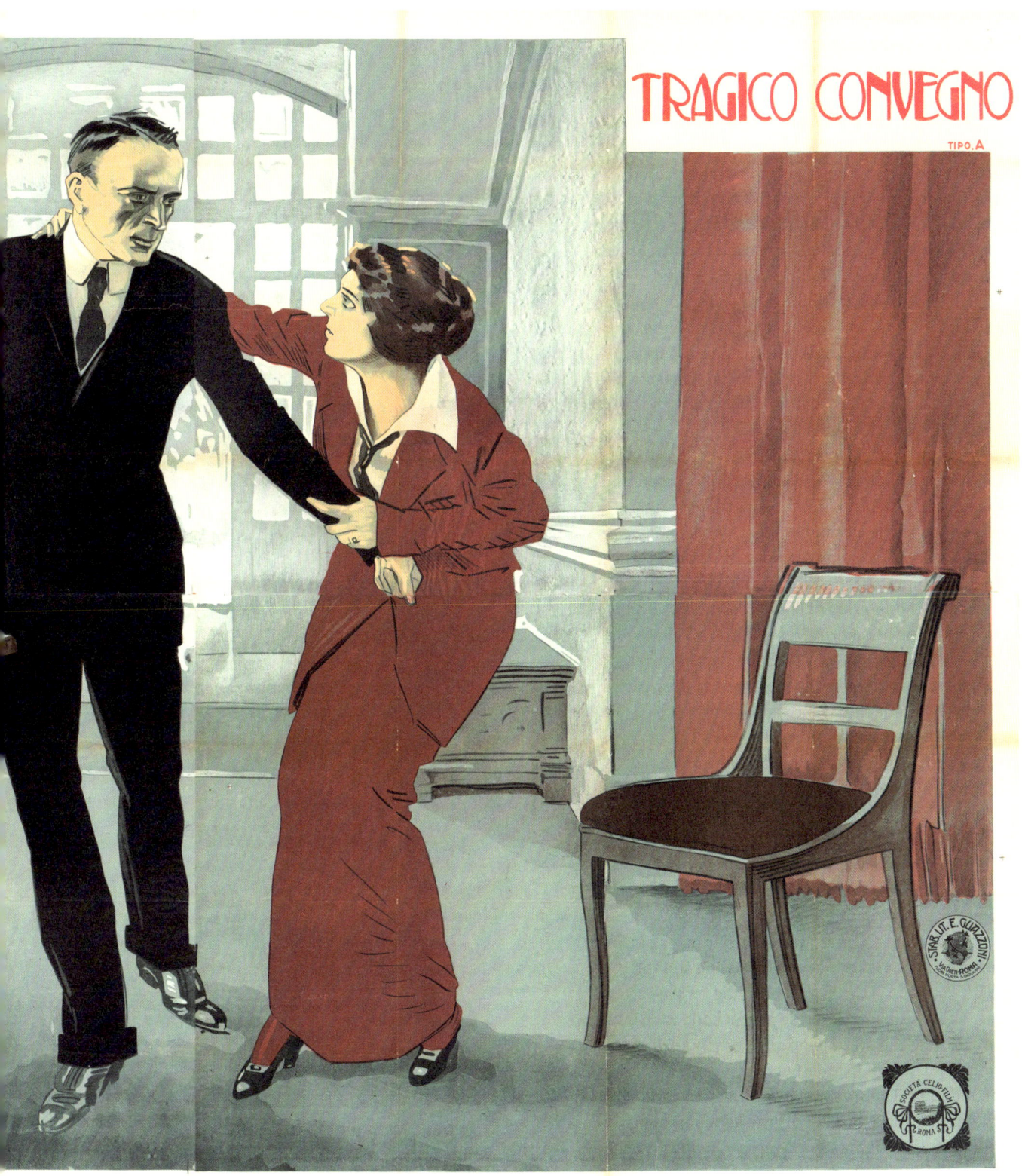

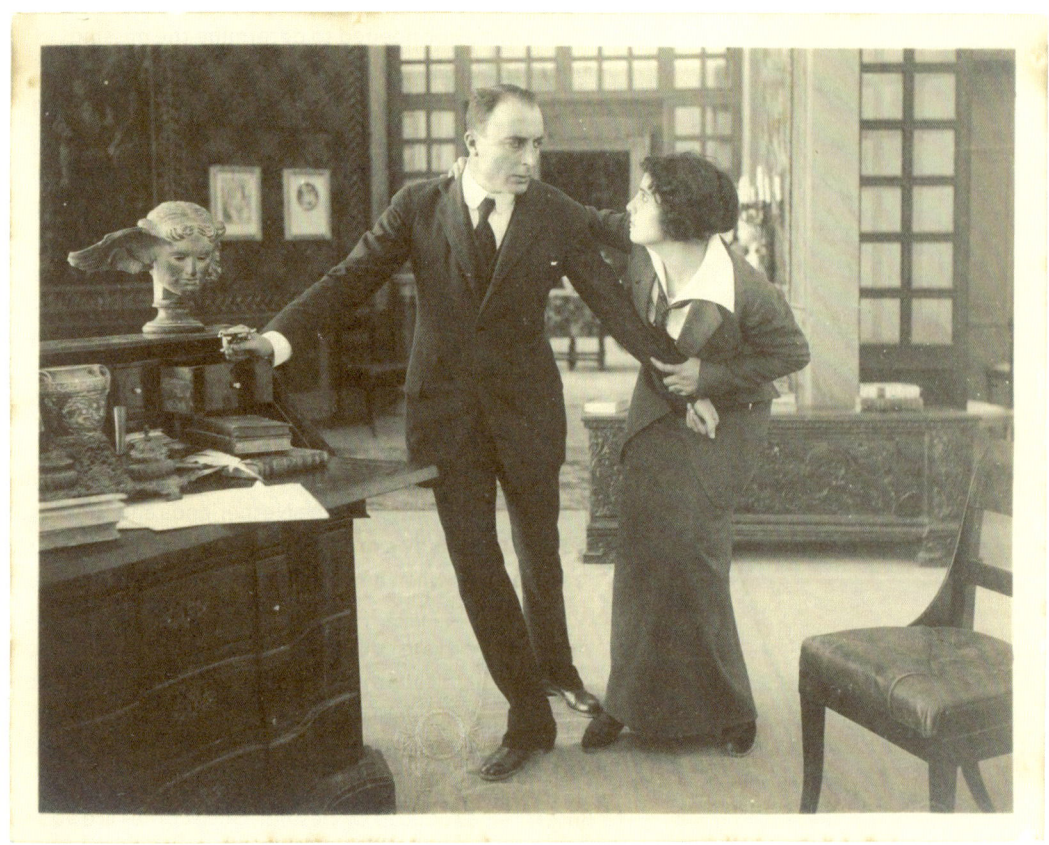

In the late 1980s, a new method was adopted: laying posters down flat in special acid-free poster folders. The problem of the adhesive tape, which had been used on many of the posters, most of them from the Desmet Collection, was tackled as part of the restoration project Deltaplan voor Cultuurbehoud (Delta Plan for the Preservation of Cultural Heritage, 1996-2000). The tape was removed and the posters repaired through a labour-intensive procedure. As part of the European Film Gateway project relating to the First World War, 850 Desmet posters were digitized in high resolution and made accessible online in 2012.[9]

Caring for a Collection of 'Global Significance and Exceptional Universal Value'

Since the inscription of the Desmet Collection on the Memory of the World Register in 2011, EYE has placed greater emphasis on the cohesion between the different parts of the collection. Over the years, the components of the Desmet Collection had been driven apart, so to speak, and had become more or less indistinguishable from other EYE holdings: Desmet films were kept with other films, Desmet posters with other posters and so forth. The present curatorial policy stresses the importance of keeping the different parts of the collection together, in the firm belief that the collection is more than the sum of its parts and can yield new insights and enrich our knowledge. Although certain elements sometimes require special treatment, there are extraordinary advantages to having a general overview and direct access to the full range of complementary collections.

One recent illustration of these advantages is the conservation and reconstruction of *Tragico convegno* (1915). The nitrate print of this film did not reach the archive until the year 2000, and the last of the original three reels was missing. Nevertheless, EYE decided to restore this film in 2013, with the aid of materials from the film-related collections. At first, it seemed that the end of the story would remain unknown, but a

p. 150
Still of *Tragico convegno*, 1915. Five of the twelve available original photographs were used in the reconstruction of *Tragico convegno* to replace missing scenes.

p. 151
Programme leaflet from Helder's first cinema in Den Helder for the week 25 February–2 March 1917, which included a description of *Tragico convegno*, 1915

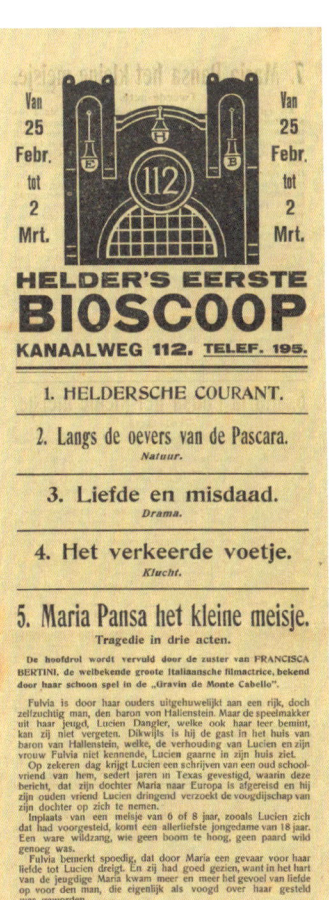

programme flyer from the Desmet Collection supplied the information needed to determine the missing ending of this lost film. The use of stills from the collection made it possible to reconstruct the ending through a combination of text and images.

The case of *Tragico convegno* also illustrates that the film collection is still growing. There is no definitive list of all the films released by Desmet, and we know that by 1957, when the collection was donated to the Filmmuseum, a few major films were already missing. During the First World War, Desmet had sold some of his reels of film for use as leaders for other films. Until 1927, he occasionally sold films to other distributors, such as Van Duinen and Ed. Pelster.[10] When Desmet felt that a feature film was particularly important, he would buy exclusive rights for 'the Netherlands and the Dutch East Indies', and he probably sold some of these films to other parties when he left the film distribution business. Even today, EYE now and then receives copies of such films from private collectors. These sometimes include added intertitles with the logos of other film distributors; in that case, the copy is not officially added to the Desmet Collection. But other film copies, such as that of *Tragico convegno*, include the original and exclusive intertitles produced by Desmet. Such copies are added to the Desmet Collection, where they clearly belong. Missing posters for Desmet films are also donated on a fairly regular basis; these too provide new information relevant to the other parts of the collection.

Conclusion

The Desmet Collection was initially seen as a goldmine in which the lost masterpieces of well-known directors and actors could be rediscovered, but today, the 'Desmet Collection' label has grown in importance, and the collection as a cohesive whole has come to outweigh its parts.

In the past, single films from the collection got selected for screening at festivals, often without any reference to their origin in the Desmet Collection. But nowadays, there are more and more requests for a specially curated Desmet compilation. Researchers and programme curators are encouraged to use Desmet materials of all kinds; as a result, the posters and stills can be found with growing frequency in festival catalogues and magazines, and DVDs sometimes even include bonus galleries of such images, with an emphasis on their Desmet origins.[11]

In an internal memo from 1988, curator Frank van der Maden commented on the films preserved in the two preceding years: 'the use of the phrase "already preserved" suggests that the titles on this list can be regarded as fully dealt with. Unfortunately, that is not always the case . . .'

By now, it has become clear that work on a collection of this size is never 'fully dealt with'. Furthermore, concepts such as 'preservation' and 'access' are becoming ever more complex with the emergence of new analogue and digital technologies and new modes of presentation (online or otherwise). Today, the policies of archival institutions are regularly put to the test by the incredibly rapid pace of technological innovation. Applying the latest technologies to a collection on the Desmet scale represents a major challenge. Nevertheless, EYE is fully committed to keeping the collection together, preserving it under optimal conditions and making it as broadly accessible to the public as possible, in the ever-growing awareness of its universal value.

1
UNESCO's Memory of the World Register nomination form, submitted in 2010. Available at http://www.unesco.org/new/en/communication-and-information/flagship-project-activities/memory-of-the-world/register/full-list-of-registered-heritage/registered-heritage-page-2/desmet-collection/.

2
In 2011, EYE received a special medal from Le Giornate del Cinema Muto, Pordenone, Italy. In 2012, EYE won the FOCAL International Award for the best archival restoration or preservation project from Focal International in London.

3
The Desmet Collection consists of: 922 films on 35mm nitrate (fiction and non-fiction), 1,032 posters in various languages, c. 2,500 items of publicity material, 1,454 stills, and company documents: 24 shelf metres, more than 120,000 items. See the filmography and list of posters in the back of this book.

4
Until the late 1990s, film archives focused on preserving chemically unstable and inflammable nitrate films by copying them onto stable, non-flammable bases. In some countries, this led to the rapid duplication of nitrate films onto an acetate base, and sometimes to the destruction of the original nitrate copy after the process. Recent research and improved methods of passive preservation have yielded the insight that nitrate copies can be preserved much longer than previously supposed. Furthermore, acetate material is subject to 'vinegar syndrome', a form of decay at least as serious as nitrate decomposition. To avoid this problem, films are now preserved on a polyester base.

5
The Nederlands Filmmuseum's policy of studying, preserving, restoring and exhibiting the original colours led to the worldwide reappraisal of colour in early cinema. In 1995 the Filmmuseum organized the Amsterdam workshop 'Disorderly Order: Colours in Silent Film'. EYE still adheres to this preservation and research policy, as illustrated by the conference 'The Colour Fantastic', which the institute will hold in March 2015, and the publication of the book *Fantasia of Color* by T. Gunning, G. Fossati and J. Yumibe, which contains a host of frame enlargements from films in EYE's nitrate collection.

6
Jan de Vaal, 'Richtlijnen voor de ontwikkeling van het Nederlands Filmmuseum', January 1957.

7
Annual reports of the Nederlands Filmmuseum for 1962, 1968 and 1970.

8
See http://www.filmgerelateerdecollecties.blogspot.nl, under 'Archief inventarissen'. Please note: Only the inventory is available online at this time. For now, the digitized documents can be consulted only in the EYE library. Metamorfoze is the national programme for the conservation of paper heritage, financed by the Dutch Ministry of Education, Culture & Science.

9
See www.europeanfilmgateway.eu. The direct link to the EYE posters is http://www.europeanfilmgateway.eu/node/33/efg1914%20EYE%20Film%20Instituut%20Nederland/multilingual:1/showOnly:image.

10
I. Blom, *Jean Desmet and the Early Dutch Film Trade* (Amsterdam, 2003), 330-331.

11
Examples include the DVDs of the Thanhouser Collection and *Sangue bleu*, both released in 2014.

Rich and Poor

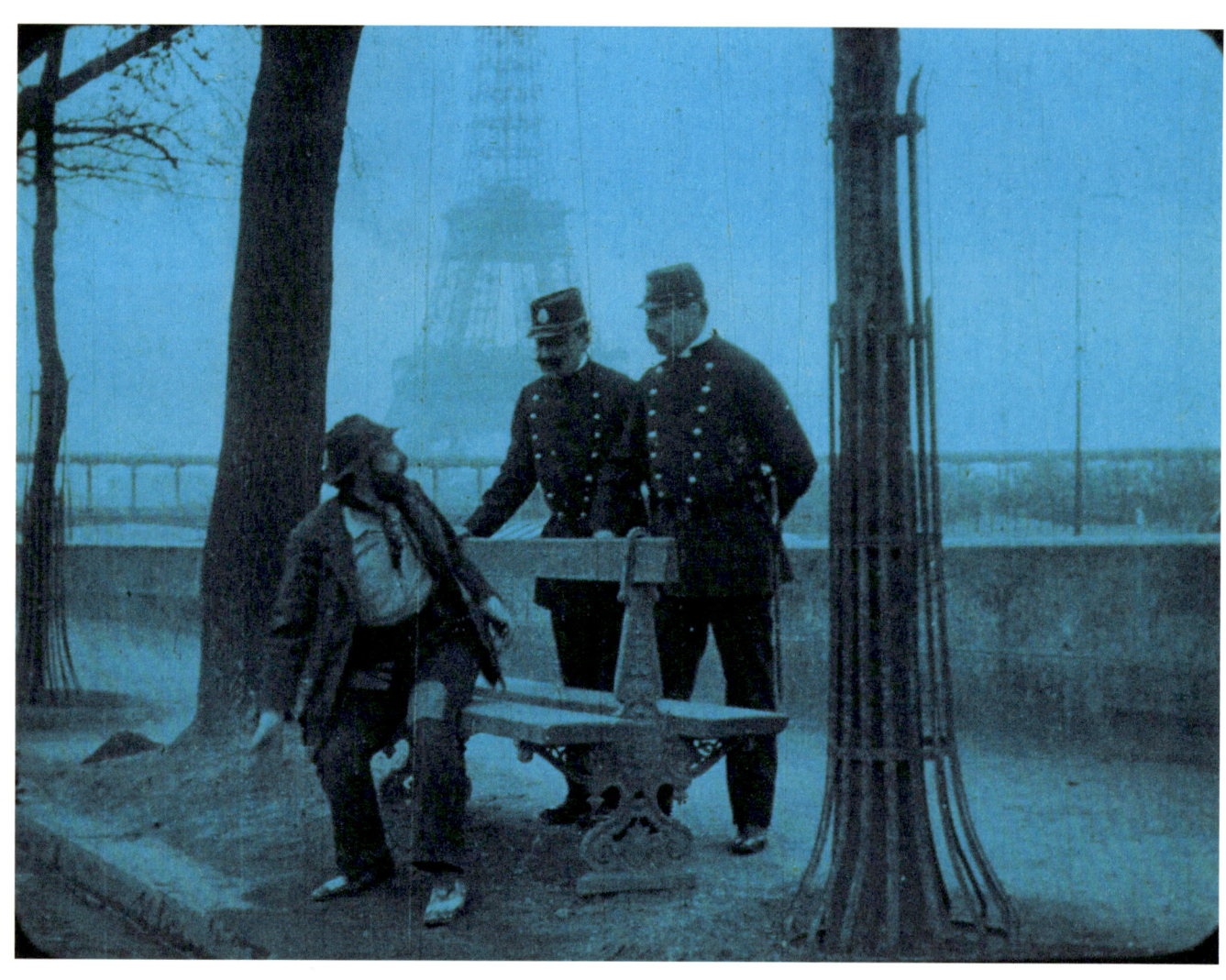

p. 154
André Heuzé, *Lutte pour la vie*, 1907

p. 155
The High Born Child and the Beggar, 1913

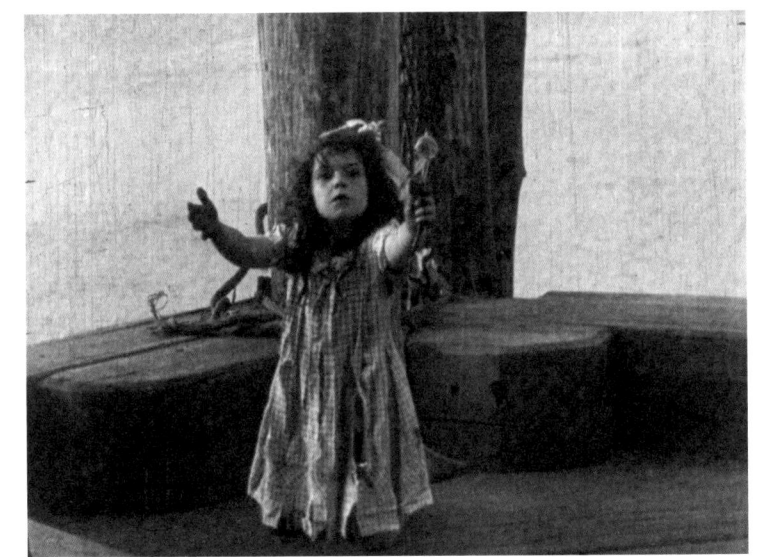

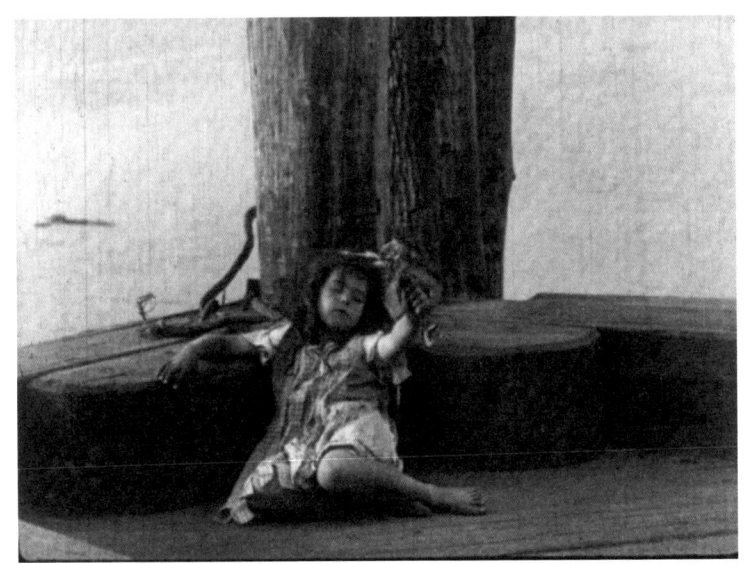

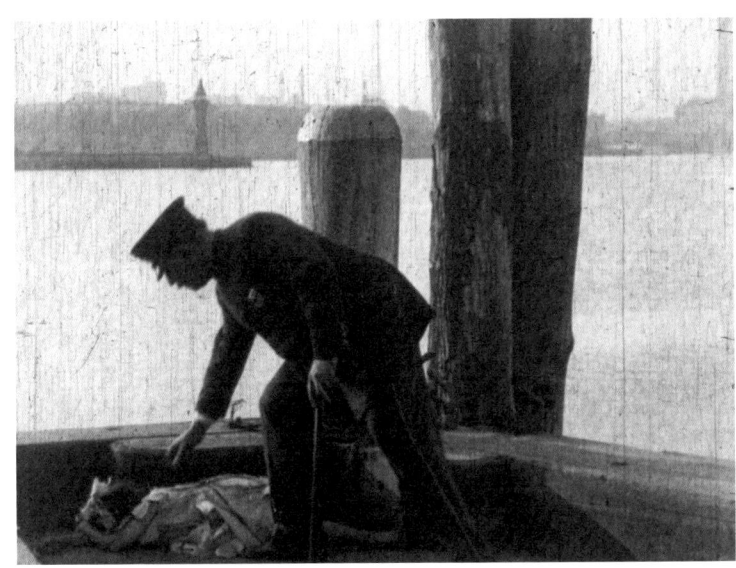

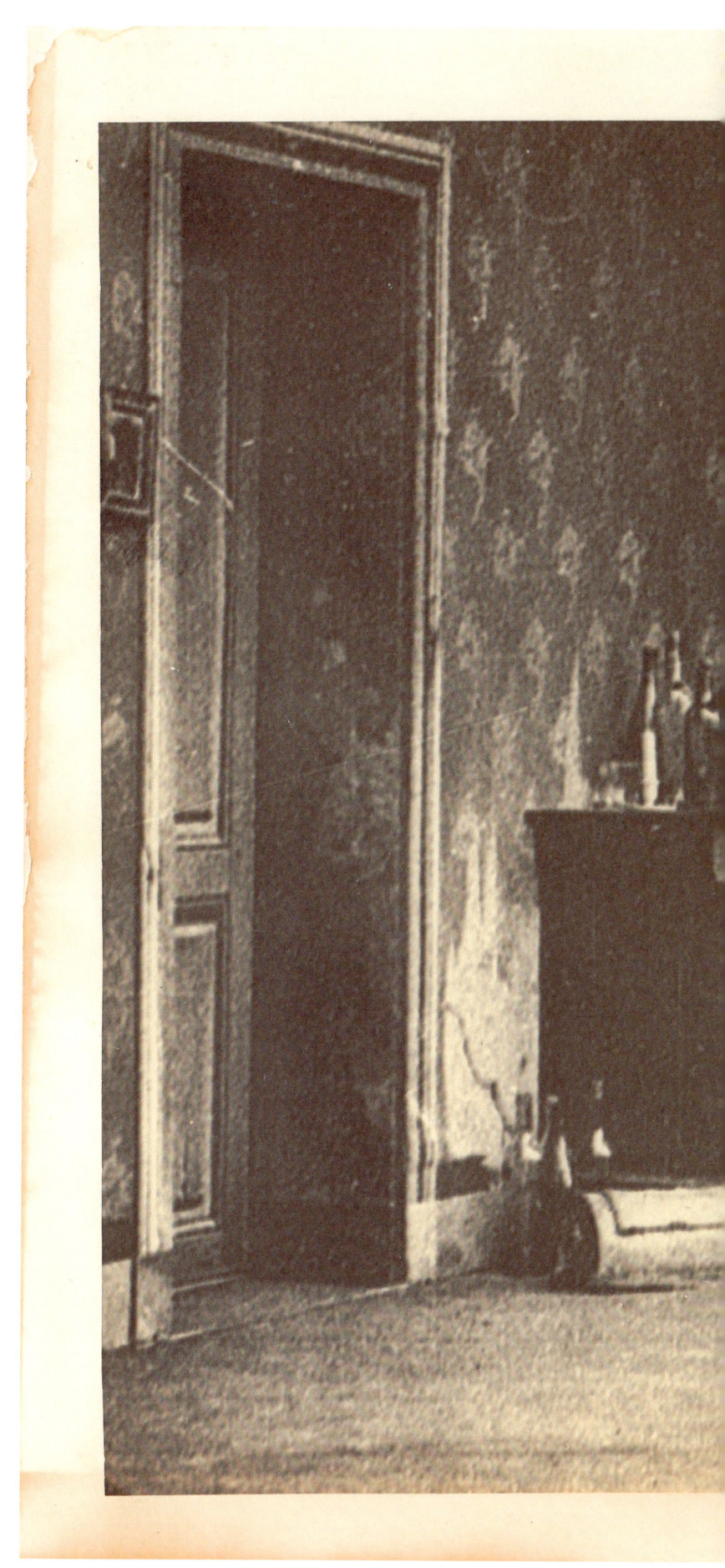

Still of Albert Capellani,
L'assommoir, 1909

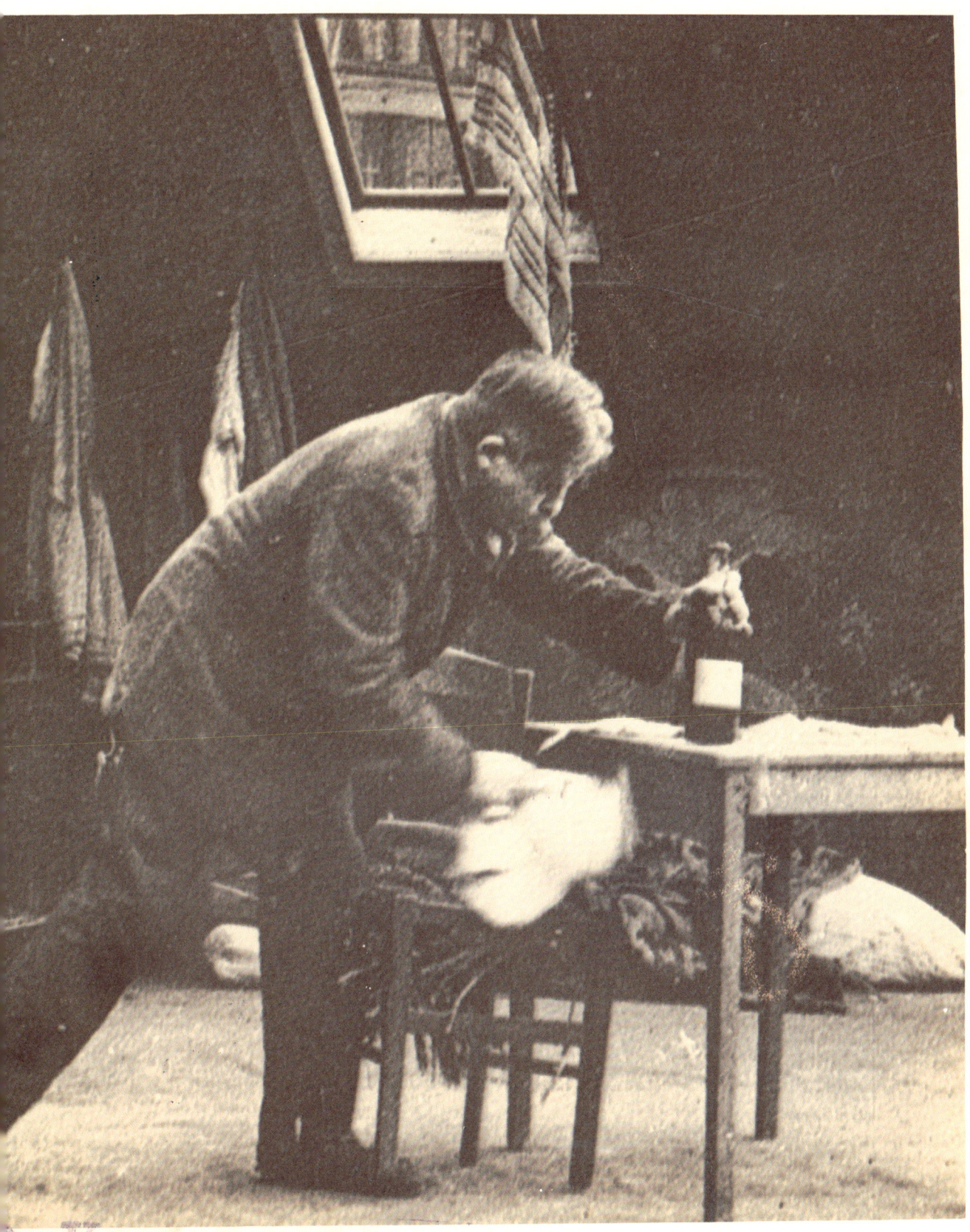

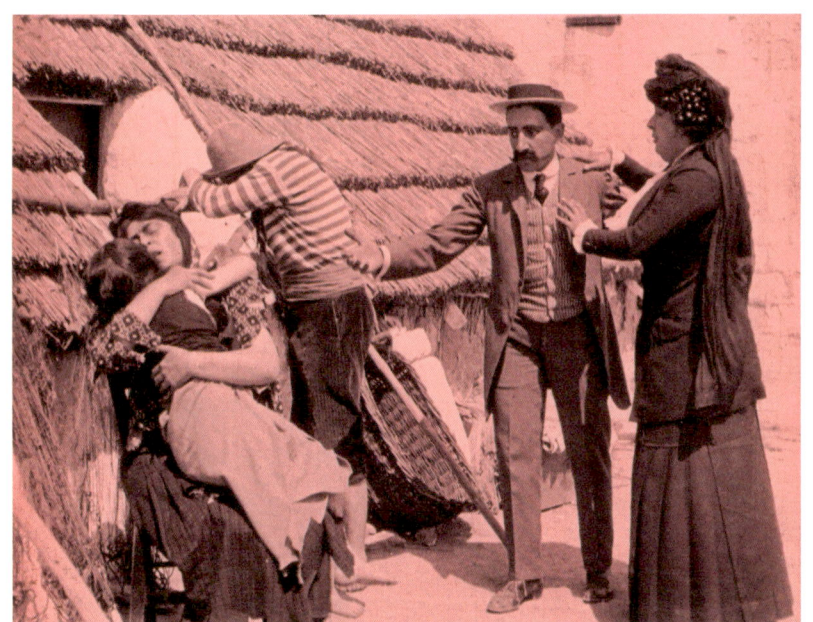
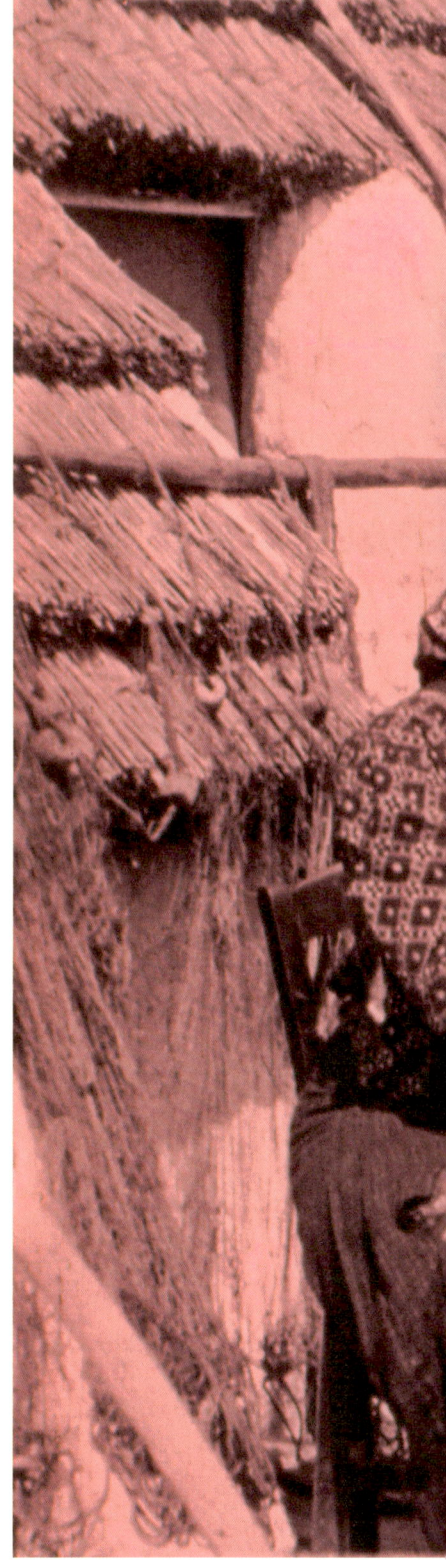

Louis Feuillade, *Mater Dolorosa*, 1910

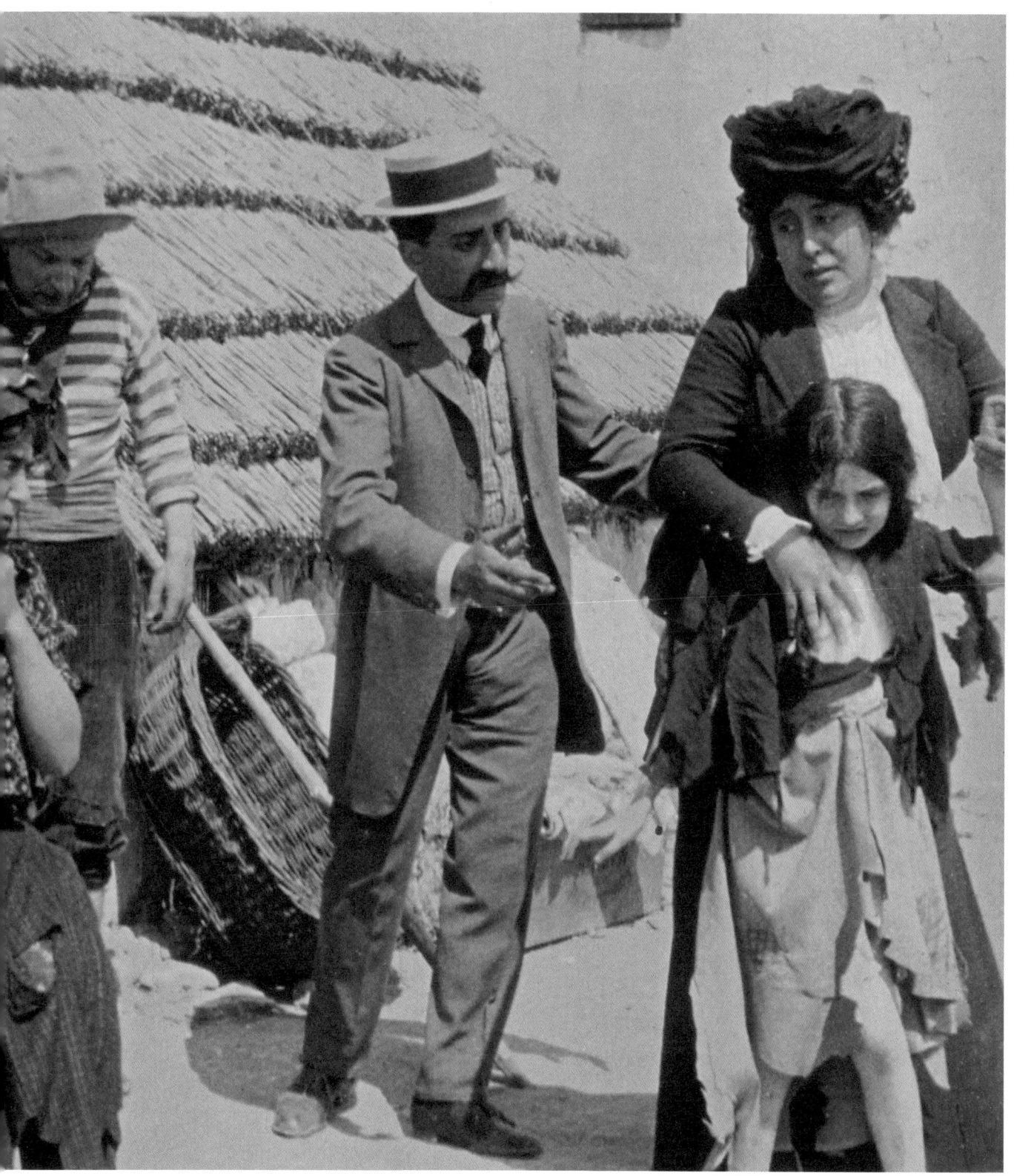

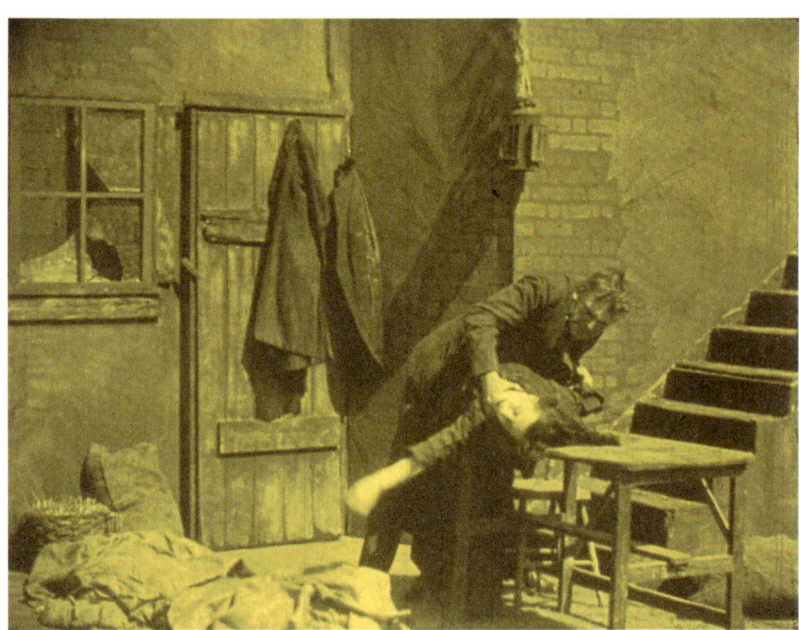

Dave Aylott, *Broken Faith*, 1912

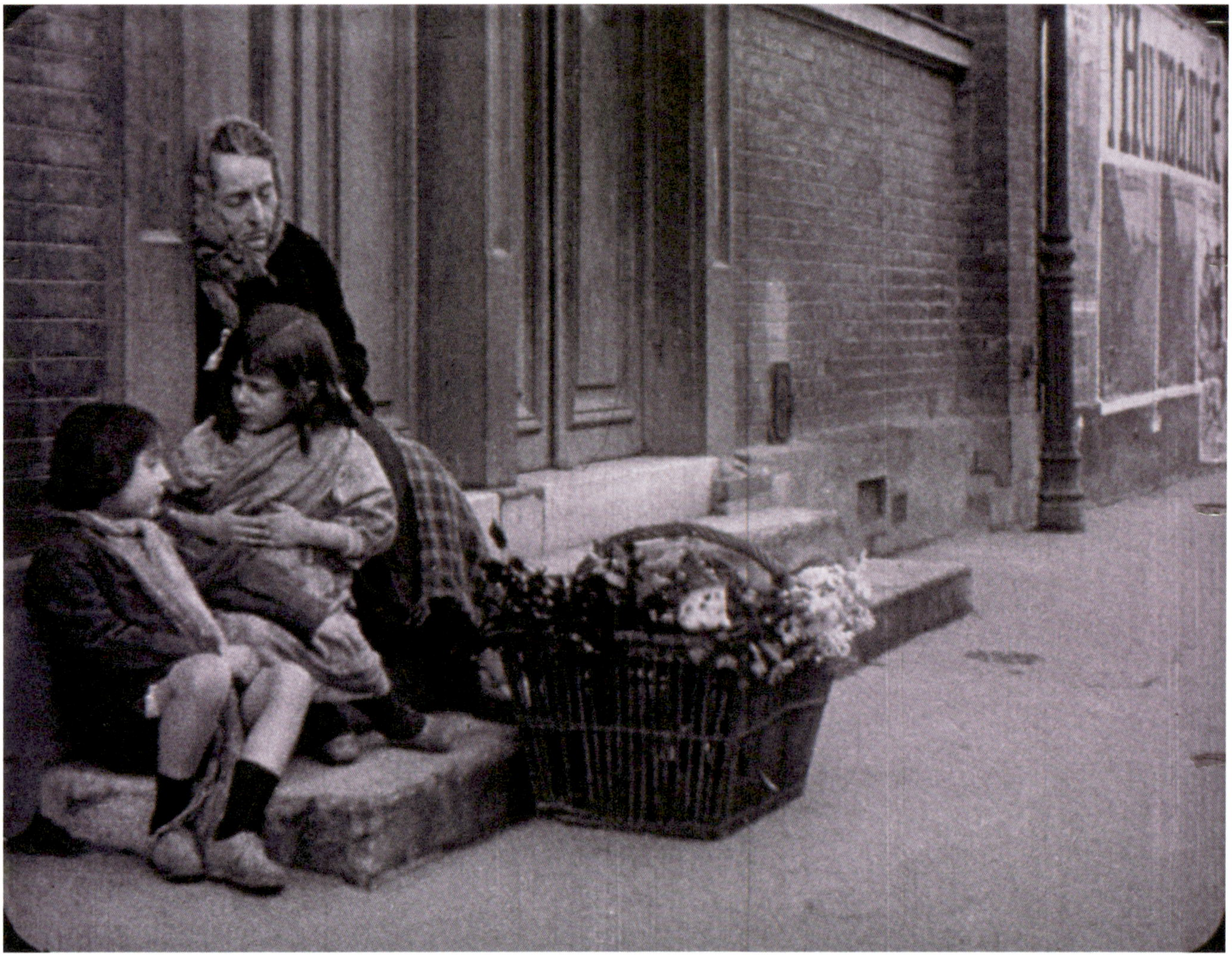

Chagrin d'enfants, 1912

Films and Posters in the Desmet Collection in the EYE Filmmuseum

Films and Posters in the Desmet Collection in the EYE Filmmuseum

It is hard to affix exact figures to the Desmet Film Collection. In an inventory Desmet made in 1938, he mentions 1013 items. However, by 1957, when the collection was donated to the museum, around 900 items were accounted for. An inventory in 1999 lists 886 items. The UNESCO's Memory of the World application of 2010 speaks of 930 films, but since then this figure has changed yet again: EYE still receives Desmet film prints from private collectors, films that were probably sold by Jean Desmet during his lifetime to film distributors who then redistributed these films. Some film prints may have simply been forgotten in cinemas and other venues. A number of the most recent additions are *Robinet scioperante*, *Das Geheimschloss* and *Loyalty of Sylvia* in 2011, and *Tragico convegno*, which was partly recovered and restored in 2013 (for more on this topic see the essay by Elif Rongen-Kaynakçi and Soeluh van den Berg in this book).

The film list below contains 922 entries; some cans containing unpresentable material (such as only title cards) are excluded. Similarly, a few titles that are from the 1930s and 1940s have been left off of the list as these were probably found within Desmet's personal belongings, but do not historically belong to the Jean Desmet International Film Rental and Sales Company Collection.

The filmography and list of film posters lists all the film and poster material currently kept in the EYE archival vaults.

Films

Format for film entries
Film title* (alternative title), year / director / production company / country / colour / length in minutes-running time

The films are listed in alphabetical order by their **original titles**, in the original language. (As the identification process is ongoing – currently about 5 per cent of the films are still unidentified – some titles are still subject to change.) The title on the film print is given as the alternative title between round brackets.

If the original title is unknown, the title on the print is given between square brackets. Most of the prints carry **Dutch titles**, since they were distributed in the Netherlands, these titles are reproduced as they are on the film. If the film print doesn't have a title card, the otherwise known Dutch title or a given title is indicated between round brackets.

The **year** of production is given between brackets, if the dating has not been confirmed. The confirmed dates are either found in the international sources, or are found on the film content or stock.

The name of the **director, production company and original country of production** are included if known.

The distinction **colour or b&w** of the films is based on the presentation print currently available at EYE. As colours are unique to each print, this category refers only to prints in the Desmet Collection and should not be taken as a general value.

Information on the **completeness** of the film prints is not included on this list, since not all the films are equally complete or their length may differ due to loss of material over time. However, most films are complete in the sense that the story can be clearly understood. Only in a few cases, where the existing material is merely a fraction of the original length, is this indicated with the abbreviation '**FRG**' (fragment). Within the silent cinema, reference to **exact length** has always been problematic; as length in metres or in running time were subject to alterations due to the length of the added intertitles (or lack thereof) but also due to the variable projection speed. For this reason, silent film lengths are generally indicated in reels. However, to give a sense of the length of each film for today's audiences the running length of the extant prints (varying dramatically from 2-minute travelogues to epic films of more than 130 minutes) is indicated in rounded off numbers. An (*) after the title refers to the presence of a **film poster** within the Desmet Collection. The details can be consulted in the list of posters. Finally, the non-fiction compilations such as the *Laatste bioscoop wereldberichten* or Pathé Newsreels are problematic to list as these were newsreels compiled by Desmet from different materials and do not correspond to anything in written sources. In this list they are referred to as groups, whereas in the EYE database they are each described individually by their contents.

Posters

Format for poster entries
Film title*, year / director / production company / country of origin (abbreviated)
Poster title (year), designer / design company / country / dimensions: h x w in cm

The posters are listed in alphabetical order, by their **original film titles,** in the original language. The title on the poster is given as the alternative title; if the original film title is unknown. Similarly, the **year** of production is given between brackets, if the dating has not been confirmed. Most of the 1,032 posters included in the Desmet Collection originated outside the Netherlands. Some of them come from the country where the film in question was made, but many others do not. For instance, there are posters designed in Great Britain for American films and French posters for Italian films. Most of the Dutch posters are text-based, essentially banners of text.

The names of the **designer** and **production company** (posters) are included if known. Multiple posters for the same film are included in some cases, with different designs and dimensions. In this respect, the religious epic *Sign of the Cross* is the clear record holder, with 11 different designs in the collection, varying in size from 20 x 51 cm (the Dutch text poster) to 223 x 392 cm. This latter poster shows a beautifully depicted Roman bacchanal; in contrast, other designs have an emphatically religious tone. A few additions have been made to the collection, when posters became available that were once used by Desmet in the distribution of the film but were not included in the materials acquired in 1957.

An (*) after the title signals the presence of a **film print** in the collection. The details can be found in the **Filmography**. The list of posters does not entirely correspond to the list of films, because for some films, posters have been preserved but not film prints. Conversely, there are many film prints in the collection for which there are no corresponding posters. This is partly because no posters were made for non-fiction films. Various posters in the collection do not include film titles. Numerous posters were intended for export and designed so that the local title could be added in each country. In many such cases, the film in question can be identified thanks to other sources. When the identification is uncertain, the probable film title is listed in square brackets: [title]. In just a few cases, at the top of the list, the title is indicated as unknown.

There are also a few posters at the top of the list with subjects other than films: a well-known individual (such as Suzanne Grandais), a character in a series (Gontran), or a studio (Eclair). Desmet had original posters designed for his flagship cinema, the Cinema Parisien.

Films in the Desmet Collection

A

[**Aan het paradijsachtige Irische meer**] (*Aan het paradijsachtige Irische meer*), [1911] / Walter Tyler / Tyler / [GB] / col. / 3

Abenteuer eines Journalisten, Das* (*Gestolen uitvinding, De*), 1914 / Harry Piel / Kinokop / DE / col. / 46

Abernathy Kids' Rescue, The, 1911 / Pathé Frères – American Kinema / US / col. / 9

Abgeführte Liebhaber, Der (*Ontlaste minaar een artiestenstreek, De*), 1912 / Carl Wilhelm / B.B. Film / DE / col. / 14

Abito bianco di Robinet, L'* (*Witte costuum van Nauke, Het*), 1911 / Marcel Fabre / Ambrosio / IT / b&w / 5

Absinthe* (*Drankduivel, De*), 1913 / Herbert Brenon / Universal / US / col. / 12

Acque miracolose, Le* (*Wonderbronnen, De*), 1914 / Eleuterio Rodolfi / Ambrosio / IT / col. / 10

Adventures of Lieutenant Petrosino, The* (*Slachtoffer der Comorra, Een*), 1912 / Sidney M. Goldin / Feature Photoplay / US / col. / 43

Adventures of PC Sharpe, The (*Politie en valsche munters*), 1911 / A.E. Coleby / Cricks & Martin / GB / col. / 12

Aérostable des frères Moreau, L' (*Groote vraagstukken der luchtscheepvaart, De*), 1913 / Gaumont / FR / b&w / 4

Agriculture moderne, L' (*Landbouw*), 1912 / Gaumont / FR / col. / 4

Agrippina (*Keizerin Agrippina*), 1911 / Enrico Guazzoni / Cines / IT / col. / 17

Al cinematografo guardate – ma non toccate (*In de cinema – wel naar kijken maar niet aankomen*), 1912 / Itala Film / IT / col. / 5

Alexandra* (*Alexandra*), 1914 / Curt A. Stark / Messter / DE / col. / 63

Alma's Champion (*Millionair en machinist*), 1912 / Vitagraph Company of America / US / col. / 13

Amalfi (*Amalfie*), 1910 / Cines / IT / col. / 4

Amazzone mascherata, L'* (*Geheimzinnige Amazona, De*), 1914 / Baldassarre Negroni / Celio Film / IT / col. / 56

Amore e cospirazione (*Verachting en liefde*), 1915 / Giovanni Enrico Vidali / Pasquali / IT / col. / 27

Amore e disciplina (*Liefde en plicht*), 1911 / Itala Film / IT / col. / 28

Amore tragico (*Morfiniste, De*), 1912 / Cines / IT / col. / 13

Amour de page (*Liefde van den page, De*), 1911 / Georges Denola / Pathé Frères – SCAGL / FR / col. / 12

Amour et musique (*Met muziek en hindernissen*), 1911 / Pathé Frères – Pathé Nizza / FR / b&w / 5

Amour et science (*Liefde en wetenschap*), 1912 / M.J. Roche / Eclair / FR / col. / 14

[**An der Schwelle der Schuld**] (*Ontdekking der ongelukkigen*), [1912] / [Messter] / DE / col. / 14

Andalousie pittoresque, L', 1914 / Pathé Frères / FR / col. / 6

Andy Goes on the Stage (*André op de planken*), 1913 / Charles H. France / Edison Manufacturing Company / US / col. / 14

Ane domestique, L' (*Ezel als huisknecht, De*), 1912 / Lux / FR / b&w / 5

Anna Karenina* (*Anna Karenina*), 1910 / Maurice André Maître / Pathé Frères – Le Film Russe / RU / col. / 14

Anna Maria (*Anne Marie*), 1912 / Cines / IT / col. / 15

Apiculture, L' (*Bijenteelt*), 1913 / Eclair Scientia / FR / b&w / 4

Apprenti architecte, L' ([*Kleine Hans als bouwkundige*]), 1908 / Louis J. Gasnier / Pathé Frères / FR / b&w / 6

Appuntamento di Kri Kri, L'* (*Rendes-vouz van Patachon, Het*), 1914 / Cines / IT / col. / 10

Arthème Dupin échappe encore (*Arthene Dupin ontsnapt opnieuw*), 1912 / Ernest Servaes / Eclipse / FR / b&w / 7

Arthème opérateur* (*Arthème als operateur*), 1913 / Ernest Servaes / Eclipse / FR / col. / 7

Arthème promène son oncle (*Arthème gaat met zijn oom wandelen*), 1913 / Ernest Servaes / Eclipse / FR / b&w / 7

Arthème sorcier (*Arthem als toovenaar*), 1913 / Ernest Servaes / Eclipse / FR / b&w / 6

As Fate Would Have It*, 1912 / Vitagraph Company of America / US / col. / 14

Ascension du Pic du Midi de Bigorre, L' (*Bestijging van de Pic du Midi, De*), 1913 / Gaumont / FR / col. / 6

Aspettando il diretto di mezzanotte (*In afwachting van den middernachtsneltrein*), 1911 / Itala Film / IT / col. / 7

Assommoir, L' ([*Kroeg, De*]), 1909 / Albert Capellani / Pathé Frères – SCAGL / FR / b&w / 16

Assurance, L' (*Verzekering, De*), 1911 / Pathé Frères – Pathé Nizza / FR / b&w / 11

At Coney Island (*Kermis avontuurtje, 'N*), 1912 / Mack Sennett / Keystone Film / US / col. / 7

At Home in the Water (*Zwemcursus van de beroemde Professor Corsan*), 1912 / Edison Manufacturing Company / US / col. / 6

At the End of the Trail, 1912 / Rollin S. Sturgeon / Vitagraph Company of America / US / col. / 14

At the Hour of Three (*Onschuld bewezen door de bioscoop, De*), 1912 / Wilfred Noy / Clarendon Film / GB / 15

At the Masquerade Ball (*Op het gemaskerd bal*), 1912 / Ashley Miller / Edison Manufacturing Company / US / 16

Attenti alla vernice* (*Pas geverfd*), 1913 / Ernesto Vaser / Itala Film / IT / col. / 7

Au pays des ténèbres ([*Gluck Auf!*]), 1911 / Victorin Jasset / Eclair / FR / 34

Auch Faulheit kann von Nutze sein (*Moderne Broedmachine, Een*), 1913 / Deutsche Mutoskop und Biograph / DE / 7

Auf einsamer Insel* (*Wraak van den visscher, De*), 1913 / Joseph Delmont / Eiko Film / DE / col. / 33

Aunty's Romance (*Wensch van de oude tante, De*), 1912 / George D. Baker / Vitagraph Company of America / US / col. / 13

Aus eines Mannes Mädchenzeit* ([*Moderne keukenmeid, Een*]), 1913 / Messter / DE / col. / 23

Automobile della morte, L'* (*Doodenrit, De*), 1912 / Ambrosio / IT / col. / 13

Auvergne pittoresque, L' (*Schilderachtige Auvergne, Het*), 1912 / Lux / FR / col. / 5

Aux feux de la rampe (*Veldslagen des levens, De*), 1912 / Victorin Jasset / Eclair / FR / col. / 13

Ave Maria di Gounod, L' (*Ave Maria, Het (Counod)*), 1910 / Ambrosio / IT / col. / 7

[**Avonturen van Fifi, De**] (*Avonturen van Fifi, De*), 1912 / Eclipse / FR / b&w / 6

Avventure di un monello, Le (*Zijn eerste baas*), 1912 / Itala Film / IT / b&w / 7

B

Bachelor's Baby, The (*Kindje van den vrijgezel, Het*), 1913 / Van Dyke Brooke / Vitagraph Company of America / US / col. / 15

Bacillo della debolezza, Il (*Microbe van de zwakte, De*), 1912 / Cines / IT / b&w / 6

Back in the North Woods*, 1911 / Vitagraph Company of America / US / col. / 10

Back to the Primitive (*In het wilde bosch verloren*), 1911 / Otis Turner / Selig Polyscope / US / col. / 15

Bambola di Luisetta, La* (*Louisa's pop*), 1911 / Ambrosio / IT / b&w / 10

Barbe grise (*Liefhebbende grijsaard, De*), 1911 / Georges Monca / Pathé Frères – SCAGL / FR / b&w / 10

Barber Cure, A* (*Streek van den barbier, De*), 1913 / Edward Dillon / Biograph / US / b&w / 7

Barcaiolo del Danubio, Il* (*Drama in de Alpen, Een*), 1914 / Roberto Roberti / Aquila Films / IT / col. / 62

Barrabas*, 1919 / Louis Feuillade / Gaumont / FR / col. / FRG

Bateau de Léontine, Le (*Lotje's zeiljacht*), 1911 / Pathé Frères / FR / b&w / 5

Battaglione di sciatori Alpini (*Ski-loopende militairen*), 1911 / Itala Film / IT / col. / 4

Bébé a le béguin (*Fritsje bemint*), 1911 / Louis Feuillade / Gaumont / FR / col. / 8

Bébé apache (*Fritsje op het oorlogspad*), 1910 / Louis Feuillade / Gaumont / FR / col. / 7

Bébé en vacances (*Bébé heeft vacantie*), 1913 / Louis Feuillade / Gaumont / FR / col. / 8

Bébé est neurasthénique (*Fritsje is niet zoo dom*), 1911 / Louis Feuillade / Gaumont / FR / b&w / 11

Bébé juge (*Bébé als scheidsrechter*), 1912 / Louis Feuillade / Gaumont / FR / b&w / 4

Bébé prestidigitateur (*Fritsje als toovenaar*), 1911 / Louis Feuillade / Gaumont / FR / b&w / 5

Bébé soigne son père ([*Vader van Bébé gevoelt zich vervelend ziek, De*]), 1912 / Louis Feuillade / Gaumont / FR / b&w / 5

Bébé, Napoléon et les cosaques ([*Triomf voor de kleine tamboer*]), 1912 / Louis Feuillade / Gaumont / FR / col. / 15

Bébé, roi de Rome (*Koning van Rome, De*), 1911 / Louis Feuillade / Gaumont / FR / col. / 9

Bella Galleana, La (*Schoone Galiana, De*), 1911 / Cines / IT / col. / 14

Bergen (*Bergen*), 1912 / Nordisk Films Kompagni / DK / col. / 4

Bergère d'Ivry, La* (*Opoffering eener pleegdochter*), 1913 / Maurice Tourneur / Eclair / FR / col. / 28

[**Bericht van schoonmoeder, Een**] ([*Bericht van schoonmoeder, Een*]), [1912] / FR / b&w / 5

Berretto di Bidoni, Il (*Kepi van Bidoni, Het*), 1912 / Cines / IT / b&w / 5

Bezoek van de Koninklijke Familie te Rotterdam, 1913 / NL / b&w / 5

Bienfait n'est jamais perdu, Un (*Goede daad wordt steeds beloond, Een*), 1908 / Pathé Frères / FR / col. / 8

Billet mrk troskab 909* (*Post restante. Smachtend verlangen No.11*), 1913 / Sofus Wolder /

Nordisk Films Kompagni / DK / col. / 17

Billige Badereise, Eine (*Goedkoop badreisje, Een*), 1911 / Messter / DE / col. / 8

Bill's Reformation ([*Na jaren*]), 1912 / Bert Haldane / Hepworth / GB / col. / 14

Billy's Seance (*Bill doet aan spiritisme*), 1911 / Imperial / US / b&w / 6

Billy's Stratagem* (*List van Billy, De*), 1912 / D.W. Griffith / Biograph / US / b&w / 13

[**Binnenland van Afrika**] ([*Binnenland van Afrika*]), [1910] / Eclair / FR / col. / 5

Bit of Blue Ribbon, A (*Blauwe lint, Het*), 1912 / Rollin S. Sturgeon / Vitagraph Company of America / US / b&w / 11

Blacksmith's Love, The (*Vreugde en smart*), 1911 / Frank Boggs / Selig Polyscope / US / col. / 16

Bloemenvelden Haarlem, 1909 / F.A. Nöggerath jr / Filmfabriek F.A. Nöggerath / NL / col. / 2

Blue Wing's Revenge ([*Jaloezie van Blauwe Vleugel, De*]), 1924 / William James Craft / Universal / US / col. / 7

Bobby als Aviatiker (*Bobby als aviateur*), 1911 / Messter / DE / b&w / 5

Bobby bei den Frauenrechtlerinnen (*Mijnheer baas en de vrije vrouwen*), 1911 / Messter / DE / b&w / 6

Bødes der for, Det* (*Zijn eer gewroken*), 1911 / August Blom / Nordisk Films Kompagni / DK / col. / 23

Bond of Music, The (*Oude musicus, De*), 1912 / Charles Kent / Vitagraph Company of America / US / col. / 13

Bout-de-Zan au bal masqué (*Bout de Zan op het bal-masque*), 1913 / Louis Feuillade / Gaumont / FR / col. / 10

Bout-de-Zan et le crime au téléphone* (*Bout-de-Zan en de telefoonmisdaad*), 1913 / Louis Feuillade / Gaumont / FR / col. / 7

Bout-de-Zan s'amuse* (*Bout-de-Zan vermaakt zich*), 1913 / Louis Feuillade / Gaumont / FR / col. / 5

Bout-de-Zan vole un éléphant (*Bout de Zan steelt een olifant*), 1913 / Louis Feuillade / Gaumont / FR / col. / 8

Bouteille de Patouillard, La (*Gibrouille en de champagneflesch*), 1911 / Roméo Bosetti / Lux / FR / b&w / 5

Brave Little Lady, A (*Kleine dappere vrouw, Eene*), 1912 / [Tom Ricketts] / Nestor / US / b&w / 8

Bravery of Dora, The (*Bravery of Dora, The*), 1912 / Lubin Manufacturing Company / US / b&w / 15

Brennan of the Moor* (*Brennan de straatroover*), 1913 / Edward Warren / Solax / US / b&w / 30

Broken Faith, 1912 / Dave Aylott / British and Colonial Kinematograph / GB / col. / 17

Broncho Billy and the Rustler's Child* ([*Invloed van het kind, De*]), 1913 / Gilbert M. 'Broncho Billy' Anderson / Essanay Film Manufacturing / US / b&w / 11

Broncho Billy's Christmas Dinner* (*Kerstfeest bij den sheriff, Het*), 1911 / Gilbert M. 'Broncho Billy' Anderson / Essanay Film Manufacturing / US / b&w / 13

Broncho Billy's Last Hold Up* (*Laatste aanranding van Broncho-Bill, De*), 1912 / Gilbert M. 'Broncho Billy' Anderson / Essanay Film Manufacturing / US / b&w / 8

Broncho Billy's Narrow Escape (*Moeilijke ontsnapping van Brocho-Bill, Een*), 1912 / Gilbert M. 'Broncho Billy' Anderson / Essanay Film Manufacturing / US / b&w / 14

Brother Bill* (*Oudste broeder, De*), 1913 / Ralph Ince / Vitagraph Company of America / US / col. / 12

Bunny in Disguise* (*Bedrieger bedrogen, De*), 1914 / George D. Baker / Vitagraph Company of America / US / b&w / 14

Bunny's Suicide (*Vroolijke zelfmoordenaar, De*), 1912 / Larry Trimble / Vitagraph Company of America / US / b&w / 5

[**Burmah: Scenes in Burmah**] ([*Beelden uit Burmah*]), 1909 / Urban Trading / GB / b&w / 4

Buster in Nodland (*In het land der dromen*), 1912 / Charles H. France / Lubin Manufacturing Company / US / b&w / 7

Butalin fa i suoi comodi (*Bobillard houdt zijn gemack*), 1912 / Ambrosio / IT / col. / 6

Butalin spazzacamino per amore (*Schoorsteenveger uit liefde*), [1912] / Ambrosio / IT / b&w / 6

Butalin troppo onesto (*Bobillard is zoo eerlijk*), 1912 / Ambrosio / IT / b&w / 6

By a Woman's Wit (*Liefde maakt vindingrijk*), 1911 / Van Dyke Brooke / Kalem / US / b&w / 15

By Fire and Water, 1913 / Ashley Miller / Edison Manufacturing Company / US / col. / 15

Caduta di Troia, La (*Val van Troje, De*), 1911 / Giovanni Pastrone / Itala Film / IT / col. / 32

C

Cajus Julius Caesar* (*Cajus Julius Caesar*), 1914 / Enrico Guazzoni / Cines / IT / col. / 104

Calino couche à la belle étoile (*Frits slaapt onder den blooten hemel*), 1911 / Pathé Frères – Comica / FR / col. / 5

Calino courtier en paratonnerres (*Piefke als uitvinder van bliksemafleiders*), 1912 / Jean Durand / Gaumont / FR / b&w / 5

Calino dompteur par amour (*Calino, dierentemmer uit liefde*), 1912 / Jean Durand / Gaumont / FR / b&w / 6

Calino sourcier* (*Carlino ontdekt waterbronnen*), 1913 / Jean Durand / Gaumont / FR / col. / 4

Calvario (*Lijdensweg eener vrouw, De*), 1911 / Pasquali / IT / col. / 40

Calvario di Polidor, Il (*Lijden van Polidor, Het*), 1912 / Pasquali / IT / b&w / 7

Cambrioleur en voit de dures, Le ([*Dief in benauwdheid, Een*]) 1911 / Pathé Frères – Pathé Nizza / FR / b&w / 6

Canine Sherlock Holmes, A* ([*Hond als detective, Een*]), 1912 / Stuart Kinder / Urban Trading / GB / col. / 16

Captain Kate ([*Onder wilde dieren*]), 1911 / Otis Turner / Selig Polyscope / US / col. / 14

Carnaval de Nice ([*Carnaval te Nizza*]), [1912] / Pathé Frères / FR / b&w / 7

Cavalerie belge (*Belgische cavallerie in de rijschool te Yperen*), 1911 / Gaumont / FR / col. / 4

Cavallo del reggimento, Il (*Regimentsknol, De*), 1911 / Emilio Vardannes / Itala Film / IT / b&w / 4

Cave Man Wooing, A ([*Getrouwd door kracht*]), 1912 / Otis Turner / Universal IMP / US / col. / 11

Cendrillon ([*Assepoester*]), 1912 / Ferdinand Zecca / Pathé Frères / FR / col. / 12

Chagrin d'enfants* (*Kindersmarten*), 1912 / Eclipse / FR / col. / 31

Chamber of Forgetfulness (*Uur van vergeving, Het*), 1912 / Etienne Arnaud / Eclair Company / US / col. / 12

Chambre 31, La (*Zimmer nr. 31*), 1911 / Lux / FR / col. / 11

Champignol malgré lui* ([*Champignol tegen wil en dank*]), 1914 / Aubert / FR / col. / 42

Charley Smiler Is Robbed (*Meyer's avontuur*), 1911 / Dave Aylott / Cricks & Martin / GB / b&w / 3

Charme de Maud, Le (*Bekoring van Maud, De*), 1913 / René Hervil / Eclipse / FR / col. / 15

Chasse à l'aigrette en Afrique (*Jacht op zilverreigers in Afrika*), 1911 / Alfred Machin / Pathé Frères / FR / b&w / 7

Châtiment de Corse (*Corsikaansche eer*), 1907 / Radios / FR / col. / 8

[**Châteaux sur le Rhin, Les**] (*Van Bingen tot Coblenz*), 1910 / Eclair / FR / b&w / 3

Chemin de fer du Loetschberg, Le, 1913 / Eclipse / FR / col. / 7

Chest of Fortune, The* (*Verborgen schat, De*), 1914 / Kenean Buel / Kalem / US / b&w / 25

Cheyenne's Bride, The (*Tijgerhart en Zilverroos*), 1911 / James Young Deer / Pathé Frères – American Kinema / US / b&w / 9

Chez les Touaregs (*Bij de Tuaregs*), 1908 / Pathé Frères / FR / b&w / 7

Chi fu il colpevole? (*Wie was de schuldige?*), 1910 / Itala Film / IT / col. / 8

Chien de garde (*Waakhond gevraagd, Een*), 1906 / Pathé Frères / FR / b&w / 4

Chien d'occasion, Un (*Neu Gekaufte Hund, Der*), 1910 / Pathé Frères / FR / b&w / 6

Chien insaisissable, Le (*Ongenaakbare hond, De*), 1912 / Lux / FR / b&w / 5

Chien voleur, Le (*Hond als dief, De*), 1912 / Lux / FR / b&w / 5

Child's Devotion, A (*Tweede moeder, De*), 1912 / Lubin Manufacturing Company / US / col. / 9

Classmate's Frolic, The (*Scholierengrap*), 1913 / Ralph Ince / Vitagraph Company of America / US / b&w / 7

Cocciutelli affissatore (*Kraue als aanplakker*), 1911 / Milano Films / IT / b&w / 6

Cocciutelli cerca lavoro (*Krause zoekt werk*), 1911 / Milano Films / IT / b&w / 7

Cocò marina la scuola (*Coco wil niet naar school*), 1912 / Cines / IT / b&w / 5

Coeur Ardent ([*Gloeiend hart*]), 1912 / Jean Durand / Gaumont / FR / col. / 13

Coeur d'enfant (*Kinderhart*), 1911 / Léonce Perret / Gaumont / FR / col. / 12

Coeur et les yeux, Le (*Ziek hart en zieke oogen*), 1911 / Emile Chautard / Eclair / FR / col. / 9

Coffin Ship, The (*Im Meere Verloren*), 1911 / Thanhouser Film / US / b&w / 14

Colonel's Escape, The (*Ontvluchting van den kolonel, De*), 1912 / Kenean Buel / Kalem / US / b&w / 13

Come una sorella (*Noodlottige luchtvaart*), 1912 / Vincenzo Denizot / Itala Film / IT / col. / 30

Comment Gontrau a perdu son épouse (*Hoe Gaston zijn bruid verloor*), 1911 / Eclair / FR / b&w / 5

Comrade's Treachery, A (*Offer van den Hartstocht, Een*), 1911 / H.O. Martinek / British and Colonial Kinematograph / GB / b&w / 9

Concini (*Concini*), [1910] / [Eclair] / FR / col. / 15

Concorso di bellezza fra bambini a Torino (*Kinder tentoonstelling*), 1909 / Aquila Films / IT / b&w / 4

Conspiracy of Pontiac, The (*Mislukte*

Indianenlist, Een), 1910 / Sidney Olcott / Kalem / US / b&w / 13
Conspiration sous Henri III (1578), Une (*Samenzwering onder Hendrik III, Een*), 1911 / Camille de Morlhon / Pathé Frères / FR / col. / 13
Constantine (*Constantine*), 1913 / Eclair / FR / col. / 6
Contrat mouvementé (*Gestoorde verlovingspartij, Een*), 1911 / Pathé Frères – Comica / FR / b&w / 5
Coup de feu, Le (*Zu Hilfe!*), 1911 / Pathé Frères – SCAGL / FR / b&w / 10
Coup de fusil, Le, 1909 / Pathé Frères – SCAGL / FR / col. / 8
Course à la Cocarde, Une (*In Camarague. De wedrennen om de Kokarde*), 1912 / Gaumont / FR / col. / 5
Course Provençale (*Komisch stierengevecht, Een*), 1913 / Jean Durand / Gaumont / FR / b&w / 5
Cowboy and the School-Marm (*Perlenfährte, Die*), 1910 / Fred J. Balshofer / NYMPC – New York Motion Picture Bison / US / col. / 12
Cowboy Coward, The (*Lafaard, De*), 1911 / Gilbert M. 'Broncho Billy' Anderson / Essanay Film Manufacturing / US / b&w / 10
Cowboy Millionaire, The* ([*Cowboy millionair, De*]), 1909 / Otis Turner / Selig Polyscope / US / col. / 20
Craven, The (*Vrouw van den lafaard, De*), 1912 / Rollin S. Sturgeon / Vitagraph Company of America / US / col. / 14
Cross Roads, The (*Oude roofvogel, De*), 1912 / Frederick A. Thomson / Vitagraph Company of America / US / b&w / 12
Cruelle plaisanterie (*Wreede scherts*), 1908 / Pathé Frères / FR / b&w / 9
Cunégonde aime son maître (*Haar eerste liefde*), 1912 / Lux / FR / b&w / 7
Cunégonde fait du spiritisme* (*Cunegonde doet aan spiritisme*), 1913 / Lux / FR / col. / 7
Cunégonde femme cochère* (*Cunegonde als huurkoetsier*), 1913 / Lux / FR / b&w / 6
Cunégonde femme crampon ([*Cunegonde wil niet dat haar man alleen uitgaat*]), 1912 / Lux / FR / b&w / 9
Cunégonde femme du monde (*Cunegonde als modedame*), 1912 / Lux / FR / b&w / 7
Cunégonde jalouse (*Cunegonde is jaloersch*), 1912 / Lux / FR / b&w / 5
Cunégonde reçoit sa famille (*Cunegonde krijgt bezoek*), 1912 / Lux / FR / b&w / 6
Cunégonde trop curieuse (*Cunegonde is nieuwsgierig*), 1912 / Lux / FR / b&w / 7

Cuore ferito, Un (*Gewond hart, Een*), 1912 / Itala Film / IT / b&w / 5
Cupid Through Padlocks (*Hangslot, Het*), 1912 / Allan Dwan / American Film Manufacturing / US / b&w / 12
Cutey and the Chorus Girls* (*Op de gezondheid van Freddy*), 1913 / James Young / Vitagraph Company of America / US / col. / 14
Cutey Plays Detective, 1913 / Larry Trimble / Vitagraph Company of America / US / col. / 10
Czernowska, Die* (*Ontmaskerd*), 1913 / Charles Decroix / Charles Decroix-Film / DE / col. / 25

D

Dans la cave (*In den kelder*), 1912 / Victorin Jasset / Eclair / FR / col. / 10
Dans les airs ([*Geschaakt in een vliegmachine*]), 1911 / Jean Durand / Lux / FR / col. / 6
Dans les Pyrénées (*In de Pyreneen*), 1913 / Gaumont / FR / col. / 3
Dattilografa, La (*Maschinen-schreiberin, Die*), 1911 / Cines / IT / b&w / 14
Days of Terror, The (*Tijdperk van verschrikking, Een*), 1912 / Charles Kent / Vitagraph Company of America / US / col. / 16
De Gibraltar à Algésiras (*Van Gibraltar naar Algeciras*), 1911 / Gaumont / FR / col. / 3
De Pau à Cauterets (*Van Pau naar Cauterets*), 1913 / Lux / FR / col. / 6
Déjeuner qui ne profite guère, Un ([*Kleine Hans steelt eten*]), 1911 / Pathé Frères / FR / b&w / 5
Delayed Proposals* ([*Verloving met hindernissen, Een*]), 1913 / James Young / Vitagraph Company of America / US / b&w / 9
Demoiselle de l'Hôtel Imperia, La (*Liefde van den Markies, De*), 1913 / Eclipse / FR / col. / 20
Demoiselles des PTT, Les (*Juffrouw van de post, De*), 1913 / Raoul d'Auchy / Gaumont / FR / col. / 10
Deputy's Peril, The (*Dochter van den valschen munter, De*), 1912 / Romaine Fielding / Lubin Manufacturing Company / US / b&w / 15
Des Meeres und der Liebe wellen* (*Schipbreuk op de Hollandsche kust, Een*), 1912 / DKG – Deutsche Kinematographen Gesellschaft / DE / col. / 37
Descente en barque à travers les gorges de l'Ardeche (*Boottocht langs de wateren van de Ardeche*), 1910 / Gaumont / FR / col. / 3
Désespoir de Pétronille, Le* (*Verloving van Petronella, De*), 1914 / Georges Rémond / Eclair / FR / col. / 8
Destiny is Changeless (*Blauwe vos,*

De), 1911 / Rollin S. Sturgeon / Vitagraph Company of America / US / col. / 15
[**Deutsche turnwedstryd**] (*Deutsche turnwedstryd*), [1912] / WKF Welt Kino / DE / col. / 6
[**Deux chiens se battant pour un os**] (*Als twee honden vechten om een been*), [1913] / Lux / FR / b&w / 8
Dette, La (*Schuld, Die*), 1910 / Serie d'art Pathé Frères / FR / col. / 6
Diamond Cut Diamond (*Bedriegster bedrogen, De*), 1912 / Wilfred North / Vitagraph Company of America / US / col. / 14
Dichiarazione impossibile di Robinet, Una (*Onmogelijke verklaring van Robinet, Een*), 1912 / Marcel Fabre / Ambrosio / IT / col. / 5
Didums and the Bathing Machine ([*Fritsje in het badkoetsje*]), 1911 / Wilfred Noy / Clarendon Film / GB / b&w / 6
Distant Relative, The (*Gouvernante, De*), 1912 / Allan Dwan / American Film Manufacturing / US / b&w / 8
District Attorney's Conscience, The* (*Einde van een opruier, Het*), 1913 / Arthur V. Johnson / Lubin Manufacturing Company / US / b&w / 29
Diver, The* ([*Drama aan de Niagara*]), 1913 / Harry Lambart / Vitagraph Company of America / US / col. / 19
Doctor Bridget (*Middel van Betje, Het*), 1912 / Frederick A. Thomson / Vitagraph Company of America / US / col. / 13
Doctor's Duty, The (*Plicht van den dokter, De*), 1913 / Walter Edwin / Edison Manufacturing Company / US / col. / 14
Dødsspring til hest fra cirkuskuplen* (*Groote circusdrama, Het*), 1912 / Eduard Schnedler-Sørensen / Nordisk Films Kompagni / DK / col. / 42
Dødsvarslet* (*Momento Mori*), 1912 / Aage Brandt / Skandinavien / DK / col. / 30
Doopplechtigheid Prinses Juliana, met incident der rijtuigen ([*Geboortedag van Prinses Juliana*]), 1909 / Willy Mullens / Alberts Frères / NL / b&w / 4
Door het Alb-dal naar St. Blasiën (*Door het Alpendal naar St. Blasien*), 1920 / Weltkino / DE / col. / 4
Dr. Lafleur's Theory (*Theorie van Dr. Lafleur*), 1912 / Van Dyke Brooke / Vitagraph Company of America / US / col. / 12
Dr. Schotte (*Verwoeste levensgeluk, Het*), 1918 / William Wauer / Greenbaum Film / DE / col. / 80
Dramma al Marocco, Un (*Drama in Marokko, Een*), 1908 / Itala Film / IT / col. / 6
Due innamorate di Cretinetti, Le

(*Vereering van Gibrouille, De*), 1911 / Itala Film / IT / col. / 9
Duel sensationnel (*Strijd tusschen wilde dieren, Een*), 1908 / Eclipse / FR / b&w / 4
[**Duel in het venster, Een**] ([*Duel in het venster, Een*]), 1910 / Eclair / FR / col. / 9
Duello dei paurosi, Il (*Vreesachtige duellanten, De*), 1908 / Rossi & C. / IT / b&w / 5
Durbar feesten, De (*Durbar feesten, De*), 1911 / Edison Manufacturing Company / US / b&w / 6
Dusty Dick's Awakening (*Bestofte Johnny, De*), 1911 / A.E. Coleby / Cricks & Martin / GB / b&w / 4
Dyrekobt aere (*Duur gekochte eer*), 1911 / Willam Augustinus / Nordisk Films Kompagni / DK / b&w / 14
Dyrekobt glimmer (*Asphaltplant, De*), 1911 / Peter Urban Gad / Nordisk Films Kompagni / DK / col. / 26
Dytique, Le (*Dytique, De*), 1912 / Eclair Scientia / FR / col. / 7

E

Éclipse de soleil du 17 avril 1912, L'* (*Éclipse de soleil du 17 avril 1912, L'*), 1912 / Gaumont / FR / col. / 7
École de sauvetage en Australie, Une (*Oefenschool voor menschlievend hulpbetoon*), 1911 / Pathé Frères – Imperium Film / FR / b&w / 4
Ekspeditricen (*Onbedachtzame jeugd, De*), 1911 / August Blom / Nordisk Films Kompagni / DK / col. / 50
Élevage des poulards de Bresse à Cousance (Jura), L' (*Fokkerij van pluimvee, Een*), 1912 / Eclipse / FR / col. / 5
Eleventh Hour, The* (*Zijn verdiende loon*), 1914 / Henry MacRae / Universal 101 Bison / US / b&w / 18
En voyage de noces ([*Jonggehuwden vertrekken naar Italie, De*]), 1912 / Gaumont / FR / col. / 10
Ende vom Liede, Das* ([*Einde van het lied, Het*]), 1915 / Rudolf Biebrach / Messter / DE / col. / 52
Endelig alene* (*Gestoorde huwelijksreis, De*), 1914 / Holger-Madsen / Nordisk Films Kompagni / DK / col. / 29
Enfant de Paris, L'* (*Kind van Parijs, Het*), 1913 / Léonce Perret / Gaumont / FR / col. / 120
Enfant sauveur, L'* ([*Kind als redder, Het*]), 1912 / André Hugon / Eclair / FR / col. / 12
Enfants du capitaine Grant, Les (*Kinderen van Kapitein Grant, De*), 1914 / Victorin Jasset / Eclair / FR / col. / 65
Engelein (*Engeltje*), 1913 / Peter

Urban Gad / PAGU – Projektions AG 'Union' / DE / b&w / 51

Envieuse, L' (*Gevolgen van ijdelheid, De*), 1911 / Albert Capellani / Pathé Frères – SCAGL / FR / col. / 14

Environs de Luchon, Les, 1912 / Gaumont / FR / col. / 4

*Épingles, Les** (*For two pins*), 1913 / Léonce Perret / Gaumont / FR / col. / 13

Epouvante du remords, L' (*Gewetenswroeging*), 1912 / Gaumont / FR / col. / 4

Epouvante, L' (*Schrecken, Der*), 1911 / Albert Capellani / Pathé Frères – SCAGL / FR / col. / 10

Equilibristi meravigliosi (*Wonderbare equilibristen*), 1911 / Cines / IT / b&w / 5

*Erblich belastet?** (*Erfelijk belast?*), 1913 / Harry Piel / Eiko Film / DE / col. / 41

*Erreur tragique** (*Noodlottige vergissing, Een*), 1912 / Louis Feuillade / Gaumont / FR / b&w / 22

Erzieherin, Die (*Gouvernante, De*), 1911 / Deutsche Mutoskop und Biograph / DE / b&w / 13

Escarpin de Gontran, L' (*Pantoffel van Gontran, De*), 1912 / Lucien Nonguet / Eclair Coloris / FR / col. / 10

Esercito vittorioso, L' (*Zegevierende leger, Het*), 1912 / Ambrosio / IT / b&w / 7

[*Eternal conflict, The*] (*Bende valsemunters opgerold door de pers, Een*), [1912] / Rex Motion Picture Company / US / b&w / 15

Eugénie, redresse-toi (*Eugenie, houdt U recht*), 1911 / Jean Durand / Gaumont / FR / col. / 4

Everything Comes to Him Who Waits (*Nieuwe kellner, De*), 1912 / C. Jay Williams / Edison Manufacturing Company / US / b&w / 7

*Evil of the Slums, An** (*Onderste lagen der maatschappij*), 1913 / Edwin August / Powers Company / US / b&w / 12

Express matrimonial (*In den tunnel of Kennismaking in een express*), 1912 / Léonce Perret / Gaumont / FR / col. / 11

Eye of Conscience, The ([*Zevende gebod, Het*]), 1911 / Selig Polyscope / US / col. / 14

F

Famille de jeunes chiens (*Honden familie, Een*), 1912 / Gaumont / FR / col. / 4

Fascino della violenza, Il (*Invloed der liefde, De*), 1912 / Cines / IT / col. / 13

Fatalité (*Noodlot, Het*), 1912 / Victorin Jasset / Eclair / FR / col. / 35

*Father's Hatband** (*Brievenbesteller van Cupido, De*), 1913 / Van Dyke Brooke / Vitagraph Company of America / US / col. / 15

Fausse information, La (*Valsche informaties*), 1912 / Jean Durand / Gaumont / FR / col. / 6

Faute de Baptiste, La (*Stem van het geweten, De*), 1911 / Pathé Frères / FR / col. / 9

Fazzoletto rivelatore, Il (*Verraderlijke zakdoek, De*), 1913 / Cines / IT / col. / 29

Ferrets, The (*Valsche munters*), 1913 / Oscar Eagle / Selig Polyscope / US / b&w / 15

Fièvre de joueur (*Speelkoorts*), 1911 / Gaumont / FR / col. / 26

*Filibus** (*Filibus, de geheimzinnige luchtpirate*), 1915 / Mario Roncoroni / Corona Films / IT / col. / 70

*Fille du squatter, La** (*Dochter van den eenzame, De*), 1911 / Pathé Frères – American Kinema / FR / col. / 6

*Fils de Locuste, Le** (*Locusta, de gifmengster*), 1911 / Louis Feuillade / Gaumont / FR / col. / 14

Fils du diable, Le, 1906 / Charles-Lucien Lépine / Pathé Frères / FR / b&w / 15

Fils du pêcheur, Le ([*Zoon van de visser, De*]), 1910 / Camille de Morlhon / Pathé Frères / FR / col. / 6

Finalmente soli! (*Eindelijk alleen*), 1912 / Itala Film / IT / b&w / 8

*Fior di male** (*Kinderen der zonde*), 1915 / Carmine Gallone / Cines / IT / col. / 65

Fiore del deserto, Il, 1911 / Cines / IT / col. / 8

*Fire djævle, De** (*Vier luchtacrobaten, De*), 1911 / Robert Dinesen / Dansk Kinograf Films / DK / col. / 39

*Fixing a Flirt** ([*Verrukte minnaar, De*]), 1912 / Lubin Manufacturing Company / US / b&w / 14

Fleurs des champs, 1912 / Gaumont / FR / col. / 4

*Focolare domestico, Il** (*Slachtoffers van een woekeraard, De*), 1914 / Nino Oxilia / Savoia Film / IT / col. / 40

For the Love of an Enemy (*Spionnenbruid, De*), 1911 / Kalem / US / col. / 15

Fortunes of a Composer (*Schepping van een componist, De*), 1912 / Charles Kent / Vitagraph Company of America / US / col. / 13

*Fortune's Turn** (*Door den brand zijn schuld geboet*), 1913 / Wilfred North / Vitagraph Company of America / US / col. / 14

Fouinard fait des conquêtes (*Beminnelijke schoone, De*), 1911 / Alfred Machin / Pathé Frères – Pathé Nizza / FR / b&w / 6

Fouquet, l'homme au masque de fer, 1910 / Pathé Frères / FR / col. / FRG, 15 meter

Foyer perdu, Le (*Vergeten en vergeven*), 1911 / Pathé Frères / FR / b&w / 14

Freckles (*Roode puisten*), 1912 / Frederick A. Thomson / Vitagraph Company of America / US / col. / 13

*Fred... couche-toi** ([*Fred ga naar bed*]), 1914 / René Hervil / Eclipse / FR / col. / 16

*Freight Train Drama, A** (*Misdadig plan verijdeld, Een*), 1912 / Selig Polyscope / US / b&w / 14

*Fremmede, Den** (*Vreemdeling, De*), 1914 / Vilhelm Glückstadt / Filmfabriken Danmark / DK / col. / 38

Frettchen, Das (*Spelende walrus, Een*), 1913 / Cosmograph / DE / col. / 5

Freuden der Reserveübung, Die (*Twintig dagen op manoeuvre*), 1913 / Charles Decroix / Decroix / DE / b&w / 26

Fricot innamorato (*Fricot is verliefd*), 1912 / Ambrosio / IT / b&w / 7

Fricot soldato (*Fricot als soldaat*), 1913 / Ambrosio / IT / col. / 7

Frieda, die Tirolerin (*Frieda, die Tirolerin*), 1911 / Pathé Frères – Germania Film / DE / b&w / 7

[*Fringent in balcostuum*] ([*Fringent in balcostuum*]), [1912] / Eclair / FR / b&w / 10

Frisaplat magicien (*Mijnheer Klipp als tooverkunstenaar*), 1912 / Pathé Frères – Comica / FR / b&w / 8

Frontier Girl's Courage, A, 1911 / Frank Montgomery / Selig Polyscope / US / b&w / 13

Frontier Hero, A (*Hond als levensredder, Een*), 1910 / Edison Manufacturing Company / US / col. / 6

Funérailles de S.M. le roi Don Carlos II et de S.A.R. le duc de Bragance, 1908 / Gaumont / FR / col. / 5

Funérailles d'Edouard VII roi d'Angleterre 20 mai 1910 (*Funérailles d'Edouard VII roi d'Angleterre 20 mai 1910*), 1910 / Gaumont / FR / b&w / 5

Furberie di Robinet, Le (*Nauke haalt een grap uit*), 1911 / Marcel Fabre / Ambrosio / IT / b&w / 5

Fureur de mme. Plumette, La (*Sterke mevrouw Plumette, De*), 1912 / Eclipse / FR / b&w / 5

Fütterung von Riesenschlangen (*Voeding van reuzenslangen*), 1911 / Komet-Film / DE / b&w / 3

G

Gamekeeper's Revenge, The (*Wraak van den jachtopziener, De*), 1912 / Wilfred Noy / Clarendon Film / GB / col. / 12

Garde-chasse, Le (*Jagdhüter, Der*), 1911 / Pathé Frères / FR / col. / 10

Gardien de phare, Le (*Vuurtorenwachter, De*), 1911 / Eclipse / FR / col. / 9

Gare! Les lions! (*Achtung! Löwen!*), 1912 / Lux / FR / b&w / 5

*Gaspare** (*Gaspard de huisknecht*), 1912 / Cines / IT / col. / 12

Gavroche au Luna-Park (*Gavroche in Lunapark*), 1912 / Paul Bertho / Eclair / FR / b&w / 7

*Gavroche et Casimir s'entraînent** (*Gavroche en Casimir trainen zich*), 1913 / Paul Bertho / Eclair / FR / b&w / 7

Gavroche peintre célèbre (*Gavroche als kunstschilder*), 1912 / Paul Bertho / Eclair / FR / b&w / 7

Gavroche rêve de grandes chasses (*Gavroche op jacht*), 1912 / Paul Bertho / Eclair / FR / b&w / 8

Gavroche veut faire un riche mariage (*Gavroche doet een rijk huwelijk*), 1912 / Roméo Bosetti / Eclair / FR / b&w / 9

Gebrochene Schwingen (*Verbroken geluk, de doodelijke val met de parachute*), 1913 / Adolf Gärtner / Messter / DE / col. / 40

Gefährliche Alter, Das (*Gevaarlijke leeftijd, De*), 1911 / Adolf Gärtner / Messters Projektion / DE / col. / 33

*Geheimnisvolle Klub, Der** (*Geheime club, De*), 1913 / Joseph Delmont / Eiko Film / DE / col. / 40

*Geheimschloss, Das** (*Miss Clever contra 'De Zwarte Hand'*), 1914 / Apollo–Film / DE / col. / 54

*Gendarme est sans culotte, Le** (*Gendarme in angst, Een*), 1914 / Louis Feuillade / Gaumont / FR / b&w / 20

Generosity of Mr. Smith, The ([*Twee vrouwen en een man*]), 1913 / Warwick Buckland / Hepworth / GB / b&w / 10

Geographie : France. Normandie (*Aan de oevers van de Orne*), 1912 / Gaumont / FR / col. / 4

Geographie : France. Région de la Seine. Les bords de l' Yerres, 1912 / Gaumont / FR / col. / 3

*Gift, The** ([*Renpaard Bol d'Or*]), 1913 / Jack Hulcup / Hepworth / GB / col. / 45

Girl in the West, A (*Paardendieven*), 1912 / Rollin S. Sturgeon / Vitagraph Company of America / US / b&w / 14

Girl Spy Before Vicksburg, The (*Dappere dochter van den commandant*), 1910 / Sidney Olcott / Kalem / US / b&w / 14

Glima-Truppe, Die (*Gilma-troep, De*), 1910 / Regia / DK / col. / 3

Golden Supper, The (*Gouden feestmaal, Het*), 1910 / D.W. Griffith / Biograph / US / b&w / 14

Gontran a volé un enfant (*Gontran heeft een kind gestolen*), 1912 /

Lucien Nonguet / Eclair / FR / b&w / 6
Gontran aime les animaux (Contram houdt van dieren), 1911 / Lucien Nonguet / Eclair / FR / b&w / 6
Gontran chauve par amour (Contran kaalhoofdig door liefde), 1912 / Lucien Nonguet / Eclair / FR / b&w / 8
Gontran combat l'oisiveté* (Contran bestrijdt de luiheid), 1913 / Lucien Nonguet / Eclair / FR / b&w / 8
Gontran dans la gueule du loup* (Contran in 't hol van een leeuw), 1913 / Lucien Nonguet / Eclair / FR / b&w / 6
Gontran doute de la fidélité de sa femme (Contran is jaloers), 1912 / Lucien Nonguet / Eclair / FR / b&w / 6
Gontran engendre une sombre postérité ([Mevrouw Contran heeft een zwart kindje]), 1912 / Lucien Nonguet / Eclair / FR / b&w / 9
Gontran et la voisine inconnue ([Gontran en zijn onbekende buurvrouw]), 1913 / Eclair / FR / col. / 8
Gontran et le dîner forcé (Contran gaat uit eten), 1913 / Lucien Nonguet / Eclair / FR / b&w / 8
Gontran et son complice (Contran en zijn medeplichtige), 1913 / Lucien Nonguet / Eclair Coloris / FR / b&w / 8
Gontran professeur de flûte (Contran als muzikant), 1912 / Lucien Nonguet / Eclair / FR / b&w / 5
Good for Nothing, The (Macht der pers, De), 1912 / Lloyd B. Carleton / Lubin Manufacturing Company / US / b&w / 15
Gorges de Sierroz, Les (Reis langs de watervallen van de Sierroz (Savoye), 1913 / Eclipse / FR / col. / 4
Got 'Em Again* (Slaapzieke politieagent, De), 1913 / E. Colbert / Cricks & Martin / GB / b&w / 6
Grammofono di Polidor, Il (Gramophone van Polidor, De), 1912 / Pasquali / IT / b&w / 8
Grand National, The (Grand National 1911, The), 1911 / Will Barker / Barker Motion Photography / GB / b&w / 7
Grandeur d'âme (Edele zelfopoffering), 1910 / Henri Andréani / Serie d'art Pathé Frères / FR / col. / 10
Grand-père, Le (Grootvader, De), 1911 / Georges Denola / Pathé Frères – SCAGL / FR / b&w / 12
Gratis (Gratis), 1911 / Pasquali / IT / b&w / 5
Gratitude obsédante (Overdreven dankbaarheid), 1912 / Lux / FR / col. / 7
Graziella la gitane (Graziella la gitana. De verlatene), 1912 / Léonce Perret / Gaumont / FR / col. / 20

Greater Love, The ([Verloofde van den sheriff, De]), 1912 / Rollin S. Sturgeon / Vitagraph Company of America / US / col. / 14
[*Groote witte vlinder, De*] (Groote witte vlinder, De), [1912] / Gaumont / FR / col. / 10
Groslard ha buoni polmoni (Man met de sterke adem, De), 1912 / Ambrosio / IT / b&w / 5
Gueuse, La* (Eerloze, De), 1913 / Eclair / FR / col. / 21
Gui, Le (Mistelboompje, Het), 1913 / Gaumont / FR / b&w / 14
Gutes Geschäft, Ein (Goede zaak, Een), 1911 / Messter / DE / b&w / 4
Guvernørens datter (Dochter van den gouverneur, De), 1912 / August Blom / Nordisk Films Kompagni / DK / col. / 28

H

Habits de Little Moritz, Les (Kleine Hans in een nieuw costuum), 1911 / Henri Gambart / Pathé Frères / FR / b&w / 9
Hand Bag, The (Groote vergissing, De), 1912 / Vitagraph Company of America / US / b&w / 8
Hans vanskeligste rolle* (Zijn zwaarste rol), 1912 / August Blom / Nordisk Films Kompagni / DK / col. / 23
Harte Zeiten (Harde tijden), 1913 / Eiko Film / DE / col. / 25
Heart Beats of Long Ago ([Herinneringen aan lang vervlogen dagen]), 1911 / D.W. Griffith / Biograph / US / b&w / 14
Heart of the King's Jester, The ([Hart van den hofnar, Het]), 1911 / William Humphrey / Vitagraph Company of America / US / col. / 14
Her Child's Honor (Eer van haar kind, De), 1911 / Harry Solter / Lubin Manufacturing Company / US / col. / 15
Her Nephews from Labrador ([Neven van Labrador, De]), 1913 / Thanhouser Film / US / b&w / 12
Hero Track Walker, The (Verijdelde overval, De), 1911 / Kenean Buel / Kalem / US / b&w / 12
Herz einer Gattin, Das (Goede hart eener vrouw, Het), 1911 / Charles Decroix / Deutsche Mutoskop und Biograph / DE / b&w / 9
Herzenseroberung, Eine (Verovering van een hart), 1911 / Pharos-Film der Deutschen Mutoskop und Biograph / DE / b&w / 8
High Born Child and the Beggar, The* (Arme en rijke kinderen), 1913 / Kalem / US / b&w / 10
His Daughter (Zijn dochter), 1911 / D.W. Griffith / Biograph / US / b&w / 14

His Daughter (Zijn dochter), 1912 / Bannister Merwin / Edison Manufacturing Company / US / col. / 13
His Hour of Triumph* (Triumph en smart), 1913 / George Loane Tucker / Universal IMP / US / b&w / 23
His Mother (Zijn moeder (Opname in Ierland en Amerika)), 1912 / Sidney Olcott / Kalem / US / b&w / 11
His Secret* (Verzoeking, De), 1913 / Frank Powell / Biograph / US / b&w / 7
Hochspannung* ([Levensgevaarlijk! 127000 volt!]), 1913 / Messter / DE / b&w / 25
Homard, Le* (Kreeft, De), 1912 / Léonce Perret / Gaumont / FR / col. / 10
Homme de peine, L' (Hotelbediende, De), 1911 / Michel Carré / Pathé Frères – SCAGL / FR / b&w / 14
Honnêteté d'un gueux, L' (Ehrlichkeit eines Bettlers, Die), 1910 / Eclair / FR / col. / 7
How a Horseshoe Upset a Happy Family (Geluksfoefijzer, Het), 1912 / Edison Manufacturing Company / US / col. / 7
How Ned Got the Raise (Salarisverhooging), 1912 / Universal IMP / US / b&w / 10
How States Are Made (Op weg naar het 'Verre Westen'), 1912 / Rollin S. Sturgeon / Vitagraph Company of America / US / b&w / 11
How the Champion of the World Trains: Jack Johnson in Defence and Attack (Jack Johnson der Meister Boxer der Welt), 1912 / Kineto / GB / b&w / 4
Hubertusjagd (Hubertusjagd), 1911 / WKF Welt Kino / DE / col. / 3
Hurra! Einquartierung! (Hoera inkwartiering), 1913 / Franz Hofer / Luna-Film / DE / b&w / 23
Hydraulic Lift Lock at Peterborough, Ontario, Canada (Hydraulische sluis te Petersborough. Ontario. Canada), 1911 / Frank Butcher / Empire / GB / col. / 5

I

Ida's Christmas (Kerstman, De), 1912 / Van Dyke Brooke / Vitagraph Company of America / US / col. / 8
Ilse und ihre drei Freier (Elza en haar drie vrijers), 1913 / Gustav Trautschold / Eiko Film / DE / col. / 15
In assenza dei padroni (Dieven die op heeterdaad betrapt werden), 1912 / Cines / IT / b&w / 7
In hoc signo vinces* (In dit teeken zult gij ooverwinnen), 1913 / Nino Oxilia / Savoia Film / IT / col. / 28
[*In verkeerde handen*]* (In verkeerde handen), 1911 / Gaumont / FR / col. / 11

In Vertretung (Fideele schoonzoon, Een), 1913 / Hans Oberländer / Messter / DE / b&w / 27
Inconvenienti della bellezza, Gli (Oude kamermeisje krijgt haar ontslag, Het), 1912 / Itala Film / IT / b&w / 8
Indian Woman's Pluck, An (Indiaansche min, De), 1912 / Frank Wilson / Hepworth / GB / col. / 13
Innocent Theft, An (Onnoozele diefstal, Een), 1912 / Vitagraph Company of America / US / b&w / 13
Intrigante, L' (Intrigante, De), 1911 / Albert Capellani / Pathé Frères – SCAGL / FR / col. / 8
[*Insaisissable picpocket, L'*] (Wondermensch, Het), [1908] / Pathé Frères / FR / b&w / 5
Inutile sacrifice, L' (Gebroken hart, Een), 1911 / Clément Maurice / Eclair / FR / col. / 12
[*Invention de Lichetout, L'*] (Uitvinding van mijnheer Pimpelaar, De), 1911 / Eclair / FR / b&w / 5
It All Came Out in the Wash (Overhemdsknoopje, Het), 1912 / Maurice Costello / Vitagraph Company of America / US / col. / 7
Ivanhoe* (Ivanhoe), 1913 / Herbert Brenon / Universal IMP / US / col. / 50

J

Jack* (Kleine Jacques, De), 1913 / André Liabel / Eclair / FR / col. / 50
Japon pittoresque, Le (Schilderachtig Japan), 1913 / Eclair / FR / b&w / 3
Jardinier hérite, Le (Tuinman als erfgenaam, De), 1911 / Pathé Frères / FR / b&w / 6
Jerry's Mother-In-Law (Hoe Jerry zijn schoonmoeder temt), 1913 / James Young / Vitagraph Company of America / US / col. / 15*
Jeux d'enfants* (Kinderspelen), 1913 / Henri Fescourt / Gaumont / FR / col. / 13
Jewel Thieves Outwitted, The* (Juweelen van Lady Morton, De), 1913 / Frank Wilson / Hepworth / GB / b&w / 10
Jim's Vindication* (Berooving van den express-rijder, De), 1912 / William Duncan / Selig Polyscope / US / b&w / 11
Jobard change de bonne (Nieuwe dienstmeisje van Christiaan, Het), 1911 / Emile Cohl / Pathé Frères / FR / b&w / 6
Jobard est demandé en mariage (Dame met de zenuwe trek, De), 1911 / Emile Cohl / Pathé Frères / FR / b&w / 5
Jobard, amoureux timide (Christiaan, de bedeesde minnaar), 1911 / Emile Cohl / Pathé Frères / FR / b&w / 5
Journée de Fifi, La (Fifi aan de rol),

1912 / Eclipse / FR / b&w / 7
Juan and Juanita* (*Moed van Jan, De*), 1912 / Wilbert Melville / Lubin Manufacturing Company / US / b&w / 12
Julot a le sourire (*Leuke mop, Een*), 1913 / Eclipse / FR / b&w / 5
Just a Shabby Doll (*Vertellingen van een ouden pop*), 1913 / Thanhouser Film / US / col. / 13

K

Kaerlighed og penge (*Geld en liefde*), 1912 / Leo Tscherning / Nordisk Films Kompagni / DK / col. / 13
Kaiserin Elisabeth von Österreich* (*Keizerin Elisabeth van Oostenrijk*), 1920 / Rolf Raffé / Indra Film / DE / col. / 130
Kasperl–Lotte ([*Lotje van het marionettentheater*]), 1913 / Emil Albes / Deutsche Bioscop / DE / col. / 12
[*Kiekjes uit een Afrikaansche dierkwekerij*] (*Kiekjes uit een Afrikaansche dierkwekerij*), [1907] / Pathé Frères / FR / b&w / 5
[*Kijkjes in Afrika*] (*Kijkjes in Afrika*), [1908] / Pathé Frères / FR / b&w / 6
[*Kijkjes uit Manawatu (Nieuw-Zeeland)*] (*Kijkjes uit Manawatu (Nieuw-Zeeland)*), [1912] / [Kalem] / US / col. / 5
Kinder des Majors, Die* (*Kinderen van den majoor, De*), 1914 / Eiko Film / DE / col. / 39
Kings of the Forest* (*Aan den dood ontsnapt*), 1912 / Colin Campbell / Selig Polyscope / US / col. / 21
Kri Kri ama la tintora* (*Patachon is verliefd op een verfster*), 1913 / Cines / IT / col. / 5
Kri Kri domestico (*Patachon wordt kamerdienaar*), 1913 / Cines / IT / col. / 5
Kri Kri e Lea militari* (*Patachon als soldaat*), 1913 / Cines / IT / b&w / 4
Kri Kri fuma l'oppio (*Patachon als opiumschuiver*), 1913 / Cines / IT / b&w / 6
Kri Kri imita Pegoud* (*Patachon imiteert Pégout*), 1914 / Cines / IT / col. / 5
Kri Kri senza testa* (*Patachon heeft zijn hoofd verloren*), 1913 / Cines / IT / col. / 8
Kri Kri s'improvvisa cameriere* ([*Patachon als kelner*]), 1914 / Cines / IT / col. / 7
Kri Kri stalliere per amore* (*Patachon als stalknecht*), 1914 / Cines / IT / col. / 5
Künstlerliebe* ([*Kunstenaarsliefde*]), 1911 / Adolf Gärtner / Messter / DE / col. / 12
Kuss des Fürsten, Der (*Kus van den vorst, De*), 1912 / Curt A. Stark / Messter / DE / col. / 13

Kvindes aere, En*, 1912 / Einar Zangenberg / Dansk Kinograf Films / DK / col. / 34

L

Laatste bioscoop wereldberichten, 1914–1918, 12 episodes / NL / b&w / 5-10
Lac de Kandy, Le (*Meer van Voendy, Het*), 1912 / Eclair / FR / col. / 3
Lady and Her Maid, A* (*Onverwachte verandering, Een*), 1913 / Bert Angeles / Vitagraph Company of America / US / col. / 13
Landru, der Blaubart von Paris (*Geknakte levens*), 1922 / Hans-Otto Löwenstein / Ottol Film / AT / col. / 82
Landstrasse, Die* (*Landlooper of Onschuldig veroordeeld, De*), 1913 / Paul von Woringen / Deutsche Mutoskop und Biograph / DE / b&w / 50
Lea bambola (*Lea's pop*), 1913 / Cines / IT / b&w / 6
Lea si diverte (*Lea amuseert zich kostelijk*), 1912 / Cines / IT / b&w / 8
League of Mercy, The (*Barmhartigheid en naastenliefde*), 1911 / Vitagraph Company of America / US / b&w / 12
Leçon d'amour, Une* (*Les in de liefde*), 1912 / Léonce Perret / Gaumont / FR / col. / 11
Lecture absorbante (*Interessantste artikel in de courant, Het*), 1911 / Eclipse / FR / b&w / 5
Légende des ondines, La (*In banden der sirenen*), 1911 / Georges Denola / Pathé Frères / FR / col. / 6
Léonce à la campagne* ([*Leon gaat naar buiten*]), 1913 / Léonce Perret / Gaumont / FR / col. / 12
Léonce et Toto (*Leon en Toto*), 1912 / Léonce Perret / Gaumont / FR / col. / 9
Léonce flirte* (*Leon's flirt*), 1913 / Léonce Perret / Gaumont / FR / col. / 15
Lesson in Jealousy, A* (*Lesje in de liefde, Een*), 1913 / Harry Lambart / Vitagraph Company of America / US / b&w / 13
Lesson, The* (*Zoon van den predikant, De*), 1910 / D.W. Griffith / Biograph / US / b&w / 13
Lessons in Courtship (*Hoe men het hof maakt*), 1912 / Vitagraph Company of America / US / b&w / 6
[*Leven der dieren, Het*] (*Leven der dieren, Het*), [1912] / Gaumont / FR / col. / 3
[*Leven in een kafferdorp, Het*] (*Leven in een kafferdorp, Het*), [1912] / Eclair / FR / b&w / 4
Liebe und Leidenschaft* (*Liefde en hartstocht*), 1911 / Adolf Gärtner / Messter / DE / col. / 26

Lieutenant Rose and the Moorish Raiders ([*Marine-luitenant Van Brinken en de Marokaansche opstanden*]), 1912 / Percy Stow / Clarendon Film / GB / col. / 11
Lieutenant Rose and the Patent Aeroplane ([*Spionage*]), 1912 / Percy Stow / Clarendon Film / GB / b&w / 13
Lieutenant's Last Fight, The* ([*Buffalo Big vertrekt naar de Militaire Academie*]), 1912 / Thomas H. Ince / NYMPC – New York Motion Picture Bison 101 / US / b&w / 25
Literature and Love (*Geluk eener romanschrijfster, Het*), 1913 / Lloyd B.Carleton / Lubin Manufacturing Company / US / b&w / 12
Lonedale Operator, The (*Moedige dochter van den stationschef, De*), 1911 / D.W. Griffith / Biograph / US / col. / 14
Lonely Princess, The* (*Eenzame prinses, De*), 1913 / Maurice Costello / Vitagraph Company of America / US / col. / 14
Lost and Won (*Verloren en wedergevonden*), 1911 / Selig Polyscope / US / col. / 11
Lost illusions (*Misstap eener vrouw, De*), 1911 / Edwin S. Porter / Rex Motion Picture Company / US / col. / 13
Lost in the Jungle (*Mensch en dier*), 1911 / Otis Turner / Selig Polyscope / US / col. / 15
Loup dans la bergerie, Le (*Wolf in de schaapskooi, De*), 1913 / Gaumont / FR / col. / 10
Love Finds a Way (*Wegen der liefde, De*), 1912 / Tefft Johnson / Vitagraph Company of America / US / col. / 13
Loyal Deserter, A* (*Aan de vlag getrouw*), 1913 / Selig Polyscope / US / b&w / 15
Loyalty of Sylvia, The*, 1912 / Van Dyke Brooke / Vitagraph Company of America / US / col. / 14
Lulu's Doctor (*Pop van Loulou, De*), 1912 / James Young / Vitagraph Company of America / US / b&w / 13
Lumpenbaron, Der* ([*Lompenbaron, De*]), 1914 / Waldemar Hecker / Karl Werner Film / DE / col. / 28
[*Luny als Chinese*] (*Luny als Chinese*), 1913 / Gerhard Dammann / Luna-Film / DE / b&w / 13
Lutte pour la vie (*Kostbaar aandenken, Een*), 1907 / André Heuzé / Pathé Frères / FR / col. / 14

M

Ma concierge est trop jolie (*Mijne huisbewaarster is te mooi*), 1912 / Lux / FR / b&w / 7

Madame Tallien, 1794 (*Madame Tallien 1793 Een episode uit de Fransche Revolutie*), 1911 / Camille de Morlhon / Pathé Frères / FR / col. / 10
Madamigella Robinet (*Juffrouw Robinet*), 1913 / Marcel Fabre / Ambrosio / IT / col. / 8
Madeleine* (*Madeleine*), 1912 / Emil Albes / Deutsche Bioscop / DE / col. / 41
Maid at the Helm, The (*In groot gevaar*), 1911 / Frank Boggs / Selig Polyscope / US / col. / 10
Maison des lions, La (*Leeuwenhuis, Het*), 1912 / Louis Feuillade / Gaumont / FR / col. / 14
Maison ensorcelée, La ([*Betooverde huisje, Het*]), 1907 / Segundo de Chomón / Pathé Frères / FR / b&w / 6
Maison Fifi. Lustspiel aus einer kleinen Garnison (*Luitenantsstreken*), 1914 / Viggo Larsen / Treumann-Larsen-Film-Vertrieb / DE / col. / 40
Making a Man of Her* (*Kok of kokkin*), 1912 / Al Christie / Universal Nestor / US / b&w / 13
Marchand des poupées, Le* (*Poppenkoopman, De*), 1913 / Gaumont / FR / col. / 14
Marengo di Tontolini, II ([*Kroon van Tontolini, De*]), 1912 / Cines / IT / b&w / 6
Mariée du château maudit, La ([*Bruid van het vervloekte kasteel, De*]), 1910 / Albert Capellani / Pathé Frères – SCAGL / FR / col. / 11
Marius adore les chiens ([*Marius houdt van honden*]), 1914 / Eclipse / FR / b&w / 5
Marozia, 1911 / Gerolamo Lo Savio / Pathé Frères – Film d'Arte Italiana / IT / col. / 13
Marseillaise, La ([*Marseillaise, De*]), 1912 / Etienne Arnaud / Gaumont / FR / col. / FRG
Maschera pietosa, La* (*Stervensuur, Het*), 1914 / Ambrosio / IT / col. / 28
Master Painter, The (*Vervallen grootheid, Een*), 1913 / L. Rogers Lytton / Vitagraph Company of America / US / col. / 15
Mate of the Alden Besse, The (*Stuurman van de 'Bessie Harden', De*), 1912 / Hobart Bosworth / Selig Polyscope / US / b&w / 12
Mater Dolorosa (*Mater Dolorosa*), 1910 / Louis Feuillade / Gaumont / FR / b&w / 9
Max a trouvé une fiancée (*Max heeft een bruid gevonden*), 1911 / Pathé Frères / FR / b&w / 7
Médor au téléphone (*Hektor aan de telephoon*), 1907 / Pathé Frères / FR / b&w / 3
Meeting of the Ways, The (*Twee

broeders), 1912 / Vitagraph Company of America / US / col. / 14

Mellem storbyens artister ([*Groot sensatienummer*]), 1912 / Eduard Schnedler-Sørensen / Nordisk Films Kompagni / DK / col. / 17

Men Were Deceivers Ever (*Oh, diese Männer*), 1911 / Dave Aylott / British and Colonial Kinematograph / GB / col. / 5

Mensonge de Jean le Manchot, Le (*Door bedrog voor een treurig leed bespaard*), 1911 / Michel Carré / Pathé Frères – SCAGL / FR / b&w / 13

Mensonge magnanime (*Groothartige leugen, Een*), 1911 / Eclair / FR / col. / 9

Menzogna fatale (*Noodlottige leugen, Een*), 1912 / Ambrosio / IT / col. / 10

Merveilles de l'Hindustan, Les ([*Wonderen van Hindoestan, De*]), 1914 / Radios / FR / col. / 2

Message de l'empereur (*Boodschap des Keizers, De*), 1912 / Gaumont / FR / col. / 16

Metamorphoses comiques, Les ([*Komische gedaanteverwisselingen*]), 1912 / Emile Cohl / Eclipse / FR / col. / 4

Mexican Courtship, A (*Mexicaansche liefde*), 1912 / Wilbert Melville / Lubin Manufacturing Company / US / b&w / 17

Mexican Filibusterers (*Mexicaansche opstandelingen*), 1911 / Kenean Buel / Kalem / US / b&w / 13

Millions de la bonne, Les* (*Millioenenjuffrouw, De*), 1913 / Louis Feuillade / Gaumont / FR / col. / 27

Mills of the Gods, The* (*Door het ongeluk achtervolgd*), 1912 / Ralph Ince / Vitagraph Company of America / US / col. / 38

Mister Smith fait l'ouverture* (*De heer Smith opent de jacht*), 1914 / Jean Durand / Gaumont / FR / col. / 6

[***Mieux valait la nuit***] (*Was ik maar blind gebleven*), 1911 / Eclair / FR / col. / 11

Mixed Identities ([*Zij hebben hun diploma als stenographiste behaald*]), 1913 / William Humphrey / Vitagraph Company of America / US / col. / 10

Moda vuole l'ala larga, La (*Hoed naar de laatste mode, Een*), 1912 / Itala Film / IT / b&w / 4

Moeurs des araignées des champs (*Kruisspin, De*), 1913 / Eclair Scientia / FR / col. / 8

Moglie del capitano, La (*Vrouw van den kapitein, De*), 1913 / Savoia Film / IT / col. / 7

Monsieur (*Dochter van den Graaf. De*), 1911 / Edison Manufacturing Company / US / col. / 13

Monsieur qui n'a pas de mémoire, Un (*Vergeetachtige heer, De*), 1911 / Pathé Frères / FR / b&w / 6

Montana State Fair, The (*Jaarmarkt te Montana, De*), 1914 / Rollin S. Sturgeon / Vitagraph Company of America / US / b&w / 5

More Than Friends (*Meer dan een vriend*), 1915 / George Reehm / Biograph / US / col. / 15

Morte civile, La* (*Schuldig aan moord*), 1913 / Ubaldo Maria Del Colle / Savoia Film / IT / col. / 23

Moscone, Il (*Bromvlieg, De*), 1911 / Ambrosio / IT / b&w / 3

[***Motorbootrennen***] (*Motorbootrennen*), [1911] / Welt Film / DE / b&w / 4

Mouches, Les (*Vliegen, De*), 1913 / Eclipse / FR / col. / 6

Mousmée et le brigand, La* (*Liefde van den roover, De*), 1911 / Pathé Frères – The Japanese Film / JP / col. / 14

Mr. Bolter's Infatuation* (*Bolten is onnoozel*), 1912 / George D. Baker / Vitagraph Company of America / US / b&w / 12

Mr. Pyp als Champignon-zuechter (*Mijnheer Pijp als kweeker van champignons*), 1913 / Charles Decroix / Monopolfilm / DE / col. / 17

Mr. Smith, Barber (*Billy de vroolijke coiffeur*), 1912 / IMP – Independent Motion Picture Corporation / US / b&w / 6

Mrs. 'Enry 'Awkins, 1912 / Van Dyke Brooke / Vitagraph Company of America / US / b&w / 12

Mystère des Roches de Kador, Le* ([*Geheim van de rotsen van Kador, Het*]), 1912 / Léonce Perret / Gaumont / FR / col. / 38

Mystère du pont Notre Dame, Le (*Geheim der brug 'Notre-Dame', Het*), 1912 / Victorin Jasset / Eclair / FR / b&w / 35

Mystery of Lonely Gulch, The (*Geheim van canon, Het*), 1911 / Pathé Frères – American Kinema / US / b&w / 9

N

Nain détective, Le (*Bobby de kleinste detective der wereld*), 1909 / Film des Auteurs / FR / b&w / 9

Napoleon, the Man of Destiny (*Napoleon de grootste man uit de Fransche geschiedenis*), 1909 / J. Stuart Blackton / Vitagraph Company of America / US / b&w / 24

Nat Pinkerton (*Nat Pinkerton*), 1911 / Pierre Bressol / Eclipse / FR / col. / 10

Navajo's Bride, The* (*Panterkat, de moedige Indiaan*), 1910 / [Sidney Olcott] / Kalem / US / b&w / 14

Nave dei leoni, La ([*Leeuwenschip, Het*]), 1912 / Luigi Maggi / Ambrosio / IT / col. / 21

Nel paese dell'oro* ([*Goudzoekers, De*]), 1914 / Cines / IT / col. / 25

Nel vortice del destino*, 1913 / Savoia Film / IT / col. / FRG

Nelly la domatrice (*Nelly de leeuwentemster*), 1912 / Mario Caserini / Ambrosio / IT / col. / 25

Neuer Apparat zur Verhütung von Kinobränden, Ein (*Neuer Apparat zur Verhütung von Kinobränden, Ein*), 1912 / DE / b&w / 4

Neuer Erwerbszweig, Ein (*Nieuwe werkkring, Een*), 1912 / Messter / DE / col. / 8

[***Nieuwste begroeting, De***] (*Nieuwste begroeting, De*), [1910] / Cines / IT / col. / 10

Non è sempre facile rincasare ([*Plezierreis van Pinsonnet, De*]), 1912 / Itala Film / IT / b&w / 11

Non tu ne sortiras pas sans moi (*Toch d'r zin*), 1911 / Jean Durand / Gaumont / FR / col. / 4

Nordlandrose* (*Roos van het Noorden, De*), 1914 / Curt A. Stark / Messter / DE / col. / 36

Nuage, Un* (*Donkere wolkjes*), 1913 / Léonce Perret / Gaumont / FR / col. / 11

O

Oasis d'El-Kantara, L' (*Oase van El-Cantora, De*), 1913 / Eclair / FR / col. / 4

Obsession d'or, L' (*Visioen van rijkdom, Een*), 1906 / Lucien Nonguet / Pathé Frères / FR / col. / 3

Obsession du souvenir, L'* (*Kwellende herinnering aan het verleden*), 1913 / Gaumont / FR / col. / 13

Odissea, L' (*Odyssee von Homer, Die*), 1911 / Francesco Bertolini / Milano Films / IT / col. / 42

Oh, You Ragtime!* ([*Kracht van muziek, de*]), 1912 / Etienne Arnaud / Eclair Company / US / b&w / 5

Old Silver Watch, The (*Oude zilveren horloge, Het*), 1912 / Van Dyke Brooke / Vitagraph Company of America / US / b&w / 13

Omelette de Polycarpe, L' (*Ommelette van Polycarp, De*), 1913 / Ernest Servaes / Eclipse / FR / b&w / 6

On Secret Service* (*On Secret Service*), 1912 / Walter Edwards / NYMPC – New York Motion Picture Kay-Bee / US / col. / 32

Onafhankelijkheidsfeesten te Rotterdam, op Maandag 17 November 1913 (*Onafhankelijkheidsfeesten te Rotterdam, op Maandag 17 November 1913*), 1913 / NL / b&w / 5

One of the Bravest* (*Dapperste, De*), 1914 / Powers Company / US / col. / 26

Onésime débute au théâtre* ([*Karel voor het eerst in het Grand Theater*]), 1913 / Jean Durand / Gaumont / FR / col. / 6

Onésime écrit un roman d'amour ([*Onesime schrijft een liefdesroman*]), 1912 / Jean Durand / Gaumont / FR / b&w / 5

Onésime et la toilette de mademoiselle Badinois ([*Onesime en het toilet van mej. Radinois*]), 1912 / Jean Durand / Gaumont / FR / b&w / 8

Onésime et son collègue (*Van je vrienden moet je het hebben*), 1913 / Jean Durand / Gaumont / FR / col. / 8

Onésime horloger (*Onesime als horlogemaker*), 1912 / Jean Durand / Gaumont / FR / col. / 8

[***Onheil aanbrengende paar pantoffels, Het***] (*Onheil aanbrengende paar pantoffels, Het*), [1911] / Raleigh & Robert / FR / b&w / 4

Only Veteran in Town, The (*Oude veteraan, Een*), 1913 / Charles Kent / Vitagraph Company of America / US / col. / 14

[***Oogst van cocosnoten in Amerika***] (*Oogst van cocosnoten in Amerika*), [1912] / Selig Polyscope / US / col. / 4

[***Oplaten eener verkenningsballon, Het***] (*Oplaten eener verkenningsballon, Het*), [1912] / Vitascope / DE / col. / 5

Opening van het Vredespaleis (*Opening van het Vredespaleis*), 1913 / Willy Mullens / Alberts Frères / NL / b&w / 2

Organ Grinder, The (*Orgeldraaier, De*), 1912 / Kalem / US / b&w / 14

Orgie romaine, L' (*Löwen des Tyrannen, Die*), 1911 / Louis Feuillade / Gaumont / FR / col. / 9

Oro maledetto, L' (*Noodlottige wantrouwen, Het*), 1911 / Aquila Films / IT / col. / 11

Oscar a pris les femmes en horreur (*Oscar haat de vrouwen*), 1913 / Gaumont / FR / col. / 13

Oscar pris au piège* ([*Zooiets kan mij niet gebeuren*]), 1913 / Louis Feuillade / Gaumont / FR / col. / 9

Otage, L'* (*Gijzelaar, De*), 1912 / Lux / FR / col. / 14

Out West ([*Out West*]), 1918 / Roscoe 'Fatty' Arbuckle / Comique Film / US / col. / 17

Over the Back Fence* (*Over de schutting*), 1913 / C. Jay Williams / Edison Manufacturing Company / US / b&w / 13

P

Padre* (*Vader*), 1912 / Gino Zaccaria, Dante Testa / Itala Film / IT / col. / 39

Pain quotidien, Le (*Strijd om het bestaan, De*), 1911 / [Louis Feuillade] / Gaumont / FR / col. / 10

Pair of Boots, A (*Inbrekersgrap, Een*), 1912 / Kalem / US / b&w / 8

Panne d'auto* (*Autopech, Een*), 1912 / Baldassarre Negroni / Celio Film / IT / col. / 13

[Pantoffelhelden] ([*Pantoffelhelden*]), [1912] / Rudi Bach / Eiko Film / DE / col. / 14

Pappa's Sweetheart (*Moeder was nog niet vergeten*), 1911 / Bannister Merwin / Edison Manufacturing Company / US / b&w / 9

Par amour de son enfant (*Uit liefde voor zijn kind*), 1911 / Radios / FR / b&w / 4

Paradies der Damen, Das* ([*Paradijs der dames*]), 1914 / Max Mack / Vitascope/PAGU / DE / col. / 16

Parc Royale de Caserte, Le, 1909 / Eclipse / FR / col. / 2

Pardonne grand-père (*Vergiffenis van grootvader, De*), 1908 / Pathé Frères / FR / b&w / 7

Paresse de Polycarpe, La (*Polycarp is lui*), 1914 / Ernest Servaes / Eclipse / FR / b&w / 5

[Pari de M. Papillon, Le] ([*Vroolijke avontuur in hotel Bristol, Het*]), 1914 / Eclipse / FR / col. / 16

Paris inondé (*Paris inondé 22-23-24 Janvier 1910*), 1910 / Gaumont / FR / b&w / 5

Partie de tandem, Une (*Ik fiets met mijn vrouw*), 1909 / Eclipse / FR / col. / 5

Pathé Courant (*Pathé-Journaal*), 1912–1917, 8 newsreel episodes / Pathé Frères / FR / b&w / ca. 4

Patouillard a mangé du homard (*Gibrouille heeft zeekreeft gegeten*), 1911 / Roméo Bosetti / Lux / FR / b&w / 5

Patouillard a une femme jalouse (*Patouillard heeft een jaloersche vrouw*), 1911 / Roméo Bosetti / Lux / FR / b&w / 5

Patouillard a une femme qui veux suivre la mode (*Patouillard heeft een vrouw die met de mode wil mededoen*), 1912 / Roméo Bosetti / Lux / FR / b&w / 6

Patouillard crieur de journaux (*Lemke als courantenjongen*), 1911 / Roméo Bosetti / Lux / FR / b&w / 7

Patouillard embêté par Jacobus (*Dierenbeschermer, De*), 1912 / Roméo Bosetti / Lux / FR / b&w / 9

Patouillard fait du Sandow (*Gibrouille maakt athletische oefeningen*), 1911 / Roméo Bosetti / Lux / FR / b&w / 6

Patouillard ordonnance par amour (*Christiaan pakjesdrager uit liefde*), 1911 / Roméo Bosetti / Lux / FR / b&w / 6

Patouillard paie ses dettes (*Hoe Lemke zijn schulden betaalt*), 1911 / Roméo Bosetti / Lux / FR / b&w / 6

Pauline* (*Opoffering eener moeder, De*), 1914 / Henri Étiévant / Vitascope/PAGU / DE / col. / 48

Paysages du Japon, 1911 / Pathé

Pêche à la morue à la ligne de fond en Islande (*Kabeljauwvangst met den grong-angel in IJsland*), 1911 / Pathé Frères / FR / b&w / 4

Pendu, Le ([*Jongmensch heeft zich opgehangen, Een*]), 1906 / Pathé Frères / FR / b&w / 7

Pension de famille modele, Un (*Model pension, Een*), 1912 / Eclipse / FR / col. / 6

Per amore di Jenny* (*Het was een droom*), 1915 / Cines / IT / col. / 17

Per l'onore della marmitta (*Twee concurrenten, De*), 1912 / Itala Film / IT / col. / 6

Perils of Pauline*, 1914 / Louis J. Gasnier / Wharton / US / b&w / FRG

Perle de la Méditerrannée: Barcelone, La, 1913 / Eclipse / FR / b&w / 6

Perle, Une* (*Parel van een keukenmeid, Een*), 1912 / Léonce Perret / Gaumont / FR / col. / 11

Perlen bedeuten Tränen (*Paarlen beteekenen tranen*), 1911 / Adolf Gärtner / Messter / DE / b&w / 14

Permission de Polycarpe, La (*Polycarpe heeft verlof*), 1913 / Ernest Servaes / Eclipse / FR / b&w / 6

Pescara, Il (*Pescara, De*), 1912 / Ambrosio / IT / col. / 4

Petite mère (*Waar is mijn moedertje*), 1910 / Léonce Perret / Gaumont / FR / col. / 13

Petites causes, grands effets (*Kleine oorzaken, groote gevolgen*), 1912 / Gaumont / FR / col. / 6

Pétronille gagne le grand steeple (*Petronella wint de groote prijs*), 1912 / Roméo Bosetti / Eclair / FR / b&w / 7

Peur des ombres, La (*Vrees voor schaduwen, De*), 1911 / Pathé Frères – Pathé Nizza / FR / b&w / 4

Pfarrers Töchterlein, Des ([*Dochter van den dominee, De*]), 1912 / Adolf Gärtner / Messter / DE / col. / 28

Pickpocket, The* (*Lotje wordt genezen*), 1913 / George D. Baker / Vitagraph Company of America / US / col. / 13

Picture Idol, The (*Ideaal van de bioscoop, Het*), 1912 / James Young / Vitagraph Company of America / US / col. / 14

Picture Palace Piecans (*Moderne bioscoop te koop*), 1914 / W.P. Kellino / Vaudefilms / GB / b&w / 4

Pietà di un angelo (*Medelijden*), 1911 / Pasquali / IT / col. / 14

Pik Nik è fanatico pei fiori (*Teddy houdt van bloemen*), 1911 / Mario Morais / Aquila Films / IT / b&w / 5

Pik Nik ha il do di petto (*Teddy Holzbock als ritter vom Hoben C.*), 1911 / Mario Morais / Aquila Films / IT / b&w / 5

Pik Nik veste la jupe-culotte* (*Teddy en de harembroek*), 1911 / Mario Morais / Aquila Films / IT / b&w / 5

Pipe d'opium, La (*Opiumpfeife, Die*), 1912 / René Leprince / Pathé Frères / FR / col. / 17

Pique-nique d'Arthème, Le ([*Pic-nic van Arthéme*]), 1912 / Ernest Servaes / Eclipse / FR / col. / 7

Più che la morte ([*Erger dan de dood*]), 1912 / Cines / IT / col. / 13

Più forte che Sherlock Holmes (*Sterker dan Sherlock Holmes*), 1913 / Giovanni Pastrone / Itala Film / IT / col. / 6

[Piu vasto altipiano, Il] (*Groote plateau van den Carnische Alpen, Het*), [1914] / [Milano Film] / IT / col. / 4

Playmates (*Zwervende hond, De*), 1912 / Vitagraph Company of America / US / b&w / 13

Poedinok ([*Duel, Het*]), 1910 / Maurice André Maître / Pathé Frères – Le Film Russe / RU / col. / 7

Polidor attendente ([*Polidor als ordonance*]), 1913 / Ferdinand Guillaume / Pasquali / IT / b&w / 5

Polidor contro la suocera (*Polidor contra zijne schoonmoeder*), 1912 / Pasquali / IT / b&w / 8

Polidor e l'americana (*Polidor doet een goed huwelijk*), 1915 / Ferdinand Guillaume / Polidor Film / IT / b&w / 6

Polycarpe architecte (*Polycarpe als architect*), 1913 / Ernest Servaes / Eclipse / FR / b&w / 6

Polycarpe en villégiature ([*Polycarpe gaat naar buiten*]), 1913 / Ernest Servaes / Eclipse / FR / col. / 8

Polycarpe fait de la morale au centimètre* (*Polycarp als inspecteur van de mode*), 1914 / Ernest Servaes / Eclipse / FR / b&w / 5

Polycarpe veut faire un carton (*Polycarpe is aan het schijfschieten*), 1914 / Ernest Servaes / Eclipse / FR / b&w / 5

Polyte esclave de la consigne (*Polyte en het consigne*), 1912 / Eclipse / FR / col. / 5

Poney de Bob, Le (*Poney van Bob, De*), 1912 / Eclipse / FR / b&w / 4

Poor Musician, The (*Dochter van de musicus, De*), 1909 / Van Dyke Brooke / Vitagraph Company of America / US / b&w / 14

Port de Barcelone, Le (*Haven van Barcelona, De*), 1913 / Eclipse / FR / col. / 5

Portrait inachevé, Le (*Onvoltooide portret, Het*), 1910 / Gaumont / FR / col. / 19

Post Telegrapher, The* (*Twee helden of de strijd om het fort*), 1912 / Francis Ford / NYMPC – New York Motion Picture Bison / US / b&w / 24

Première aventure, La (*Eerste avontuur, Het*), 1911 / [Léonce Perret] / Gaumont / FR / col. / 9

Price of Gold, The (*Price of Gold, The*), 1913 / Essanay Film Manufacturing / US / b&w / 14

Prima bicicletta di Robinet, La (*Zijn eerste fiets*), 1910 / Ambrosio / IT / b&w / 4

Primevères, Les (*Hoe de naam 'Hemelbloemetje' ontstond*), 1910 / Lux / FR / col. / 7

Primo duello di Polidor, Il (*Eerste duel van Polidor, Het*), 1913 / Ferdinand Guillaume / Pasquali / IT / b&w / 8

Promenade dans Los-Angeles, Une (*Los Angelos*), 1912 / IMP – Independent Motion Picture Corporation / US / col. / 5

Promesse, La (*Gelofte, De*), 1913 / Eclair / FR / col. / 8

Property Man, The, 1914 / Charles Chaplin / Keystone Film / US / b&w / FRG

Proposal from the Duke, A* (*Martha wil 'n aristocraat trouwen*), 1913 / Walter Edwin / Edison Manufacturing Company / US / b&w / 15

Pumps* (*Wie mooi wil zijn, moet pijn lijden*), 1913 / Larry Trimble / Vitagraph Company of America / US / col. / 8

Pursuit of the Smugglers, The (*Smokkelaars, De*), 1913 / J.P. McGowan / Kalem / US / col. / 14

Q

Question of Seconds, A* (*Kwestie van eenige seconden, De*), 1912 / Edison Manufacturing Company / US / b&w / 12

R

Raccommodeur, la pipe et le vase, Le (*Hersteller, de pijp en de vaas, De*), 1912 / Lucien Nonguet / ACAD – Association Cinématographique des Auteurs Dramatiques / FR / b&w / 8

Rachat de l'honneur, Le, 1913 / Gaumont / FR / col. / 30

Railroad Wooing, A* (*Trouwen met*

hindernissen), 1913 / Kalem / US / b&w / 14
Railway de la mort, Le (Weg des doods, De), 1912 / Jean Durand / Gaumont / FR / col. / 20
Railway Mail Clerk, The (Spoorwegpostbeambte, De), 1910 / Kalem / US / b&w / 14
Ranchman's Vengeance, The ([Wraak van een boer, De]), 1911 / Allan Dwan / American Film Manufacturing / US / col. / 15
Rançon du bonheur, La* (Vervlogen geluk), 1912 / Léonce Perret / Gaumont / FR / col. / 27
Rapaces, Les ([Roofzucht, De]), 1912 / Oliver G. Pike / Pathé Frères / FR / col. / 5
Rapallo (Rapollo), 1914 / Cines / IT / col. / 4
Rätsel seines Lebens, Das (Raadsel des levens, Het), 1912 / Deutsche Mutoskop und Biograph / DE / b&w / 36
Ratto delle Sabine, Il (Sabijnsche maagdenroof, De), 1910 / Ugo Falena / Pathé Frères – Film d'Arte Italiana / IT / col. / 17
Ravalement précipité, Un (Rosalia, de knappe huisbewaarster), 1911 / Roméo Bosetti / Pathé Frères / FR / b&w / 5
Re Enzo (Koning Enzo), 1911 / Giuseppe de Liguoro / Milano Films / IT / col. / 9
Recht aufs Dasein, Das* (Op bevel van aanhouding), 1913 / Joseph Delmont / Eiko Film / DE / col. / 44
Red Barrier, The (Visioen, Het), 1912 / Vitagraph Company of America / US / col. / 15
Redemption of Red Rube, The (Kind en de bandiet, Het), 1912 / Rollin S. Sturgeon / Vitagraph Company of America / US / col. / 13
Regina per quindici giorni (Koningin voor twee weken), 1911 / Mario Caserini / Cines / IT / col. / 13
[*Reisje door het hooge noorden, Een*] (Reisje door het hooge noorden, Een), [1912] / Vitascope / DE / col. / 5
[*Reisje door omstreken van Corvu, Een*] (Reisje door omstreken van Corvu, Een), [1912] / DK / col. / 3
Renegades, The* (Slechte huishouding, Een), 1912 / Lubin Manufacturing Company / US / b&w / 14
Reve du cocher, Le (Droom van den koetsier, De), 1913 / Gaumont / FR / col. / 7
Revenge Is Sweet (Wraak van den kantoorjongen, De), 1912 / Charles M. Seay / Edison Manufacturing Company / US / b&w / 9
Reward of Perseverance, The* (Taschje van Miss Nelly, Het), 1912 / Bert Haldane / Barker Motion Photography / GB / b&w / 6
Richard Wagner* (Richard Wagner), 1913 / Carl Froelich / Messter / DE / col. / 105
Rigadin explorateur, 1912 / Georges Monca / Pathé Frères / FR / col. / 6
Rigadin n'aime pas le vendredi 13 (Moritz is bijgeloovig), 1911 / Georges Monca / Pathé Frères – SCAGL / FR / b&w / 6
Right Number, But the Wrong House, The* (809 of 608), 1913 / Edison Manufacturing Company / US / b&w / 10
Riley's Decoys* (Goede reclame, Een), 1913 / Biograph / US / b&w / 7
Rinaldo Rinaldini, 1927 / Max Obal / Aafa Film / DE / col. / 81
Riposo festivo (Jim wil een dag vrij hebben), 1912 / Cines / IT / b&w / 9
Robinet chauffeur miope* ([Robinet bijziende chauffeur]), 1914 / Marcel Fabre / Ambrosio / IT / col. / 7
Robinet in vacanza (Robinet heeft vacantie), 1912 / Marcel Fabre / Ambrosio / IT / col. / 9
Robinet innamorato di una chanteuse ([Nauke wordt verliefd op een chanteuse]), 1911 / Marcel Fabre / Ambrosio / IT / b&w / 8
Robinet padre e figlio (Wenn der Vater mit dem Sohne...), 1912 / Ambrosio / IT / b&w / 8
Robinet pescatore (Robinet gaat uit visschen), 1914 / Marcel Fabre / Ambrosio / IT / col. / 5
Robinet ricattatore (Afpersers, De), 1912 / Ambrosio / IT / col. / 12
Robinet ricco per dieci minuti (Robinet rijk voor 10 minuten), 1912 / Marcel Fabre / Ambrosio / IT / col. / 7
Robinet Scioperante*, 1912 / Ambrosio / IT / b&w / 6
Robinet troppo amato da sua moglie (Robinet wordt te veel bemind), 1912 / Marcel Fabre / Ambrosio / IT / b&w / 8
Robinet vuol fare il jockey (Nauke als jockey), 1910 / Marcel Fabre / Ambrosio / IT / b&w / 4
Roches et grottes de Baume, Les (Rotsen van Baume-les-Messiers (Jura), De), 1913 / Eclipse / FR / col. / 5
Roman de la petite vendeuse, Le, 1912 / Gaumont / FR / col. / 28
Roman de l'écuyère, Le (Abgewiesene Verehrer, Der), 1909 / Camille de Morlhon / Pathé Frères / FR / col. / 7
Roman d'un caissier, Le* (Vaderleed), 1914 / Emile Chautard / Eclair / FR / col. / 43
Romance of the Cliff Dwellers, A (Primitief man, Een), 1911 / Edwin S. Porter / Edison Manufacturing Company / US / b&w / 14
Romanzo di un fantino, Il (Roman van een jockey, De), 1910 / Ambrosio / IT / col. / 12
Rosa Pantöffelchen, Das*, 1913 / Franz Hofer / Luna-Film / DE / col. / 28
Rosalie et ses meubles fidèles, 1911 / Roméo Bosetti / Pathé Frères – Comica / FR / b&w / 5
Rosalie et son phonographe (Rosalie en haar phonograaf), 1911 / Roméo Bosetti / Pathé Frères / FR / b&w / 4
Rose of Old St. Augustine, The (Rose von St. Augustine, Die), 1911 / Otis Turner / Selig Polyscope / US / b&w / 14
Rose O'Salem Town (Roos van Salem, De), 1910 / D.W. Griffith / Biograph / US / b&w / 14
[*Rotsen en golven*] (Rotsen en golven), [1911] / Gaumont / FR / col. / 3
Royaume des fleurs, Le (Bloemenweelde), [1914] / Gaumont / FR / col. / 1
Rozhdyestvo obitateli Iyesa (Heilige nacht), 1912 / Ladislas Starevitch / A. Khanzhonkov & Co. / RU / col. / 6
Runaway Engine, The (Führerlose lokomotive, Die), 1911 / Kalem / US / b&w / 14
Rupe del Malconsiglio, La* (Wraak van den veedrijver, De), 1913 / Cines / IT / col. / 26
Ruse de Miss Plumcake, La (List van de Amerikaansche, De), 1911 / Georges Monca / Pathé Frères – SCAGL / FR / b&w / 5

S

Salti e laghi del fiume Velino (Rivier Velino, De), 1912 / Cines / IT / col. / 3
San Sebastiano (Uit den tijd van Keizer Deocletianus), 1911 / Giuseppe de Liguoro / Milano Films / IT / col. / 8
Sangue bleu* (Vorstin van Monte Cabello, De), 1914 / Nino Oxilia / Celio Film / IT / col. / 65
Santa Lucia (Santa-Lucia), 1910 / Ambrosio / IT / col. / 5
Saved by the Pony Express (Gered door een expressrijder), 1911 / Frank Boggs / Selig Polyscope / US / b&w / 14
Scandale au village, Un* (Dorpsschandaal, Een), 1913 / Maurice Mariaud / Gaumont / FR / col. / 13
Schein trügt, Der* (Schijn bedriegt), 1914 / Eiko Film / DE / col. / 15
[*Schoone Noord-Afrikaansche kustgebergte, Het*] (Schoone Noord-Afrikaansche kustgebergte, Het), [1911] / Pathé Frères / FR / col. / 2
[*Schoonste uit de natuur, Het*] (Schoonste uit de natuur, Het), [1912] / Gaumont / FR / col. / 4
Schuldig*, 1913 / Hans Oberländer / Messter / DE / col. / 70
Schwarze Kugel oder die geheimnisvollen Schwestern, Die* (Geheimzinnige zusters, De), 1913 / Franz Hofer / Luna-Film / DE / col. / 35
Schwarze Natter, Die* (Gevaarlijke vrouw, Een), 1913 / Franz Hofer / Luna-Film / DE / col. / 34
Scimmia per amore (Gotlieb Wurm is een aap), 1911 / Aquila Films / I / b&w / 5
She Cried* (Huilebalk, De), 1912 / Albert W. Hale / Vitagraph Company of America / US / col. / 10
Shipwrecked (Schipbreuk, De), 1911 / Frank Boggs / Selig Polyscope / US / b&w / 10
Show Girl, The ([Liefdessmart]), 1911 / Van Dyke Brooke / Vitagraph Company of America / US / b&w / 13
Sign of the Cross, The* (Teeken des kruises, Het), 1914 / Frederick A. Thomson / Famous Players / US / col. / 65
Signal Fire, The* ([Roman van de zee]), 1912 / William V. Ranous / Vitagraph Company of America / US / col. / 9
Signora dall'eterno sorriso, La ([Haar minnaar]), 1912 / Itala Film / IT / b&w / 5
Signora Fricot è gelosa, La (Juffrouw Fricot is jaloersch), 1913 / Ambrosio / IT / b&w / 8
Singe de Pétronille, Le (Aap van Petronella, De), 1913 / Georges Rémond / Eclair / FR / col. / 7
Slim Jim's Last Chance (Laatste waarschuwing, De), 1911 / Kenean Buel / Kalem / US / b&w / 5
Smyrne (Smyrna), 1911 / Eclair / FR / col. / 3
Sogno di un tramonto d'autunno (Fluch eines betrogenen Weibes, Der), 1911 / Luigi Maggi / Ambrosio / IT / col. / 16
Soir de noel dans un salon de mode (Weihnachten im Putzsalon), 1911 / Gaumont / FR / col. / 11
Soldier's Duty, A, 1912 / Charles Brabin / Edison Manufacturing Company / US / b&w / 11
Solitaires* (Onwetend verloofd), 1913 / Van Dyke Brooke / Vitagraph Company of America / US / b&w / 7
Son passé* ([Haar verleden]), 1913 / Henri Fescourt / Gaumont / FR / col. / 31
Sorte domino, Den*, 1910 / Nordisk Films Kompagni / DK / b&w
Sous le ciel Basque (Onder de baskische hemel), 1913 / Eclipse / FR / col. / 4
Spauracchio, Lo (Vogelverschrikker,

De), 1912 / Cines / IT / col. / 12

Spoiled Darling's Doll, The (Elsa's pop), 1913 / Thanhouser Film / US / b&w / 15

[**Sportfilm**] ([*Sportfilm*]), [1910] / b&w / 5

Sposa del Nilo, La (*Bruid van den Nijl*), 1911 / Enrico Guazzoni / Cines Princeps Film / IT / col. / 17

Steckbrief, Der*(*Noodlottige liefde*), 1913 / Franz Hofer / Luna-Film / DE / col. / 42

Stenographer Troubles*(*Nieuwe machineschrijfster, Eene*), 1913 / Frederick A. Thomson / Vitagraph Company of America / US / b&w / 14

Stenographer Wanted (*Keuze van eene machineschrijfster, De*), 1912 / Vitagraph Company of America / US / b&w / 12

Stern des Südens (*Stern des Südens*), 1911 / R. Güntzel / Vitascope / DE / col. / 74

Stierkämpfe in Barcelona (*Stierengevecht*), 1909 / Gaumont / FR / b&w / 7

[**Stoccolma pittoresca**] ([*Stoccolma pittoresca*]), [1909] / Pasquali / [IT] / b&w / 4

Streets of New York*(*Geheimen eener wereldstad, De*), 1913 / Travers Vale / Pilot Films / US / col. / 40

Strength of Men, The*([*Zucht naar 't goud*]), 1913 / Ralph Ince / Vitagraph Company of America / US / col. / 21

Strong Man's Burden, The*(*Last van den sterkere, De*), 1913 / D.W. Griffith / Biograph / US / col. / 15

Styrmandens sidste fart (*Tusschen hemel en water*), 1913 / Eduard Schnedler-Sørensen / Nordisk Films Kompagni / DK / col. / 9

Sua Maestà il sangue*(*Van koninklijke bloede*), 1913 / Roberto Roberti / Aquila Films / IT / b&w / 39

Successo diplomatico, Un (*Bommenwerpster, De*), 1913 / Ambrosio / IT / col. / 16*

Sui gradini del trono*(*Strijd om een troon, De*), 1912 / Ubaldo Maria Del Colle / Pasquali / IT / col. / 59

Suing Susan (*Door de schutting*), 1912 / Larry Trimble / Vitagraph Company of America / US / b&w / 12

Suisse merveilleuse (*Grindelwald et le Rothorn*) (*Mooi Zwitserland*), 1913 / Eclair Scientia / FR / col. / 4

Suisse merveilleuse, La (*Isola Bella en Locarno*) (*Zwitserland*), 1913 / Eclair Scientia / FR / col. / 3

Sulla via dell'oro*(*Goudzoeker, De*), 1913 / Baldassarre Negroni / Cines / IT / col. / 24

Sulle rive del Pescara (*Aan de oevers der Pascara*), 1912 / Cines / IT / col. / 4

Sumpfblume, Die (*Vloek van haar verleden, De*), 1913 / Viggo Larsen / Treumann-Larsen-Film-Vertrieb / DE / col. / 54

Suoceri, I (*Julius en zijn schoonpapa*), 1912 / Cines / IT / b&w / 9

Supplizio dei leoni, Il (*Overwinning na strijd*), 1914 / Luigi Mele / Pasquali / IT / col. / 62

Sur la mer Caspienne (*Panorama van Rusland; De Caspische Zee*), 1912 / Gaumont / FR / col. / 3

Sur le lac Léman (*Op het meer van Leman*), 1913 / Radios / FR / col. / 4

Surprises de l'amour, Les (*Verrassingen der liefde, De*), 1912 / Gaumont / FR / col. / 13

Suzanne et les vieillards (*Suzanne met oude heeren*), 1912 / Henri Fescourt / Gaumont / FR / col. / 13

T

Tangled Tangoists (*John gaat naar een soirée*), 1914 / George D. Baker / Vitagraph Company of America / US / b&w / 14

Target Practice of Atlantic Fleet US Navy (*Amerikaansche vlootmanoeuvre*), 1912 / Edison Manufacturing Company / US / col. / 6

[**Te midden de heerlijke Zwitsersche Alpen**] (*Te midden de heerlijke Zwitsersche Alpen*), [1912] / WKF Welt Kino / DE / col. / 4

Teddy a mangé des grenouilles (*Teddy heeft kikvorschen gegeten*), 1912 / Lux / FR / b&w / 7

[**Tempête dans le golfe de Gascogne**] (*Storm op zee*), [1911] / Gaumont / FR / col. / 3

Tenacité de Polycarpe, La (*Volharding van Polycarpe, De*), 1914 / Ernest Servaes / Eclipse / FR / b&w / 6

Terra promessa, La*(*Goud en liefde*), 1913 / Baldassarre Negroni / Celio Film / IT / col. / 35

Test of a Friendship, A (*Moeilijke redding, Een*), 1911 / Bannister Merwin / Edison Manufacturing Company / US / b&w / 16

Teufelsauge, Das*(*Duivelsoog, de beroemde diamant*), 1914 / Harry Piel / Vay & Hubert / DE / col. / 45

Teufelskirche, Die (*Djävulskyrkan*), 1919 / Hans Mierendorff / Lucifer-Film-Co / DE / col. / 55

Teutoburgerwoud (*Teutoburgerwoud*), 1912 / DE / b&w / 5

Thor, Lord of the Jungles (*Heer der wildernis, De*), 1913 / Colin Campbell / Selig Polyscope / US / col. / 27

Those Troublesome Tresses*(*Jaloersche echtgenooten, De*), 1913 / George D. Baker / Vitagraph Company of America / US / b&w / 13

Tilly in a Boarding House (*Tilly en Dolly hebben vacantie*), 1912 / Hay Plumb / Hepworth / GB / col. / 7

Tirailleurs anamites, Les (*Anamitische tirailleurs*), 1913 / Eclair / FR / col. / 7

Tomboy on Bar Z, The (*Dochter uit het goudkamp, De*), 1912 / Gilbert M. 'Broncho Billy' Anderson / Essanay Film Manufacturing / US / b&w / 15

Tontolini commesso viaggiatore (*Tontolini doet in lijm*), 1911 / Cines / IT / b&w / 5

Tontolini filantropo (*Tontolini als volksopvoeder*), 1911 / Cines / IT / b&w / 7

Tontolini sbaglia piano (*Tontolini is vroolijk*), 1911 / Cines / IT / b&w / 6

Topolini riconoscenti, I*(*Grootmoeder's kerstvertellingen*), 1908 / Ambrosio / IT / col. / 7

Torchon brûle, Le (*Echtelijke twist*), 1911 / Roméo Bosetti / Pathé Frères – Comica / FR / b&w / 5

[**Tot inkeer gebracht**] (*Tot inkeer gebracht*), [1911] / Radios / FR / col. / 9

Totò critico della nuova moda (*Toto is aanhanger van de nieuwe mode*), 1911 / Emilio Vardannes / Itala Film / IT / b&w / 5

Tournée du docteur, La (*Grossmutige Arzt, Der*), 1911 / Pathé Frères – SCAGL / FR / b&w / 10

Toys of Destiny (*Speelgoedwinkel, De*), 1915 / Biograph / US / b&w / 11

Tra le pinete di Rodi (*In de bosschen van het eiland Rhodes*), 1912 / Savoia Film / IT / col. / 4

Trabocchetto punitore, Il (*Gevaarlijke valluiken, De*), 1912 / Cines / IT / col. / 12

Tragedia al cinematografo, Una (*Treurspel in de bioscoop, Een*), 1913 / Enrico Guazzoni / Cines / IT / col. / 8

Tragedia di Kri Kri, La*(*Patachon wil zich dood houden*), 1913 / Cines / IT / b&w / 9

Tragico convegno*(*Maria Pansa, het kleine meisje*), 1915 / Ivo Illuminati / Celio Film / IT / col. / 34

Trail of Cards, The (*Trail of Cards, The*), 1913 / Gilbert P. Hamilton / American Film Manufacturing / US / b&w / 15

Travail des éléphants, Le (*Werkzaamheden van Olifanten in West-Indië*), 1913 / Eclair / FR / col. / 4

Tribulations d'un huissier, Les (*Deurwaarde beetgenomen, Een*), 1911 / Eclair / FR / b&w / 6

Tried in the Fire*([*Millioenen erfgenaam, De*]), 1913 / Warwick Buckland / Hepworth / GB / col. / 15

Trionfo della forza, Il ([*Triomf der kracht, De*]), 1913 / Arrigo Frusta / Ambrosio / IT / col. / 17

Tripoli*(*Hoogland van Barka, Het*), 1912 / Ambrosio / IT / col. / 4

Tristano e Isotta (*Tristan und Isolde*), 1911 / Ugo Falena / Pathé Frères – Film d'Arte Italiana / IT / col. / 28

Triumph of Right, The*(*Overwinning van het recht, De*), 1912 / Rollin S. Sturgeon / Vitagraph Company of America / US / b&w / 15

Trompeurs trompés (*Met z'n tweeën op stap*), 1912 / Pathé Frères / FR / b&w / 8

Troublesome Stepdaughters, The (*Vijf dochters van den consul, De*), 1912 / George D. Baker / Vitagraph Company of America / US / b&w / 14

Trouvaille de Polycarpe, La ([*Vondst van Polycarpe, De*]), 1913 / Ernest Servaes / Eclipse / FR / b&w / 6

Turi, der Wanderlappe*(*Turi, der Wanderlappe*), 1913 / Alfred Lind / Deutsche Bioscop / DE / b&w / FRG

Tutela, La*([*Onder voogdijschap*]), 1913 / Baldassarre Negroni / Celio Film / IT / col. / 36

Twins, The ([*Tweeling zusters, De*]), 1911 / Edwin S. Porter / Rex Motion Picture Company / US / col. / 15

Two Brothers and a Spy (*Twee broeders*), 1912 / Hay Plumb / Hepworth / GB / col. / 10

Two Brothers, The (*Twee broeders*), 1910 / D.W. Griffith / Biograph / US / b&w / 11

Two Brothers, The (*Liefde en vriendschap*), 1912 / Pathé Frères – American Kinema / US / col. / 10

Two Little Rangers ([*Twee meisjes van het verre westen*]), 1912 / Alice Guy-Blaché / Solax / US / col. / 15

Two Naughty Boys (*Twee kleine nietsnutters*), 1909 / Dave Aylott / Clarendon Film / GB / b&w / 4

Types des Indes et de Ceylon (*Leven in Indië; Indische en Ceylon typen, Het*), 1913 / Eclair / FR / b&w / 4

U

[**Uitstapje door China, Een**] (*Uitstapje door China, Een*), 1911 / Eclair / FR / col. / 5

Ultimi giorni di Pompei, Gli (*Laatste dagen van Pompey, De*), 1908 / Luigi Maggi / Ambrosio / IT / col. / 16

Und das Licht erlosch (*Licht van den vuurtoren, Het*), 1914 / Fritz Bernhardt / Imperator Film / DE / col. / 43

Ungdommens ret (*Recht der jeugd, Het*), 1911 / August Blom / Nordisk Films Kompagni / DK / col. / 26

Up Against It (*Soirée met hindernissen, Een*), 1912 / Otis Turner / Universal IMP / US / col. / 10

Uragano, L' (*Wraak eener vrouw, De*), 1911 / Ubaldo Maria Del Colle / Pasquali / IT / col. / 38
Urolig vagt, En* (*Onrustige wacht, Een*), 1912 / Eduard Schnedler-Sørensen / Nordisk Films Kompagni / DK / col. / 5

V

V dni Getmanov (*Hoofdman Nicolajeff*), 1911 / Maurice André Maître / Pathé Frères – Le Film Russe / RU / b&w / 13
Ved Faenglets Port ([*Verleiding eener wereldstad, De*]), 1911 / August Blom / Nordisk Films Kompagni / DK / col. / 36
[Veelbelovend jongmens] (*Veelbelovend jongmens*), [1912] / Eclipse / FR / col. / 7
Veleno delle parole, Il (*Lastertongen*), 1913 / Baldassarre Negroni / Celio Film / IT / col. / 29
Vendetta d'amico (*Freundesrache*), 1911 / Ambrosio / IT / b&w / 9
Vengeance des esprits, La (*Rache der Geister, Die*), 1911 / Emile Cohl / Pathé Frères / FR / b&w / 5
Vengeance du concierge, La (*Wraak van den huisbewaarder, De*), 1911 / Pathé Frères / FR / b&w / 7
Vengeance du forgeron, La (*Vengeance du forgeron, La*), 1907 / Lucien Nonguet / Pathé Frères / FR / b&w / 7
Vengeance du sergent de ville, La* (*Wraak van den politie-agent, De*), 1913 / Louis Feuillade / Gaumont / FR / col. / 13
Venise et ses monuments (*Wonderen van Venetië, De*), 1914 / Eclair Scientia / FR / col. / 5
Venskab og kaerlighed (*Strijd om haar geluk, De*), 1911 / Eduard Schnedler-Sørensen / Nordisk Films Kompagni / DK / col. / 35
Ver à soie, Le (*Zijdewormenteelt, De*), 1912 / Gaumont / FR / col. / 8
Vergebens (*Vergebens*), 1911 / Walter Schmidthässler / Vitascope/PAGU / DE / col. / 17
Verhängnisvoller Schwur, Ein (*Verhängnisvoller Schwur, Ein*), 1919 / Emmerich Hanus / Dagny Servaes Exklusiv Film Fabrikat Deitz & Co / DE / col. / 116
Verräterin, Die* (*Verraadster, De*), 1911 / Peter Urban Gad / Deutsche Bioscop / DE / col. / 44
Verso l'amore* (*Ware liefde zegeviert, De*), 1913 / Ubaldo Pittei / Latium Film / IT / col. / 29
Versöhnt (*Verzoend*), 1911 / Pharos-Film der Deutschen Mutoskop und Biograph / DE / b&w / 10
Vertige, Le (*In 's levens maalstroom*), 1910 / Léonce Perret / Gaumont / FR / col. / 14
Veuve et son enfant, La (*In de wereldstad verloren*), 1911 / Gaumont / FR / col. / 11
Vicar of Wakefield, The (*Landprediger von Wakefield, Der*), 1910 / Theodore Marston / Thanhouser Film / US / b&w / 14
Vie et la passion de Notre Seigneur Jésus Christ, La* (*Van de kribbe tot het kruis*), 1907 / Ferdinand Zecca / Pathé Frères / FR / col. / 52
[Violoneux, Le] (*Zoon van den vioolspeler*), [1911] / Eclipse / FR / col. / 9
Vitagraph Romance, A (*Goede zijde van de bioscoop, De*), 1912 / James Young / Vitagraph Company of America / US / col. / 13
Vittoria o morte* (*Overwinnen of sterven*), 1913 / Itala Film / IT / col. / 38
Voetbalwedstrijd te Dordrecht, 1912 / NL / b&w / 4
Voix d'or, La* (*Verloren en gewonnen*), 1913 / Georges André Lacroix / Gaumont / FR / col. / 54
Vor tids dame (*Dollarprinses, Een*), 1912 / Eduard Schnedler-Sørensen / Nordisk Films Kompagni / DK / col. / 36
Voyage à toute vapeur, Une (*Plezierreis met een moderne oceaanstoomer*), 1909 / Eclipse / FR / b&w / 3
[Vriend Jaap haalt suiker] (*Vriend Jaap haalt suiker*), [1911] / Eclair / FR / b&w / 5

W

Was He a German Spy?* (*Duitsche spion, Een*), 1912 / Hay Plumb / Hepworth / GB / b&w / 8
Wasted Sacrifice, A ([*Noodelooze opoffering, Een*]), 1912 / Rollin S. Sturgeon / Vitagraph Company of America / US / col. / 15
Water Lilies (*Waterlelie, De*), 1911 / Vitagraph Company of America / US / col. / 14
Watersnood in Noord-Holland (*Watersnood in Noord-Holland*), 1916 / Kinematograaf Pathé Frères / NL / b&w / 4
Weihnachtsträume. Geschichte eines Kriegsinvaliden (*Kerstgedachten*), 1911 / Deutsche Bioscop / DE / b&w / 10
[Weltreise unseres Kronprinzen, Die] (*Weltreise unseres Kronprinzen, Die*), 1911 / Eclipse / FR / b&w / 4
Wenn Völker streiten* (*Wanneer volkeren strijden*), 1915 / Cäsar Lupow / Apollo-Film / DE / col. / 39
When Father Fetched the Doctor* (*Gelukkige vader, De*), 1913 / Dave Aylott / Cricks & Martin / GB / b&w / 4
When Lovers Part ([*Liefde heelt alles*]), 1910 / Kalem / US / b&w / 15
When Mary Grew Up* (*Meisje dat een jongen had moeten zijn, Een*), 1912 / James Young / Vitagraph Company of America / US / col. / 15
When Persistency and Obstinacy Meet* (*Geduld overwint alles*), 1912 / Vitagraph Company of America / US / col. / 14
When She Was About Sixteen ([*Gestoorde huwelijksreis, De*]), 1912 / Edison Manufacturing Company / US / col. / 15
When the Earth Trembled* (*Aardbeving, De*), 1913 / Barry O'Neill / Lubin Manufacturing Company / US / col. / 19
When the Night Call Came* (*Misdaad en liefde*), 1914 / Edward LeSaint / Selig Polyscope / US / col. / 15
When the West Was Young* (*Dankbaarheid van den Indiaan, De*), 1913 / William J. Bauman / Vitagraph Company of America / US / col. / 12
When Wealth Torments (*Geld en liefde*), 1912 / Essanay Film Manufacturing / US / b&w / 14
White Cloud's Secret (*Geheim der Witte Wolk, Het*), 1912 / Milton J. Fahrney / Nestor / US / b&w / 14
Wife of the Hills, A (*Vrouw van de bergen, Een*), 1912 / Gilbert M. 'Broncho Billy' Anderson / Essanay Film Manufacturing / US / b&w / 14
William Voss* (*William Voss contra Sherlock Holmes*), 1915 / Rudolf Meinert / Meinert-Film / DE / col. / 53
Willie the Hunter (*Willem de jager*), 1912 / Lubin Manufacturing Company / US / b&w / 7
Willie's Sister (*Zijn zuster*), 1912 / Vitagraph Company of America / US / b&w / 11
Willy est un enfant martyr ([*Willy is een kleine martelaar*]), 1912 / Joseph Faivre / Eclair / FR / b&w / 7
Willy et le vieux soupirant (*Willy en de oude vrijgezel*), 1912 / Joseph Faivre / Eclair / FR / b&w / 9
Willy roi des concierges (*Willy koning der huisbewaarders*), 1912 / Joseph Faivre / Eclair / FR / b&w / 6
Winning Back His Love (*Teruggewonnen liefde*), 1910 / D.W. Griffith / Biograph / US / b&w / 13
[Winter in Stockholm, Een] (*Winter in Stockholm, Een*), 1913 / Svea Film / SE / b&w / 4
Winterlandschappen, 1913 / WKF Welt Kino / DE / b&w / FRG
Wintersport in Zwitserland, 1915 / Continental-Kunstfilm / DE / b&w / FRG
Witch of the Everglades, The ([*Blanke dochter der Indianen, De*]), 1911 / Otis Turner / Selig Polyscope / US / b&w / 15
With the Assistance of Shep (*Hond als huwelijksmakelaar, De*), 1913 / Edison Manufacturing Company / US / b&w / 8
Wolf Among Lambs, A* ([*Bekeering, De*]), 1913 / Essanay Film Manufacturing / US / b&w / 15
Work in an US Arsenal, 1912 / Lubin Manufacturing Company / US / b&w / 11

Y

Yellowstone National Park, Wyoming, U.S. ([*Yellowstone Park*]), 1912 / Edison Manufacturing Company / US / col. / 7

Z

Zenscina zavtrashnego dnja* (*Vrouw, De*), 1914 / Pyotr Chardynin / A. Khanzhonkov & Co. / RU / col. / 42
Zigomar contre Nick Carter (*Bende van Z., De*), 1912 / Victorin Jasset / Eclair / FR / col. / 47
Zigomar, roi des voleurs (*Zigomar en Nick Carter*), 1911 / Victorin Jasset / Eclair / FR / col. / 13
Zigoto en pleine lune de miel ([*Zigoto in de wittebroodsweken*]), 1912 / Jean Durand / Gaumont / FR / col. / 7
Zigoto et la locomotive (*Zigoto en de lokomotief*), 1912 / Jean Durand / Gaumont / FR / col. / 7
Zigoto policier trouve une corde (*Zigoto als toreador*), 1912 / Jean Durand / Gaumont / FR / col. / 4
[Zigoto promène ses amis] (*Zigoto en zijn automobiel*), [1912] / Jean Durand / Gaumont / FR / col. / 6
Zu spät (*Te laat*), 1912 / Carl Froelich / Messter / DE / col. / 9
Zuviel des Guten (*Te veel van het goede*), 1914 / Messter / DE / col. / 13
Zweimal gelebt ([*Tweemaal geleefd*]), 1912 / Max Mack / Continental-Kunstfilm / DE / col. / 26

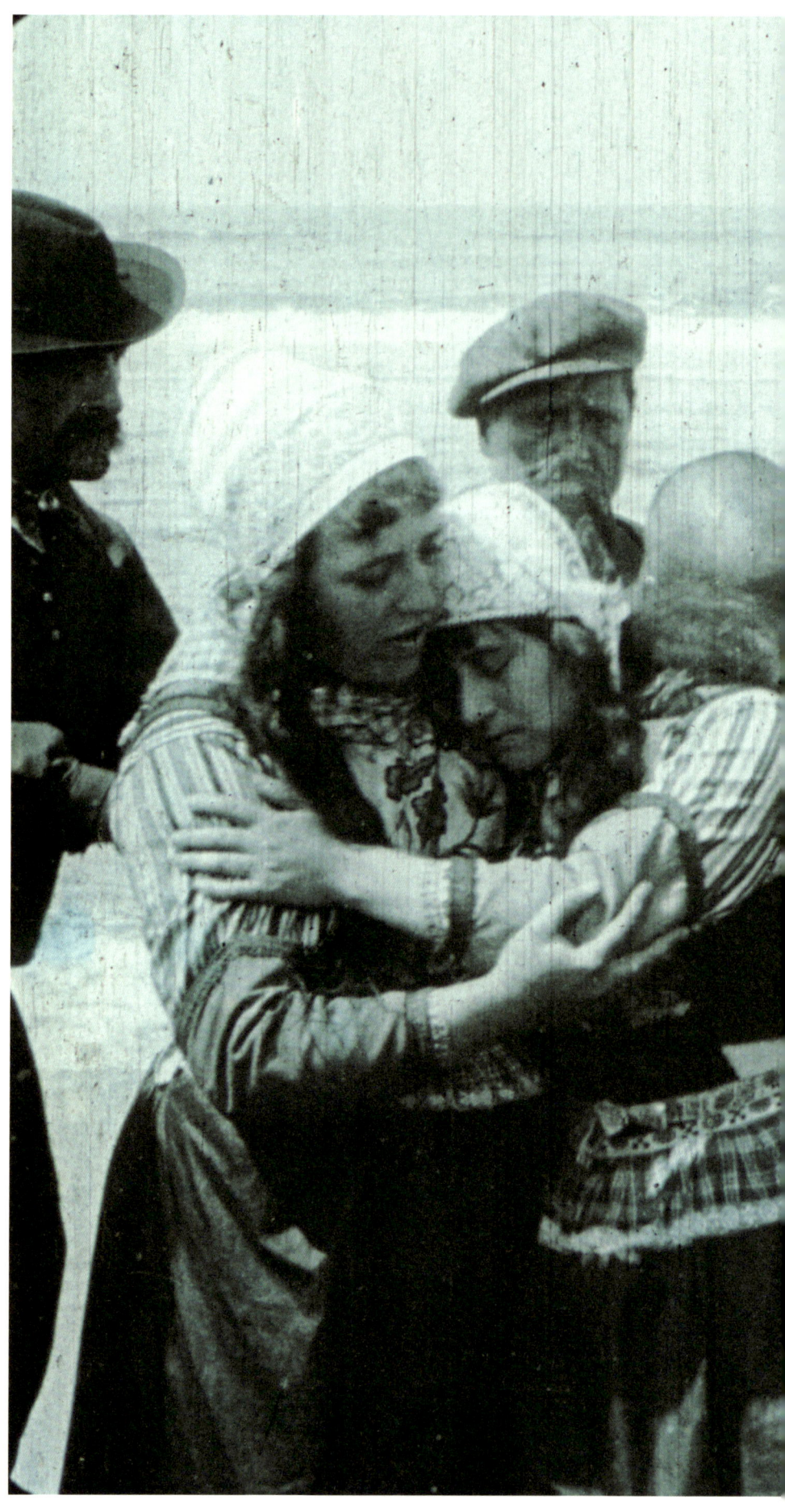

Joseph Delmont, *Auf einsamer Insel*, 1913

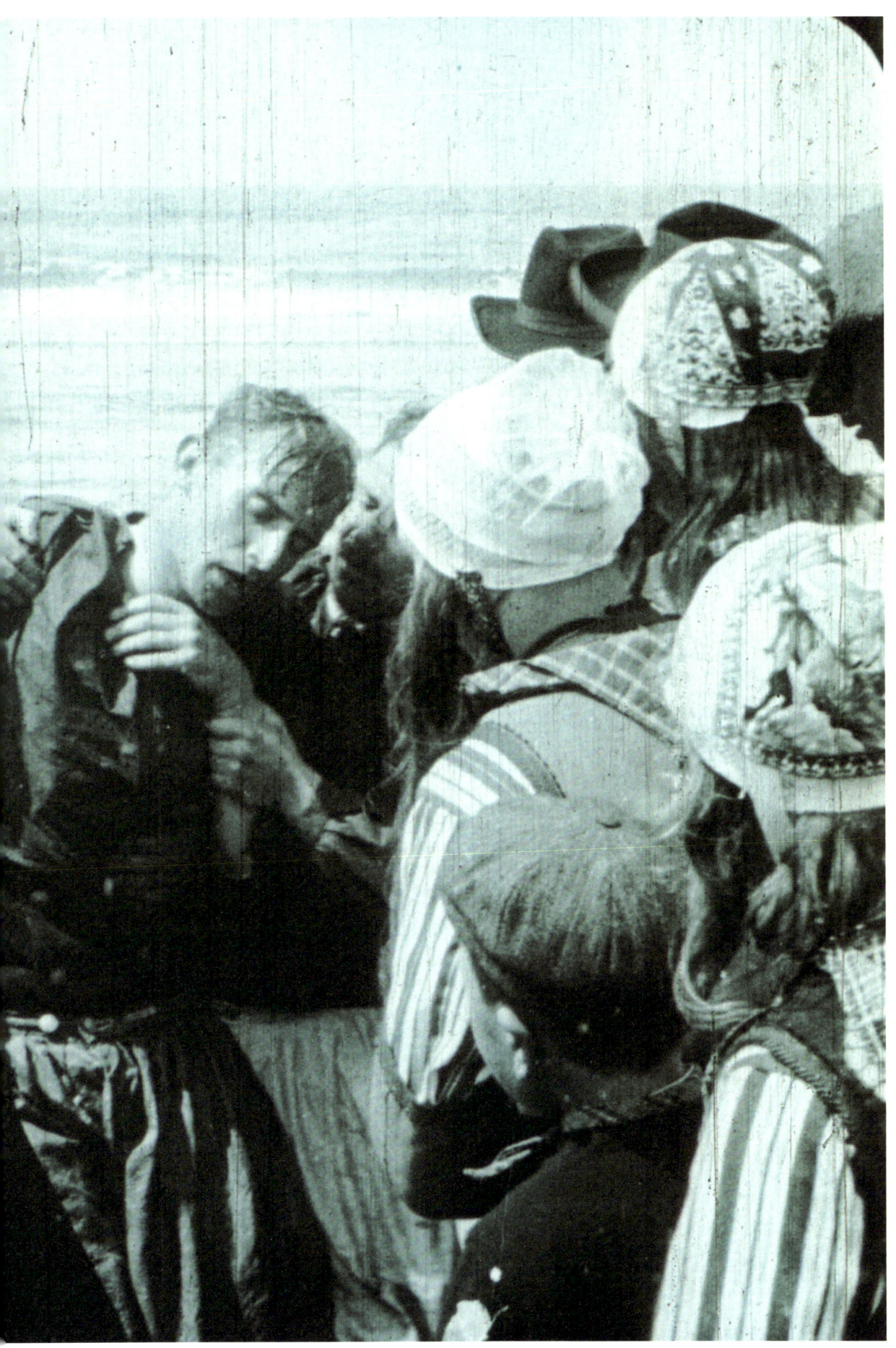

Posters in the Desmet Collection

General Posters

Unknown / Gaumont / FR
[Untitled] / FR / 150 x 111
Unknown / Savoia Film / IT
[Untitled] / [IT] / 150 x 102
Unknown, 1911 / Ambrosio / IT
[Untitled], 1911, P. Pavodi / IT / 143 x 101
A
Aujourd'hui Gontran Comic, 1911–1913 / 100 x 75
B
Biograph showing / 76 x 51
C
Cinema Palace / 100 x 65
Cinema Parisien / 22 x 62
Cinema Parisien / 31 x 86
Cinema Parisien / 40 x 47
Cinema Parisien / 24 x 124
Cinema Parisien / 84 x 58
Cinema Parisien, 1909 / Julien t' Felt / 130 x 62
E
Eclair coloris / 100 x 75
Eclair drame / 100 x 75
Eclair Revue / Auguste Leymarie / 159 x 119
Elettra Raggio / Giovanni Vianello / 100 x 70
G
Great Scott! / G. Mitchell / 100 x 73
H
Hepworth drama / 224 x 102
Heute Drama / 104 x 70
Heute Drama / 104 x 69
Heute Kalem Drama / 104 x 70
Heute. Heute. Heute, 1912 – 1919 / 69 x 54
I
Iederen dinsdag en vrijdag / 32 x 85
K
Kalem's latest feature / 77 x 51
M
Mario Bonnard / 204 x 101
Master Judson Melford / 104 x 70
P
Polidor, 1912–1913 / Giovanni Grande / 140 x 100
Polycarpe, Verde Vase / 120 x 80
S
Serie Harry Piel / 200 x 140
Società Anonima Ambrosio Torino / IT / 140 x 101
Suzanne Grandais dans…, 1916 / H. de Nothac / 159 x 120
T
Tag im Film, Der / 91 x 60
V
Very sincerely yours Pearl White / 103 x 70
Z
Zonder titel / 84 x 62

Film Posters

1861, 1911 / Selig Polyscope / US
1861, 1911 / NL / 32 x 85
1861, 1911 / US / 107 x 72

A

Abenteuer eines Journalisten, Das*, 1914 / [Harry Piel] / Kinokop / DE
Abenteuer des Journalisten, Das, 1914, Stenzel / DE / 149 x 109
Abito bianco di Robinet, L'*, 1911 / Marcel Fabre / Ambrosio / IT
[Abito bianco di Robinet, L'], 1911 / IT / 140 x 100
Absinthe*, 1913 / Herbert Brenon, George Edwardes Hall / Universal / US
[Absinthe], 1914 / GB / 225 x 198
Absinthe, 1914 / US / 210 x 210
Absinthe, 1914 / US / 212 x 108
Verloren zoon, De, 1914 / NL / 32 x 84
Verloren zoon, De, 1914 / NL / 31 x 84
Absinthe*, 1913 / Universal Gem / US
Absinthe, 1913 / US / 104 x 72
Acque miracolose, Le*, 1914 / Eleuterio Rodolfi / Ambrosio / IT
Acqua miracolosa, 1914 / Atelier Butteri / IT / 210 x 140
Adventures of Lieutenant Petrosino, The*, 1912 / Sidney M. Goldin / Feature Photoplay / US
Zwarte Hand ontmaskerd, De / NL / 30 x 84
Alene i Verden, 1908 / Viggo Larsen / Nordisk Films Kompagni / DK
Allein in der Welt, 1908 / DE / 95 x 71
Alexandra*, 1914 / Curt A. Stark / Messter / DE
Alexandra, 1914, Hans Kalmár / DE / 220 x 150
Alexandra, 1914 / NL / 85 x 31
Alkali Ike's Pants, 1912 / Essanay Film Manufacturing / US
Alkali Ike's pants, 1912 / US / 101 x 76
All for Love, 1912 / Universal Victor / US
All for love, 1912 / US / 104 x 71
Allan Field's Warning, 1913 / Bert Haldane / Barker Motion Photography / GB
Allan Field's warning, 1913 / GB / 98 x 73
Amazzone mascherata, L'*, 1914 / Baldassarre Negroni / Celio Film / IT
[Amazzone mascherata, L'], 1914 / IT / 175 x 70
Amazzone mascherata, L', 1914 / IT / 208 x 100
Amazzone mascherata, L', 1914 / IT / 280 x 200
Amazzone mascherata, L', 1914 / IT / 277 x 400
Amico intimo di Polidor, L', 1913 / Ferdinand Guillaume / Pasquali / IT
[Amico intimo di Polidor, L'], 1913 / IT / 140 x 99
Amore e boxe, 1912 / Cines / IT
Amore e box, 1912 / IT / 100 x 70
Amour tragique de Mona Lisa, Un, 1912 / Albert Capellani / Pathé Frères / FR
Tragique amour de Mona Lisa, Le, 1912, Candido Aragonês de Faria / FR / 161 x 118
Ancient Bow, The, 1912 / Rollin S. Sturgeon / Vitagraph Company of America / US
Ancient bow, The, 1912 / US / 107 x 71
And His Wife Came Back, 1913 / James Young / Vitagraph Company of America / US
And his wife came back, 1913 / US / 107 x 71
Animated Bathtub, The, 1912 / Solax / US
Animated bathtub, The, 1912 / GB / 101 x 76
Anna Karenina*, 1911 / Maurice André Maître / Pathé Frères – Russian Film / RU
Anna Karenine, 1911, Vincent Lorant-Heilbronn / FR / 117 x 80
Antro funesto, L', 1913 / Sandro Camasio / Itala Film / IT
Fatal grotto, The / GB / 102 x 76
Apache Dog's Sagacity, An, 1913 / Eclipse / FR
Apache dog's sagacity, An, 1913 / GB / 102 x 77
Apache Renegade, The, 1912 / Kalem / US
Weisse Apache, Der, 1912 / GB / 102 x 70
Apachen-opstand
Apachen-opstand / NL / 31 x 85
Appuntamento di Kri Kri, L'*, 1914 / Cines / IT
Appuntamento di Kri-Kri, L', 1914, Marchetti / IT / 137 x 100
Arabia the Equine Detective, 1913 / Oscar Eagle / Selig Polyscope / US
Arabia the equine detective, 1913 / US / 104 x 71
Ariadne: Eine ergreifende Künstlertragödie, 1912 / Viggo Larsen / DKG – Deutsche Kinematographen Gesellschaft / DE
Ariadne, 1913 / DE / 220 x 150
Arthème opérateur*, 1913 / Ernest Servaes / Eclipse / FR
Arthème opérateur, 1913 / FR / 120 x 80
Artists Wife, The, 1915 / Elmer Clifton / Majestic Motion Picture / US
Vrouw van den kunstschilder, De, 1915 / NL / 84 x 31
As Fate Would Have It*, 1912 / Vitagraph Company of America / US
Deux messages, Les, 1912 / FR / 140 x 100
As fate would have it, 1912 / US / 107 x 72
At Scrogginses' Corner, 1912 / Hal Reid / Vitagraph Company of America / US
Enfant du village, L', 1912 / FR / 140 x 100
Attenti alla vernice*, 1913 / Ernesto Vaser / Itala Film / IT
[Attenti alla vernice], 1913, Emilio Vacchetti / IT / 140 x 100
Auberge sanglante de peirebeilhe, L' [1913] / FR
Auberge sanglante de peirebeilhe, L', 1913 / FR / 198 x 297
Auf Abwegen, 1911 [Paul Leni] / Britannia-Films / DE
Auf Abwegen, 1911, Paul Leni / DE / 70 x 95
Auf Abwegen, 1911 / DE / 224 x 110
Auf einsamer Insel*, 1913 / Joseph Delmont / Eiko Film / DE
Auf einsamer Insel, 1913 / DE / 220 x 150
Aunts, Too Many, 1913 / Edward Dillon / Biograph / US
Aunts, too many, 1913 / GB / 104 x 70
Aus eines Mannes Mädchenzeit*, 1913 / Messter / DE
Aus eines Mannes Mädchenzeit, 1913 / DE / 97 x 64
Aus eines Mannes Mädchenzeit, 1913 / DE / 149 x 110
Automartirio, 1917 / Ivo Illuminati / Raggio Film / IT
Automartirio, 1917, Carlo Nicco / IT / 100 x 70
Automartirio, 1917, Carlo Nicco / IT / 100 x 70
Automartirio, 1917, Carlo Nicco / IT / 100 x 70
Automartirio, 1917, Carlo Nicco / IT / 100 x 70
Automate incassable, L'*, 1913 / Lux / FR
Automate incassable, L', 1913, Lucien Charbonnier / FR / 140 x 100
Automobile della morte, L', 1912 / Ambrosio / IT
Automobile della morte, L', 1912 / IT / 198 x 140
Auto-scat di Robinet, Gli, 1911 / Ambrosio / IT
Nauke als auto roller, 1911, P. Pavodi / IT / 141 x 100
Aventure de miss Simpton, 1913 / Lux / FR
Miss Simpton's jewels, 1913, Lucien Charbonnier / FR / 107 x 71
Awakening of Bianca, The, 1912 / Charles Kent / Vitagraph Company of America / US
Prix d'une chevelure, Le / FR / 140 x 100
Awakening, The, 1912 / Hardee Kirkland / Selig Polyscope / US

Awakening, The, 1912 / US / 105 x 71

Baby's Shoe, A, 1912 / Edison Manufacturing Company / US
Baby's shoe, a, 1912 / US / 100 x 71

B

Back in the North Woods*, 1911 / Vitagraph Company of America / US
Dans les forêts du Nord, 1911, R. Hem / FR / 140 x 100

Back to His Old Home Town, 1912 / IMP – Independent Motion Picture Corporation / US
Back to his old home town, 1912 / US / 108 x 71

Bagerstrædes Hemmelighed, 1913 / Alfred Cohn / Dansk Filmfabrik / DK
Geheimnis der Bäckerstrasse, Das, 1914 / DE / 150 x 110

Bal d'Apaches dans le grand monde, Un, 1912 / Lux / FR
Bal d'Apaches dans le grand monde, Un, 1912 / FR / 159 x 120

Bambola di Luisetta, La*, 1911 / Ambrosio / IT
[*Bambola di Luisetta, La*], 1911, P. Pavodi / IT / 140 x 100

Bandit of Point Loma, The, 1912 / Allan Dwan / American Film Manufacturing / US
Bandit of Point Loma, The, 1912 / US / 108 x 71

Barber Cure, A*, 1913 / Edward Dillon / Biograph / US
Barber cure, A, 1913 / US / 104 x 70

Barcaiolo del Danubio, Il *, 1914 / Roberto Roberti / Aquila Films / IT
[*Count Thurnia*], 1914–1915 / US / 200 x 100

Baron's Bear Escape, The, 1914 / L-KO Comedies / US
Barons bear escape, The, 1914 / GB / 98 x 84

Barrabas*, 1919 / Louis Feuillade / Gaumont / FR
Barrabas, 1919 / FR / 220 x 150
Barrabas, 1919, A. Rapeño / FR / 220 x 150
Barrabas; 1er épisode, 1919 / FR / 214 x 145
Barrabas; 2ème episode, 1919, Emilio Vila / FR / 218 x 150
Barrabas; 4ème episode, 1919 / FR / 228 x 150
Barrabas; 5ème episode, 1919 / FR / 217 x 150
Barrabas; 6ème episode, 1919 / FR / 215 x 147
Barrabas; 7ème episode, 1919 / Atelier Fournier / FR / 220 x 150
Barrabas; 9ème episode, 1919, Maurice Lalau / FR / 212 x 141
Barrabas; 11e épisode, 1919 / FR / 219 x 150
Barrabas; 12ème épisode, 1919 / FR / 218 x 150

Barrier of Flames, The, 1914 / John Harvey / Thanhouser Film / US
Barrier of flames, The / GB / 225 x 102
Barrier of flames, The [1914] / US / 107 x 72

Barrier That Was Burned, The, 1912 / Vitagraph Company of America / US
Barrier that was burned, The, 1912 / US / 107 x 71

Battle at Elderbush Gulch, The, 1913 / D.W. Griffith / Biograph / US
Battle at Elderbush Gulch, The, 1913 / GB / 226 x 102
Battle of Elderbush Gulch, The, 1913 / GB / 101 x 70

Bear Escape, A, 1912 / Mack Sennett / Keystone Film / US
Bear escape, 1912 / US / 101 x 76

Beau Brummell, 1913 / James Young / Vitagraph Company of America / US
Beau Brummell, 1913 / US / 107 x 72

Beau tzigane, Le, 1909 / Radios / FR
Beau tzigane, Le, 1909 / FR / 120 x 80

Bébé et ses grands-parents, 1912 / Louis Feuillade / Gaumont / FR
Bébé et ses grands parents, 1912 / FR / 107 x 77

Behind the Curtain, 1916 / Henry Otto / Universal 101 Bison / US
Behind the curtain, 1916 / US / 107 x 72

Bergère d'Ivry, La*, 1913 / Maurice Tourneur / ACAD – Association Cinématographique des Auteurs Dramatiques / FR
Bergère d'Ivry, La, 1913 / FR / 150 x 200
Bergère d'Ivry, La, 1913 / FR / 149 x 100

Better Man, The, 1912 / Vitagraph Company of America / US
Better man, The, 1912 / US / 107 x 72

Betty Becomes a Maid, 1911 / Vitagraph Company of America / US
Betty becomes a maid, 1911 / R. Hem / FR / 140 x 100

Bezoek van HM de Koningin Wilhelmina aan Parijs, Het, 1912 / Pathé Frères / FR
Bezoek van H.M. Wilhelmina aan president Fallières, Het, 1912 / NL / 86 x 55

Billet mrk troskab 909*, 1913 / Sofus Wolder / Nordisk Films Kompagni / DK
Postlagernd "Treues Herz" 909, 1913 / DE / 93 x 73

Billy's Stratagem*, 1912 / D.W. Griffith / Biograph / US
[*Billy's stratagem*], 1912 / GB / 200 x 101

Bingles and the Cabaret, 1913 / Frederick A. Thomson / Vitagraph Company of America / US

Zepherin n'aime pas le bruit / Harry Bedos / FR / 140 x 100

Biograph Feature About the Sea / Deutsche Mutoskop und Biograph / DE
[*Biograph feature about the sea*] / DE / 220 x 150

Bismarck, 1913 / Gustav Trautschold, William Wauer, Richard Schott / Eiko Film / DE
Bismarck, 1913 / DE / 95 x 72

Bjørnetæmmeren*, 1912 / Alfred Lind / Skandinavisk-Russiske Handelshus / DK
Reizend circus, Het / NL / 80 x 62
Reizend circus, Het, 1912 / NL / 62 x 162

Black Mask, The, 1914 / American Film Manufacturing / US
Black mask, The, 1914 / GB / 102 x 76

Bødes der for, Det*, 1911 / August Blom / Nordisk Films Kompagni / DK
Rächer seiner Ehre, Der, 1911 / DE / 210 x 101

Bohemian Girl, The, 1912 / US
Bohemian girl, The, 1912 / US / 98 x 66

Boob, The, 1913 / Rex Motion Picture Company / US
Boob, The / US / 107 x 71

Bouquetière de Montmartre, La, 1913 / Victorin Jasset / Eclair / FR
Bouquetière de Montmartre, La, 1913 / Roger Chapelet / FR / 300 x 300
Bouquetière de Montmartre, La, 1913 / Roger Chapelet / FR / 160 x 223
Bouquetière de Montmartre, La, 1913 / Roger Chapelet / FR / 160 x 120

Bout-de-Zan et le crime au téléphone*, 1913 / Louis Feuillade / Gaumont / FR
Bout de Zan et le crime du téléphone, 1914 / FR / 101 x 77

Bout-de-Zan et le ramoneur, 1914 / Louis Feuillade / Gaumont / FR
Bout de Zan et le ramoneur, 1914 / René Poyen / FR / 101 x 76
Tiny Tim as an enquiry agent, 1914 / FR / 102 x 76

Bout-de-Zan s'amuse*, 1913 / Louis Feuillade / Gaumont / FR
Bout de Zan s'amuse, 1913 / FR / 102 x 77

Box Car Baby, The, 1912 / Selig Polyscope / US
Box car baby, The, 1912 / GB / 102 x 76

Boxkampf zwischen Johnson und Jeffries, 1911 / PAGU – Projektions AG 'Union' / DE
Champion match Johnson – Jeffries, 1910–1914 / DE / 96 x 71
Champion-match Johnson – Jeffries, 1910–1914 / DE / 96 x 71
Champion-match Johnson – Jeffries, 1910–1914 / DE / 267 x 96

Brandmal, Das, 1912 / Skandinavisk Films / DE
Brandmal, Das, 1912 / DE / 220 x 150

Brennan of the Moor*, 1913 / Edward Warren / Solax / US
Brennan of the Moor, 1914 / GB / 228 x 204
Brennan de straatroover, 1913 / NL / 84 x 31
Brennan of the Moor, 1913 / US / 204 x 102
Brennan of the Moor, 1913 / US / 102 x 76

Bridget and the Egg, 1911 / Lubin Manufacturing Company / US
Bridget and the egg, 1911 / GB / 104 x 70

Broken Lease, The, 1912 / IMP – Independent Motion Picture Corporation / US
Broken lease, The, 1912 / US / 107 x 72

Broncho Billy and the Rustler's Child*, 1913 / Gilbert M. 'Broncho Billy' Anderson / Essanay Film Manufacturing / US
Kindes Einfluss, Des, 1912 / US / 110 x 75

Broncho Billy for Sheriff, 1912 / Gilbert M. 'Broncho Billy' Anderson / Essanay Film Manufacturing / US
Broncho Billy for Sheriff, 1912 / US / 107 x 72

Broncho Billy's Christmas Dinner*, 1911 / Gilbert M. 'Broncho Billy' Anderson / Essanay Film Manufacturing / US
Broncho Billy's X mas dinner, 1912 / US / 102 x 78
Weihnachtsschmaus beim Sheriff, 1912 / US / 104 x 74

Broncho Billy's Last Hold Up*, 1912 / Gilbert M. 'Broncho Billy' Anderson / Essanay Film Manufacturing / US
Broncho Billy's last deed, 1913 / GB / 102 x 76

Brother Bill*, 1913 / Ralph Ince / Vitagraph Company of America / US
Frère aîné, le, 1913, Harry Bedos / FR / 140 x 100

Bryggerens datter, 1912 / Rasmus Ottesen / Skandinavisk-Russiske Handelshus / DK
Dagmar die Brauerstochter, 1912 / DE / 200 x 150
Dagmar die Brauerstochter, 1912 / DE / 100 x 65
Brouwersdochter, de, 1913 / NL / 31 x 85

Bunny at the Derby, 1912 / Larry Trimble / Vitagraph Company of America / US
En route pour le derby, 1912 / FR / 140 x 100

**Bunny in Disguise*, 1914 / George

D. Baker / **Vitagraph Company of America** / US
Facheux deguisement, Le, 1914, Harry Bedos / FR / 140 x 100
Ruse déjouée, La, 1913 / FR / 140 x 101

Bunny's Birthday Surprise, 1913 / Wilfred North / Vitagraph Company of America / US
Bonne surprice, Une, 1913, Harry Bedos / FR / 140 x 100

Burnt Cork, A, 1912 / Lubin Manufacturing Company / US
Burnt cork, The, 1912 / US / 200 x 100

Cajus Julius Caesar*, 1914 / Enrico Guazzoni / Cines / IT
Cajus Julius Caesar, 1914 / NL / 112 x 80

Calino sourcier*, 1913 / Jean Durand / Gaumont / FR
Calino sourcier, 1913 / FR / 101 x 77

Calvaire d'une mère, Le, 1912 / Adrien Caillard / Pathé Frères / FR
Calvaire d'une mère, Le, 1913 / FR / 160 x 120

Canine Sherlock Holmes*, A, 1912 / Stuart Kinder / Urban Trading / GB
Canine Sherlock Holmes, A, 1913 / GB / 102 x 76

Caprices of Fortune, 1912 / Etienne Arnaud / Universal Eclair American / US
Caprices de la fortune, Les, 1912 / FR / 300 x 150

Captain Barnacle's Legacy, 1912 / Van Dyke Brooke / Vitagraph Company of America / US
Universalerbe, Der / Harry Bedos / FR / 140 x 100

Captain Jenk's Dilemma, 1912 / Vitagraph Company of America / US
Huit enfants de capitaine, Les, 1912 / FR / 140 x 100

Captain Kidd, 1913 / Otis Turner / Universal 101 Bison / US
Capt Kidd, 1913 / US / 152 x 102
Capt. Kidd, 1913 / US / 102 x 72

Capture du bandit Bonnot, 1912 / Pathé / FR
Gewelddadige dood van Bonnot, het hoofd der Parijsche automobieldieven, 1912 / NL / 85 x 56

Caretaker, The, 1912 / Lubin Manufacturing Company / US
Caretaker, The, 1912 / GB / 102 x 76

Casimir gentleman pick-pocket, 1913 / Roméo Bosetti / Eclair / FR
Casimir gentleman pick-pocket, 1913 / Auguste Leymarie / FR / 158 x 118

Casimir tangue, 1914 / Roméo Bosetti / Eclair / FR
Casimir tangue, 1914 / Auguste Leymarie / FR / 150 x 100

Cat's Cup Final, The, 1912 / Arthur Cooper / Empire / GB
Cats' cup final, The, 1912 / GB / 101 x 76

Caught, 1912 / [Dave Aylott] / Cricks & Martin / GB
Caught, 1912 / GB / 102 x 76

Chagrin d'enfants*, 1912 / Eclipse / FR
[*Chagrin d'enfants*] / FR / 159 x 234
[*Chagrin d'enfants*], 1912 / FR / 120 x 80

Champignol malgré lui*, 1914 / Aubert / FR
Champignol malgré lui, 1914 / Edwin Marin / FR / 227 x 106
Champignol malgré lui, 1913 / Edwin Marin / FR / 234 x 320

Charge of the Light Brigade, The, 1912 / J. Searle Dawley / Edison Manufacturing Company / US
Totesritt bei Balaklave, Der, 1912 / DE / 100 x 70

Chase Across the Continent, A, 1912 / Edison Manufacturing Company / US
Chase across the continent, A, 1912 / US / 102 x 70

Chasse à l'éléphant au Cambodge / Le Lion / FR
Chasse à l'éléphant au Cambodge / Albert Dorfinant / FR / 160 x 119

Checco e Cocò spiritisti, 1912 / Cines / IT
Checco e Cocò spiritisti, 1912 / IT / 100 x 70

Chelsea 7750, 1916 / J. Searle Dawley / Famous Players / US
Chelsea 7750, 1916 / US / 206 x 202
Chelsea 7750, 1916 / US / 206 x 202

Chest of Fortune, The*, 1914 / Kenean Buel / Kalem / US
Chest of fortune, 1914 / US / 210 x 107
Chest of fortune, The, 1914 / US / 201 x 206
Chest of fortune, The, 1914 / US / 104 x 70
Verborgen schat, De, 1914 / NL / 31 x 86

Chief's blanket, The, 1912 / D.W. Griffith / Biograph / US
Chief's blanket, The, 1912 / GB / 102 x 76

Chiffonnier de Paris, Le, 1913 / ACAD – Association Cinématographique des Auteurs Dramatiques / FR
Chiffonnier de Paris, Le, 1913 / FR / 200 x 300
Chiffonnier de Paris, Le, 1913 / FR / 150 x 100

Child's Remorse, A, 1911 / D.W. Griffith / Biograph / US
Child's remorse, A, 1911 / GB / 102 x 76

Church Across the Way, The, 1912 / Vitagraph Company of America / US
Church across the way, The, 1912 / US / 107 x 72

Circuit de Gavroche, Le, 1912 / Eclair / FR
Circuit de Gavroche, Le, 1912 / Auguste Leymarie / FR / 153 116

Cirque miniature, Le, 1908 / Pathé Frères / FR
Cirque miniature, Le, 1908 / Candido Aragonês de Faria / FR / 117 x 160

[Clown, De] / Pasquali / IT
Pasquali Film Turin / IT / 210 x 145

Come Robinet sposò Robinette, 1913 / Ambrosio / IT
[*Come Robinet sposò Robinette*], 1913 / P. Pavodi / IT / 140 x 100

Come Totò riscuote l'affitto, 1912 / Emilio Vardannes / Itala Film / IT
Como Toto riscuote l'affitto, 1912 / Emilio Vacchetti / IT / 145 x 100

Coming back of Kit Denver, The, 1912 / [Warwick Buckland] / Hepworth / GB
Coming back of Kit Denver, The, 1912 / GB / 101 x 76

Condamné, Le, 1913 / Universal Eclair American / US
Condamné, Le, 1913 / FR / 300 x 150

Consultation improvisée, 1908 / Pathé Frères / FR
Consultation improvisée, 1908 / Vincent Lorant-Heilbronn / FR / 112 x 77

Coronets and Hearts, 1912 / Earle Williams / Vitagraph Company of America / US
Coronets and hearts, 1912 / US / 107 x 71

Counterfeit Plot, The, 1914 / Kalem / US
Bank-note forgers, The / GB / 102 x 77

County Fair, The, 1912 / Kalem / US
County fair, The, 1912 / US / 104 x 70

Courageous Blood, 1913 / Lubin Manufacturing Company / US
Courageous blood, 1913 / GB / 101 x 76
Courageous blood, 1913 / GB / 103 x 70

Course de taureaux à Séville, 1907 / Pathé Frères / FR
Course de taureaux, 1907 / Candido Aragonês de Faria / FR / 160 x 120

Cowboy Millionaire, The*, 1909 / Frank Boggs, Otis Turner / Selig Polyscope / US
Cowboy millionair, De, 1913 / NL / 31 x 85
Cowboy millionaire, The, 1909 / US / 224 x 104
Cowboy millionaire, The, 1913 / US / 224 x 200

Crazy Apples, 1913 / Vitagraph Company of America / US
Satanéees pommes, 1913 / Mett / FR / 140 x 100

Cross Your Heart, 1912 / Thanhouser Film / US
Cross your heart, 1912 / GB / 102 x 77

[**Cunégonde et la bouche de chaleur**], 1912 / Lux / FR

Cunégonde et la bouche de chaleur / Lucien Charbonnier / FR / 140 x 100

Cunégonde fait du spiritisme*, 1913 / Lux / FR
Cunégonde fait du spiritisme, 1913 / Lucien Charbonnier / FR / 140 x 100

Cunégonde femme cochère*, 1913 / Lux / FR
Cunégonde femme cochère, 1913 / Lucien Charbonnier / FR / 140 x 100

Cutey and the Chorus Girls*, 1913 / James Young / Vitagraph Company of America / US
A la santé de Freddy, 1913 / Harry Bedos / FR / 140 x 99

[Czernowska, Die]*, 1913 / Charles Decroix / Charles Decroix-Film / DE
Czernowska, [1914] / GB / 102 x 77
[*Czernowska, Die*] / US / 203 x 105

D

Dalle stelle alla stalla, 1912 / Cines / IT
Dalle stelle alla stalla, 1912 / IT / 100 x 70

Dame aux camélias, La, 1911 / André Calmettes, Louis Mercanton, Henri Pouctal / Pathé Frères – Le Film d'Art / FR
Dame aux camelias, La, 1911 / Atelier Minot (Frankrijk) / FR / 237 x 160

Dance at Silver Gulch, The, 1912 / Essanay Film Manufacturing / US
Dance at Silver Gulch, The, 1912 / GB / 102 x 76

Daughter of the hills, The, 1914 / J. Searle Dawley / Famous Players / US
Dochter van de bergen, Een, 1914 / NL / 31 x 85

Daughters of Senor Lopaz, The, 1912 / Allan Dwan / American Film Manufacturing / US
Daughters of senor Lopaz, The, 1912 / US / 107 x 72

Day Off, A, 1912 / Selig Polyscope / US
Day off, a, 1912 / US / 104 x 71

Day That is Dead, A, 1913 / Charles H. France / Edison Manufacturing Company / US
Day that is dead, A, 1913 / US / 102 x 70

Debito dell'Imperatore, Il, 1911 / Luigi Maggi / Ambrosio / IT
Schuld des Kaisers, Die, 1911 / DE / 159 x 79

Débuts du Venduron, Les, 1913 / Gaumont / FR
Débuts du Venduron, Les, 1913 / FR / 101 x 76

Defender of the Name, 1912 / Rex Motion Picture Company / US
Defender of the name / GB / 102 x 76

**Delayed Proposals*, 1913 / James

Young / Vitagraph Company of America / US
Demande interrompue, La, 1913 / FR / 140 x 100

Denn die Elemente hassen..., 1913 / Continental-Kunstfilm / DE
Denn die Elemente hassen, 1914 / DE / 220 x 150

Des Meeres und der Liebe wellen*, 1912 / Deutsche Kinematographen Gesellschaft / DE
Des Meeres und der liebe Wellen, 1912 / DE / 157 x 102

Deserteur, De
Deserteur, De / NL / 85 x 31

Désespoir de Pétronille, Le*, 1914 / [Roméo Bosetti], Georges Rémond / Eclair / FR
Désespoir de Pétronille, Le, 1914 / Auguste Leymarie / FR / 149 x 99

Detective Brown / New Century Film Service / GB
Detective Brown, 1910–1914 / GB / 223 x 101

Deux braves petits coeurs, 1912 / Eclair / FR
Deux braves petits coeurs, 1912 / Roger Chapelet / FR / 160 x 120

Deux enfants dans la forêt, 1912 / Albert Capellani / Pathé Frères / FR
Babes in the wood, The, 1912 / GB / 101 x 76

Dévouement filial, 1909 / Etienne Arnaud / Gaumont / FR
Devouement filial, 1909 / FR / 150 x 111

Diamantbedrageren, 1910 / Nordisk Films Kompagni / DK
Diamantenbedrieger, De / NL / 31 x 85

Disastrous imitation, A, 1912 / Cosmo / GB
Disastrous imitation, A, 1912 / GB / 102 x 77

Dispute animée, Une / Savoia Film / IT
Dispute animée, Une / Achille Luciano Mauzan / IT / 110 x 75

District Attorney's Conscience, The*, 1913 / Arthur V. Johnson / Lubin Manufacturing Company / US
District attorney's conscience, The, 1913 / GB / 102 x 75

Diver, The*, 1913 / Harry Lambart / Vitagraph Company of America / US
Dans les flots du Niagara, 1913 / FR / 199 x 140
Plongeuse ideal, La, 1913 / R. Hem / FR / 140 x 102

Doctor's Photograph, The, 1913 / Walter Edwin / Edison Manufacturing Company / US
Doctor's photograph, The, 1913 / US / 102 x 71

Dødsspring til hest fra cirkuskuplen*, 1912 / Eduard Schnedler-Sørensen / Nordisk Films Kompagni / DK
Grosse Circusattraction, Die, 1912 / DE / 63 x 49

Dödsvarslet*, 1912 / Aage Brandt / Skandinavien / DK
[*Dödsvarslet*], 1912 / DK / 214 x 101

Does Advertising Pay?, 1913 / Larry Trimble / Vitagraph Company of America / US
Bienfaits de la reclame, Les, 1913 / Harry Bedos / FR / 140 x 100

Doggie's Debut, 1912 / Thanhouser Film / US
Doggie's debut, 1912 / GB / 102 x 77

Door zucht naar rijkdom haar eed gebroken
Door zucht naar rijkdom haar eed gebroken / NL / 31 x 85

Drink's lure, 1913 / D.W. Griffith / Biograph / US
Drink's lure, 1913 / US / 104 x 70

Dronningens Kærlighed, 1908 / Viggo Larsen / Nordisk Films Kompagni / DK
Liebe der Königin, Die, 1908 / DE / 96 x 72

Due vite per un cuore, 1912 / Cines / IT
Due vite per un cuore, 1912 / IT / 140 x 100
Zwei Leben für ein Herz, 1912 / IT / 200 x 280

Duel de Max, Le, 1913 / Max Linder / Pathé Frères / FR
Duel de Max, Le, 1913 / Adrien Barrère / FR / 160 x 120

[Duel, Het] / Cines / IT
[*Duel, Het*] / Anselmo Ballester / IT / 200 x 270

Duello, Il, 1914 / Cines / IT
Duello, Il, 1914 / Achille Luciano Mauzan / IT / 75 x 111

Duetto in quattro, 1914 / Marcel Fabre / Ambrosio / IT
[*Duetto in quattro*], 1914 / Atelier Butteri / IT / 140 x 101

Duke's Dilemma, The, 1913 / Walter Edwin / Edison Manufacturing Company / US
Duke's dilemma, The, 1913 / US / 102 x 70

E

Éclipse de soleil du 17 avril 1912, L'*, 1912 / Gaumont / FR
Zonsverduistering van 17 april 1912, De, 1912 / NL / 55 x 85

Effroyable châtiment de Yann le troubadour, L', 1911 / Alfred Machin / FR
Straf van den troubadour, De / NL / 31 x 84

Ehrenwort, Das, 1913 / Emil Albes / Deutsche Bioscop / DE
Ehrenwort, Ein, 1913 / DE / 110 x 150

Eid des Stephan Huller, Der (deel 2), 1912 / Viggo Larsen / Vitascope / DE
Eid des Stephan Huller, Der, 1912 / DE / 220 x 150
Eid des Stephan Huller, Der, 1912 / DE / 95 x 65

Eiko-Woche. Kriegs-Sonderausgabe / Eiko Film / DE
Kriegs-Sonderausgabe der Eiko-Woche, 1914–1918 / DE / 71 x 47

Eleventh Hour, The*, 1914 / Henry MacRae / Universal 101 Bison / US
Eleventh hour, The, 1914 / US / 107 x 71
Eleventh hour, The, 1914 / US / 223 x 100
Eleventh hour, The, 1914 / US / 210 x 210

End of the Feud, The, 1912 / Essanay Film Manufacturing / US
End of the feud, The, 1912 / US / 101 x 76

Ende vom Liede, Das*, 1915 / Rudolf Biebrach / Messter / DE
Ende vom Lied, Das / Hans Kalmár / DE / 215 x 144

Endelig alene*, 1914 / Holger-Madsen / Nordisk Films Kompagni / DK
Endlich Allein, 1914 / DE / 220 x 102

Enemy in our midst, The, 1914 / Wilfred Noy / Clarendon Film / GB
Enemy in our midst, The, 1914 / GB / 300 x 300

Enfant de Paris, L'*, 1913 / Léonce Perret / Gaumont / FR
Enfant de Paris, L', 1913 / FR / 150 x 111

Enfant de Paris, L'*, 1913 / Léonce Perret / Gaumont / FR
Enfant de Paris, L', 1913 / FR / 143 x 100
Enfant de Paris, L', 1913 / FR / 150 x 111
Enfant de Paris, L', 1913 / FR / 150 x 110

Enfant d'une autre, L', 1914 / ACAD – Association Cinématographique des Auteurs Dramatiques / FR
Enfant d'une autre, L', 1914 / Roger Chapelet / FR / 150 x 100

Enfant sauveur, L'*, 1912 / André Hugon / ACAD – Association Cinématographique des Auteurs Dramatiques / FR
Enfant sauveur, L' / Roger Chapelet / FR / 160 x 118

Enhver, 1915 / Vilhelm Glückstadt, Kai van der Aa Kühle / Filmfabriken Danmark / DK [*Lidenskabens magt*], 1915 / DK / 196 x 140

Épingles, Les*, 1913 / Léonce Perret / Gaumont / FR
For two pins, 1913 / FR / 106 x 76

Er weiss sich zu helfen / Messter / DE
Er weiss sich zu helfen / Julius Klinger / DE / 125 x 94

Erblich belastet*, 1913 / Harry Piel / Eiko Film / DE
Erblich belastet, 1913 / DE / 218 x 150

Erreur tragique*, 1912 / Louis Feuillade / Gaumont / FR
Erreur tragique, L', 1912 / FR / 111 x 149
Noodlottige dwaling, Een / NL / 31 x 85

Estrangement, The, 1914 / Oscar Eagle / Selig Polyscope / US
Estrangement, The, 1914 / GB / 225 x 102

Europäisches Sklavenleben, 1912 / Emil Justitz / Bonanza-Kunstfilm / DE
Europäisches Sklavenleben, 1912 / Hans Erdt / DE / 125 x 94

Eventail, L', 1912 / Lux / FR
Ching Chang's little fan, 1912 / Lucien Charbonnier / FR / 107 x 71

Eventful Evening, An, 1911 / Edison Manufacturing Company / US
Eventful evening, An, 1911 / US / 104 x 70

Evil of the Slums, An*, 1913 / Edwin August / Powers Company / US
Evil of the slums, An, 1914 / GB / 102 x 76

Ex-Convict, The, 1913 / Oscar Eagle / Selig Polyscope / US
Ex-convict, The, 1913 / US / 101 x 76

Express Car Mystery, The, 1913 / Kalem / US
Express car mystery, The, 1913 / US / 56 x 36
Mystery of the express car, The, 1913 / US / 102 x 76

F

Face of Madonna, The, 1915 / Kenean Buel / Kalem / US
Face of madonna, The / US / 206 x 200
Face of madonna, The, 1915 / US / 200 x 107

Fairy Bottle, The, 1913 / Dave Aylott / Cricks & Martin / GB
Fairy bottle, The, 1913 / GB / 101 x 76

Family Mix up, A, 1912 / Mack Sennett / Keystone Film / US
Family mix-up, A, 1912 / US / 102 x 77

Fanciulla sublime, La, 1912 / Aquila Films / IT
Fanciulla sublime, La, 1912 / IT / 220 x 280

Fatale distrazione, 1912 / Cines / IT
Fatale distrazione, 1912 / IT / 100 x 70

Fate, 1913 / D.W. Griffith / Biograph / US
Fate, 1913 / US / 104 x 70

Fate's Warning, 1912 / Rex Motion Picture Company / US
Fate's warning / US / 105 x 71

Father's Favorite, 1912 / American Film Manufacturing / US
Father's favorite, 1912 / US / 107 x 72

Father's Hatband*, 1913 / Van Dyke Brooke / Vitagraph Company of America / US
Facteur de Cupidon, Le, 1913 / FR / 140 x 100
Fauvette et le coucou, La, 1912 / Oliver G. Pike / Pathé Frères / FR
Fauvette et le coucou, La, 1912 / Adrien Barrère / FR / 164 x 118
[Fee, De] / DE
[Fee, De] / DE / 200 x 110
Festungsplan 612, 1912 / Berolina Film / DE
Festungsplan 612, 1912 / DE / 100 x 65
Festungsplan 612, 1912 / Berolina Film / DE
Festungsplan 612, 1912 / DE / 150 x 217
Fettered Lives / New Film Service / GB
Fettered lives / GB / 225 x 102
Fighting Instinct, The, 1912 / William Duncan / Selig Polyscope / US
Fighting instinct, The, 1912 / US / 102 x 72
Figlia di Jorio, La, 1911 / Ambrosio / IT
Tochter des Kosakenfürsten, Die, 1911 / P. Pavodi / IT / 140 x 101
Filial Love, 1912 / Etienne Arnaud / Universal Eclair American / US
Amour filial, 1912 / FR / 225 x 200
Filibus*, 1915 / Mario Roncoroni / Corona Films / IT
Filibus, 1915 / IT / 196 x 140
Filibus, 1915 / IT / 276 x 197
Filibus, 1915 / IT / 278 x 200
Fille du squatter, La*, 1911 / Pathé Frères – American Kinema / FR US
Dochter van den eenzame, De, 1911 / NL / 31 x 85
Fils de Locuste, Le*, 1911 / Louis Feuillade / Gaumont / FR
Locusta, 1911 / DE / 140 x 100
Finer things, The, 1913 / Allan Dwan / American Film Manufacturing / US
Finer things, 1913 / US / 107 x 71
Fior di male*, 1915 / Carmine Gallone / Cines / IT
Fior di male, 1915 / IT / 197 x 140
Fior di male, 1915 / IT / 141 x 198
Fire djævle, De*, 1911 / Robert Dinesen. Alfred Lind / Dansk Kinograf Films / DK
Vier Teufel, Die, 1911 / DE / 60 x 78
Vier Teufel, Die, 1911 / DE / 50 x 65
Vier Teufel, Die, 1911 / DE / 99 x 75
Fisher Folks, 1911 / D.W. Griffith / Biograph / US
Fisher folks, 1911 / GB / 104 x 70
Fixing a Flirt*, 1912 / Lubin Manufacturing Company / US
Fixing a flirt / GB / 102 x 77
Flo's Discipline, 1912 / Harry Solter / Universal Victor / US
Flo's discipline, 1912 / US / 104 x 71
Focolare domestico, Il*, 1914 / Nino Oxilia / Savoia Film / IT
[Focolare domestico, Il], 1914 / Achille Luciano Mauzan / IT / 145 x 210
Slachtoffers van 'n woekeraar, De / NL / 29 x 86
Folkesagn, Et, 1908 / Viggo Larsen / Nordisk Films Kompagni / DK
Gnomen, Die, 1908 / DE / 72 x 96
For hendes skyld*, 1911 / Willam Augustinus / Nordisk Films Kompagni / DK
Door eigen kracht zijn eer gered, 1911 / NL / 31 x 84
For Her People, 1914 / Larry Trimble / Biograph / US
For her people, 1914 / US / 107 x 72
Fortune's Turn*, 1913 / Wilfred North / Vitagraph Company of America / US
Feu qui purifie, Le, 1913 / Harry Bedos / FR / 200 x 130
Foster Child, The, 1912 / Van Dyke Brooke / Vitagraph Company of America / US
Ihr Enkelkind, 1912 / FR / 140 x 100
Fred... couche-toi*, 1914 / René Hervil / Eclipse / FR
Fred, couche-toi!, 1914 / FR / 120 x 80
Frédéric le grand, 1909 / Gérard Bourgeois, Jean Durand / Lux / FR
Frédéric le grand, 1910 / FR / 136 x 99
Freight Train Drama, A*, 1912 / Selig Polyscope / US
Freight train drama, The, 1912 / US / 104 x 71
Fremmede, Den*, 1914 / Vilhelm Glückstadt / Filmfabriken Danmark / DK
[Fremmede, Den], 1914 / GB / 200 x 101
Geheimzinnige vreemdeling, De, 1914 / NL / 31 x 85
French Spy, The, 1912 / Vitagraph Company of America / US
Französische Spionin, Die / DE / 64 x 48
Friend John, 1913 / Arthur V. Johnson / Lubin Manufacturing Company / US
Friend John, 1913 / GB / 105 x 70
From Jerusalem to the Dead Sea, 1912 / Sidney Olcott / Kalem / US
Von Jerusalem nach dem Toten Meer, 1912 / DE / 102 x 39
Fugitive from Justice, A, 1912 / Lubin Manufacturing Company / US
Fugitive from justice, A, 1914 / GB / 101 x 76
[Für sein Kind], 1914 / Majestic Motion Picture / US
Voor zijn kind / NL / 42 x 62

G

Gaffney's Gladiator, 1913 / Majestic Motion Picture / US
Gaffney's gladiator / GB / 102 x 77
Galeotto fu il mare, 1916 / Achille Mauzan / Raggio Film / IT
Galeotto fu il mare, 1916 / Achille Luciano Mauzan / IT / 140 x 101
Gallop of Death, The, 1913 / Henri Vernot / Universal Eclair American / US
[Gallop of death, The], 1913 / FR / 230 x 200
Garden of Love, 1913 / Vitagraph Company of America / US
Plaisirs? (du Jardinage), Les, 1913 / R. Privat / FR / 140 x 100
Gaspare*, 1912 / Cines / IT
Gaspare, 1912 / IT / 140 x 100
Gaumont-Woche Ausgabe 3A, 1913 / Gaumont / FR
Gaumont Woche Ausgabe 3A, 1913 / Achille Luciano Mauzan / FR / 103 x 109
Gavroche et Casimir s'entraînent*, 1913 / Paul Bertho Roméo Bosetti / Eclair / FR
Gavroche et Casimir s'entrainent, 1913 / Auguste Leymarie / FR / 156 x 119
Gebannt und erlöst. Abenteuer eines Kunstreiters, 1912 / Heinrich Bolten-Baeckers / B.B. Film / DE
Gebannt und erlöst, 1912 / DE / 149 x 217
Gefangene des alten Tempels, Die, 1912 / Percy Stow / Clarendon Film / GB
Gefangene des alten Tempels, Die / DE / 69 x 101
Geheimnis des Schlosses, Das, 1911 / Messter / DE
Geheimnis des Schlosses, Das, 1912 / DE / 149 x 110
Geheimnis von Château Richmond, Das, 1913 / Willy Zeyn / Karl Werner Film / DE
Geheimnis von Château Richmond, Das, 1913 / DE / 150 x 218
Geheimnisvolle Klub, Der*, 1913 / Joseph Delmont / Eiko Film / DE
Geheimnisvolle Club, Der, 1913 / DE / 224 x 110
Geheime club, De / NL / 31 x 84
Geheimschloss, Das*, 1914 / Apollo-Film / DE
[Geheimschloss, Das], 1914 / DE / 218 x 149
Geheimschloss, Das, 1914 / DE / 96 x 65
Gelbe Rose, Die, 1913 / Eiko Film / DE
Gelbe Rose, Die, 1913 / DE / 218 x 150
Gendarme est sans culotte, Le*, 1914 / Louis Feuillade / Gaumont / FR
Gendarme est sans culotte, Le, 1914 / FR / 200 x 150
Gendarme irascible, Le, 1908 / Eclipse / FR
Gendarme irascible, Le, 1908, Louis Galice / FR / 81 x 120
Getting Rid of Trouble, 1912 / Mack Sennett / Biograph / US
Getting rid of trouble, 1912 / US / 104 x 70
Gift, The*, 1913 / [Warwick Buckland] / Jack Hulcup / Hepworth / GB
Kissing Cup, 1913 / GB / 225 x 200
Girl at the Brook, The, 1912 / Essanay Film Manufacturing / US
Girl at the brook, The, 1912 / GB / 101 x 76
Girl in the Armchair, The, 1912 / Solax / US
Girl in the arm-chair, The, 1912 / GB / 102 x 70
Girl's Bravery, A, 1912 / Lubin Manufacturing Company / US
Girl's bravery, A, 1912 / GB / 102 x 76
Glade løjtnant, Den, 1912 / Robert Dinesen / Nordisk Films Kompagni / DK
Arzt seiner Ehre, Der, [1912–1913] / DE / 145 x 179
Arzt seiner Ehre, Der, [1912–1913] / DE / 220 x 102
Glückstaumel, 1911 / Düsseldorfer Film Manufactur / DE
Glückstaumel, 1912 / DE / 217 x 150
Gold Is Not All, 1913 / Wilfred Lucas / Universal IMP / US
Gold is not all, 1913 / GB / 102 x 76
Gontran combat l'oisiveté*, 1913 / Lucien Nonguet / Eclair / FR
Serment de Gontran, Le, 1913 / Maurice Lauro / FR / 160 x 120
Gontran dans la gueule du loup*, 1913 / [Lucien Nonguet] / Eclair / FR
Gontran dans la gueule du loup, 1913 / Maurice Lauro / FR / 160 x 120
Good for the Gout*, 1913 / Kalem / US
Good for the gout, 1913 / GB / 102 x 77
Got 'Em Again*, 1913 / [Charles Calvert], [E. Colbert] / Cricks & Martin / GB
Got 'em again, 1913 / GB / 102 x 76
Graf Woronzow – mein Verlobter!, 1912 / Vitascope / DE
Graf Woronzow – mein Verlobter!, 1912 / DE / 65 x 50
Great Drought, The, 1912 / Colin Campbell / Selig Polyscope / US
Great drought, The, 1912 / US / 105 x 71
Grevinde X, 1909 / Holger Rasmussen / Nordisk Films Kompagni / DK
Rote domino, Der, 1909 / Louis Galice / DE / 100 x 140
Groom par amour / Lux / FR
Groom par amour / Lucien Charbonnier / FR / 184 x 100
Groote mijnen en hunne gevare, De

Groote mijnen en hunne gevaren, De / NL / 32 x 85
Groote schoonmaak, De /　Ambrosio / IT
[*Groote schoonmaak, De*] / Atelier Butteri / IT / 140 x 100
Grosse Wette, Die, 1915 / Harry Piel / Bayerische Film-Vertriebs-Gesellschaft Fett u. Wiesel / DE
Grosse Wette, Die, 1916 / DE / 210 x 150
Grosse Wette, Die, 1916 / DE / 142 x 96
Grosse Wette, Die, 1916 / Fritz G. Kirchbach / DE / 100 x 70
Grüne Teufel, Der, 1913 / Harry Piel / Vitascope / DE
Grüne Teufel, Der, 1914 / DE / 210 x 300
Groene duivel, De, 1913 / NL / 84 x 31
Groene duivel, De, 1913 / NL / 85 x 31
Gruss aus der Tiefe, Ein, 1915 / Emmerich Hanus / Zelnik-Film / DE
Gruß aus der Tiefe, Ein, 1915 / DE / 72 x 94
Gueuse, La*, 1913 / Eclair / FR
Gueuse, La, 1913 / FR / 150 x 200
Gueuse, La, 1913, Roger Chapelet / FR / 150 x 100
Eerlooze, De, 1913 / NL / 31 x 85

H

Half a Hero, 1912 / James Young / Vitagraph Company of America / US
Half a hero, 1912 / US / 107 x 72
Hallali, L', 1913 / Alfred Machin / Pathé Frères / FR
Hallali, L', 1913 / Atelier Faria / FR / 161 x 120
Hand of Fate, The, 1913 / Essanay Film Manufacturing / US
Hand of Fate, The, 1913 / GB / 102 x 77
Hands Across the Sea in '76, 1911 / Lawrence B. McGill / Eclair Company / US
Hands across the Sea in '76, 1911 / US / 106 x 72
Hans faders ære, 1914 / Filmfabriken Danmark / DK
His father's honour, 1914 / DK / 49 x 44
Hans vanskeligste rolle*, 1912 / August Blom / Nordisk Films Kompagni / DK
Zijn zwaarste rol, 1912 / NL / 84 x 31
Hantise du grandpère, La, 1912 / Lux / FR
Hantise du grandpère, La / Lucien Charbonnier / FR / 150 x 120
Hater of Women, The, 1912 / Solax / US
Hater of women, The, 1912 / GB / 102 x 76
Havd mollebranden afslorede, 1912 / Eduard Schnedler-Sørensen / Nordisk Films Kompagni / DK

Geheimnis der Mühle, Das, 1913 / DE / 220 x 102
Heart of the Forest, A, 1913 / Ralph Ince / Vitagraph Company of America / US
Heart of the forest, A, 1913 / US / 107 x 72
Heaven Avenges, 1912 / D.W. Griffith, Frank Powell / Biograph / US
Heaven avenges, 1911 / GB / 102 x 76
Heisses Blut, 1911 / Peter Urban Gad / Deutsche Bioscop / DE
Heisses Blut, 1911 / DE / 149 x 110
Hell's Hinges, 1916 / William S. Hart, Charles Swickard / NYMPC – New York Motion Picture Kay-Bee / US
[*Hell's hinges*], 1916 / US / 200 x 100
Helvedes datter, 1909 / Nordisk Films Kompagni / DK
Höllenkind, Das, 1909 / DE / 72 x 96
Her Husband*, 1914 / Theodore Marston / Vitagraph Company of America / US
Son mari, 1914 / FR / 200 x 139
Her Secret, 1912 / Thanhouser Film / US
Her secret, 1912 / GB / 102 x 76
Her Spoiled Boy, 1911 / Gaston Méliès / Méliès Manufacturing Company / US
Her spoiled boy, 1911 / GB / 102 x 77
Hero Coward, The, 1913 / Theodore Wharton / Essanay Film Manufacturing / US
Hero coward, The, 1913 / GB / 225 x 102
Hero coward, The, 1913 / GB / 102 x 77
Herz und Pflicht / Gaumont / FR
Herz und Pflicht / DE / 151 x 110
Hexenfeuer, 1912 / Messter / DE
Hexenfeuer, 1912 / DE / 96 x 64
High Born Child and the Beggar, The*, 1913 / Kalem / US
High-born child and the beggar, The, 1913 / GB / 220 x 100
High-born child and the beggar, The, 1913 / US / 102 x 70
Hindoo's Charm, The, 1912 / Lubin Manufacturing Company / US
Hindoo's charm, The, 1912 / GB / 102 x 76
His Enemy, 1913 / Charles Brabin / Edison Manufacturing Company / US
His enemy, 1913 / US / 102 x 70
His Hour of Triumph*, 1913 / George Loane Tucker / Universal IMP / US
His hour of triumph, 1913 / GB / 225 x 102
His hour of triumph, 1913 / GB / 100 x 75
His Last Burglary, 1910 / D.W. Griffith / Biograph / US
His last burglary, 1910 / GB / 104 x 70
His Mother's Hope, 1912 / Charles Brabin / Edison Manufacturing Company / US

His mother's hope, 1912 / US / 102 x 70
His New Profession, 1914 / Charles Chaplin / Keystone Film / US
His new profession, 1914 / US / 200 x 102
His Only Son, 1912 / Milton J. Fahrney / Universal Nestor / US
His only son, 1912 / US / 107 x 71
His Punishment, 1912 / Charles K. French / New York Motion Picture Bison 101 / US
[*His punishment*], 1912 / US / 74 x 107
His punishment, 1912 / US / 100 x 70
His Secret*, 1913 / [Lionel Barrymore], [Frank Powell] / Biograph / US
His secret, 1913 / GB / 102 x 70
His secret, 1913 / GB / 225 x 101
His Tempermental Mother-In-Law, 1916 / L-KO Comedies / US
His tempermental mother-in-law, 1916 / US / 211 x 101
His tempermental mother-in-law, 1916 / US / 209 x 210
His Vacation, 1912 / Lubin Manufacturing Company / US
His vacation, 1912 / US / 104 x 70
Hochspannung*, 1913 / Messter / DE
Hochspannung, 1913 / Max Fließ / DE / 210 x 150
Hochspannung, 1913 / DE / 97 x 64
Homard, Le*, 1912 / Léonce Perret / Gaumont / FR
Homard, Le, 1912 / FR / 146 x 103
Honneur, L', 1913 / [Henri Pouctal] / Delac & Cie / FR
Honneur, L', 1913 / Gabriel Rousseau / FR / 105 x 70
Honneur, L', 1913 / FR / 220 x 210
Hot Finish, A, 1914 / Universal IMP / US
Hot finish, A, 1914 / US / 107 x 69
House of Mystery, The, 1913 / Wilfred Noy / Clarendon Film / GB
House of mystery, The, 1913 / GB / 98 x 73
How Betty Won the School, 1911 / Vitagraph Company of America / US
Quarantaine au pensionnat, La, 1911 / R. Hem / FR / 140 x 100
How Did It Finish?, 1913 / Ashley Miller / Edison Manufacturing Company / US
Comment s'ecrit l'histoire, [1913] / [FR] / 120 x 79
How Motion Pictures Are Made, 1913 / Keystone Film / US
How motion pictures are made, 1913 / US / 107 x 72
Human Kindness, 1913 / Allan Dwan / American Film Manufacturing / US
Human kindness, 1913 / US / 107 x 71
Hussard, Le / René Plaisetty / Pathé Frères / FR
Hussard, Le / Clerice Frères / FR / 160 x 120

I

Im Fegefeuer, 1913 / Pathé Frères / FR
Im Fegefeuer / DE / 219 x 149
Im Fegefeuer / DE / 150 x 110
In carnevale, 1915 / Cines / IT
In carnevale / IT / 139 x 100
In dem grossen Augenblick, 1911 / Peter Urban Gad / Deutsche Bioscop / DE
Onder den invloed van sterke wil / NL / 31 x 85
In flagranti ertappt, 1912 / Messter / DE
In flagranti ertappt, 1912 / DE / 125 x 94
In hoc signo vinces*, 1913 / Nino Oxilia / Savoia Film / IT
In hoc signo vinces, 1913 / NL / 64 x 50
In Peril of Their Lives, 1912 / Kalem / US
In peril of their lives, 1912 / GB / 102 x 76
In the Tents of the Asra, 1912 / Selig Polyscope / US
In the tents of the Asra, 1912 / US / 102 x 71
In verkeerde handen*, 1911 / Gaumont / FR
In valsche handen / NL / 32 x 86
Infamia Araba, 1912 / Mario Caserini / Ambrosio / IT
[*Infamia Araba*], 1912 / Atelier Butteri / IT / 140 x 100
Infernal Tangle, An, 1913 / William Humphrey / Vitagraph Company of America / US
Mêlée infernale, Une, 1913 / Harry Bedos / FR / 140 x 100
Inferno, L', 1911 / Adolfo Padovan / Milano Films / IT
Dante, 1911 / DE / 75 x 47
Interrupted Elopement, An, 1912 / Mack Sennett / Biograph / US
Interrupted elopement, An, 1912 / GB / 101 x 75
Ipnosi, 1912 / Cesare Carini Tebro / IT
Hypnose, 1912 / IT / 140 x 100
It Did Look Suspicious, 1911 / Vitagraph Company of America / US
It did look suspicious, 1911 / R. Hem / FR / 140 x 100
Italiaansche-Turksche oorlog!
Italiaansche-Turksche oorlog!, 1911–1912 / NL / 85 x 59
Ivanhoe*, 1913 / Herbert Brenon / Universal IMP / US
Ivanhoe, 1913 / GB / 225 x 102
Ivanhoe, 1913 / GB / 102 x 76
Ivanhoe, 1913 / NL / 31 x 85
Ivrogne, L', 1912 / Vitagraph Company of America / US
Ivrogne, L, 1912 / Harry Bedos / FR / 140 x 100

J

Jack Brown / Lux / FR
Jack Brown / Lucien Charbonnier / FR / 150 x 120
Jack*, 1913 / André Liabel / Eclair / FR
Jack, 1913 / FR / 200 x 300
Jack, 1913 / FR / 150 x 100
Kleine Jacques, De, 1913 / NL / 31 x 85
Kleine Jacques, De, 1913 / NL / 85 x 31
Kleine Jacques, De, 1913 / NL / 31 x 84
Kleine Jacques, De, 1913 / NL / 31 x 84
Jack's Chrysanthemum, 1913 / Maurice Costello, William V. Ranous / Vitagraph Company of America / US
Petite Japonaise, La, 1913 / FR / 139 x 100
Jaloezie
Jaloezie / NL / 43 x 62
Jambes, Les / Gaumont / FR
Jambes, Les / FR / 110 x 150
Je me présente... Gavroche / Eclair / FR
Je me presente... Gavroche / Auguste Leymarie / FR / 160 x 120
Jerry's Mother-In-Law*, 1913 / James Young / Vitagraph Company of America / US
Comment Jerry dompta sa Belle-mère, 1913 / Harry Bedos / FR / 198 x 130
Jerry's Uncle's Namesake*, 1913 / James Young / Vitagraph Company of America / US
Pseudo-bébé de Jerry, Le, 1913 / Harry Bedos / FR / 200 x 130
Jeux d'enfants*, 1913 / Henri Fescourt / Gaumont / FR
Jeux d'enfants, 1913 / FR / 225 x 103
Jewel Thieves Outwitted, The*, 1913 / Frank Wilson / Hepworth / GB
Jewel thieves outwitted, The, 1913 / GB / 101 x 76
Jim's Vindication*, 1912 / William Duncan / Selig Polyscope / US
Jim's vindication, 1912 / US / 104 x 71
Juan and Juanita*, 1912 / Wilbert Melville / Lubin Manufacturing Company / US
Juan and Juanita / GB / 103 x 77
Justice of the Desert, The, 1912 / Rollin S. Sturgeon / Vitagraph Company of America / US
Justice au desert, La, 1912 / R. Hem / FR / 141 x 101
Juvenile Love Affair, A, 1912 / Charles Kent / Vitagraph Company of America / US
Amour en herbe, L', 1912 / FR / 140 x 100

K

Kaiserin Elisabeth von Österreich*, 1920 / Rolf Raffé / Indra Film / DE
Kaiserin Elisabeth von Oesterreich, 1920 / DE / 105 x 71
Kämpfende Herzen, 1912 / Curt A. Stark / Messters Projektion / DE
Kämpfende Herzen, 1912 / DE / 190 x 125
Kerry Gow, The, 1912 / Sidney Olcott / Kalem / US
Kerry gow, The, 1912 / GB / 102 x 77
Kill or Cure, 1914 / Harry Lambart / Vitagraph Company of America / US
Madamme vous empoisonne!, 1914 / Harry Bedos / FR / 140 x 100
Kinder des Majors, Die*, 1914 / Eiko Film / DE
Kinder des Majors, Die, 1915 / Tjerk Bottema / DE / 216 x 149
King of the Circus, 1920 / J.P. McGowan / Universal / US
King of the circus, 1920 / US / 205 x 103
Kings of the Forest*, 1912 / Colin Campbell / Selig Polyscope / US
Kings of the forest / GB / 225 x 102
Aan d'n dood ontsnapt, 1912 / NL / 31 x 85
Aan d'n dood ontsnapt, 1912 / NL / 31 x 85
Kings of the forest, 1912 / US / 204 x 204
Kino-Schieber-Gesellschaft m.b.h., Die, 1912 / Hepworth / GB
Kino-Schieber-Gesellschaft m.b.h., Die, 1912 / GB / 102 x 77
Kloster bei Sendomir, Das, 1912 / Deutsche Mutoskop und Biograph / DE
[Kloster bei Sendomir, Das] / DE / 150 x 110
Kosakfyrsten, 1910 / Nordisk Films Kompagni / DK
Kozakkenvorst, De, 1910 / NL / 29 x 84
Kozakkenvorst, De, 1910 / NL / 29 x 84
Kri Kri ama la tintora*, 1913 / Cines / IT
Kri Kri ama la tintura, 1913 / Marchetti / IT / 140 x 100
Kri Kri e Lea militari*, 1913 / Cines / IT
Kri Kri e Lea militari, 1913 / Marchetti / IT / 140 x 100
Kri Kri imita i voli di Pegoud*, 1914 / Cines / IT
Kri Kri imita Pegoud, 1914 / Marchetti / IT / 138 x 100
Kri Kri martire della suocera, 1915 / Cines / IT
Patachon et sa belle-mere, 1915 / IT / 100 x 71
Kri Kri sbadiglia, 1914 / Cines / IT
Kri Kri sbadiglia, 1914 / Marchetti / IT / 140 x 100
Kri Kri senza testa*, 1913 / Cines / IT
Kri-Kri à perduto la testa, 1913 / IT / 138 x 100
Kri Kri s'improvvisa cameriere*, 1914 / Cines / IT
Kri Kri cameriere, 1914 / Marchetti / IT / 140 x 100
Kri Kri stalliere per amore*, 1914 / Cines / IT
Kri Kri stalliero per amore, 1914 / Marchetti / IT / 140 x 100
Kriegsfackel, Die, 1912 / Alfred Lind / Royal Films / DE
Kriegsfackel, Die, 1912 / DE / 210 x 150
Kümmere dich um Fifi!, 1911 / Elge-Gaumont / FR
Kümmere dich um Fifi!, 1911 / FR / 106 x 76
Künstlerliebe*, 1911 / Adolf Gärtner / Messter / DE
Künstlerliebe, 1911 / DE / 100 x 72
Kvindes aere, En*, 1912 / Einar Zangenberg / Dansk Kinograf Films / DK
Woman's Honour, A, 1912 / GB / 200 x 150

L

Lad from Old Ireland, The, 1910 / Sidney Olcott / Kalem / US
Lad from Old Ireland, The, 1911 / GB / 101 x 77
Lady and Her Maid, A*, 1913 / Bert Angeles / Vitagraph Company of America / US
Transformation inespérée, Une, 1913 / Harry Bedos / FR / 140 x 100
Lake of Dreams, The, 1912 / Selig Polyscope / US
Lake of dreams, The, 1912 / US / 105 x 71
Landstrasse, Die*, 1913 / Paul von Woringen / Deutsche Mutoskop und Biograph / DE
[Landstrasse, Die], 1913 / A. Hubert / DE / 214 x 147
Landlooper, De, 1913 / NL / 64 x 50
Last Rose of Summer, The, 1912 / Lubin Manufacturing Company / US
Last rose of summer, The, 1912 / GB / 102 x 76
Lealtà di soldato, 1912 / Cines / IT
Twixt Love and War, 1910–1914 / GB / 221 x 199
Leben heisst kämpfen, 1914 / Luna-Film / DE
[Leben heisst kämpfen], 1914 / DE / 148 x 110
Wedloop om het leven, Een, 1914 / NL / 31 x 85
Leçon d'amour, Une*, 1912 / Léonce Perret / Gaumont / FR
Leçon d'amour, La, 1912 / FR / 150 x 111
Legend of Sleepy Hollow, The, 1912 / Etienne Arnaud / Eclair Company / US
Legend of Sleepy Hollow, The, 1912 / US / 106 x 72
Lektion, En, 1911 / August Blom / Nordisk Films Kompagni / DK
Aviaticker und die Frau des Journalisten, 1911 / DE / 216 x 292
Vliegenier en de vrouw van den journalist, De, 1911–1913 / NL / 32 x 85
Leo, der Witwenfreund, 1912 / Carl Wilhelm / B.B. Film / DE
Leo, der Witwenfreund, 1912 / Art Gratz / DE / 95 x 75
Léonce à la campagne*, 1913 / Léonce Perret / Gaumont / FR
Léonce à la campagne, 1913 / FR / 102 x 76
Léonce flirte*, 1913 / Léonce Perret / Gaumont / FR
Léonce flirt, 1912 / FR / 151 x 111
Leonie, 1913 / Bannister Merwin / Edison Manufacturing Company / US
Leonie, 1913 / US / 102 x 71
Lesson in Jealousy, A*, 1913 / Harry Lambart / Vitagraph Company of America / US
Leçon du jalousie, Une, 1913 / Harry Bedos / FR / 140 x 101
Lesson, The*, 1910 / D.W. Griffith / Biograph / US
Eert uwen vader en uwe moeder / NL / 31 x 86
Letzte Tag, Der, 1913 / Max Mack / Vitascope / DE
Letzte Tag, Der, 1913 / DE / 147 x 107
Liebe und Leidenschaft*, 1911 / Adolf Gärtner / Messter / DE
Liefde en hartstocht, 1911 / NL / 31 x 85
Liefde en hartstocht / NL / 31 x 85
Liefde en trouw
Liefde en trouw / NL / 31 x 85
Lieut. Daring R.N. and the Photographing Pigeon, 1912 / Charles Raymond / British and Colonial Kinematograph / GB
Lieut. Daring R.N. and the photographing pigeon, 1912 / GB / 102 x 76
Lieutenant's Last Fight, The*, 1912 / Thomas H. Ince / NYMPC – New York Motion Picture Bison 101 / US
Laatste rit van den officier, De, 1912 / NL / 31 x 86
[Lijk, het] / Luna-Film / DE
[Lijk, het] / DE / 215 x 148
Little Enchantress, The, 1913 / Majestic Motion Picture / US
Little enchantress, The / GB / 101 x 77
Little Girl Next Door, The, 1912 / Lucius Henderson / Thanhouser Film / US
Little girl next door, The, 1912–1913 / GB / 102 x 77
Little hands, 1912 / Etienne Arnaud / Eclair Company / US

Little hands, 1912 / US / 106 x 73

Little Spreewald Maiden, The, 1910 / Sidney Olcott / Kalem / US
Kleine Spreewaelderin, Die, 1910 / GB / 105 x 70

Little Wanderer, The, 1912 / Kalem / US
Little wanderer, The, 1912 / GB / 102 x 76

Livets løgn*, 1912 / August Blom / Nordisk Films Kompagni / DK
Lüge des Lebens, Die, 1912 / DE / 221 x 102

Locket, The, 1913 / Frederick A. Thomson / Vitagraph Company of America / US
Locket, The, 1913 / US / 107 x 72

Lonely Princess, The*, 1913 / Maurice Costello / Vitagraph Company of America / US
Princesse solitaire, La, 1913 / FR / 140 x 100

Lord and the Peasant, The, 1912 / J. Searle Dawley / Edison Manufacturing Company / US
Lord and the peasant, The, [1912] / US / 102 x 70

Loyal Deserter, A*, 1913 / Selig Polyscope / US
Loyal deserter, A, 1913 / US / 101 x 77

Loyalty of Sylvia, The*, 1912 / Van Dyke Brooke / Vitagraph Company of America / US
Loyalty of Sylvia, The, 1912 / GB / 102 x 77

Lucette's Fuss, 1913 / Vitagraph Company of America / US
Pied de Lucette, Le, 1910–1914 / FR / 140 x 100

Lucky Fall, A, 1912 / [Francis J. Grandon] / Lubin Manufacturing Company / US
Lucky fall, A, 1912 / US / 103 x 70

Lucky Mistake, A, 1913 / Lorimer Johnston / Selig Polyscope / US
Lucky mistake, A, 1913 / US / 104 x 71

Lulu's Anarchist, 1912 / Edward R. Phillips / Vitagraph Company of America / US
Anarchiste de Loulou, L', 1912 / FR / 140 x 100

Lumpenbaron, Der*, 1914 / Waldemar Hecker / Karl Werner Film / DE
Lumpenbaron, Der, 1914 / DE / 221 x 103

Lure of the City, The, 1911 / Edwin S. Porter / Edison Manufacturing Company / US
Nellys Abenteuer in der Stadt, 1911 / DE / 100 x 71

Lure of Vanity, The, 1911 / Vitagraph Company of America / US
Démon de la vanité, Le, 1911 / R. Hem / FR / 140 x 99

[Lusthof, Het] / FR
[Lusthof, Het], [1910–1919] / [FR] / 240 x 320

M

Mabel's Lovers, 1912 / Mack Sennett / Keystone Film / US
Mabel's Lovers, 1912 / US / 101 x 76

Madeleine*, 1912 / Emil Albes / Deutsche Bioscop / DE
Duitschers in Frankrijk, De, 1912 / NL / 31 x 35
Duitschers in Frankrijk, De, 1912 / NL / 31 x 85

Maid of Honour, The, 1913 / Charles Brabin / Edison Manufacturing Company / US
Maid of honour, The, 1913 / US / 102 x 70

Making a Man of Her*, 1912 / Al Christie / Universal Nestor / US
Making a man of her, 1912 / US / 107 x 71

Making of Broncho Billy, The, 1913 / Gilbert M. 'Broncho Billy' Anderson / Essanay Film Manufacturing / US
Making of Broncho Billy, The, 1913 / GB / 101 x 76
Making of Broncho Billy, The, 1913–1915 / GB / 102 x 76

Man Higher Up, The, 1913 / Frederick A. Thomson / Vitagraph Company of America / US
Man higher up, The, 1913 / US / 108 x 72
Supérieur et subalterne, 1913 / Harry Bedos / FR / 140 x 100

Man Who Might Have Been, The, 1913 / Selig Polyscope / US
Man who might have been, The, 1913 / US / 106 x 72

Manden med de ni fingre IV, 1916 / Anders Wilhelm Sandberg / Nordisk Films Kompagni / DK
Valsch geld / NL / 86 x 31

Man's Genesis, 1912 / D.W. Griffith / Biograph / US
Man's genesis, 1912 / GB / 102 x 76

Marchand des poupées, Le*, 1913 / Gaumont / FR
Marchand des poupées, Le, 1913 / FR / 101 x 77

Marga, Lebensbild aus Künstlerkreisen, 1913 / Danny Kaden / Uranus Film Gesellschaft / DE
Marga!, 1913 / Atelier Louis Wagner / DE / 184 x 125
Marga de schilderes, 1913 / NL / 84 x 31

Marriage of Convenience, A, 1912 / James Young / Vitagraph Company of America / US
Marriage of convenience, A, 1912 / US / 107 x 71

Mary's New Hat, 1913 / Charles H. France / Edison Manufacturing Company / US
Marie a envie d'un chapeau, 1913 / FR / 120 x 80

Ma's Apron Strings, 1913 / Frederick A. Thomson / Vitagraph Company of America / US
Ma's apron strings, 1913 / US / 107 x 72

Maschera pietosa, La*, 1914 / Ambrosio / IT
[Maschera pietosa, La], 1914 / Atelier Butteri / IT / 200 x 140

Maske, Die, jaar onbekend / Düsseldorfer Film Manufaktur Ludwig Gottschalk / DE
Maske, Die / DE / 203 x 95

Massacre, The, 1912 / D.W. Griffith / Biograph / US
[Massacre, The], [1912–1913] / GB / 200 x 200

Maudie's Adventure, 1913 / Percy Stow / Clarendon Film / GB
Maudie's adventures, 1913 / GB / 102 x 76

Memories That Haunt*, 1914 / Harry Lambart / Vitagraph Company of America / US
Hantise du passé, La, 1914 / FR / 200 x 140

Men Were Deceivers Ever*, 1911 / Dave Aylott / British and Colonial Kinematograph / GB
Men were deceivers ever, 1912 / FR / 151 x 109

Ménage Dranem, Le, 1912 / Pathé Frères / FR
Ménage Dranem, Le, 1912 / Adrien Barrère / FR / 160 x 120

Message of the Palms, The, 1913 / Robert Vignola / Kalem / US
Message of the palms, The, 1913 / US / 104 x 70

Messaggio del vento, Il, 1913 / Oreste Mentasti / Savoia Film / IT
Message de vent, Le, 1913 / Achille Luciano Mauzan / IT / 200 x 140

Mike's Brainstorm, 1912 / Selig Polyscope / US
Mike's brainstorm, 1912 / US / 101 x 77

Millions de la bonne, Les*, 1913 / Louis Feuillade / Gaumont / FR
Millions de la bonne, Les, 1913 / FR / 102 x 77
Millions de la bonne, Les, 1913 / FR / 220 x 150
Millioenen juffrouw, De / NL / 31 x 85

Mills of the Gods, The*, 1912 / Ralph Ince / Vitagraph Company of America / US
Genie du mal, Le, 1912 / FR / 140 x 99
Mills of the gods, The, 1912 / GB / 102 x 76

Mimosa san, 1912 / Curt A. Stark / Messter / DE
Mimosa san, 1912 / DE / 76 x 50

Minenbesitzer, Der / Eiko Film / DE
Mine owner, The / GB / 101 x 76

Miracolo d'amore, 1919 / Ivo Illuminati / Raggio Film / IT
[Miracolo d'amore], 1919 / IT / 101 x 70

Mirage, Le, 1912 / Victorin Jasset / Eclair / FR
Mirage, Le, 1912 / Roger Chapelet / FR / 158 x 237

Mistaken Accusation, 1913 / Essanay Film Manufacturing / US
Mistaken accusation, 1913 / US / 102 x 77

Mister Smith fait l'ouverture*, 1914 / Jean Durand / Gaumont / FR
Mr. Smith fait l'ouverture, 1914 / GB / 101 x 77

Modell, Das / DE
Modell, Das / DE / 142 x 95

Money Kings, The, 1912 / Van Dyke Brooke / Vitagraph Company of America / US
Stahlkönig, Der, 1912 / DE / 65 x 50

Monsieur Lecoq, 1913 / Maurice Tourneur / Eclair / FR
Monsieur Lecoq, 1913 / FR / 200 x 300
Monsieur Lecoq, 1915 / FR / 150 x 100

Monte Christo, 1912 / Colin Campbell / Selig Polyscope / US
Monte Cristo, 1912 / GB / 101 x 76

Mormonens offer, 1911 / August Blom / Nordisk Films Kompagni / DK
Opfer des Mormonen, Das, 1911 / DE / 225 x 300
Opfer des Mormonen, Das, 1911 / DE / 214 x 102

Morsa, La, 1912 / Ubaldo Maria Del Colle / Pasquali / IT
Im Zwange der Not, 1912 / DE / 97 x 64

Mort qui venge, La / Lux / FR
Mort qui venge, La / Lucien Charbonnier / FR / 140 x 100

Morte civile, La*, 1913 / Ubaldo Maria Del Colle / Savoia Film / IT
[Morte civile, La], 1913 / Achille Luciano Mauzan / IT / 290 x 210

Morte civile, La*, 1913 / Ubaldo Maria Del Colle / Savoia Film / IT
Schuldig aan moord / NL / 30 x 85
Schuldig aan moord, 1913 / NL / 30 x 85

Mother of the Ranch, The, 1912 / Essanay Film Manufacturing / US
Mother of the ranch, The, 1912 / US / 102 x 76

Mother's awakening, A, 1912 / Rex Motion Picture Company / US
Mothers awakening, A, 1912 / GB / 102 x 77

Mountain Witch, The, 1913 / Kalem / US
Mountain witch, The, 1913 / US / 104 x 70

Mousmée et le brigand, La*, 1911 / CGPC / FR
Mousmée et le brigand, La / Adrien Barrère / FR / 155 x 100

Mr. Bolter's Infatuation*, 1912 / George D. Baker / Vitagraph Company of America / US

Unüberlegtes Wort, Ein, 1912 / DE / 110 x 75
Mr. Bolter's niece, 1913 / Frederick A. Thomson / Vitagraph Company of America / US
Mr. Bolter's niece, 1912 / US / 107 x 72
Mr. Grouch at the Seashore, 1912 / Dell Henderson / Biograph / US
Mr. Grouch at the seashore, 1912 / GB / 101 x 76
Mrs. Lirriper's Lodgers, 1912 / Van Dyke Brooke / Vitagraph Company of America / US
Pensionnaires de madame Lirriper, Les, 1912 / Harry Bedos / FR / 140 x 100
Mrs. Lirriper's lodgers, 1912 / US / 107 x 72
Musketeers of Pig Alley, The*, 1912 / D.W. Griffith / Biograph / US
Musketeers of Pig Alley, 1912 / GB / 102 x 76
My Baby, 1912 / Frank Powell / Biograph / US
My baby, 1912 / GB / 102 x 70
Mystère des Roches de Kador, Le*, 1912 / Léonce Perret / Gaumont / FR
Geheim van de rotsen van Kador, Het, 1912 / NL / 31 x 85
Mystère des roches de Kador, Le, 1912 / FR / 221 x 220

N

Naar manden gaar paa børsen*, 1913 / Eduard Schnedler-Sørensen / Nordisk Films Kompagni / DK
[Naar manden gaar paa børsen], 1913 / DK / 210 x 100
Nan in Fairyland, 1912 / Edwin J. Collins / Cricks & Martin / GB
Nan in Fairyland, 1912 / GB / 101 x 76
Navajo's Bride, The*, 1910 / [Sidney Olcott] / Kalem / US
Navajoe's bride, 1910 / GB / 102 x 71
Near to Earth, 1913 / D.W. Griffith / Biograph / US
Near to earth, 1913 / GB / 105 x 70
Nel paese dell'oro, 1914 / Cines / IT
Nel paese dell'oro, 1914 / IT / 197 x 140
Nel vortice del destino*, 1913 / Savoia Film / IT
Nel vortice del destino, 1913 / Achille Luciano Mauzan / IT / 140 x 200
Nina's Evening Prayer, 1912 / Wilfred Noy / Clarendon Film / GB
Nina's prayer, 1912 / GB / 102 x 76
Noble Deed, A / Gaumont / [Frankrijk]
Noble deed, A / FR / 101 x 77
Noël de Francesca, Le, 1912 / Louis Feuillade / Gaumont / FR
Francesca's Weihnacht, 1912, / Achille Luciano Mauzan / FR / 200 x 140

Nordlandrose*, 1914 / Curt A. Stark / Messter / DE
Nordlandrose, 1914 / Erich Wohlfahrt / DE / 220 x 149
Medeminnaars, 1914 / NL / 30 x 85
Nordlandrose*, 1914 / Curt A. Stark / Messter / DE
Medeminnaars, 1914 / NL / 32 x 86
Northwoods romance, A, 1913 / Universal Gem / US
Northwoods romance, A, 1913 / US / 101 x 68
Now Watch the Professor, 1912 / Thanhouser Film / US
Now watch the professor, 1912 / GB / 102 x 76
Nr. 482, 1912 / Deutsche Mutoskop und Biograph / DE
Nr. 482, 1912 / DE / 61 x 95
Nuage, Un*, 1913 / Léonce Perret / Gaumont / FR
Nuage, un, 1912 / FR / 150 x 110

O

Obsession du souvenir, L'*, 1913 / Gaumont / FR
Obsession du souvenir, L', 1913 / FR / 102 x 76
Kwellende herinneringen aan het verleden, 1913 / NL / 31 x 85
Off the Road, 1913 / Ralph Ince / Vitagraph Company of America / US
Off the road, 1913 / US / 107 x 72
Oh, You Ragtime!*, 1912 / Etienne Arnaud / Eclair Company / US
Oh, you ragtime!, 1912 / US / 106 x 73
Old Guard, The, 1913 / James Young / Vitagraph Company of America / US
Old guard, The, 1913 / US / 107 x 72
Ombre du passé, L' / Ashley Miller / Edison Manufacturing Company / US
Ombre du passé, L', 1915 / FR / 120 x 80
Ombrellino, L' / Savoia Film / IT
Ombrellino, L' / Achille Luciano Mauzan / IT / 100 x 70
Omens of the Mesa, 1912 / Rollin S. Sturgeon / Vitagraph Company of America / US
Omens of the mesa, 1912 / US / 107 x 72
On Secret Service*, 1912 / Walter Edwards / New York Motion Picture Kay-Bee / US
On secret service, 1912 / GB / 200 x 102
[On secret service], 1913 / US / 200 x 100
On secret service, 1913 / US / 200 x 100
On secret service, 1912 / US / 152 x 102
On the Threshold, 1913 / George Nichols sr / Lubin Manufacturing Company / US
On the threshold / GB / 101 x 76
One of the bravest, The*, 1914 / Otis Turner / Universal Gold Seal / US
Dapperste, De, 1912 / NL / 31 x 86
Dapperste, De, 1912 / NL / 31 x 86
One Over on Cutey, 1913 / Van Dyke Brooke / Vitagraph Company of America / US
Amoureux de Colombine, 1913, Harry Bedos / FR / 139 x 100
One She Loved, The, 1912 / D.W. Griffith / Biograph / US
One she loved, The, 1912 / GB / 104 x 70
Onésime débute au théâtre*, 1913 / Jean Durand / Gaumont / FR
Onésime débute au théâtre, 1913 / FR / 102 x 76
Onésime et l'éléphant détective, 1912 / Jean Durand / Gaumont / FR
Augustin und der Detektiv-Elefant, 1912 / FR / 102 x 76
Onésime, Calino et la panthère, 1913 / Jean Durand / Gaumont / FR
Simple Simon and Calino's panther, 1913 / FR / 102 x 77
Op leven en dood / Messter / DE
[Op leven en dood] / GB / 300 x 200
From the jaws of death / GB / 101 x 76
Origineller Fächer, Ein / Messter / DE
Origineller Fächer, Ein / DE / 124 x 94
Oscar pris au piège*, 1913 / Louis Feuillade / Gaumont / FR
Oscar pris au Piège, 1913 / FR / 102 x 77
Otage, L'*, 1912 / Lux / FR
Otage, L', 1912 / Lucien Charbonnier / FR / 155 x 118
Out of the Dark, 1912 / Thanhouser Film / US
Out of the dark, 1912 / GB / 102 x 76
Over the Back Fence*, 1913 / C. Jay Williams / Edison Manufacturing Company / US
Palissade, La, 1913 / DE / 101 x 71
Overwinning, De, 1912 / Eduard Schnedler-Sørensen / Nordisk Films Kompagni / DK
Overwinning, De / NL / 85 x 31

P

[Paar schoenen, Een] / Vitascope / DE
[Paar schoenen, Een] / DE / 200 x 110
Padre*, 1912 / Dante Testa, Gino Zaccaria / Itala Film / IT
Father, 1912 / GB / 102 x 77
[Padre], 1912 / Emilio Vacchetti / IT / 140 x 100
Vater, 1912 / DE / 65 x 48
Page, Le, 1912 / Henri Desfontaines / Eclipse / FR
[Page, Le], 1912 / David Hand / FR / 162 x 120

Panne d'auto*, 1912 / Baldassarre Negroni / Celio Film / IT
Panne d'auto, 1912 / IT / 197 x 140
[Panter] / Gaumont / FR
[Panter] / FR / 150 x 220
Pantera, La, 1912 / Savoia Film / IT
Pantera, La, 1912 / Achille Luciano Mauzan / IT / 197 x 140
Paradies der Damen, Das*, 1914 / Max Mack / Vitascope/PAGU / DE
[Paradies der Damen, Das], 1914 / DE / 221 x 110
Pas de deux / Compagnie des Cinématographes / FR
Pas de deux / FR / 120 x 80
Patouillard et le pensionnat, 1912 / Roméo Bosetti / Lux / FR
Patouillard et le pensionnat / Lucien Charbonnier / FR / 140 x 100
Pauline*, 1914 / Henri Étiévant / Vitascope/PAGU / DE
Pauline, 1914 / Otto Dely / DE / 217 x 140
Pay Train, The, 1915 / J.P. McGowan / Kalem / US
Pay train, The, 1914 / US / 170 x 106
Paying the board bill, 1912 / Kalem / US
Paying the board bill, 1912 / GB / 102 x 77
Paymaster's Son, The, 1913 / Thomas H. Ince / New York Motion Picture Kay-Bee / US
Indian raid, 1913 / GB / 220 x 102
Met den dood bekocht, 1913 / NL / 31 x 85
Met den dood bekocht, 1913 / NL / 31 x 85
Pay master's son, The, 1913 / US / 210 x 110
Per amore di Jenny*, 1915 / Cines / IT
Per amore di Fanny, 1915 / IT / 139 x 100
Per mia figlia!, 1914 / Ivo Illuminati / Cines / IT
Per sua figlia, 1914 / IT / 270 x 194
Peril of the cliffs, The, 1912 / Kalem / US
Peril of the cliffs, The, 1912 / GB / 102 x 70
Perilous Cargo, A, 1913 / Edison Manufacturing Company / US
Perilous cargo, A, 1913 / US / 100 x 71
Perils of Pauline*, 1914 / Louis J. Gasnier / Wharton / US
Phare de la mort, 1914 / Atelier Faria / FR / 240 x 320
Perle, Die, 1914 / Max Mack / Vitascope/PAGU / DE
Perle, Die, 1914 / DE / 216 x 143
Perle, Die, 1914 / DE / 96 x 66
Perle, Die, 1914 / DE / 95 x 65
Perle, Une*, 1912 / Léonce Perret / Gaumont / FR
Perle, Une, 1912 / FR / 106 x 76
Petite Fifi, La, 1913 / Pathé Frères – Le Film d'Art / FR
Petite Fifi, Ka, 1913 / FR / 225 x 300

***Phantom Ship, The*, 1913 / Harold M. Shaw / Edison Manufacturing Company / US**
Phantom ship, The, 1913 / US / 100 x 70

***Physician of Silver Gulch, The*, 1912 / Francis J. Grandon / Lubin Manufacturing Company / US**
Physician of Silver Gulch, The, 1912 / GB / 102 x 76

***Pickaninnies and the Watermelons*, 1912 / Rep Films / US**
Pickaninnies and watermelons, 1912 / US / 107 x 71

***Pickpocket, The**, 1913 / George D. Baker / Vitagraph Company of America / US**
Pour guérir Lolotte, 1913 / Harry Bedos / FR / 140 x 100

***Pik Nik veste la jupe-culotte**, 1911 / Mario Morais / Aquila Films / IT**
Harembroek, De, 1911 / NL / 31 x 84

***Pimple Becomes an Acrobat*, 1912 / Fred Evans, Joe Evans / Folly / GB**
Hello! Pimple again / GB / 77 x 51

***Pimple Collects the Rent*, 1914 / Fred Evans / Folly / GB**
Pimple at it again, 1914 / GB / 77 x 51
Pimple collects the rent, 1914 / GB / 77 x 51

***Pimple Has a Try*, 1914 / Fred Evans / Folly / GB**
Pimple has a try, 1914 / GB / 77 x 51

***Pimple Wins a Bet*, 1912 / Fred Evans / Folly / GB**
Pimple wins a bet, 1912 / GB / 77 x 51

***Pinned*, 1912 / Lubin Manufacturing Company / US**
Pinned, 1912 / GB / 102 x 76

***Pipe de Barnabé, La*, 1912 / Lux / FR**
Pipe de monsieur Barnabé, La, 1912 / Lucien Charbonnier / FR / 107 x 76

***Plot and Pash*, 1912 / Hay Plumb / Hepworth / GB**
Plot and pash, 1912 / GB / 102 x 77

***Polidor al club della morte*, 1912 / Ferdinand Guillaume / Pasquali / IT**
Polidor, 1912 / Giovanni Grande / IT / 140 x 100
Polidor, 1913 / Giovanni Grande / IT / 140 x 100

***Polidor e l'attaccapanni*, 1914 / [Ferdinand Guillaume] / Pasquali / IT**
[*Robinet*] / IT / 140 x 100

***Polycarpe fait de la morale au centimètre**, 1914 / Ernest Servaes / Eclipse / FR**
[*Polycarpe fait de la morale au centimètre*], 1914 / FR / 120 x 80

***Portafortuna di Totò, Il*, 1912 / Emilio Vardannes / Itala Film / IT**
Portafortuna di Totò, il, 1912 / Emilio Vacchetti / IT / 140 x 100

***Portrait, The*, 1913 / George Lessey / Edison Manufacturing Company / US**
Portrait, The, 1913 / US / 102 x 70

***Post Telegrapher, The**, 1912 / Francis Ford, Thomas H. Ince, [Frank Morty] / New York Motion Picture Bison / US**
Telegrafist van het fort Jates, De / NL / 31 x 85

***Power of Conscience, The*, 1912 / Independent Motion Picture Corporation / US**
Power of conscience, The, 1912 / US / 107 x 71

***Premier duel de Willy, Le*, 1914 / Joseph Faivre / Eclair / FR**
Premier duel de Willy, Le, 1914, Edouard Bernard / FR / 150 x 100

***Primavera*, 1916 / Achille Mauzan / Raggio Film / IT**
Primavera, 1916 / Achille Luciano Mauzan / IT / 106 x 70

***Prison Ship, The*, 1912 / Kalem / US**
Prison ship, The, 1912 / GB / 102 x 76

***Prisoners of War*, 1913 / George Melford / Kalem / US**
Prisoners of war, 1913 / GB / 101 x 71

***Prisoner's Story, The*, 1912 / Méliès Manufacturing Company / US**
Prisoner's story, The, 1912 / GB / 101 x 76

***Prompted by Jealousy*, 1913 / Selig Polyscope / US**
Prompted by jealousy, 1912 / US / 104 x 71

***Pumps**, 1913 / Larry Trimble / Vitagraph Company of America / US**
Escarpins, 1913 / FR / 140 x 100

Q

***Question of Seconds, A**, 1912 / Edison Manufacturing Company / US**
Question de seconde, Une, 1912 / DE / 100 x 72

R

***Rache* / DE**
Rache / DE / 100 x 72

***Rags and Riches*, 1913 / Herbert Brenon / Universal IMP / US**
Rags and riches, 1913 / GB / 102 x 76

***Ragtime Romance, A*, 1913 / Dell Henderson / Biograph / US**
Ragtime romance, A, 1913 / GB / 102 x 70

***Railroad Wooing, A**, 1913 / Kalem / US**
Railroad wooing, A, 1913 / GB / 102 x 70

***Rajah's Hatred, A*, 1912 / Vitagraph Company of America / US**
Rajah's hatred, A, 1912 / GB / 102 x 76

***Ranch Girl's Trial, The*, 1912 / Essanay Film Manufacturing / US**
Ranch girl's trial, The, 1912 / US / 107 x 71

***Rançon du bonheur, La**, 1912 / Léonce Perret / Gaumont / FR**
Rançon du bonheur, La, 1912 / FR / 220 x 150
Verklungene Lieder, 1912 / FR / 210 x 150
Vervlogen geluk, 1912 / NL / 32 x 84
Vervlogen geluk, 1912 / NL / 31 x 85

***Rancune, La*, 1912 / Eclair / FR**
Rancune, La / Roger Chapelet / FR / 160 x 120

***Recht aufs Dasein, Das**, 1913 / Joseph Delmont / Eiko Film / DE**
Recht aufs Dasein, Das, 1913 / DE / 220 x 150
Recht aufs Dasein, Das, 1913 / DE / 48 x 30

***Red and White Roses*, 1913 / William Humphrey / Vitagraph Company of America / US**
Rose rouge et la rose blanche, La, 1913 / Harry Bedos / FR / 200 x 130

***Reddingschool in Australië* / Independent Motion Picture Corporation / US**
Reddingschool in Australië, 1912 / NL / 32 x 85

***Redskin Raiders, The*, 1912 / Kalem / US**
Redskin raiders, The, 1912 / GB / 102 x 76

***Reflets vivants, Les*, 1908 / Camille de Morlhon / Pathé Frères / FR**
Reflet vivant, Le, 1908 / Candido Aragonês de Faria / FR / 120 x 160

***Regeneration of Nancy, The*, 1913 / Lubin Manufacturing Company / US**
Regeneration of Nancy, 1913 / GB / 101 x 70

***Regeneration of Worthless Dan, The*, 1912 / Universal Nestor / US**
Regeneration of Worthless Dan, The, 1912 / US / 107 x 71

***Renegades, The**, 1912 / Lubin Manufacturing Company / US**
Renegades, The, 1912 / GB / 102 x 76

***Réprouvé, Le*, 1912 / René Leprince / Pathé Frères – SCAGL / FR**
Réprouvé, Le, 1912 / Atelier Faria / FR / 237 x 320

***Résurrection de Nick Winter, La*, 1912 / Paul Garbagni / Pathé Frères / FR**
Wederopstanding van Nick Winter, De, 1915 / NL / 86 x 61

***Return of Draw Egan, The*, 1916 / William S. Hart / Triangle Film / US**
Return of Draw Egan, The, 1916 / US / 205 x 207

***Reward of Perseverance, The**, 1912 / Bert Haldane / Barker Motion Photography / GB**
Reward of preserverance, The, 1912 / GB / 102 x 77

***Reward, The*, 1914 / Reginald Barker / Lubin Manufacturing Company / US**
Reward, The, 1914 / GB / 101 x 76

***Ricatto, Il*, 1912 / Cines / IT**
Ricatto, 1912 / IT / 140 x 100

***Richard Wagner**, 1913 / Carl Froelich, William Wauer / Messter / DE**
Richard Wagner, 1913 / NL / 100 x 65

***Right Number, But the Wrong House, The**, 1913 / Edison Manufacturing Company / US**
809 et le 608, Le, 1913 / DE / 100 x 71

***Riley's Decoys**, 1913 / Biograph / US**
Riley's decoys, 1913 / US / 104 x 70

***Riri ha un rivale nero*, 1912 / Savoia Film / IT**
Rival de Riri, Le, 1912 / Achille Luciano Mauzan / FR / 110 x 75

***Rivalité des pécheurs*, 1913 / Le Cosmograph / FR**
Rivalité de pécheurs, 1913 / FR / 200 x 130

***Robin Hood Outlawed*, 1912 / Charles Raymond / British and Colonial Kinematograph / GB**
Robin Hood, 1912 / GB / 76 x 25

***Robinet Alpino*, 1912 / Ambrosio / IT**
[*Robinet Alpino*], 1912 / P. Pavodi / IT / 140 x 100

***Robinet chauffeur miope**, 1914 / Marcel Fabre / Ambrosio / IT**
Robinet automobilista miope, 1914 / Atelier Butteri / IT / 140 x 100

***Robinet contro un rubinetto*, 1912 / Ambrosio / IT**
Robinet contro Rubinetto, 1912 / IT / 140 x 100

[*Robinet en de dienstmeid*] / Ambrosio / IT
[*Robinet en de dienstmeid*], 1913 / R. Muller / IT / 140 x 100

***Robinet operatore*, 1912 / Ambrosio / IT**
[*Robinet operatore*], 1912 / IT / 140 x 101

***Robinet scioperante**, 1912 / Ambrosio / IT**
[*Robinet scioperante*], 1912 / P. Pavodi / IT / 140 x 101
[*Robinet scioperante*], 1911 / IT / 138 x 98

***Robinet studia matematica*, 1913 / Ambrosio / IT**
[*Robinet studia matematica*], 1913 / IT / 140 x 100

***Robinet tenore*, 1913 / Ambrosio / IT**
[*Robinet tenore*], 1913 / P. Pavodi / IT / 139 x 100

***Roman d'un caissier, Le**, 1914 / Emile Chautard / Association Cinématographique des Auteurs Dramatiques / FR**
Roman d'un caissier, Le, 1914 / FR / 300 x 200
Roman d'un caissier, Le, 1914 / FR / 150 x 100

***Rosa Pantöffelchen, Das**, 1913 / Franz Hofer / Luna-Film / DE**
Rosa Pantöffelchen, Das, 1913 / DE / 94 x 64

Rosa Pantöffelchen, Das, 1913 / DE / 150 × 110
Rose of Old Mexico, The, 1913 / Allan Dwan / American Film Manufacturing / US
Rose of Mexico, The, 1913 / US / 107 × 71
Rough Ride With Nitroglycerine, A, 1912 / William Duncan / Selig Polyscope / US
Rough ride with nitroglycerine, A, 1912 / US / 101 × 76
Rowdy Comes Home, 1913 / Reliance Motion Picture Company / US
Rowdy comes home / GB / 101 × 76
[Ruiter, De] / GB
[Ruiter, De] / GB / 225 × 101
Rule Thyself, 1913 / C. Jay Williams / Edison Manufacturing Company / US
Mauvais caractère, Un, 1913 / FR / 120 × 80
Runaway Freight, The, 1913 / John G. Adolfi / Kalem / US
Runaway freight, The, 1913 / GB / 222 × 196
Rupe del Malconsiglio, La*, 1913 / Cines / IT
Rupe del malconsiglio, La, 1913 / IT / 150 × 100
Rupe del malconsiglio, La, 1913 / IT / 195 × 138
Ruse du fakir, La, 1913 / Vitagraph Company of America / US
Ruse du fakir, La, 1913 / Harry Bedos / FR / 140 × 100

S

Sacrifice of Kathleen, The, 1914 / Van Dyke Brooke / Vitagraph Company of America / US
Brave petit coeur, Un, 1914 / FR / 140 × 100
Verschoppelinge, De / NL / 31 × 85
Sacrifice, The, 1913 / Kalem / US
Sacrifice, The, 1913 / GB / 102 × 70
Sailor's Heart, A, 1912 / Wilfred Lucas / Biograph / US
Sailor's heart, A, 1912 / US / 104 × 70
Sally In Our Alley, 1913 / Colin Campbell / Selig Polyscope / US
Sally in our alley, 1913 / US / 105 × 71
Samaritan of Coogan's Tenement, The, 1912 / Fred E. Wright / Lubin Manufacturing Company / US
Samaritan of Coogan's tenement, The, 1912 / GB / 102 × 77
Sands of the Time, The, 1913 / Lorimer Johnston / Selig Polyscope / US
Sands of the time, The, 1913 / US / 104 × 71
Sangue bleu*, 1914 / Nino Oxilia / Celio Film / IT
Sangue bleu, 1914 / IT / 200 × 280
Santa Claus and the Clubman, 1911 / Edison Manufacturing Company / US
Santa Claus and the clubman, [1912] / US / 102 × 70
Satanasso, 1913 / Achille Consalvi / Aquila Films / IT
Prince of darkness, The, 1913 / GB / 200 × 210
Prince of darkness, The, GB / 221 × 198
Prince of darkness, The, 1913 / GB / 223 × 102
[Satanasso], 1913 / IT / 200 × 280
Satansteins bande, 1915 / Filmfabriken Danmark / DK
Bande de Zatanstein, La, 1915 / DK / 45 × 43
Sauvetage, Un, 1913 / Henri Pouctal / Pathé Frères – Le Film d'Art / FR
Sauvetage, Un / Edouard Bernard / FR / 160 × 240
Saving the Game, 1912 / Charles M. Seay / Edison Manufacturing Company / US
Saving the game, 1912 / US / 100 × 70
Scales of Justice, The, 1912 / Oscar Eagle / Selig Polyscope / US
Scales of justice, The, 1913 / US / 104 × 71
Scandale au village, Un*, 1913 / Maurice Mariaud / Gaumont / FR
Village scandal, A, 1913 / FR / 106 × 77
Schatten des Lebens, 1912 / Adolf Gärtner / Messters Projektion / DE
Schatten des Lebens, 1912 / DE / 151 × 110
Schatten des Meeres, Der, 1912 / Curt A. Stark / Messter / DE
Schatten des Meeres, Der, 1912 / DE / 185 × 125
Schatten des Meeres, Der, 1912 / DE / 97 × 64
Schein trügt, Der*, 1914 / Eiko Film / DE
Schein trügt, Der, 1914 / Tjerk Bottema / DE / 149 × 110
Schuldig*, 1913 / Hans Oberländer / Messter / DE
Schuldig / NL / 155 × 216
Schwarze Katze, Die, 1912 / Viggo Larsen / Vitascope / DE
Schwarze Katze, Die, 1912 / J. Bubna / DE / 220 × 148
Schwarze Katze, Die, 1912 / DE / 93 × 65
Schwarze Katze, Die, 1912 / DE / 94 × 64
Schwarze Kugel oder die geheimnisvollen Schwestern, Die*, 1913 / Franz Hofer / Luna-Film / DE
Schwarze Kugel, Die, 1913 / DE / 92 × 60
Schwarze Maske, Die, 1912 / Royal Films / DE
Schwarze Maske, Die / DE / 116 × 90
Schwarze Maske, Die / DE / 218 × 147
Schwarze Natter, Die*, 1913 / Franz Hofer / Luna-Film / DE
Schwarze Natter, Die, 1913 / DE / 128 × 94
Schwarze Natter, Die, 1913 / DE / 149 × 110
Scotland Forever, 1914 / Harry Lambart / Vitagraph Company of America / US
Bébés Ecossais, Les, 1913 / Mett / FR / 140 × 100
Segreto della cassaforte, Il, 1913 / Cines / IT
Secret of the safe, The / US / 102 × 76
Sejrens dag, 1918 / Messter / DE
Sejrens dag / H. Joensen / DK / 87 × 59
Série Yvette Andreyor / FR
[Série Yvette Andreyor], [1914] / FR / 240 × 160
She Cried*, 1912 / Albert W. Hale / Vitagraph Company of America / US
Pleurnicheuse, La, 1912 / Harry Bedos / FR / 140 × 100
Sheriff of Yavapai County, The, 1913 / William Duncan / Selig Polyscope / US
Sheriff of Yavapai County, The, 1913 / US / 104 × 71
Sheriff's Story, The, 1913 / Essanay Film Manufacturing / US
Sheriff's story, The, 1912 / GB / 102 × 76
Shotgun Ranchman, The, 1912 / Essanay Film Manufacturing / US
Shotgun ranchman, The, 1912 / GB / 101 × 76
Sign of the Cross, The*, 1914 / Frederick A. Thomson / Famous Players / US
Sign of the cross, The, 1914 / GB / 216 × 102
Sign of the cross, The, 1914 / GB / 245 × 102
Sign of the cross, The, 1914 / GB / 222 × 199
Sign of the cross, The, 1914 / A. Morrow / GB / 221 × 197
Sign of the cross, The, 1914 / GB / 223 × 392
Sign of the cross, The, 1914 / GB / 225 × 295
Sign of the cross, The, 1914 / Hyland Collins / GB / 216 × 102
Sign of the cross, The, 1914 / GB / 221 × 198
Sign of the cross, The, 1914 / Stewart Browne / GB / 300 × 220
Teeken des kruises, Het, 1914 / NL / 20 × 51
Sign of the cross, The, 1914 / US / 107 × 71
Signal Fire, The*, 1912 / William V. Ranous / Vitagraph Company of America / US
Roman de la Mer, Un / Harry Bedos / FR / 140 × 101
Signal of Distress, The, 1912 / Larry Trimble / Vitagraph Company of America / US
Signal of distress, The, 1912 / US / 107 × 72
Sin of Another, The / New Century Film Service / GB
Sin of another, The, 1910–1914 / GB / 222 × 102
Sin of another, The, 1910–1914 / GB / 76 × 51
Sinews of War, jaar onbekend / London Exclusive / GB
Sinews of war / GB / 220 × 120
Skelly Buys a Hotel, 1914 / Edward Dillon / Biograph / US
Skelly buys a hotel, 1914 / GB / 102 × 69
Skovsoens datter, 1912 / Dansk Kinograf Films / DK
Tochter des Waldsees, Die, 1912 / DE / 213 × 143
Sleep Walker, The, 1911 / Van Dyke Brooke / Vitagraph Company of America / US
Somnambule, Le, 1911 / Harry Bedos / FR / 140 × 100
Sleeper, The, 1912 / Lubin Manufacturing Company / US
Sleeper, The, 1912 / US / 104 × 70
Sleeping beauty, The, 1912 / Elwin Neame / Hepworth / GB
Sleeping beauty, The, 1912 / GB / 101 × 76
Smarten van een moeder
Smarten van een moeder / NL / 30 × 85
Smiling Bob, 1912 / Méliès Manufacturing Company / US
Smiling Bob, 1912 / GB / 102 × 77
Snowball and his pal, 1912 / Thomas H. Ince / New York Motion Picture Bison 101 / US
Snowball and his pal, 1912 / US / 207 × 99
So Near, Yet So Far, 1912 / D.W. Griffith / Biograph / US
So near, yet so far, 1912 / GB / 101 × 76
Sogno di Bidoni, Il / Cines / IT
Sogno di Bidoni, Il / Marchetti / IT / 140 × 197
Solitaires*, 1913 / Van Dyke Brooke / Vitagraph Company of America / US
Fiancés sans le savoir, 1913 / FR / 140 × 100
Sømandsbrud, En, 1914 / Filmfabriken Danmark / DK
Seemannsbraut, Eine, 1915 / DK / 39 × 41
Son passé*, 1913 / Henri Fescourt / Gaumont / FR
Son passé!, 1913 / FR / 150 × 111
Song of the Wildwood Flute, The, 1910 / D.W. Griffith / US
Zauberflöte, Eine, 1910 / DE / 104 × 70
Sophomore, The / Nat Nathanson / Hi-Mark Productions / US

Sophomore, The / US / 104 x 69
***Sorte domino, Den*, 1910** / Nordisk Films Kompagni / DK*
Gute Bruder, Der, 1910 / Louis Galice / DE / 99 x 140
***Sorte drom, Den, 1911** / Peter Urban Gad / Fotorama / DK*
Schwarze Traum, Der, 1911 / DE / 90 x 60
***Sorte kansler, Den, 1912** / August Blom / Nordisk Films Kompagni / DK*
[Sorte kansler, Den], 1912 / DE / 200 x 100
[Sorte kansler, Den], 1912 / DE / 200 x 100
[Sorte kansler, Den], 1912 / DE / 400 x 420
[Sorte kansler, Den], 1912 / DE / 220 x 200
Schwarze Kanzler, Der, 1912 / DE / 147 x 200
***Souvenir de la morte, Le** / Lux / FR*
Souvenir de la morte, Le / Lucien Charbonnier / FR / 140 x 100
***Spätes Glück, 1912** / Eclipse / FR*
Spätes Glück / DE / 149 x 99
Spätes Glück, 1912 / DE / 102 x 70
***Speed Demon, The, 1912** / Mack Sennett / Biograph / US*
Speed demon, The, 1912 / GB / 104 x 76
***Spiel ist aus, Das, 1912** / Messter / DE*
Spiel ist aus, Das, 1912 / DE / 220 x 150
***Spoorweg ongeluk door jaloezie, Een** / US*
Spoorwegongeluk door jalouzie, Een, 1915 / NL / 95 x 53
***Stærkeste, Den, 1915** / Filmfabriken Danmark / DK*
Strongest, The, 1915 / DK / 50 x 47
***Standuhr, Die, 1913** / Rudolf Meinert / Prometheus Film / DE*
Weg der tranen, De / NL / 19 x 69
***Star of Bethlehem, The, 1912** / Lawrence Marston / Thanhouser Film / US*
Star of Bethlehem, 1912 / GB / 102 x 76
Star of Bethlehem, 1912–1913 / GB / 225 x 102
***Steckbrief, Der*, 1913** / Franz Hofer / Luna-Film / DE*
Steckbrief, Der, 1913 / DE / 218 x 149
Steckbrief, Der, 1913 / DE / 224 x 110
***Stenographer Troubles*, 1913** / Frederick A. Thomson / Vitagraph Company of America / US*
Jolies dactylographes, Les, 1913 / Harry Bedos / FR / 140 x 100
***Stolen Bride, The, 1913** / Anthony O'Sullivan / Biograph / US*
Stolen bride, The, 1913 / GB / 102 x 71
***Stolen Glory, 1912** / Mack Sennett / Keystone Film / US*
Stolen glory, 1912 / US / 101 x 76
***Storm og stille, I, 1915** / Vilhelm Glückstadt / Filmfabriken Danmark / DK*
Petit réconcilliateur, Le, 1915 / DK / 53 x 33
***Story of Lavinia, The, 1913** / Colin Campbell / Selig Polyscope / US*
Story of Lavinia, The, 1913 / US / 102 x 76
***Strange Story of Elsie Mason, The, 1912** / Kalem / US*
Strange story of Elsie Mason, The, 1912 / GB / 102 x 77
***Streets of New York*, 1913** / Travers Vale / Pilot Films / US*
Geheimen eener wereldstad, De, 1913 / NL / 84 x 31
Streets of New York, The, 1913 / US / 210 x 107
Streets of New York, The, 1913 / US / 200 x 208
Streets of New York, The, 1913 / US / 106 x 71
***Strength of Men, The*, 1913** / Ralph Ince / Vitagraph Company of America / US*
Or meurtrier, L', 1913 / Harry Bedos / FR / 200 x 131
***Strength of Men, The*, 1913** / Ralph Ince / Vitagraph Company of America / US*
Or meurtrier, L', 1913 / Harry Bedos / FR / 200 x 131
***Strength of Men, The*, 1913** / Ralph Ince / Vitagraph Company of America / US*
Het moordende goud, 1913 / NL / 31 x 85
***Strong Man's Burden, The*, 1913** / [D.W. Griffith], [Anthony O'Sullivan], [Frank Powell] / Biograph / US*
Strong man's burden, The, 1913 / GB / 104 x 76
***Stronger, The, 1913** / O.A.C. Lund / Universal Eclair American / US*
Plus fort, Le, 1911 / FR / 300 x 150
***Sua Maestà il sangue*, 1913** / Roberto Roberti / Aquila Films / IT*
[Sua maesta il sangue], 1913 / IT / 280 x 200
Van koninklijken bloede, 1913 / NL / 31 x 84
***Substitute Heiress, The, 1912** / Lubin Manufacturing Company / US*
Substitute heiress, 1912 / GB / 102 x 77
***Successo diplomatico, Un*, 1913** / Ambrosio / IT*
[Successo diplomatico, Un], 1913 / P. Pavodi / IT / 139 x 100
***Sui gradini del trono*, 1912** / Ubaldo Maria Del Colle / Pasquali / IT*
Strijd om een troon, De, 1913 / NL / 31 x 84
[Sui gradini del trono], 1913 / G. Boano / IT / 136 x 100
***Sulla via dell'oro*, 1913** / Baldassarre Negroni / Cines / IT*
Sulla via dell' oro, 1913 / IT / 280 x 200
Sulla via dell' oro, 1913 / IT / 209 x 100
***Sündige Liebe, 1911** / Emil Albes / Deutsche Bioscop / DE*
Sündige Liebe, 1911 / DE / 104 x 70
***Sur le cable aérien, 1913** / Eclectic / FR*
Sur le cable aérien, 1913 / Atelier Faria / FR / 240 x 320
***Suspicious Henry, 1913** / Frederick A. Thomson / Vitagraph Company of America / US*
Pot de peinture, Le, 1913 / Harry Bedos / FR / 140 x 100
***Suzanne, 1916** / René Hervil, Louis Mercanton / Eclipse / FR*
Suzanne, 1919 / FR / 210 x 250

T

***Tango de la mort, Le, 1914** / Eclair / FR*
Tango de la mort, Le, 1914 / Roger Chapelet / FR / 199 x 225
Tango de la mort, Le, 1914 / Roger Chapelet / FR / 150 x 100
***Télégraphiste, Le, 1912** / Pathé Frères / FR*
Telegrafiste, De, 1912 / NL / 84 x 31
***Terra promessa, La*, 1913** / Baldassarre Negroni / Celio Film / IT*
Terra promessa, La, 1913 / IT / 209 x 100
***Teufelsauge, Das*, 1914** / Harry Piel / Vay & Hubert / DE*
Duivelsoog / NL / 31 x 87
Duivelsoog, 1916 / NL / 85 x 62
[Teufelsauge, Das], 1914 / IT / 207 x 101
[Teufelsauge, Das], 1914 / IT / 197 x 279
[Teufelsauge, Das], 1914 / IT / 197 x 130
***Those Troublesome Tresses*, 1913** / George D. Baker / Vitagraph Company of America / US*
Crin révélateur, Le, 1913 / FR / 140 x 100
***Three Friends, 1912** / D.W. Griffith / Biograph / US*
Three friends, 1913 / US / 104 x 70
***Three Valises, The, 1912** / Selig Polyscope / US*
Three valises, The, 1912 / US / 101 x 72
***Through Shadowed Vales, 1912** / Universal IMP / US*
Through shadowed vales, 1912 / GB / 101 x 76
***Thug, Der. Im Dienste der Todesgöttin, 1916** / Heinz Karl Heiland, Alwin Neuss / DECLA-Film-Gesellschaft / DE*
Alwin Neuss, 1916 / Fritz G. Kirchbach / DE / 107 x 143
***Tiger, The, 1913** / Frederick A. Thomson / Vitagraph Company of America / US*
Tigre, Le, 1913 / FR / 100 x 140
***Tillie's Punctured Romance, 1914** / Mack Sennett / Keystone Film / US*
Tillie's punctured romance / E.J. Warver Poster Co / US / 105 x 72
***To violiner, De, 1908** / Viggo Larsen / Nordisk Films Kompagni / DK*
Beiden Violinen, Die, 1908 / DE / 72 x 95
***Toll of the sea, The, 1912** / Universal Gem / US*
Toll of the sea, The, 1915 / US / 104 x 72
***Tommy's Sister, 1912** / William V. Ranous / Vitagraph Company of America / US*
Tommy's sister, 1912 / US / 107 x 72
***Tontolini non vuol la suocera, 1912** / Cines / IT*
Tontolini non vuole suocera, 1912 / IT / 101 x 70
Tontolini non vuole suocera, 1911 / IT / 100 x 70
***Too Much Wooing of Handsome Dan, 1912** / Vitagraph Company of America / US*
Six fiancées du cowboy, Les / FR / 140 x 100
***Topolini riconoscenti, I*, 1908** / Ambrosio / IT*
[Topolini riconoscenti,] / IT / 139 x 102
***Tortillard détective, 1913** / Lux / FR*
Tortillard détective, 1913 / Lucien Charbonnier / FR / 140 x 100
***Toten leben, Die*, 1914** / Walter Schmidthässler / Vitascope / PAGU / DE*
Dooden leven!, De, 1914 / NL / 29 x 84
Dooden leven!, De, 1914 / NL / 29 x 84
Dooden leven!, De, 1914 / NL / 31 x 84
Toten leben, Die, 1914 / DE / 94 x 64
Toten leben, Die, 1914 / Otto Dely / DE / 186 x 124
***Toymaker's Secret, The, 1910** / Vitagraph Company of America / US*
Fabricant de jouets, Le, 1910 / Harry Bedos / FR / 140 x 100
***Tragedia di Kri Kri, La*, 1913** / Cines / IT*
Tragedia di Kri Kri, La, 1913 / Marchetti / IT / 139 x 100
***Tragico convegno*, 1915** / Ivo Illuminati / Celio Film / IT*
Tragico convegno, 1915 / Tito Corbella / IT / 197 x 139
Tragico convegno, 1915 / Tito

Corbella / IT / 200 x 279
Traum des Junggesellen, Der, 1912 / Messter / DE
Traum des Junggesellen, Der, 1912 / DE / 125 x 93
Tredie magt, Den, 1912 / August Blom / Nordisk Films Kompagni / DK
Dritte macht, Die, 1912 / DK / 144 x 194
Dritte Macht, Die, 1912 / DE / 219 x 102
Treff Bube, 1912 / Walter Schmidt-hässler / Vitascope / DE
Treff Bube, 1912 / DE / 110 x 149
Treff Bube, 1912 / John Dape / DE / 220 x 149
Trials of a Merry Widow, The, 1912 / [Charles Calvert] / Cricks & Martin / GB
Trials of a merry widow, 1912 / GB / 102 x 77
Triangle, The, 1912 / Selig Polyscope / US
Triangle, The, 1912 / US / 102 x 76
Tried in the Fire*, 1913 / Warwick Buckland / Hepworth / GB
Tried in the fire, 1913 / GB / 100 x 76
Trionfo della forza, Il*, 1913 / Arrigo Frusta / Ambrosio / IT
[Trionfo della forza, Il], 1913 / P. Pavodi / IT / 140 x 100
Triumph of Right, The*, 1912 / Rollin S. Sturgeon / Vitagraph Company of America / US
Overwinning van het recht, 1912 / NL / 86 x 31
Overwinning van het recht, De / NL / 43 x 63
Troubled Trail, The, 1912 / Rollin S. Sturgeon / Vitagraph Company of America / US
Troubled trail, The, [1912] / GB / 102 x 76
Trovata di Kri Kri, La, 1914 / Cines / IT
Trovata di Kri Kri, La, 1914 / Marchetti / IT / 100 x 70
Turi, der Wanderlappe*, 1913 / Alfred Lind / Deutsche Bioscop / DE
Turi, der Wanderlappe, 1913 / DE / 220 x 150
Turn of the Balance, The, 1910 / Maurice Costello / Vitagraph Company of America / US
Roue de la fortune, La, 1910, Mett / FR / 140 x 100
Tutela, La*, 1913 / Baldassarre Negroni / Celio Film / IT
Tutela, La, 1913 / IT / 208 x 100
Twenty Years in Sing-Sing, 1911 / American Film Manufacturing / US
Twenty years in Sing-Sing, 1911 / GB / 101 x 76
Twilight, 1912 / Essanay Film Manufacturing / US
Twilight, 1912 / US / 101 x 76
Twilight, 1912 / US / 107 x 72
Twixt Love and Ambition, 1912 / Lubin Manufacturing Company / US
Twixt love and ambition, 1912 / GB / 102 x 76
Two Daughters of Eve, 1912 / D.W. Griffith / Biograph / US
Two daughters of Eve, 1912 / GB / 101 x 76
Two Souls with But a Single Thought; or, A Maid and Three Men, 1913 / Bert Angeles / Vitagraph Company of America / US
Deux coeurs à l' unisson, 1913 / FR / 140 x 100
Two Women and Two Men, 1912 / Van Dyke Brooke / Vitagraph Company of America / US
Two women and two men, 1912 / US / 107 x 71

U

Übertrumpft / Cines / IT
Overtroefd / NL / 31 x 85
Ueberfall, Der, 1912 / Biograph / US
Ueberfall, Der, 1912 / GB / 200 x 104
Ueberfall, Der, [1912] / GB / 104 x 70
Ultima avventura, L', 1912 / Itala Film / IT
Ultima avventura, L', 1912 / IT / 141 x 100
Un duel au far-west / Vitagraph Company of America / US
Duel in het Wilde Westen, Een, 1912 / NL / 31 x 86
Under False Colors, 1912 / Bannister Merwin / Edison Manufacturing Company / US
Fau x comte, Le, 1912 / DE / 100 x 71
Secret d'une fiancée, Le, 1910 / FR / 153 x 120
Unter der Maske, 1912 / Curt A. Stark / Messters Projektion / DE
Unter der Maske, 1912 / DE / 200 x 130

V

V dni Getmanov*, 1911 / Maurice André Maître / Pathé Frères – Russian Film / RU
Hoofdman Nilolajeff, 1911 / NL / 31 x 84
Vampires de la côte, Les, 1908 / Pathé Frères / FR
Vampires de la côte, Les, 1908 / Candido Aragonês de Faria / Atelier Faria / FR / 118 x 158
Vaterherz, Das, 1912 / Messter / DE
Vaterherz, Das, 1912 / DE / 59 x 92
Vaterherz, Das, 1912 / DE / 185 x 124
Vengeance du sergent de ville, La*, 1913 / Louis Feuillade / Gaumont / FR
Vengeance du sergent de ville, La, 1913 / FR / 107 x 77
Vengeance is Mine, 1913 / Thanhouser Film / US
Vengeance is mine, 1913 / GB / 101 x 76
Vengeance of the Fakir, The, 1912 / Henri Vernot / Universal Eclair American / US
Vengeance of the fakir, The, 1912 / US / 101 x 76
Vergangenes Glück, 1912 / DE
Vergangenes Glück, 1912 / DE / 149 x 110
Verräterin, Die*, 1911 / Peter Urban Gad / Deutsche Bioscop / DE
Verraderes, De, 1911 / NL / 32 x 86
Verso l'amore*, 1913 / Ubaldo Pittei / Latium Film / IT
Verso l'amore, 1913 / IT / 206 x 100
Vie et la passion de Notre Seigneur Jésus Christ, La*, 1907 / Lucien Nonguet, Ferdinand Zecca / Pathé Frères / FR
Passion, La, 1907 / [Vincent Lorant-Heilbronn] / FR / 159 x 120
Village Vixen, The, 1912 / Kalem / US
Village vixen, The, 1912 / GB / 102 x 76
Virtue of Rags, The, 1912 / Theodore Wharton / Essanay Film Manufacturing / US
Virtue of rags, The, 1912 / GB / 102 x 76
Vita perduta, Una, 1912 / Milano Films / IT
Vita perduta, Una, 1912 / IT / 200 x 145
Vittoria o morte*, 1913 / Itala Film / IT
[Vittoria o morte], 1913 / Leopoldo Metlicovitz / IT / 280 x 200
Vittoria o morte!, 1913 / Leopoldo Metlicovitz / IT / 205 x 145
Vittoria o morte!, 1913 / Pier Luigi Caldanzano / IT / 203 x 145
Voix d'or, La*, 1913 / Georges André Lacroi x / Gaumont / FR
Voix d'or, La, 1913 / FR / 220 x 150
Voor haar rover / Gaumont / FR
[Voor haar rover] / FR / 200 x 150

W

Wandering Musician, The, 1912 / George Melford / Kalem / US
Wandernde Musikant, Der, 1912 / GB / 105 x 70
War Correspondent, The, 1913 / Kalem / US
War correspondent, The, 1913 / GB / 101 x 70
Wartime Romance, A, 1912 / Selig Polyscope / US
War time romance, A, 1912 / US / 102 x 72
Was He a German Spy?*, 1912 / Hay Plumb / Hepworth / GB
Gefährlicher Spion, Ein, 1912 / GB / 102 x 76
Weisse Schleier, Der, 1912 / Adolf Gärtner / Deutsche Bioscop / DE
Weisse Schleier, Der, 1912 / Emilio Vacchetti / DE / 216 x 149
Weisse Schleier, Der, 1912 / DE / 97 x 61
Weisse Sklavin, Die (deel 3), 1911 / Viggo Larsen / Vitascope / DE
Weisse Sklavin III, Die, 1911 / DE / 100 x 65
Welcome Intruder, A, 1913 / D.W. Griffith / Biograph / US
Welcome intruder, A, 1913 / GB / 104 x 70
Welt ohne Männer, Die, 1913 / Max Mack / Vitascope / DE
[Welt ohne Männer, Die], 1913 / Robert Michael Bell / DE / 218 x 145
Wenn die Maske fällt, 1912 / Peter Urban Gad / Deutsche Bioscop / DE
[Wenn die Maske fällt], 1912 / Arnold Gerstl / DE / 140 x 95
Geslachtziekte en haar gevolgen, De / NL / 35 x 22
Wenn Völker streiten*, 1915 / Cäsar Lupow / Apollo-Film / DE
[Wenn Völker streiten], 1915 / R. Wolff / DE / 218 x 149
Wer ist der Täter?, 1913 / Franz Hofer / Luna-Film / DE
Wer ist der Täter?, 1913 / DE / 94 x 64
Western Law That Failed, The, 1913 / Essanay Film Manufacturing / US
Western law that failed, The, 1913 / GB / 102 x 77
What the Driver Saw, 1912 / Lubin Manufacturing Company / US
What the driver saw, 1912 / GB / 102 x 76
When Father Fetched the Doctor*, 1913 / Dave Aylott / Cricks & Martin / GB
When father fetched the doctor, 1912 / GB / 102 x 76
When He Wants a Dog He Wants a Dog, 1913 / Emile Cohl / Eclair Company / US
Zozor veut un chien, 1913 / FR / 100 x 70
When Mary Grew Up*, 1912 / James Young / Vitagraph Company of America / US
Mary, Le garcon manque, 1912 / FR / 140 x 100
When Persistency and Obstinacy Meet*, 1912 / Vitagraph Company of America / US
Patience et longueur de temps, 1912 / FR / 140 x 100
When Soul Meets Soul, 1912 / J. Farrell MacDonald / Essanay Film Manufacturing / US
When soul meets soul, 1912 / GB / 101 x 76
When the Earth Trembled*, 1913 / Barry O'Neill / Lubin Manufacturing Company / US
Quand la terre trembla, 1913 / GB / 225 x 100
Quand la terre trembla, 1913 / GB / 230 x 300

Quand la terre trembla, [1913] / GB / 102 x 77
When the Night Call Came*, 1914 / Edward LeSaint / Selig Polyscope / US
When the nightcall came, 1914 / GB / 225 x 102
When the nightcall came, 1914 / GB / 101 x 76
When the West Was Young*, 1913 / William J. Bauman / Vitagraph Company of America / US
Reconnaissance du Huron, La, 1913 / Harry Bedos / FR / 140 x 100
Where Destiny Guides, 1913 / Allan Dwan / American Film Manufacturing / US
Where destiny guides, 1913 / US / 107 x 72
Whimsical Threads of Destiny*, The, 1913 / Frederick A. Thomson / Vitagraph Company of America / US
Juge invisible, Le, 1913 / FR / 240 x 160
Onzichtbare rechter, De / NL / 31 x 85
White Aprons, 1912 / Etienne Arnaud / Eclair Company / US
White aprons, 1912 / US / 106 x 73
White Brave's Heritage, 1911 / Kalem / US
White brave's heritage, 1911 / GB / 101 x 70
Proposal from the Duke, A*, 1913 / Walter Edwin / Edison Manufacturing Company / US
Ehrgeizige Lieschen, Das / DE / 100 x 70
Wild Cat Well, The, 1911 / Vitagraph Company of America / US
Puits de pétrole, Le, 1911 / Harry Bedos / FR / 140 x 100
Wild Pat, 1912 / Charles Kent / Vitagraph Company of America / US
Wild Pat, 1912 / US / 107 x 72
Wilhelm Tell, 1908 / Viggo Larsen / Nordisk Films Kompagni / DK
Wilhelm Tell, Der Befreier der Schweiz, 1908 / DE / 72 x 95
William Voss*, 1915 / Rudolf Meinert / Meinert-Film / DE
William Voss, 1915 / DE / 96 x 65
William Voss, 1915 / T. Joh / DE / 218 x 149
William Voss, 1915 / R. Kreidl / DE / 100 x 70
Willow Tree, The, 1911 / Vitagraph Company of America / US
Saule du souvenir, Le, 1911 / Harry Bedos / FR / 140 x 100
Willy et les Parisiens, 1913 / Joseph Faivre / Eclair / FR
Willy et les Parisiens, 1913 / Maurice Lauro / FR / 150 x 100
With Love's Eyes, 1913 / Lem Parker / Selig Polyscope / US
With love's eyes, 1913 / US / 104 x 72
With The Enemy's Help, 1912 / D.W. Griffith / Biograph / US
With the enemy's help, 1912 / GB / 101 x 76
Wolf Among Lambs, A*, 1913 / Essanay Film Manufacturing / US
Wolf among lambs, A / US / 107 x 70
Woman Haters, The, 1912 / Hal Reid / Vitagraph Company of America / US
Ennemis des femmes, Les, 1912 / FR / 140 x 100
Wreck, The, 1913 / Ralph Ince / Vitagraph Company of America / US
Catastrophe vengeresse, 1913 / FR / 76 x 56
Wrong weigh, The, 1912 / William Robert Daly / Universal IMP / US
Wrong weigh, The, 1912 / US / 107 x 71

Y

Young Millionaire, The, 1912 / Kalem / US
Young millionaire, The, 1912 / GB / 102 x 76

Z

Zaza, 1913 / Adrien Caillard / Pathé Frères / FR
Zaza, 1913 / L. F. Chalicarne / FR / 240 x 320
Zenscina zavtrashnego dnja*, 1914 / Pyotr Chardynin / A. Khanzhonkov & Co. / RU
Weib, Das, 1920 / DE / 149 x 220
Zeppelin 10 / DE
DAZE / DE / 150 x 110
Zug des Herzens, Der, 1912 / Walter Schmidthässler / Vitascope / DE
Zug des Herzens, Der, 1912 / J. Bubna / DE / 218 x 149
[Zwaard, het] / Pathé Frères / FR
[Zwaard, het] / Atelier Faria / FR / 240 x 320
Zwei Bestien, 1913 / Vitascope / DE
Zwei Bestien / J. Bubna / DE / 110 x 149
[Zwerver, de] / Pathé Frères – Le Film d'Art / FR
[Zwerver, De] / Gil Baer / FR / 160 x 210

Cinemas of Jean Desmet

Over the years, Jean Desmet owned many permanent (as opposed to travelling) cinemas in the Netherlands for some length of time. He also held shares in a number of other cinemas. The dates below relate solely to the period when Jean Desmet was the owner, a shareholder, or an executive director of the cinema in question. Many cinemas continued to operate for many years after he sold them. This list does not include the cinemas owned by his brothers and sisters.

For a more detailed discussion of these cinemas, see Ivo Blom, *Jean Desmet and the Early Dutch Film Trade (1907-1916)*; www.cinemaincontext.nl; and the Jean Desmet company archive.

Owner & Executive Director

Cinema Parisien
Nieuwendijk 69, Amsterdam
26 March 1910 – 1956
190 seats (in 1987)
The Cinema Parisien closed on 25 March 1987, and the interior was moved to the Nederlands Filmmuseum. In 2014, after EYE established in Amsterdam-Noord, the interior was installed in De FilmHallen cinema, Hannie Dankbaar Passage 33, Amsterdam.

Palace
Kalverstraat 224, Amsterdam
1911 – October 1918
550 seats in 1912

Cinema Parisien
Korte Hoogstraat 28a, Rotterdam
13 March 1909 – November 1918
In 1915 the name was changed to the Modern Bioscoop Theater.

Royal
Coolsingel 17, Rotterdam
1913 – March 1916
400 seats in 1913
Abraham Tuschinski acquired this cinema from Desmet in 1916.

Amersfoortsch Bioscoop Theater
Langestraat 129, Amersfoort
April 1914 – 1956
In 1924 the name was changed to the Royal and in 1930 to the Rembrandt.

Palace
Havenstraat 12, Bussum
3 May 1913 – 1920

Delfia
Binnenwatersloot 1, Delft
1915 – August 1919

Shareholder

Bellamy
Bellamypark, Vlissingen
15 October 1913 – 1927
400 seats in 1913
In 1921 this cinema was named the Luxor.

De Munt
Kalverstraat 226, Amsterdam
May 1914 – 1916
450 seats in 1914

Parisien
Vrijstraat 22, Eindhoven
1917 – 1928
400 seats in 1917
From 1917 to 1928, Desmet and his brother Mathijs jointly managed this cinema. Mathijs was also on its executive board from 1942 to 1947.

Chicago Bioscoop Theater
Rechtestraat 19, Eindhoven
1919 – 1928
575 seats in 1913
Desmet and his brother Mathijs jointly managed this cinema. Mathijs later rejoined its executive board, from 1945 to 1947.

Selected Bibliography

Books on Jean Desmet

Ivo Blom, *Pionierswerk. Jean Desmet en de vroege Nederlandse filmhandel en bioscoopexploitatie (1907-1916)* (dissertation, University of Amsterdam, 2000)
Ivo Blom, *Jean Desmet and the Early Dutch Film Trade* (Amsterdam, 2003)

Other Publications

Soeluh van den Berg, 'Het begin van de film in Nederland. Het archief van Jean Desmet', *Metamorfoze nieuws*, no. 1 (2011), 1-3
Don Bierman, '100.000 velletjes, de ontsluiting van het Desmet-archief', *Studiecentrum Bulletin Nederlands Filmmuseum*, no. 2 (1994), 6-7
Ivo Blom, 'Filmdistributie tijdens de Eerste Wereldoorlog. Jean Desmet en de Films-Erneuerungs-Gesellschaft', *GBG-Nieuws*, no. 21 (summer 1992), 34-36
Ivo Blom, 'Filmvertrieb in Europa 1910–1915. Jean Desmet und die Messter-Film GmbH', *KINtop*, no. 3 (1994), 73-91
Ivo Blom, '"Comme l'eau qui coule". Les films de rivières de Gaumont dans la collection Desmet', in: Thierry Lefebvre, Michel Marie and Laurent Véray (eds.), *Images du réel. La non-fiction en France (1890-1930)* (1895: Bulletin de l'Association française de recherche sur l'histoire du cinéma; 18) (Paris, 1995), 157-164
Ivo Blom, 'Il primo cinema tedesco nella collezione Desmet', *Nuovo Cine critica*, no. 2/3 (1996), 129-133
Ivo Blom, 'What's in a Name? Pathé and the Netherlands as Envisioned in the Pathé-Desmet Relationship', in: Michel Marie and Laurent Le Forestier (eds.), *La firme Pathé frères, 1896-1914* (Paris, 2004), 95-106
Ivo Blom, 'Infrastructure, Open System and the Take-off Phase. Jean Desmet as a Case Study for Early Distribution in the Netherlands', in: Frank Kessler and Nanna Verhoeff (eds.), *Networks of Entertainment. Early Film Distribution 1895-1915* (Eastleigh, 2007), 137-144
Ivo Blom, *Sangue bleu and the Italian Films in the Desmet Collection*, booklet with *Sangue bleu* (Bologna, 2014)
Ivo Blom and Paul van Yperen, 'Het nimmer gebouwde Flora-Palace. De droom van Jean Desmet', *Ons Amsterdam*, 1 September 2004, 342-346
Ivo Blom and Paul van Yperen, 'Jan de Vaal en de Desmet-collectie', in: Mirjam van Kempen et al., *Altijd film voor ogen. Jan de Vaal en het Nederlands Filmmuseum* (Utrecht, 2014)
Charles Boost, *Biopioniers* (Amsterdam, 1961)
Joost Broeren, 'Unieke blik op vroegste filmgeschiedenis. Desmet-collectie wordt Werelderfgoed', *Ons Erfdeel*, no. 1 (2012), 132-134
Itzia Fernandez Escareno, *La compilation, un outil paradoxal de valorisation des films muets recyclés par Peter Delpeut et coproduits par le Nederlands Filmmuseum (1989-1999)* (dissertation, Université Sorbonne Nouvelle, Paris, 2009)
Emmy de Groot and Frank van der Maden, 'De schatkamers van Desmet', *Skrien*, no. 148 (summer 1986), 30-34
Emmy de Groot and Frank van der Maden, 'Der Schatz von Jean Desmet/The Treasure Trove of Jean Desmet', in: Daniela Sannwald (ed.), *Rot für Gefahr, Feuer und Liebe. Frühe deutsche Stummfilme/Red for Danger, Fire and Love. Early German Silent Films* (Berlin, 1995), 13-15
Sandra den Hamer, 'EYE's Desmet Collection Inscribed on UNESCO's Memory of the World Register', *Journal of Film Preservation*, 1 October 2011, 42-44
Daan Hertogs, 'Themadagen Jean Desmet', *Studiecentrum Bulletin Nederlands Filmmuseum*, no. 2 (1994), 3-5
Rixt Jonkman, 'Any ID? Building a Database out of the Jean Desmet Archive', in: Frank Kessler and Nanna Verhoeff (eds.), *Networks of Entertainment. Early Film Distribution 1895-1915* (Eastleigh, 2007), 312-319
Nico de Klerk, 'What the Papers Say. The Case of the Film-Related Papers of Jean Desmet', *KINtop*, no. 14/15 (2006), 112-121
Frank van der Maden, 'De opkomst van de filmhandel in Nederland', *Spieghel historiael*, vol. 20 (1985) no. 11, 484-491
Frank van der Maden, 'Hommage Jean Desmet, Nederlands filmpionier, zes Desmet-programma's', *Filmmuseum Cinematheek Journaal*, no. 71 (1985), 16-46
Frank van der Maden, 'Aangenaam, leerzaam en pakkend. Uit de schatkamers van Desmet', *Filmmuseum Cinematheek Journaal*, no. 77 (1987), 37-46
Frank van der Maden, 'Desmet, Jean Conrad Ferdinand Théodore', in: J. Charité and A.J.C.M. Gabriëls (eds.), *Biografisch woordenboek van Nederland*, vol. 4 (The Hague, 1994), 96-98
Ester Rutten, 'Film per meter, Jean Desmet en de filmdistributie in de jaren tien', in: Bart Koetsenruijter (ed.), *Honderd jaar film in Nederland. Het begin, Jaarboek mediageschiedenis*, vol. 8 (Amsterdam, 1997), 111-128
Edith Taekema (ed.), *Interessant voor volwassenen, leerzaam voor kinderen. Aspecten van de vroege film*, information booklet for visitors, vol. 6 (Amsterdam, 1985)
Peter Westervoorde, 'Jean Desmet en het NFM', *Filmmuseum Cinematheek, waarin opgenomen de Amsterdamse Filmliga*, no. 3 (1970), 3-5
Wim Willems, 'Jean Desmet, een Belgische vrije jongen in het bioscoopwezen', in: Wim Willems, *De kunst van het overleven. Levensverhalen uit de twintigste eeuw* (The Hague, 2004), 1-29
Paul van Yperen, 'Volle tenten! Volle zalen! Het opwindende begin van de filmvertoning', *Ons Amsterdam*, no. 10 (1991), 226-231

About the Editors and Authors

Rommy Albers is senior curator at EYE
Sanne Baar is project coordinator exhibitions at EYE
Soeluh van den Berg is curator film-related collections at EYE
Marente Bloemheuvel is associate curator at EYE
Ivo Blom is assistant professor in Comparative Arts & Media Studies at the VU University, Amsterdam, and author of *Jean Desmet and the Early Dutch Film Trade* (2003).
Peter Delpeut is a filmmaker and writer. From 1988 to 1995 he worked for the Filmmuseum. In 1990 he directed the film *Lyrical Nitrate*, a found-footage homage to the Desmet Collection.
Jaap Guldemond is director of exhibitions at EYE
Sandra den Hamer is director of EYE
Mark-Paul Meyer is senior curator at EYE
Lizette Oostendorp is information specialist at EYE
David Robinson is director of the Pordenone Silent Film Festival and author of film historical books.
Elif Rongen-Kaynakçi is silent film curator at EYE
Leanne van Schijndel is a film historian

Photo Credits

Images from films have been created specially for this publication. Original publicity photographs are denoted as such. Unless otherwise stated, all published films and posters originate in the EYE collection.

Rapsodia satanica (Nino Oxilia, 1917) is not part of the Desmet Collection, but is part of the collection of EYE Filmmuseum.

Jean Desmet in His Time

1
Jean Desmet, photo c.1915
2
Construction of legs of Eiffel Tower, Paris, 15 May 1888. Photographer unknown
3
Edward Munch, *The Scream*, 1910. Munch Museum, Oslo
4
Logo of FA Noggerath Amsterdam, cinema and film company
5
Travelling cinema of Albert Frères on main square in Haarlem, date unknown
6
Inaugural flight of LZ-1, 2 July 1900. Library of Congress, Washington
7
Stock Exchange by Berlage, Amsterdam. Photographer unknown
8
Canadian Toboggan, 1905
9
Henri Matisse, *La Desserte rouge*, 1908. Hermitage, St Petersburg
10
The Imperial Bio on main square in Groningen, May 1908
11
Pablo Picasso, *Les Demoiselles d'Avignon*, 1907. Museum of Modern Art, New York
12
Futuristic Manifest, 20 February 1909
13
Poster for the Cinema Parisien in Rotterdam, 1909
14
From: F.A. Talbot, *Practical Cinematography and its Applications*, London, 1994, p. 52
15
Wassily Kandinsky, *Komposition IV*, 1911. Kunstsammlung Nordrheinwestfalen, Düsseldorf
16
From: *The Motion Picture Story Magazine*, February 1911
17
Demonstration by suffragettes. Date and photographer unknown
18
Jean Desmet and his wife Hendrika Klabou. Date unknown
19
Front page of *New York Herald*, 15 April 1912
20
Asta Nielsen in *Afgrunden*, 1910
21
Poster for Enrico Guazzoni, *Quo vadis?*, 1912
22
Kazimir Malevich, *Black Square*, 1913. State Russian Museum, St Petersburg
23
Marcel Duchamp, *Roue de bicyclette*, 1913. Museum of Modern Art, New York
24
Richard Wagner, 1913
25
Logo of Cinema Royal Elite
26
Attack on Archduke Franz Ferdinand. Artist unknown
27
Annie Bos in *Op Hoop van Zegen*, 1918
28
British soldiers and mules with gasmasks. Photographer unknown
29
Advertisement of Jean Desmet, 8 November 1918
30
Signing of armistice in forest at Compiègne, 11 November 1918
31
Technical drawing for part of Desmet's cloud project
32
Flora theatre, Amsterdam. Date and artist unknown
33
Black Thursday. Photographer unknown
34
Jean Desmet's death notice, 1956
35
Poster for the film programme 'Hommage Jean Desmet, zes Desmet programma's' and for the exhibition 'Film per Meter', November and December 1985 at Filmmuseum Amsterdam
36
Dutch intertitle for *Fior di male (Kinderen der zonde)*, 1915
37
Parisien Room at the Nederlands Filmmuseum, Amsterdam, 1991
38
Cinema 4 in EYE, Amsterdam. Photo Rene den Engelsman
39
UNESCO certificate, 2011
40
Poster for the exhibition 'Jean Desmet's Dream Factory', 2014, design Joseph Plateau

Credits

This book was published on the occasion of the exhibition

Jean Desmet's Dream Factory
The Adventurous Years of Film (1907-1916)

13 December 2014 – 12 April 2015

EYE Filmmuseum
IJpromenade 1
1013 KT Amsterdam
Tel. 31 (0)20 5891400
info@eyefilm.nl
www.eyefilm.nl

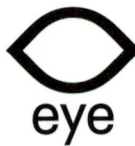

Exhibition

Concept and development
Mark-Paul Meyer, Marente Bloemheuvel, Jaap Guldemond

Director
Sandra den Hamer
Director of exhibitions
Jaap Guldemond
Senior curator
Mark-Paul Meyer
Associate curator
Marente Bloemheuvel
Project coordinator
Sanne Baar, Claartje Opdam
Concept and realization music
Martin de Ruiter
Advisors
Rommy Albers, Soeluh van den Berg, Elif Rongen-Kaynakçi
Exhibition design
Jeroen de Vries
Graphic design
Joseph Plateau, Amsterdam
Film programmer
Anna Abrahams
with Sanne Baar, Mark-Paul Meyer, Elif Rongen-Kaynakçi, Martin de Ruiter
Film digitization
Anne Gant, Anna Hoetjes, Jan Scholten
Restoration Ernemann projector
Hans van der Kraan
Restoration of travelling cinema parts
Tirza Mol
Restoration and advice on paper
Jacco Schipper, Floor Meijboom
Exhibition texts
Mark-Paul Meyer, Meike Amelie Scholten
Editing of exhibition texts
Els Brinkman
Translation of exhibition texts
Billy Nolan
Publicity and marketing
Inge Scheijde, Marnix van Wijk
Technical production
Indyvideo and Martin Schrevelius
Audiovisual equipment
Beam Systems
Installation
Landstra & De Vries
Light
Theatermachine

Publication

Editors
Marente Bloemheuvel, Jaap Guldemond, Mark-Paul Meyer
Design
Joseph Plateau, Amsterdam
Authors
Rommy Albers and Leanne van Schijndel, Sanne Baar, Ivo Blom, Peter Delpeut, Jaap Guldemond, Sandra den Hamer, Mark-Paul Meyer, David Robinson, Elif Rongen-Kaynakçi and Soeluh van den Berg
Peter Delpeuts text 'Femmes Fatales and Film Divas' was previously published in *Kunstschrift* 6 (2011).
Filmography
Elif Rongen-Kaynakçi, Sanne Baar, Mark-Paul Meyer
List of posters
Soeluh van den Berg, Sanne Baar, Mark-Paul Meyer
Bibliography
Lizette Oostendorp
Translation Dutch–English
Billy Nolan (Sandra den Hamer, Jaap Guldemond); Open Book Translation, David McKay (all essays and timeline)
Text editing
D'Laine Camp, Mehgan Bakhuizen
Lithography and printing
die Keure, Bruges (BE)
Paper
Munken Polar 130 gr
Font
Balance
Publishers
EYE Filmmuseum, Amsterdam / Barbera van Kooij, nai010 publishers, Rotterdam
www.nai010.nl

Cover
front: Mario Roncoroni, *Filibus*, 1915
back: *A Freight Train Drama*, 1912
inside: The Imperial Bio, Jean Desmet's travelling cinema on the main square in Groningen, May 1908

© 2014 EYE Filmmuseum, the authors, nai010 publishers, Rotterdam
All rights reserved. No part of this publication may be reproduced, stored in a retrieval system, or transmitted in any form or by any means, electronic, mechanical, photocopying, recording or otherwise, without the prior written permission of the publisher. For works of visual artists affiliated with a CISAC-organization the copyrights have been settled with Pictoright in Amsterdam. © 2014, c/o Pictoright Amsterdam

Every effort has been made to obtain the necessary permissions to reproduce all copyrighted material contained in this book. Should copyright have been unwittingly infringed in this book, interested parties are requested to contact nai010 publishers, Mauritsweg 23, 3012 JR Rotterdam, the Netherlands, info@nai010.com

nai010 publishers is an internationally orientated publisher specialized in developing, producing and distributing books on architecture, visual arts and related disciplines.
www.nai010.com

nai010 books are available internationally at selected bookstores and from the following distribution partners:

North, Central and South America
Artbook | D.A.P., New York, USA, dap@dapinc.com

Rest of the world
Idea Books, Amsterdam, the Netherlands, idea@ideabooks.nl

For general questions, please contact nai010 publishers directly at sales@nai010.com or visit our website www.nai010.com for further information.

Printed and bound in Belgium
ISBN 978-94-6208-174-1

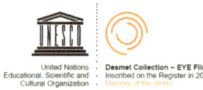

The exhibition and this publication were made possible with the financial support of Fonds 21.

FONDS 21